Developing FoxPro® Applications

P. L. Olympia and Kathy Cea

Addison-Wesley Publishing Company, Inc.

Reading, Massachusetts • Menlo Park, California • New York
Don Mills, Ontario • Wokingham, England • Amsterdam • Bonn
Sydney • Singapore • Tokyo • Madrid • San Juan

Many of the designations used by manufacturers and sellers to distinguish their products are claimed as trademarks. Where those designations appear in this book, and Addison-Wesley was aware of trademark claim, the designations have been printed in initial capital letters or all capital letters.

Library of Congress Cataloging-in-Publication Data

Olympia, P.L.
Developing FoxPro applications / P.L. Olympia and Kathy Cea.
p. cm.
Includes index.
ISBN 0-201-55070-9
1. FoxPro (Computer program) I. Cea, Kathy. II. Title.
QA76.73.F69038 1990
005.75'65--DC20 90-39592

Cover design by Doliber Skeffington
Set in 11-point Times Roman by Context Publishing Services, San Diego, CA

ISBN 0-201-55070-9
ABCDEFGHIJ-MW-90
First printing, August 1990

Contents

Acknowledgments

For every book that has ever been written there is always a group of people who, directly or indirectly, made its publication possible. This book is no exception and we take singular pleasure in acknowledging the help of the following individuals.

We thank Emmanuel Sigler and Janet Walker for technical edits to the manuscript. We are grateful to Dr. David Fulton, Janet Walker, Gloria Pfeif, and the Fox Software technical staff for providing us with answers to many technical questions, and for religiously keeping us up-to-date with FoxPro beta and production files and documentation. We benefited from insightful discussions on multiuser and other coding techniques with Kurt Reiter, Emmanuel Sigler, and the rest of the LRAP team of ARC Professional Services Group. This book would not have been possible without the continued support and encouragement provided by Adonice Hereford. We also acknowledge the assistance provided by Julie Stillman and Elizabeth Grose of Addison-Wesley.

Preface

This book begins where the FoxPro manuals end. Much of the material in this book is not covered by the FoxPro manuals or other books. In essence, this is a book about techniques—written by application developers primarily for those who want to develop FoxPro applications and who need the tools and information not readily available elsewhere. For example, we devote an entire chapter to the important subject of database design techniques. Being database developers ourselves, we learned long ago the enormous value of spending the requisite time to plan and design databases carefully.

We also provide a detailed discussion of multiuser procedures and techniques. This is partly a reflection of the ever-increasing need for network database applications in today's market, and partly a reflection of our experience in FoxBASE+ and FoxPro applications development. Much of what we do entails large-scale database development for local area networks, including porting mainframe database systems to FoxPro applications on microcomputer-based LANs. Indeed, we began what may have been the first multiuser FoxPro application using the first beta copy of FoxPro single-user version. The chapters on multiuser techniques go into considerable detail on issues such as controlling concurrent updates and deadlock prevention including techniques that take advantage of facilities provided by the LAN operating system. We also discuss transaction processing and various options for implementing transaction processing in a FoxPro application. These include the Novell NetWare TTS facility and two approaches to how you might write your transaction tracking facility.

The book describes the structure of the various files used by FoxPro, including the .dbf, .idx, .fpt (memo), .frx (report), and .lbx files. In some cases we show sample C programs to illustrate how to access data from these files from a DOS application. Knowing the format of FoxPro's most important files lets you develop your own tools or utilities that access FoxPro files directly. It also provides you with the information that you need to establish a bridge between FoxPro and any other software package you may be using.

We devote several chapters to procedures and techniques for manipulating different types of FoxPro data including date, time, memo fields, arrays, and character data. The thrust of these discussions is to show novel uses of FoxPro features that you can use in your own development work, as well as to encourage you to explore additional uses of the facilities and power that FoxPro provides.

Our clients look up to us as "experts," but if the truth be known, we are only experts to the extent that we have made a lot of mistakes and we have learned from them. In this book, we try to give you the benefit of our experience, and hopefully save you the agony of our mistakes. Whenever possible we teach by example, providing you with a sample program or program fragment to illustrate the techniques under discussion. Programs described in this book, along with supplemental files, are available separately on a program disk.

Writing a book is always an intense exercise requiring many sacrifices. Writing a book about FoxPro is no exception, but we are happy to admit that we enjoyed writing this book because we learned a lot from the experience and because FoxPro is central to many of our current applications development activities. If any of the techniques we describe help you in your work and save you some time, then the book has met its objectives.

Chapter 1

FoxPro and dBASE IV

Organizations that have standardized on dBASE or even FoxBASE+ need to know whether switching to FoxPro is worth the trouble. In this chapter, we provide an overview of FoxPro's most significant features and capabilities, and compare them with dBASE IV's. We also discuss compatibility with dBASE and FoxBASE+, which should give you an idea of how much recoding, or file conversion, is required to adopt FoxPro as a standard database management system for your organization.

Introducing FoxPro

FoxPro is a Dbase-compatible database management system that includes more than 100 extensions to the Dbase language. It comes in two versions--single user FoxPro and FoxPro/LAN. The latter is the multiuser version that includes automatic record and file locking, multiple record locks on the same data file, and a flexible system for handling unsuccessful record and file locks. Like FoxBASE+, FoxPro version 1.02 does not compile programs into native code to produce standalone .exe files. Rather, FoxPro compiled programs require either the full developmental package (FoxPro or FoxPro/LAN) or the Runtime version of the software.

FoxPro has a scrollable Command window which replaces the usual dBASE dot prompt. It also has system-wide menus in the familiar style of IBM's Standard Application Architecture/Common User Access system. FoxPro provides extensive support for a mouse pointing device but it can be operated as well using the keyboard. FoxPro uses "true" windows that can be moved, sized, overlaid and hidden. The total number of windows that may be opened at one time is limited only by available memory.

On machines with expanded memory that conform to the Lotus-Intel-Microsoft (LIM) 4.0 specifications or higher, FoxPro uses the first 64K of expanded memory as general purpose memory to manage Browse windows, user-defined windows, memory variables, menus and programs. It uses remaining expanded memory to speed up file input/output operations. FoxPro operates comfortably on a machine with 640 KB of conventional memory even with the Novell shell, and a few other Terminate and Stay Resident (TSR) programs, loaded. Users can swap FoxPro to disk to run external programs requiring 400 KB or more of memory.

Data files of all Dbase products, including FoxBASE+ and dBASE IV, do not require prior conversion since they are directly usable in FoxPro. FoxPro memo files can use less space than corresponding FoxBASE+ or dBASE IV files because FoxPro memo file blocksizes can be as small as 33 bytes; these files can be written back in a FoxBASE-compatible format. For the most part, FoxPro memo fields can be treated as character strings and their length is limited only by available disk space. Memo files can be used to contain almost anything including memory variables, arrays, screens and binary data such as scanned images.

FoxPro permits 99 files of all types to be open at one time, 25 work areas, up to 25 total index files open at one time, up to 3600 elements per array, character strings up to 64K long, and 1170 procedures per procedure file. A FoxPro data file may have up to 4000 characters and 255 fields per record. Procedures may be nested up to 32 levels deep through DO calls, and READs may be nested up to 4 levels deep.

The built-in report writer (FoxReport) implements a what-you-see-is-what-you-get work surface on which you may paint report fields, text, lines, boxes and user-defined functions. FoxReport uses report bands and stores the report definition in a .frx file. FoxPro automatically maintains a set of system memory variables to control the appearance of the printed page including margins, copies, text alignment and wordwrap. It has commands to send control sequences, including the null character, directly to the printer. It also has commands to manage network printer output.

FoxPro's built-in text editor can be used to edit multiple files simultaneously. Blocks of text may be cut and pasted among open files. The editor does not impose any limit on line length or file length. It has search and replace, undo, block operations, auto indent, and configurable keys.

FoxPro has a full set of low-level file I/O functions, built-in trace and debug facility, customizable help, and an application-accessible system menu containing desk accessories such as a calculator, ASCII chart, diary, and calendar.

General Compatibility Issues

With few exceptions, FoxPro can be considered as a compatible superset of both dBASE IV and FoxBASE+. This is quite an accomplishment given that FoxBASE+ and dBASE IV are not very compatible with each other in the first place. FoxPro uses the SET COMPATIBLE command to solve the compatibility problem. Basically, SET COMPATIBLE FoxPlus (or SET COMPATIBLE OFF) causes FoxBASE+ programs to be run in FoxPro without change. This is the default state. On the other hand, SET COMPATIBLE DB4 (or SET COMPATIBLE ON) causes FoxPro to interpret selected commands or functions the way dBASE IV would. We discuss the commands and functions affected by the SET COMPATIBLE switch in the next section.

In FoxPro, as in all Dbase family products, an uninitialized memory variable is normally set to .F. by default. However, in FoxBASE+, declaring a public variable called FOX automatically initializes that variable to .T. This is useful for isolating blocks of code that are specific to FoxBASE+. In FoxPro, the statement

```
PUBLIC fox, foxpro
```

not only defines the two memory variables FOX and FOXPRO as public but also initializes them to .T. If you normally move applications between dBASE IV and FoxPro and use the FOXPRO public variable to isolate FoxPro-specific code, you should take an extra precaution to prevent the dBASE IV compiler from parsing FoxPro syntax. For example, the syntax of the ON KEY command differs between the two software products, so you may think the following sample code fragment would handle the inconsistency:

```
If Foxpro
  ON KEY = 315 DO kathelp      && FoxPro syntax
ELSE
  ON KEY LABEL F1 DO kathelp   && dBASE IV
ENDIF
```

In dBASE IV, this code generates an error because it tries to parse the FoxPro-style command syntax. One way around this problem is to define a macro and substitute the following two lines for the first ON KEY statement:

```
F1macro = '= 315'
ON KEY &F1macro DO kathelp     && FoxPro syntax
```

Custom Keyboard Macros

If you find the FoxPro editor to be too difficult to learn or use because you are accustomed to the WordStar-style command keys of FoxBASE+, for example, you can use the keyboard macro file Foxplus.fky provided with FoxPro. Activate this file with the RESTORE MACROS FROM FoxPlus command or rename the file to Default.Fky so that FoxPro automatically loads it when it starts up. Alternatively you may define any key with a command such as

```
ON KEY LABEL L KEYBOARD "1"
```

which causes the number 1 to print whenever you press the L key. Using a series of commands like this permits you to redefine the keyboard. To override a keyboard macro or a key's definition that you reassigned with the ON KEY command, use the KEYBOARD command with the PLAIN option. For instance, the command

```
KEYBOARD "L" PLAIN
```

from a program (since you cannot type this from a keyboard while the character is redefined) causes the letter L to be interpreted literally by stuffing the keyboard with L. To cancel the key reassignment and have the keys revert to their original meanings, use the ON KEY command without any additional parameter.

If you prefer the FoxBASE+ or dBASE interactive command screen (including the familiar status bar and scoreboard), create a file, say, Oldface.prg, and add the line

```
COMMAND = DO Oldface
```

to Config.fp. Oldface.prg should be in the default directory and may contain the following SET commands:

```
SET STATUS ON          && Brings back dBASE status bar
SET SCOREBOARD ON      && dBASE-style scoreboard
SET NOTIFY OFF         && Turns off FoxPro system msg
```

```
SET BRSTATUS ON          && Status bar appears in BROWSE
SET MACKEY TO            && Disables define macro key,F10
```

Naturally you may also just define these settings in your Config.fp file and forget about invoking a startup command file such as Oldface.prg.

UDF Names

You should inspect any dBASE and FoxBASE+ programs you are thinking of running in FoxPro for any user-defined functions (UDFs) with names such as BETWEEN( ) that may conflict with FoxPro's new set of built-in functions. Although FoxPro does not consider its function names to be reserved words, any of your UDFs with syntax similar to FoxPro's will never be executed if they conflict with FoxPro's built-in functions.

The SET COMPATIBLE Switch

The SET COMPATIBLE switch affects the results of array initialization; the cursor location in menus and popups; the manner in which FoxPro searches files with a drive reference; the INKEY( ), LASTKEY( ), LIKE( ), and SELECT( ) functions; and the ACTIVATE SCREEN/WINDOW, APPEND MEMO, PLAY MACRO, READ, SET MESSAGE, @...SAY, and SUM commands.

Array Initialization

Assume that the My_Array variable is a one-dimensional array with 10 elements. With SET COMPATIBLE FoxPlus (or OFF), the command

```
STORE 1 TO My_Array
```

causes all 10 elements of the array to be initialized to 1. Otherwise, the My_Array variable is no longer an array; it becomes a scalar memory variable with a value of 1. This is an extremely important distinction because unwary FoxPro users may find their array variables disappearing with the STORE or assignment command when the compatible switch is set to DB4 (or ON).

Dbase family products define and use arrays inconsistently. For instance, dBASE IV and Clipper use a command such as DECLARE X[9] to define array X, whereas the equivalent FoxBASE+ statement is DIMENSION X(9). Apart from the difference in commands, note the difference in the use of square brackets and parentheses to reference array elements. This has been a major irritant to developers who typically move applications from one Dbase dialect to another because a global find and replace of square brackets and parentheses is not easy to perform in a program. FoxPro solves this perennial problem by automatically recognizing DECLARE and DIMENSION as equivalent statements and allowing both brackets and parentheses to reference arrays.

Built-in Functions and the Compatible Switch

The INKEY( ) function returns an integer from 0 through 255 corresponding to the ASCII code value of the key the user pressed while the machine is in a wait state awaiting user input. The LASTKEY( ) function returns the ASCII code of the last key the user pressed to exit a full-screen operation, for example, READ. The values returned by both functions for the same keypress are identical. Normally these functions return the same codes that FoxBASE+ returns. Previously coded dBASE IV programs whose logic depends on testing the values returned by the functions clearly would need to be revised extensively to run in FoxPro were it not for the SET COMPATIBLE switch. Setting the switch to ON (or DB4) allows the program to behave as expected under FoxPro without changing any other line of code.

With SET COMPATIBLE OFF, the SELECT( ) function returns the number of the currently selected work area just as it does in FoxBASE+. With the switch ON, the function returns the number of the highest unused work area, just as it does in dBASE IV.

The LIKE( ) function compares two character expressions and returns .T. if one appears in the other. With SET COMPATIBLE ON, trailing blanks are removed before making the comparison, just as dBASE IV does it; otherwise, the character expressions are left as they are.

Disk Drive Reference

FoxPro commands that reference a disk drive and a file are affected by the SET COMPATIBLE switch. If the switch is set to DB4 (or ON), any command that specifies a drive causes the command to search only the drive, even if a SET PATH TO command references another drive. If the switch is set to FoxPlus (or OFF), the command searches the specified drive and then also searches the FoxPro path.

Commands Affected by the Compatible Switch

The ACTIVATE SCREEN/WINDOW command causes the cursor position to be set to the coordinates 0,0 with SET COMPATIBLE ON; otherwise, the cursor position is not redefined. Also, with the switch set to ON, FoxPro places popups in the active output window. Then, when the popup is activated, the cursor is positioned on an option in the popup. If the popup is placed in row zero, the entire row is used as part of the menu bar. With SET COMPATIBLE FoxPlus, popups are placed on their own windows, and the cursor is not repositioned; placing the popup on row zero causes the pads of the menu alone to be treated as part of the menu bar.

The APPEND MEMO command allows data from a specified text or binary file to overwrite, or be added to, a given memo field. With SET COMPATIBLE DB4, the command assumes a default file extension of .txt if one is not provided. With the switch set to FoxPlus, no default extension is assumed.

The way that FoxPro executes the PLAY MACRO command depends on SET COMPATIBLE. With the switch set to DB4, FoxPro executes a single letter keyboard macro (A–Z) as though it were defined with ALT-F10 preceding the letter; for example, macro A becomes ALT-F10-A. Macros defined with the function keys F1–F10 are executed as though they were defined with ALT preceding the function key; for instance, macro F5 becomes ALT-F5. FoxPro does not implicitly add ALT or ALT-F10 to the keyboard macro name if the compatible switch is set to FoxPlus.

What happens when a user presses <Esc> during a READ of a field with a VALID clause in the GET statement? With SET COMPATIBLE DB4, the validation routine is still executed; otherwise, FoxPro does not perform any validation.

The expression specified in SET MESSAGE appears immediately on the last line of the screen if the compatible switch is set to DB4; otherwise, the expression is displayed only if SET STATUS is ON. The output of the SUM command contains the same number of decimal places specified in the SET DECIMALS command if the compatible switch is set to DB4; otherwise, the displayed number of decimals is the same as the number of decimals for the field as defined in the database structure.

Comparison of Program Limits

For the most part, FoxPro and dBASE IV have comparable program capacities. Some of the most important differences are in the number of work areas and index files. FoxPro allows 25 work areas, and therefore up to 25 database files, to be open at one time. A total of 25 index files may be open in all work areas at once. FoxPro does not have the dBASE IV multiple index (.mdx) file facility.

dBASE IV allows more memory variables, but FoxPro has higher limits on memo field and character string length, the number of array elements, and the number of procedures or functions in a procedure file. Note that although only one procedure file may be open at a time, procedures may be included in the currently active (Main) program, and FoxPro finds those procedures (in addition to those included in the SET PROCEDURE TO file) without requiring you to SET PROCEDURE to the currently active program.

Table 1-1 compares the program limits of FoxPro and dBASE IV.

Files and File Formats

FoxPro database files without an associated memo (.fpt) file are, for practical purposes, indistinguishable from those of FoxBASE+, dBASE III PLUS, and dBASE IV. The signature byte (byte 0) for these .dbf files is 03H. If a FoxPro .dbf file contains a memo file, the signature byte is F5H, and only FoxPro can read the file.

FoxPro can read the database and memo files of all members of the Dbase family. It can read and write directly to FoxBASE+ and dBASE III PLUS memo files without first converting them to .fpt files. When FoxPro cannot write directly to a memo file created in dBASE IV, it asks your permission to convert the file to an .fpt file. Later you can convert the file to a form recognizable by dBASE IV with the following command:

```
COPY TO <dbfname> TYPE FOXPLUS
```

FoxPro and other members of the Dbase family can now read and write directly to the resulting .dbt file. The FoxPro memo file generally occupies less space than the corresponding dBASE IV memo file. FoxPro also allows

Table 1-1. Comparison of FoxPro and dBASE IV Program Limits

	Maximum Values	
	FoxPro	**dBASE IV**
Records per .dbf file	1 billion	1 billion
Characters per record	4000	4000
Fields per record	255	255
Characters in char field	254	254
Characters in string	65,504	254
Size of numeric field	20	20
Numeric precision, digits	16	20
Char in field name	10	10
# all files open at one time	99	99
# .dbf open at one time	25	10
# open .ndx per .dbf	25	10
# open memo file per .dbf	1	1
Char per memo field	unlimited	64K
Char per index key	100	100
Index per .mdx file	n/a	47
# memory variables	3600	15,000
# of arrays	3600	1170
# elements per array	3600	1170
# dimensions per array	2	2
SET PROCEDURE file	1	1
Procedures per PROCEDURE file	1170	963
Program code bytes	64K	64K
Chars in command line	1024	1024
Report width, chars	255	255
Grouping levels/rpt bands	20	44

any type of data (text or binary) to be stored in a memo field and .fpt file. However, if you intend to convert the file to a FoxBASE-compatible .dbt file, make sure that the field does not contain the Null (ASCII decimal 0) or Ctrl-Z (ASCII decimal 26) character.

Like FoxBASE+, FoxPro uses a default file extension of .idx for index files. This is structured differently from the dBASE .ndx file and is not compatible with it. However, FoxPro can read a dBASE .ndx file directly and convert it automatically into its own .idx format, leaving the original unaltered. You can force FoxPro to use .ndx as the default index file extension by adding the following line to the Config.fp file:

```
INDEX = NDX
```

However, doing so will overwrite any existing dBASE index files that FoxPro reads and automatically converts to its own format.

FoxPro automatically compiles screen format (.fmt) files into .prx files when given the SET FORMAT TO command. FoxPro can read and use FoxBASE+ and dBASE III PLUS report (.frm) files although it will write changes to these files in its own .frx format.

Table 1-2 compares the file extensions that FoxPro and dBASE IV use for common files.

FoxPro Extensions

One of FoxPro's most distinctive features is its extensively revised user interface, including its total support of a mouse pointing device. FoxPro has a long list of commands and command extensions to support the use of a mouse.

In FoxPro, everything happens in a window. Windows may be moved, sized, zoomed, deactivated, or hidden. Even the dot prompt has been replaced by a Command window. Whereas dBASE users have to recall previously issued dot prompt commands one at a time, FoxPro users have the benefit of a scrollable window containing the entire command history. The Command window also allows users to block, cut, and paste a set of interactively entered commands onto a program being edited at another window. Thus, users can test a set of commands and then include them in a program.

The FoxPro opening screen, shown in Figure 1-1, shows the Command window and the System menu. The System menu contains desk accessories such as a calculator, diary/calendar, and an ASCII chart. It also includes a keyboard macro dialog facility for defining, editing, and restoring keyboard

Table 1-2. FoxPro and dBASE IV File Extensions

File Type	FoxPro	dBASE IV
Database	.dbf	.dbf
Index	.idx (.ndx)	.ndx, .mdx
Memo	.fpt	.dbt, .cpt
Memory	.mem	.mem
Screen format	.fmt, .prx	.fmt, .fmo
Keyboard macro	.fky	.key
Label	.lbv, .lbx	.lbl, .lbg, .lbo
Report	.frv, .frx	.frm, .frg, .fro
Program	.prg	.prg
Compiled program	.fxp	.dbo
Template	.gen, .cod, .inc	.gen, .cod
SQL command file	n/a	.prs

macros. The Filer facility allows disk maintenance such as copying or deleting files in a point-and-shoot window without leaving the FoxPro environment. Finally, the Help option of the menu invokes the Help database currently defined by the SET HELP TO command. By default, this is set to the Foxhelp.dbf file.

Normally, users can access the System menu by pressing the ALT key or the F10 key. Application developers may allow or disallow user access to the menu from within a program by way of the SET SYSMENU OFF/ON command.

Since FoxPro is windows oriented, a number of enhancements relate to windows, popups, and menus. User-defined windows are allowed in addition to system windows. FoxPro output goes to the active window and all cursor positioning commands are relative to that window's origin so you won't have to worry about calculating offsets. The View window serves as a control panel where you can open data files, set file relations, define your FoxPro environment by setting appropriate switches on and off, and specify data display formats. The Browse/Edit window showcases FoxPro's extensively enhanced BROWSE command, which lets you display a select group of fields, includ-

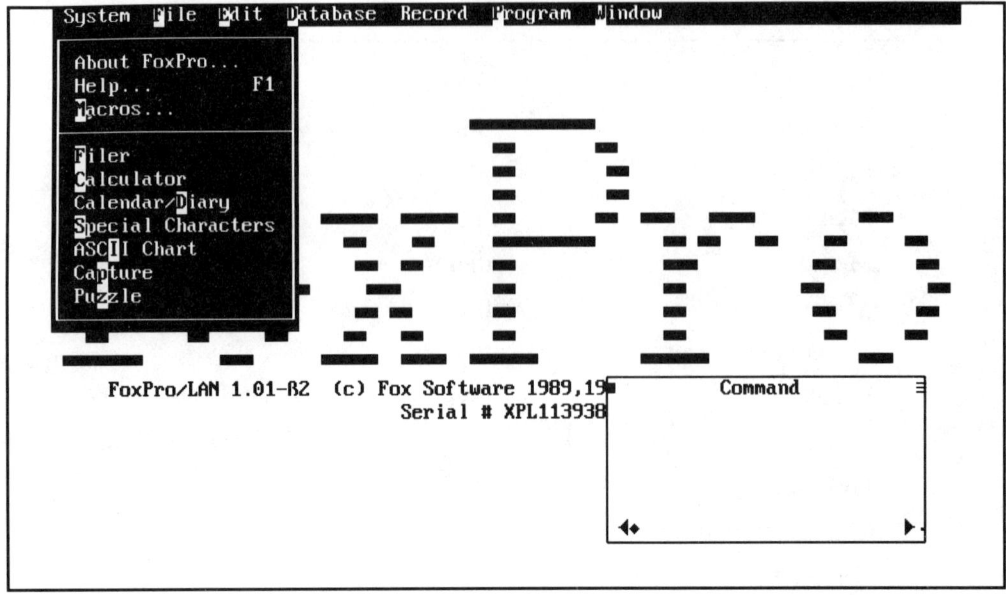

Figure 1-1. FoxPro Opening screen.

ing calculated fields, and split the window into partitions (or panes) so you can view two different sets of fields within the database.

When FoxPro encounters an error in a program run in its interactive environment, the text editor window opens and the cursor rests on the program line that generated the error. Clearly, this helps speed up program development. In addition, the Trace and Debug windows are a boon to application developers. While a program is running, press <Esc> to interrupt and then SUSPEND the program. After you pop down the Windows menu, select the Trace option and watch the program run one line at a time. Chapter 4 describes the Trace and Debug facility in detail.

Customizable Help

FoxPro's default help file, Foxhelp.dbf, is just a regular FoxPro database file consisting of two fields:

Field	Field Name	Type	Width
1	TOPIC	Character	30
2	DETAILS	Memo	10

The TOPIC field contains the names of FoxPro's commands and functions, and the actual help text is stored in the memo field. Since the file is just a .dbf/.fpt file, we are free to modify the help text according to our own requirements, add records to the file, or even create our own replacement for Foxhelp. This capability is discussed more fully in Chapter 4.

FoxPro has taken memo fields to a point where they can be treated just like regular character strings but with additional features such as the ability to store binary data including pictures and other graphics. For the most part, character functions are applicable to memo fields as well. Although dBASE IV memo fields are limited to 64 KB, the length of FoxPro memo fields is limited only by available disk space. Chapter 7 contains an extensive discussion of the FoxPro memo field facility.

The low-level file I/O functions allow a FoxPro program to directly manipulate files written by other software without first having to read those files into a scratch .dbf. These functions operate on text as well as binary data and facilitate importing alien data into a FoxPro application as well as exporting FoxPro data to even mainframe-based programs. Low-level I/O functions support unbuffered access to a communication port, say, COM1:, which is treated almost like a regular file. Chapter 12 contains many examples of how these functions can be put to good use.

FoxPro includes a number of utility programs to facilitate compiling and distributing applications. The Foxbind utility, familiar to FoxBASE+ users, combines multiple procedures and functions into one procedure file. Programs may be batch compiled using the Fls utility program, which creates a list of files for input to a FoxPro program. Finally, the Cruncher.exe utility dramatically reduces the size of compiled (.fxp) programs by removing cross-reference information used by Trace and Debug. Removing this information saves approximately 8 bytes per program source line, including comments, and is intended for thoroughly debugged programs before they are distributed. Users of FoxPro version 1.01 and later do not need this utility because they can specify that cross-reference data be removed at compile time, using the NODEBUG option of the COMPILE command.

Memory Requirements and Usage

FoxPro runs comfortably on a machine with 640 KB RAM even with a typical network shell loaded. Such a machine has enough room to shell to DOS or invoke a reasonably sized editor such as IBM's Personal Editor or Semware's Qedit program from within the FoxPro environment. Note that you can specify the amount of memory you are willing to give to an external program, which you call up from FoxPro by way of the RUN command. The command

```
RUN /n <pgmname>
```

yields control to the DOS command or external program <pgmname> allocating to it memory amounting to *n* KB. If *n* is zero, FoxPro invokes its Foxswap utility program to swap the entire contents of memory to disk before yielding control to the external program. Memory swapped out to disk is restored when the external program terminates. Invoking /0 is not usually a good idea unless absolutely necessary because of the delay involved in activating Foxswap and swapping memory to, and from, disk.

If the optional parameter /*n* is omitted, FoxPro attempts to execute the external program in whatever memory is currently available. If this memory is insufficient to run the program, control returns to FoxPro without running the program. For optimum results, you should estimate the amount of memory required by the program and invoke it with the estimated /*n* value.

Expanded Memory Support

FoxPro can take advantage of as much EMS (expanded memory specification) memory as available. The amount of EMS memory made available to FoxPro translates to better overall performance. To limit or suppress FoxPro's use of EMS memory, add either of the following lines to your Config.fp file:

```
EMS = n
EMS = OFF
```

The first line limits the amount of EMS that FoxPro can access to *n* kilobytes of memory, where *n* should be a multiple of 16. Why would you ever want to turn off FoxPro usage of expanded memory? FoxPro always places its own memory back into the EMS page frame after a CALL to a .bin file. If your .bin file is not prepared for this, you may wish to turn off EMS to play it safe. Additionally, some RAM disks and disk caching programs conflict with the way FoxPro uses EMS—they incorrectly assume that no other program performs direct memory access I/O into the EMS page frame. In this case, you may want to turn EMS off. However, note that FoxPro's performance is not significantly affected by the presence of a disk cache.

For products, such as 386MAX, which provide an option for configuring a RAM disk to use either extended or expanded memory, you should consider using extended memory for the RAM disk. If you have an 80386 machine and

Quarterdeck's popular EMS emulator, QEMM, FoxPro comes with the Foxq utility program that makes memory above 640 KB accessible to FoxPro.

If you use DOS 4.00 or 4.01, note that you can load DOS buffers into expanded, rather than conventional, memory. To do that, add the command

```
BUFFERS=nn/X
```

in your Config.sys file, where *nn* is the number of buffers you want reserved. Use of EMS this way may occasionally produce problems with software that uses expanded memory.

Unimplemented dBASE IV Features

FoxPro version 1.0 does not have dBASE IV's multiple index file facility, which allows up to 47 index tags per index file. The dBASE IV system automatically maintains a production .mdx file, ensuring that all 47 tags in that file are always in sync with the associated .dbf file. Since FoxPro does not provide .mdx file support, it also does not have built-in support for indexing files in descending order. Procedures and techniques for indexing files in descending order are described in Chapters 6 and 10.

FoxPro also does not currently provide a SQL (Structured Query Language) or a QBE (Query By Example) facility similar to those provided by dBASE IV. FoxPro version 1.0 does not implement printer drivers that allow dBASE IV users to change print styles without knowing specific printer command sequences.

Also missing in the current version of FoxPro is support for transaction processing, allowing for rollback and recovery from system failure in the midst of a transaction, and ensuring that files remain in a consistent state. Additionally, dBASE IV has the CONVERT command and the complement functions CHANGE( ) and LKSYS( ) to implement multiuser lock detection. This facility is still unavailable in FoxPro 1.01.

Chapter Summary

FoxPro is a compatible superset of FoxBASE+ and includes most of the dBASE IV command set and features except support for SQL, QBE, multiple index file and transaction processing, and automatic lock detection in multiuser mode. Its SET COMPATIBLE command determines whether select commands and functions behave like FoxBASE+ (OFF) or dBASE IV (ON).

FoxPro can use data files created by other Dbase products without prior conversion. In this chapter, we also compared FoxPro and dBASE in terms of their program capacities and the files they use.

One of FoxPro's most distinguishable features is its totally revamped user interface including full support for a mouse. It provides numerous extensions to the Dbase language, particularly in support of windows, menus and pop-ups. In the following chapters we will discuss many of FoxPro's new capabilities in detail, and how you may take advantage of them in developing your applications.

Chapter 2

Database Design

A good database design is quite possibly the most critical element in an application system, providing it flexibility and simplifying its maintenance. It is the groundwork you lay for your entire development effort. Even the best programming will not overcome a deficient design.

What factors should you consider when you start defining your database? This chapter answers this question with a set of steps you should follow to ensure a good design. It gives you some idea as to where to start and what questions to ask. We start out with the basics, then discuss more sophisticated design issues such as integrity rules and normalization of your database files, and finally look at how you implement these rules in a FoxPro application. Then we walk through a sample application to demonstrate how to implement each of the steps.

The Eight Steps to Database Design

The eight steps to a database design are shown in Figure 2-1.

Step 1: Complete a Thorough Requirements Analysis

First and foremost in any design effort is to complete a thorough requirements analysis. This means talking with your clients, managers as well as end users, to gain an understanding of the work process. The more you learn about what they do, the better equipped you are to start automating the process. Even if

8. Specify the Domain for Each Field
7. Build Your Data Network
6. Add Nonkey Fields to Your Database Files
5. Identify Foreign Keys
4. Define Primary Keys
3. Identify Relationships Among the Entities
2. Identify Entities
1. Complete a Thorough Requirements Analysis

Figure 2-1. The Eight Steps to Database Design.

certain aspects of the process will not be automated, it helps to define the procedures from beginning to end.

Clients do not necessarily have a complete idea of what the new application should look like. They usually do not know what is reasonable to expect from an automated system. Therefore, they do not know precisely what information you need to do the job. Start by gaining an understanding of the entire process from a high-level viewpoint. Ask enough questions to be sure you are not missing any of the big pieces. Then you can determine what details you need to design the system. In addition to talking to everyone involved in the process, read as many procedures manuals or other documentation as you can get your hands on. This can give you vital details that your client may have forgotten. In the end, your goal is to understand your client's work process as well as he or she does.

Step 2: Identify Entities

Once you understand the work process, you must define the entities with which you will be dealing. For example, an order processing system may have customers, orders, parts, and suppliers. Each entity represents a distinct object in the process. These entities may eventually be represented as tables in your database. Later you may add more tables or separate the entities into more than one table, but for now just make sure that everything is represented.

Step 3: Identify Relationships Among the Entities

Now that you know what entities you are working with, you must define the relationships that exist. For example, in an order processing system, each customer may have more than one order, but any given order belongs to just one customer. This is termed a one-to-many relationship. Each order may contain many items, and any given item will appear on numerous orders. This is called a many-to-many relationship. Finally, you may have a one-to-one relationship. For example, suppose that every item is produced by exactly one supplier, and every supplier provides exactly one item.

Identify all the relationships that exist among your entities, and the type of relationship (one-to-one, one-to-many, or many-to-many) in each case.

Step 4: Define Primary Keys

In each of your tables (entities) you need some identifier that distinguishes each record. Since one of the basic rules of good design is to not allow duplicate records, you must have a means of ensuring that each record is unique. The value that you use to distinguish your records is called the primary key. Later, we will discuss the requirement that no primary key be null (blank). For now, just identify the value you will use to differentiate among your records and to enforce the requirement that duplicates be rejected.

In some cases, the entity will already have a value that you can use as a primary key. For example, an Employee table could easily use employee social security number as the primary key. In other cases, your system may have to assign a value to be used as the key. For example, a Customer table may require that you assign a unique customer id to each record. It is important that you know how the client currently differentiates among occurrences of each entity. As part of Step 1, you should know whether unique customer ids are assigned as part of the current work process. Wherever possible, use "real" values, that is, values that are already in use and may have some meaning to your client. This means that you should use, for example, employee social security number rather than a system-assigned id.

If you have several choices for a unique key value, select the one that is most pertinent to the application. The primary key may be made up of more than one field value; this is called a composite key. It is perfectly acceptable to define such a primary key, but be sure that the composite value is irreducible. In other words, each field value making up the composite key must be required to ensure uniqueness. If not, drop that field from the primary key.

Finally, stay away from long character strings when defining the key. This is primarily to avoid confusion and errors when variable case and spacing is introduced to the character value. For example, Smith, J. and SMITH, J appear to be two different values. Some of the alternatives to using a character string are: find an abbreviation that retains the unique quality, use a numeric value associated with the record, or assign a unique number within your application. For example, when defining the unique key for a table of company departments, stay away from keys that look like this:

Accounting
Sales
Human Resources
Data Processing

Instead, either assign values (for example, 01, 02, 03, and 04) to the departments, or use easy-to-remember abbreviations such as:

ACCT
SALES
HR
DP

It is generally preferable to use codes in place of character strings where feasible.

Step 5: Identify Foreign Keys

C. J. Date (Date, 1987) defines a foreign key as an attribute (field), or attribute combination, in one table (T2) whose values are required to match those of the primary key of some table (T1). Tables T1 and T2 are not necessarily unique.

Consider our order processing example. The Order table will have a primary key of order number, perhaps generated by our application. In addition, each order must be traceable to the customer who placed it. We will include a field for customer id in each order. This customer id must match one of the (primary key) customer id values in the Customer table. This means that customer id is a foreign key in the Order table.

Essentially, the foreign key is used to associate a record with a value in another table. As another example, an Employee table may contain a department id field to indicate the department to which each employee is assigned.

Employee	**Department**
Emp_id	Dept_id
Dept_id	Dept_name

The Dept_id field in the Employee table links the employees with their departments, where the department information is stored in another table.

As discussed later in this chapter under the relational integrity rules, a foreign key must be either:

1. Equal to the value of a primary key in another table, or
2. Entirely null.

It is not usually desirable to allow a null foreign key. The problem with a null foreign key is obvious—it is impossible to link the record to a corresponding value in another table. This can be controlled within your application by requiring that the foreign key be provided (and validated) before permitting the record to be added. You may also have to ensure that the foreign key value is not deleted during a database update.

Step 6: Add Nonkey Fields to Your Database Files

Now that you have defined your entities and the primary and foreign keys for each, you must determine the remaining fields for each table. This is a critical step, resulting in the specification of each of your tables.

This is the time to decide on the field names for each table. You should adhere to some naming convention to facilitate your documentation and maintenance activities in the future. One good convention is to prefix each nonkey field name with the first two or three letters from the table name. Primary and foreign key field names should not have a prefix since they will appear in multiple tables. Of course your field names should be descriptive of the contents of the field. For example, a table named Order might consist of three fields: Order Id, Customer ID, and Order Date. Using our naming conventions, your field names might be:

OrdId (Primary key)
CusId (Foreign key)
Ord_OrdDt

The next consideration, and possibly the most important procedure in defining your database, is to normalize your tables. Normalization eliminates redundancy, keeps related data together, and ensures that you do not lose information when related information is deleted from the database. These points are explained in greater detail later in this chapter.

Step 7: Build Your Data Network

In this step, you simply map out what you have already defined. At this point, you know what tables you will be working with, as well as the primary and foreign keys for each table. Draw a simple diagram, displaying each table as a box and writing the primary and foreign key values in each box. Then draw lines to connect your primary keys and foreign keys. Figure 2-2 shows a sample data network for an order processing system.

This step does not add new information, but clarifies what you have already defined. Primarily, it serves to identify unnecessary tables in your database. If you see a table with no links to any other table, it is highly likely that you can eliminate the table from the database. Now is your chance to go back and redefine your tables so that you are satisfied with the "map" of your database.

Step 8: Specify the Domain for Each Field

During this step, you determine the most appropriate data type for each field. In other words, you determine the type of values the field will contain: numeric, character, date, and so on. Then you determine the acceptable range of values for each field. This is where you decide the length of a character field and the minimum and maximum values for a numeric field. Actually, you start determining much of your field validation criteria at this point. However, the validation procedures are not part of the FoxPro database design; you will incorporate your edit and validation routines into your application. When you have identified the domains, you are ready to create your tables in FoxPro.

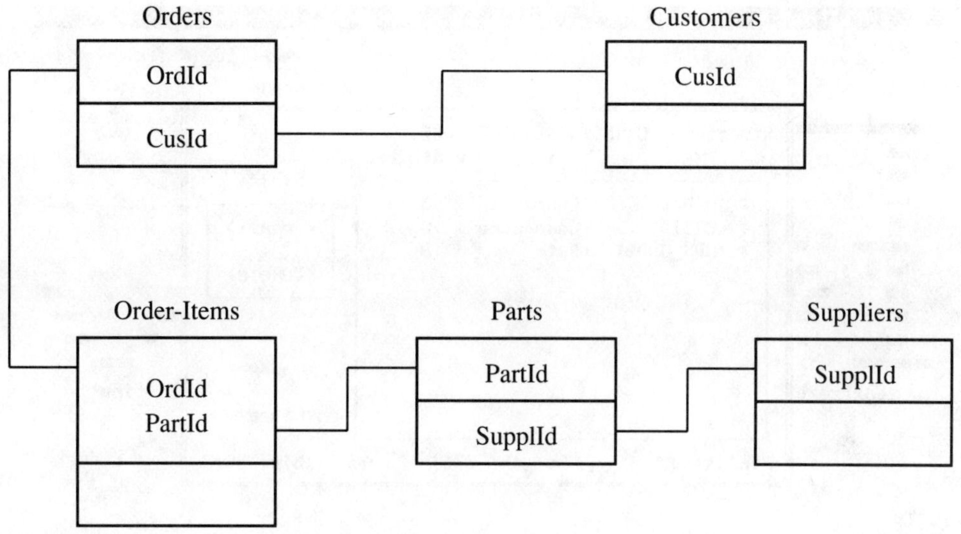

Figure 2-2. A sample data network diagram. Primary keys are shown in the top of each box and foreign keys are shown on the bottom.

Creating Your FoxPro Database

Once you have completed each of the eight steps, you know exactly what your database files (tables) should consist of. You are now ready to create your database in FoxPro.

Using the CREATE command, you create a database file for each table in your database. You have already identified the fields to be contained in each table, the names of the fields, and the field domains (numeric, character, and so on). Figure 2-3 shows a sample screen used to CREATE each file.

Of course, when you create your files, you have no means of indicating primary and foreign keys. In FoxPro, this must be controlled by your application when you start writing code. Once your files are built, you will usually want to create an index with the primary key defined as the index expression. Of course, you may decide to build additional indexes to be used for reporting or other purposes as well. The creation of the index does not enforce the requirement that the primary key be unique and nonnull; you must enforce this through program code. The index helps you determine whether or not a record with the desired key already exists.

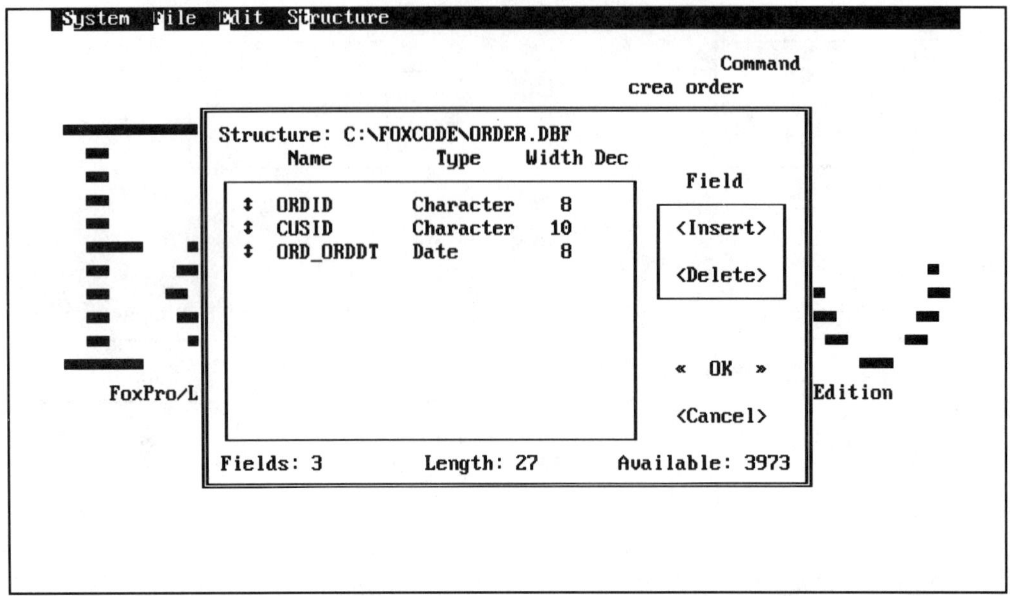

Figure 2-3. Sample FoxPro CREATE screen, used to define each database file.

How do you identify your foreign keys? Actually, you don't. There is no built-in facility for indicating which fields participate in a foreign key, or the link between foreign keys and their associated primary keys in another table. You have to handle the primary/foreign key relationships yourself in the program code, for example, with the SET RELATION TO command.

The Relational Integrity Rules

C. J. Date defined two integrity rules of the relational model. These rules, defined in terms we have been using, are as follows:

1. *Entity integrity* — No field participating in the primary key of a table may be null.
2. *Referential integrity* — If a table includes a foreign key (FK) matching the primary key (PK) of some table T, every value of FK must be either:
   a) Equal to the value of PK in some record in table T, or
   b) Entirely null.

Remember that a primary key is defined as a field (or combination of fields) that uniquely identifies each record in a table. If the primary key is a composite key (made up of more than one field), each of the fields must be required to ensure uniqueness.

We already mentioned these rules in Steps 4 and 5, where we defined the primary and foreign keys for our tables. The importance of these rules extends beyond just ensuring that our primary and foreign keys meet the listed criteria, however. We must ensure that the rules are met at all times. This means that you, as the application developer, must make sure that your system has addressed the following issues.

Null Foreign Keys

As previously mentioned, although the referential integrity rule allows foreign keys to be null, we do not recommend it. You must decide if you will allow null foreign keys in your application. In making this decision, consider the event that it represents. In other words, does it make sense within the context of your application that a foreign key might, even temporarily, contain a null value? The answer to this questions will in part determine the approach you take in designing your application.

Adhering to the Referential Integrity Rule

In ensuring that the referential integrity rule is always met, you should consider three operations: Inserts, Updates, and Deletes.

Inserts If a user attempts to insert a record with an invalid foreign key (that is, a value is entered for the foreign key that does not match any of the corresponding primary key values in the associated table), you can apply one of the following three rules:

1. Disallow the addition of the record and require the user to enter the primary key information into the corresponding table [DEPENDENT rule].
2. Automatically branch the user to another module where he or she can add the record with the required primary key [AUTOMATIC rule].
3. Accept the new record with a null foreign key value [NULLIFY rule]. (Applicable only if you accept null foreign keys.)

Deletes If a user attempts to delete a record containing a primary key that at least one table uses as a foreign key, the integrity rules can be enforced in three ways:

1. Automatically delete all records in all tables with the corresponding foreign key [CASCADE rule].
2. Allow the deletion only if there are no records with a foreign key matching the primary key about to be deleted [RESTRICT rule].
3. Nullify the foreign key values on all matching records [NULLIFY rule]. Of course, this option is valid only if you have decided to accept null foreign keys.

Updates You must also define how you will handle an attempt to modify a primary key that has related foreign keys. These three options are essentially the same as for delete operations.

1. Automatically update the matching foreign key values to the new value of the primary key [CASCADE rule].
2. Allow the update only if there are no records with matching foreign keys [RESTRICT rule].
3. Nullify the foreign key values on all matching records [NULLIFY rule]. Again, this option is valid only if you have decided to accept null foreign keys.

Normalization

Database normalization is a technique that simplifies the database structure and eliminates redundant data. As previously stated in Step 6 of database design, databases are normalized for the following reasons:

- To keep related data together.
- To eliminate redundancy.
- To ensure that information is not lost when related data is deleted from the database.

A normalized database is said to be in one of several normal forms. First, second, and third normal forms are the most common forms and the ones we will discuss. Refer to Date [Date, 1987] for information on fourth and fifth normal forms.

Order:

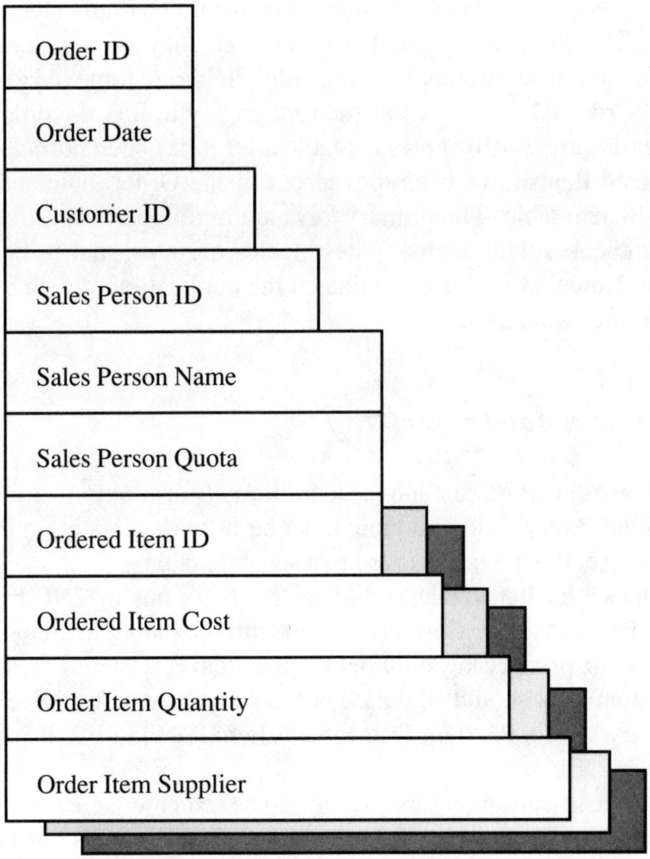

Order ID
Order Date
Customer ID
Sales Person ID
Sales Person Name
Sales Person Quota
Ordered Item ID
Ordered Item Cost
Order Item Quantity
Order Item Supplier

Figure 2-4(a). Unnormalized database.

First Normal Form (1NF)

A database is said to be in first normal form when all repeating groups have been put in separate tables. Figure 2-4(a) shows an example of a database that is not in 1NF. The Order table initially contains fields for Order ID, Order Date, Customer ID, Sales Person ID, Sales Person Name, and Sales Person Quota, and multiple occurrences of the Ordered Item ID, Ordered Item Cost, Ordered Item Quantity, and Ordered Item Supplier fields. Since an order may be made up of many ordered items, the item ids, costs, quantities, and suppliers are said to be repeating fields. The problem with this structure is that in order to store data about each ordered item, multiple Order records would be needed, which means the Order Date, Customer ID, Sales Person ID, Sales Person Name, and Sales Person Quota would be duplicated for each ordered item. This introduces a great deal of redundancy into the database.

To normalize this table, the repeating fields are removed to a separate table, with Order ID designated as the foreign key to link the ordered items to the order. Figure 2-4(b) shows the table after it has been normalized to 1NF; the Ordered Items have been moved out of the Order table and into their own Order-Item table. The primary keys are highlighted, and field dependencies are indicated with arrows. These tables are now said to be in first normal form. Note that we have eliminated the duplication of data by separating the table into two tables.

Second Normal Form (2NF)

A database can be cast into second normal form only if it is first in 1NF. In addition, every field in a table must be fully dependent on the primary key; otherwise, it must be removed to a separate table.

The Order-Item table in Figure 2-4(b) is not in 2NF because the Item Supplier and Item Cost are dependent only on the Item ID, not on the composite primary key of Order ID plus Item ID. Therefore, the Item Supplier and Item Cost should be pulled out to a separate table called Item-Data. The primary key for the Item-Data table is Item ID. Figure 2-4(c) shows the tables now in 2NF.

The justification for this change can be seen more clearly by looking at our table with sample data. The following example shows our Order-Item table before it is placed in 2NF:

Order-Item:

Order ID	Item ID	Item Cost	Item Quantity	Item Supplier
2378	A15	24.99	3	S234
2378	A48	12.50	8	S90
2379	A15	24.99	2	S234
2379	A23	41.25	4	S123
2380	A23	41.25	2	S123

As you can see, the Item Cost and Item Supplier information is duplicated. By separating this table into two, we eliminate the redundant data as follows:

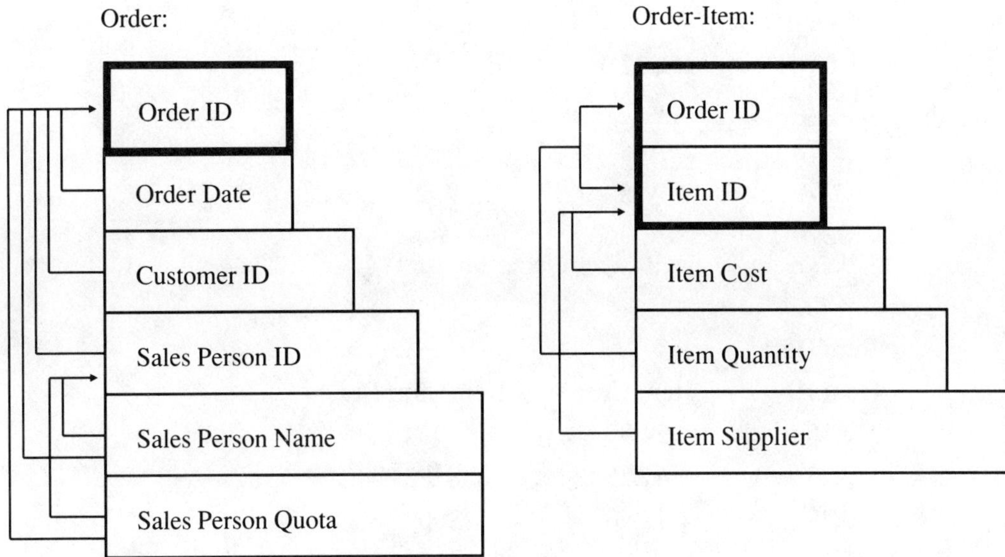

Figure 2-4(b). The same database in first normal form. Primary keys are highlighted, and field dependencies are shown with arrows.

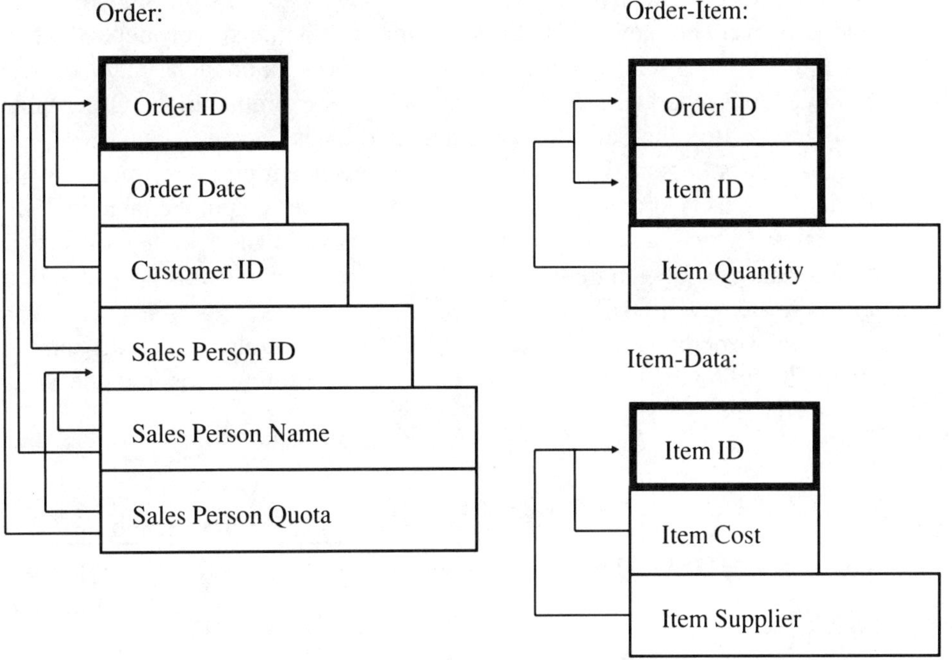

Figure 2-4(c). The same database in second normal form. Primary keys are highlighted, and field dependencies are shown with arrows.

Order-Item:

Order ID	Item ID	Item Quantity
2378	A15	3
2378	A48	8
2379	A15	2
2379	A23	4
2380	A23	2

Item Data:

Item ID	Item Cost	Item Supplier
A15	24.99	S234
A23	41.25	S123
A48	12.50	S90

Third Normal Form (3NF)

A table must be in 2NF before it can be cast into third normal form. In addition, every nonkey field in the table must be nontransitively dependent on the primary key. Fields that are transitively dependent on the primary key are removed to a separate table during this step. For example, in the Order table of Figure 2-4(c), the Sales Person Name and Sales Person Quota are dependent on Sales Person ID, which in turn is dependent on the primary key of Order ID. This is known as a transitive dependence. To put the table in 3NF, the Sales Person Name and Quota fields are moved to a separate table called Sales-Pers, as shown in Figure 2-4(d). The tables shown in this normalization example are now in 3NF.

Again, we demonstrate the advantage of 3NF with tables containing sample data. The following table shows the Order table before we separate the Sales Person data:

Order:

			Sales Person		
Order ID	**Order Date**	**Customer ID**	**ID**	**Name**	**Quota**
2378	02/12/90	C4990	S12	J. Jones	12000
2379	02/12/90	C3299	S13	M. Martin	14000
2380	02/14/90	C4163	S15	A. Smith	10000
2381	02/15/90	C2244	S12	J. Jones	12000

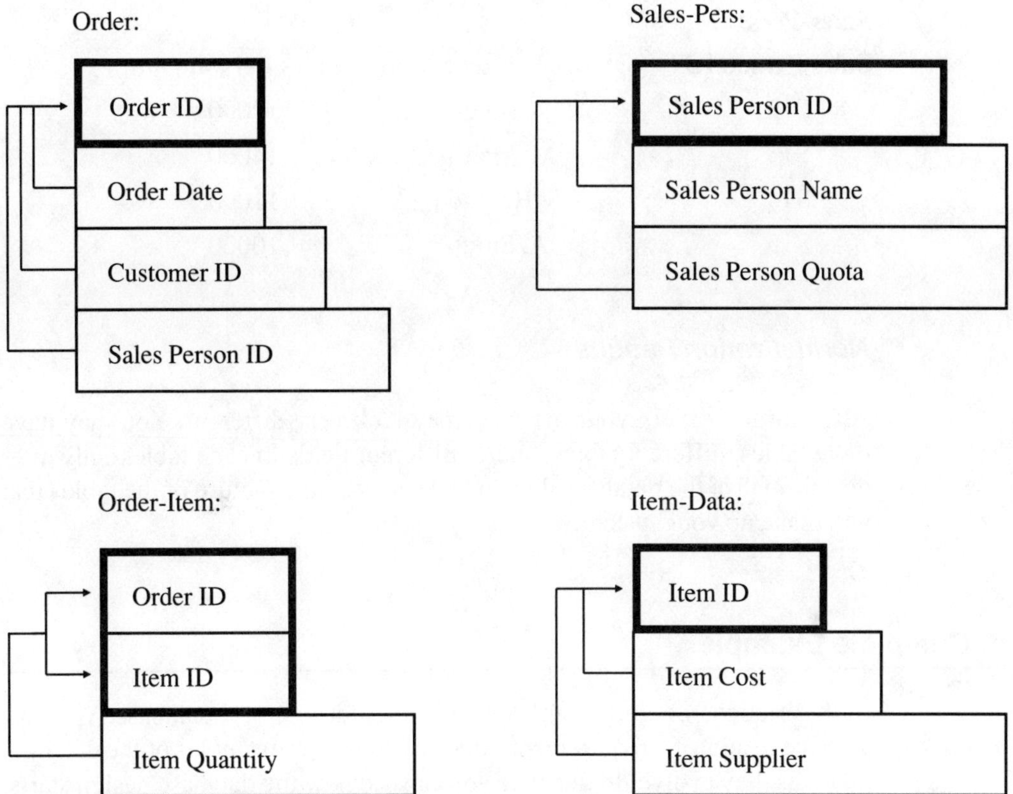

Figure 2-4(d). Third normal form. The results of normalization techniques applied to our order processing database. Primary keys are highlighted, and field dependencies are shown with arrows.

As this example demonstrates, the fields that are transitively dependent on Order ID (Sales Person Name and Sales Person Quota) contain redundant data. By separating these fields into a separate table, and thus placing the tables in 3NF, we eliminate the redundancy as follows:

Order:

Order ID	Order Date	Customer ID	Sales Person ID
2378	02/12/90	C4990	S12
2379	02/12/90	C3299	S13
2380	02/14/90	C4163	S15
2381	02/15/90	C2244	S12

Sales-Pers:

Sales Person ID	Sales Person Name	Sales Person Quota
S12	J. Jones	12000
S13	M. Martin	14000
S14	S. Harrison	11000
S15	A. Smith	10000

Normalization Results

After normalization, your database may look very different. You may have more tables, different tables, and/or different fields in each table. Only after you normalize the database do you have an accurate picture of the tables that will make up your system.

A Complete Example

In this section, we go through a step-by-step design of a database. We start with the results of a requirements analysis and show examples of the database tables as they evolve. In this way you can see how the database design starts, what decisions are made at each step, and what changes take place as we satisfy each of the rules. The example we are going to use is a common business application—the tracking of incoming correspondence as it passes through the various departments of a company, up through the time that a response/resolution is completed.

Step 1: Complete a Thorough Requirements Analysis

Assume that you have attended a series of meetings at your client's site. In addition, you have reviewed some existing procedures manuals, interviewed analysts, and examined typical types of documents currently received and processed. At the completion of this step, you have the following information:

- All correspondence is received in the company mailroom and stamped with a date of receipt. It is then routed to the receptionist, who opens each item, briefly reviews it, and determines where to route it next. The receptionist records the analyst to whom it is routed and the date it is passed to the analyst.

- Each analyst is a member of exactly one department.
- The analyst formulates a response and sends it out. Occasionally the document is routed to the wrong department and must be rerouted to an analyst in another department. When this happens, the receptionist's log book is corrected to show the new analyst and the date the document was passed to that analyst.
- Finally, the original document and a copy of the response is returned to the receptionist, who files both copies and updates his or her log with a close-out date.

The system you are to develop must replace the manual logging procedures. The most important aspect of the system is the ability to determine the status of a particular document at any given time and how it was resolved if it has been closed. The system should also provide management reports showing items not responded to within certain time frames. Management determines the specific time frames within which each document type must be responded to. For example, a request for literature must be answered within one week, a product order must be filled within two weeks, and a complaint must be answered within three days. Department managers also would like to be able to review the completed work of their analysts and be aware of which analysts have overdue items. Certain departments have specific needs, for example, the Customer Service department needs to know which issues generate the most customer complaints. With this information we are now ready to draft a database structure.

Step 2: Identify Entities

From our understanding of the work process at this point, we initially define the following entities for our system:

Documents
Responses
Analysts
Customers
Departments

Step 3: Identify Relationships Among the Entities

Now we are ready to define the relationships among the five entities we defined in Step 2. The relationships that are clear to us at this point are:

- Documents to Responses—A one-to-one relationship exists. Each document has one response, and each response corresponds to exactly one document.
- Documents to Analysts—A many-to-one relationship exists. Many documents are assigned to any given analyst, but a given document is assigned to only one analyst.
- Documents to Customers—A many-to-one relationship exists. A customer may write many letters, but each letter is written by only one customer.
- Documents to Departments—No relationship exists.
- Responses to Analysts—A many-to-one relationship exists. An analyst writes many responses, but each response is written by just one analyst.
- Responses to Customers—A one-to-many relationship exists. Each response is sent to exactly one customer, but each customer may receive several responses (if several letters are sent in by the same customer at different times).
- Responses to Departments—No relationship exists.
- Analysts to Customers—No relationship exists.
- Analysts to Departments—A many-to-one relationship exists. Each analyst is assigned to exactly one department, but each department has many analysts.
- Customers to Departments—No relationship exists.

Step 4: Define Primary Keys

For each of the five entities, we define a primary key. Again, the purpose of the primary key is to differentiate among the many occurrences of each entity (that is, to ensure uniqueness among our records in the table). We define primary keys as follows:

Entity	Primary Key	Description
Documents	DocId	A system-generated document id.
Responses	DocId	The document id of the original correspondence (same as above).

Entity	**Primary Key**	**Description**
Analysts	EmpId	Employee id.
Customers	CusId	First five digits of zip code plus last four digits of phone number plus one-digit sequence number used in case of duplicates.
Departments	DeptNum	A code assigned to each department.

Step 5: Identify Foreign Keys

The foreign keys indicate the relationships among the tables. We already indicated what types of relationships exist among the entities; now we must determine what field values we will use to associate a record with a corresponding primary key in another table.

Entity	**Foreign Key**	**Description**
Documents	EmpId	Associates the document with the responsible analyst.
	CusId	Links the document to the customer who sent it.
Responses	None.	We store the response data in the Document table, so no foreign key is required.
Analysts	DeptNum	Identifies the department to which the analyst belongs.
Customers	None.	There are no fields in the Customers table that depend on fields in other tables.
Departments	None.	There are no fields in the Departments table that depend on fields in other tables.

Step 6: Add Nonkey Fields to Your Database Files

First, we'll add the fields that seem to belong to each table. We will use a nonkey field naming convention of the first three letters of the table plus a descriptive field identifier that represents the data stored in the field. Key fields do not have the table name prefix since they appear in multiple tables. This convention helps us readily identify primary/foreign key relationships in our database. Figure 2-5(a) shows our tables before we have applied any normalization techniques.

When we normalize the database, we start by putting the database in 1NF. To do this, we examine each table and determine whether there are any repeating groups. Since we find no repeating groups in our initial database design, we determine that the database is already in 1NF.

Now we examine the database to determine what changes are required to satisfy the 2NF rules. For each table, every field must be fully dependent on the primary key. If we examine each table, we can see that our tables are already in 2NF, so no further changes are required at this point. By having already defined our entities, relationships, and key fields, we have started off with a database structure in 2NF. This demonstrates the value of going through each of the steps described so far before defining a database.

We still must ensure that the database is in 3NF. To satisfy the 3NF requirement, we eliminate any nontransitive dependencies. We find that there is one nontransitive dependency in our tables: the Doc_MaxDay field is dependent on CorrType, which in turn is dependent on DocId. We therefore remove the MaxDay field to a new table we call DayMax, as shown in Figure 2-5(b). The advantage to this change should be clear: we have eliminated a redundancy by storing the maximum days to respond in just one place, rather than for each document. Also, if management decides to change the requirements, the update is simply made to one record in one table. Finally, a subtle advantage is that we do not accidentally lose the maximum response time information for a particular document type in the event that all document records of that type are deleted.

Our database is now normalized to third normal form. The tables that make up our new database are shown in Figure 2-5(b).

Step 7: Build Your Data Network

Figure 2-6 displays our data network as we have currently defined it. We look at each table in our diagram and determine whether there is at least one relationship to another table by looking at the lines we have drawn to associate primary keys with foreign keys. In this case, every table is associated with at least one other table, so we decide that we do not have any frivolous tables and we leave the design as is.

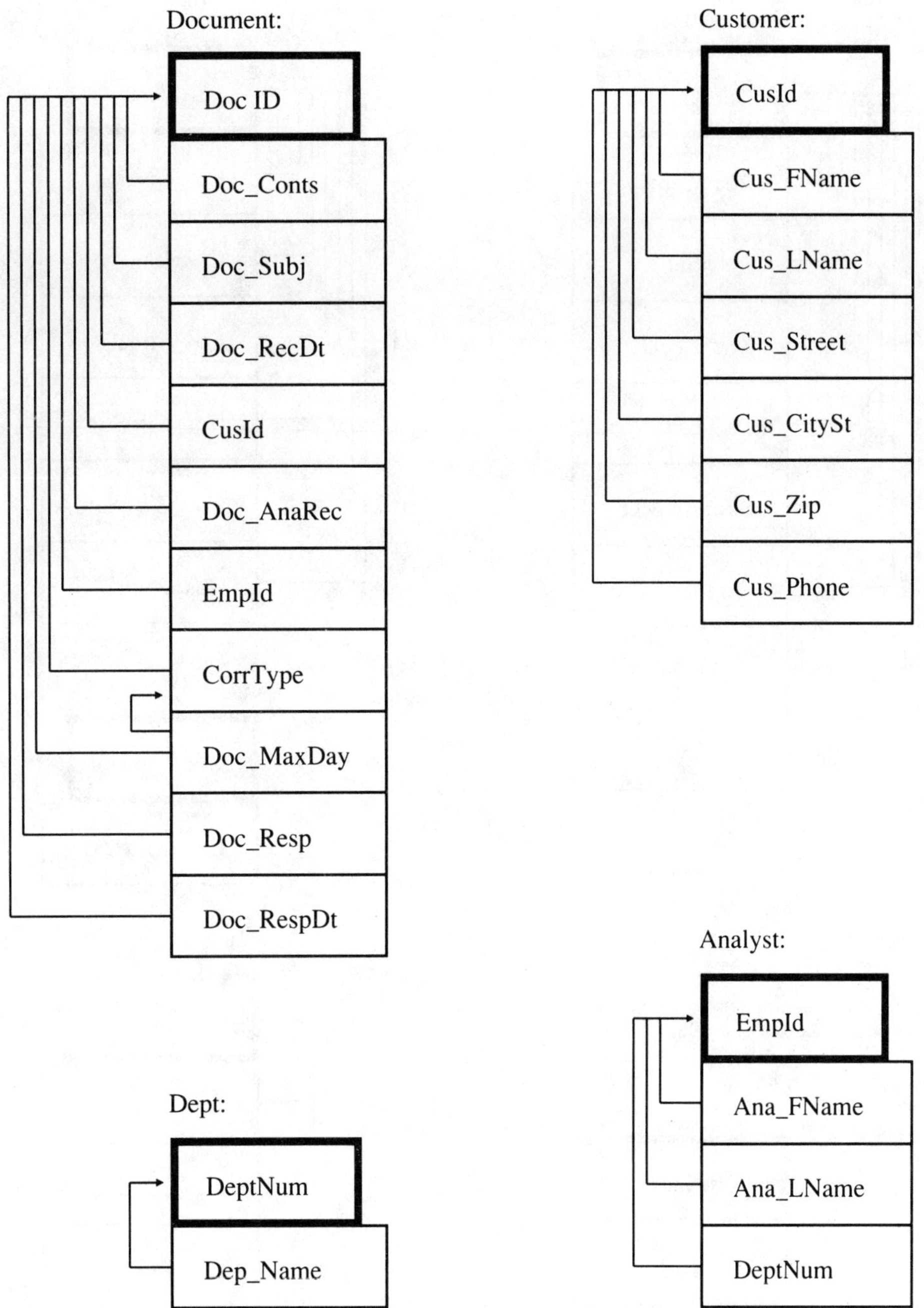

Figure 2-5(a). The correspondence tracking database before normalization techniques are applied. Primary keys are highlighted, and field dependencies are shown with arrows.

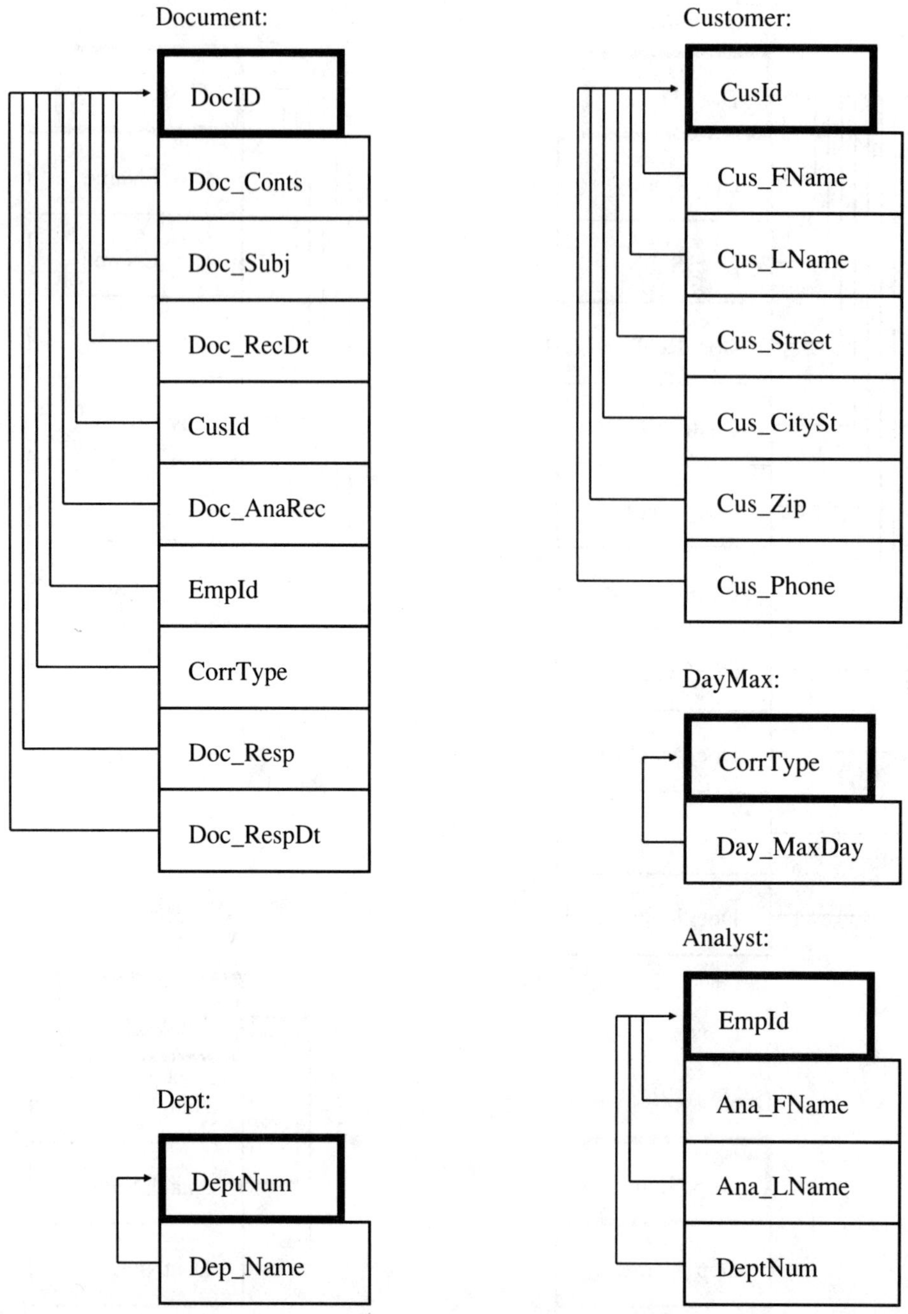

Figure 2-5(b). The results of normalization techniques applied to our correspondence tracking database. Primary keys are highlighted, and field dependencies are shown with arrows.

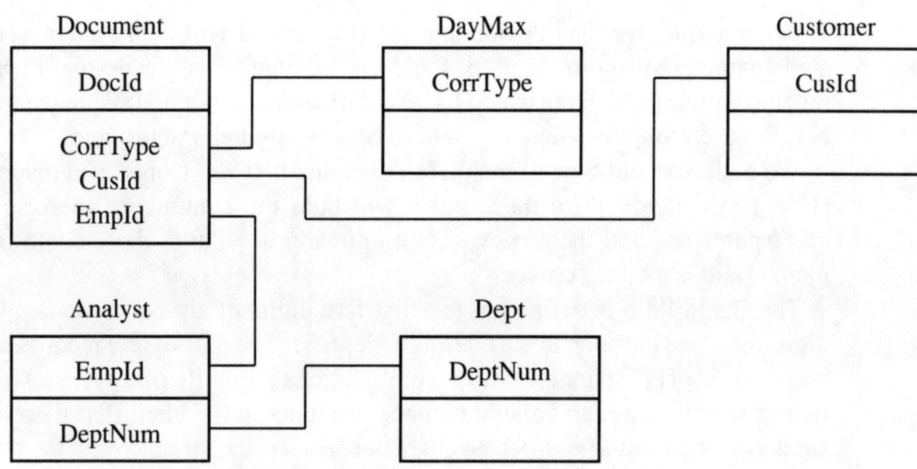

Figure 2-6. The data network diagram for the correspondence tracking database.

Looking at the data network diagram can also help point out flaws in the design; for example, you may notice that a critical element in the system is not addressed. You can always decide to back up to an earlier step, make the appropriate changes, and then pick up from there.

Step 8: Specify the Domain for Each Field

Now that we have defined all our tables and fields, we can determine the domain for each field. This means deciding the type of data to be stored in each field and the valid ranges.

FoxPro offers the following field types:

Character
Numeric
Floating
Logical
Date
Memo

As we look at each field, we should think in terms of these six data types and decide which is most appropriate. Then, for those fields defined as character, numeric, or floating, we will consider the valid range of values in order to determine the field size to be assigned.

For example, we may decide that the DocId field will be a system-generated character string made up of the correspondence type code (CorrType), received month and year (from Doc_RecDt), and an assigned sequence number. We therefore designate the field to be a 10-digit character field.

We assign a field type of memo to the contents (Doc_Conts) and response (Doc_Resp) fields since these fields will hold the contents of the original correspondence and the response. Not knowing how large these could be, a memo field is the best choice.

The CusId field is defined as the first five digits of zip code, the last four digits of phone number, and a one-digit identifier (used if several records have identical zip code/phone number combinations). For flexibility, we would like to be able to assign either a number or a letter to the identifier; therefore, we define the CusId field to be a character field of size 10.

Figure 2-7 shows our entire database with field types and sizes identified. It should be clear that the actual creation of our database in FoxPro is now very easy; we simply CREATE a .dbf file corresponding to each of our tables.

Chapter Summary

Database design is a critical step in the application development process. A good design ensures data integrity, eliminates redundancy, and facilitates system maintenance. Good programming practices cannot compensate for a poor database design.

In this chapter, we presented eight steps to designing a database. These steps are:

1. Complete a thorough requirements analysis.
2. Identify entities.
3. Identify relationships among the entities.
4. Define primary keys.
5. Identify foreign keys.
6. Add nonkey fields to your database files.
7. Build your data network.
8. Specify the domain for each field.

We also discussed the relational database integrity rules and techniques for normalizing a database, and how these rules and techniques apply in creating your FoxPro database. The Entity integrity and Referential integrity rules help maintain accurate and consistent data. Normalization eliminates redundant

Document:

DocId	Character	10
Doc_Conts	Memo	
Doc_Subj	Character	12
Doc_RecDt	Date	
CusId	Character	10
Doc_AnaRec	Date	
EmpId	Numeric	9
CorrType	Character	2
Doc_Resp	Memo	
Doc_RespDt	Date	

DayMax:

CorrType	Character	2
Day_MaxDay	Numeric	3

Analyst:

EmpId	Numeric	9
Ana_FName	Character	10
Ana_LName	Character	15
DeptNum	Character	2

Customer:

CusId	Character	10
Cus_FName	Character	10
Cus_LName	Character	15
Cus_Street	Character	40
Cus_CitySt	Character	15
Cus_Zip	Character	10
Cus_Phone	Character	12

Dept:

DeptNum	Character	2
Dep_Name	Character	15

Figure 2-7. The correspondence tracking database field domains, defined specifically for our FoxPro application.

data, keeps related data together, and ensures that data is not lost when related records are deleted from the database.

Finally, we looked at a sample application, a correspondence tracking system, and walked through each of the eight steps in order to design a logical database structure for the application.

Chapter 3

Data Dictionary

A typical business application consists of a large number of data elements in multiple data files, along with a substantial set of index files and reports. Many database development projects, particularly those involving a large team of programmers, analysts, and writers, can quickly run into trouble if no one bothers to ensure that data representation, even just a field naming convention, is consistent across all programs or system modules. Database normalization helps guarantee against data redundancy so that a nonkey field does not appear in more than one data file. However, without a systematic way of defining and maintaining data, the development team may well discover later on that a required field is unaccounted for in any of the data files, or that two fields in a file that earlier seemed different actually are the same.

One of the most glaring deficiencies of the Dbase product family, including FoxPro, is its inability to fully describe a data element, including the element's range of allowed values, picture clause, source, validation criteria, or even whether or not it is a required field. In Dbase's way of defining a database structure, all we have to work with is a 10-character field name that, in most cases, is hardly sufficient to describe the field, its data type, and its length (and number of decimal places for a numeric field).

Unfortunately, the term "data dictionary" is unknown to a generation of programmers and application developers whose first and only exposure to database management systems is the Dbase product family. Consequently, this generation's approach to data definition is backward—a collection of .dbf files is created before a complete and comprehensive set of all fields that the entire system requires is at hand. It is no wonder then that one of the most popular commands in the Dbase language, especially for beginners, is MOD-

IFY STRUCTURE. This is not a particularly attractive prospect given that changing data file definitions midway through the application development process is a wasteful exercise.

What Is a Data Dictionary?

A data dictionary may be defined as an organized system for uniformly defining and managing data elements, or fields. The dictionary acts as a central repository of information about each data element in a group of related systems. Its purpose is to facilitate access to, and control of, databases. The dictionary manages what is often referred to as metadata, that is, data about data. This metadata includes descriptive properties such as length, value range, validation criteria, or types of admissible data.

A data dictionary serves as a focal point for the development of standard data definitions and coding schemes. It can also serve as the primary tool for monitoring adherence to the organization's standards. Clearly, a fully developed data dictionary can serve as an organization's catalog of its data resources, fully documenting its data collection, processing, and dissemination activities. It is at once a tool for data resource management, data standardization, and system documentation.

In most cases, a data dictionary is itself an automated database system, although it does not have to be. It is intended to fully document all the fields and files that an application system requires. In some cases, the data dictionary is used to define all the data requirements of the entire organization, including programs and entire application systems.

A data dictionary may be manual or automated, standalone or dependent, active or passive. A standalone dictionary is self-contained, independent of the particular DBMS or other software with which it can interface. A dependent dictionary is usually a part of a standard DBMS and requires the facilities of that DBMS to perform its functions.

Depending on the degree of its integration with the database management system, a data dictionary may be considered either active or passive. An active dictionary becomes the sole source of data descriptions for all applications, including DBMS and language compilers. It is so tightly coupled with the DBMS it serves that the latter uses definitions from the dictionary at run time. To serve that function, an active dictionary clearly must contain current and accurate information that is shared by all software components of the system. One example of an active dictionary that is available for mainframes is the Integrated Data Dictionary by Cullinet Software. It serves a family of products that includes IDMS/R, IDBMS-DB, IDBMS-DC, Culprit, and Goldengate. In the Dbase world, the one product that implements what can be considered an active data dictionary (though far less active than Cullinet's) is Recital by Recital Corporation. Recital operates on Vax/VMS, UNIX, and Xenix machines.

A passive dictionary is used only to enter or retrieve entity descriptions. It is used and maintained independently of the DBMS, although the information it contains, for example, validation criteria for fields, may be the same information that the DBMS uses. An example of a passive dictionary used in mainframes is Datamanager by Manager Software Products. Datamanager does not depend on any specific DBMS, although it can be used to generate database definitions and source language statements. It has an interface with popular DBMS products such as Adabas, IDBMS, IMS, System 2000, and Total.

Although an active dictionary offers superior advantages in terms of ensuring the timeliness and accuracy of data, its use can entail significant processing overhead as the DBMS retrieves and updates information from this complex database. On the other hand, a truly passive dictionary has no processing overhead, but it has the serious disadvantage of possibly containing outdated information since it is maintained independent of the DBMS.

Data Dictionary Advantages

It is clear that an enterprise-wide data dictionary system permits centralized access and control of an organization's data. It provides the facility for fully documenting all data elements required by the organization and provides the mechanism for enforcing validation rules on those data elements. The desired result is that incorrect information never find its way to the organization's databases in the first place.

A data dictionary eliminates unnecessary data redundancy. A data element is defined once, even though it may appear on multiple databases. This ensures consistent definition of the field across all databases and across all applications. Any change in the field's properties, for example its validation rules, is instituted once—in the data dictionary—and the change is reflected on all the databases that use the field. A dictionary helps avoid the situation where two or more fields that look different are actually the same, subject to the same validation rules. Of course, the dictionary helps ensure that the text of the help prompts and/or error messages for a given field is consistent throughout all applications.

Programming teams, particularly those who work at remote sites, will find even a passive dictionary indispensable as the authoritative source of information for data element attributes (formats, codes, allowed values, and so on) that need to be enforced in application code. The dictionary is also a useful tool for communicating data element attributes among data users, programmers, and analysts.

Setting Up a Primitive FoxPro Dictionary

In the Dbase product family, we normally define a data file by using the CREATE command. This allows us to specify the name of the fields, their types (character, date, and so on), and field width, including the number of decimal places in the case of numeric fields. In reality, FoxPro (and other Dbase product family members) has a poorly documented facility that allows us to define much more information about the fields, including field description, picture clauses, or validation criteria. The additional information can be maintained as part of the system documentation, not as an integral part of an active dictionary system.

If we use a previously defined .dbf and then issue the COPY STRUCTURE EXTENDED command, the result is a new .dbf file with four fields and as many records as there were fields in the original file. For example, assume that we have a file called People.dbf, which has the following structure:

```
Structure for database : PEOPLE.DBF
Number of data records : 1
Date of last update    : 2/10/90
Field  Field Name  Type        Width    Dec    Index
    1  NAME        Character      25
    2  DOB         Date            8
    3  SALARY      Numeric        10      2
    4  CITYSTATE   Character      15
    5  NOTES       Memo           10
** Total **                       69
```

The following commands:

```
USE people
COPY STRUCTURE EXTENDED TO peoplex
```

produce the file called Peoplex.dbf with the four fields, Field_name, Field_type, Field_len, and Field_dec, and five records.

```
Structure for database : PEOPLEX.DBF
Number of data records : 5
Date of last update    : 2/10/90
Field  Field Name  Type        Width    Dec
    1  FIELD_NAME  Character      10
    2  FIELD_TYPE  Character       1
    3  FIELD_LEN   Numeric         3
    4  FIELD_DEC   Numeric         3
** Total **                       18
```

The first record has a Field_name value of Name, and the last record has a Field_name value of Notes. The philosophy behind an extended structure is to allow data files to be built from it using the FROM clause of the CREATE command. Thus, the command

```
CREATE people2 FROM peoplex
```

simply creates the file called People2.dbf with the same structure as People.dbf. However, what is not well documented is the fact that, we are free to add more records to an extended structure, in effect including more descriptive information about data fields. Adding records to an extended structure does not hinder CREATE FROM's ability to produce a perfectly usable .dbf file provided that we do not reorder the first four fields in the extended structure.

Therefore, we can modify the structure of Peoplex.dbf to our heart's content, adding fields such as Field_desc to more fully describe the field, Field_pict to document the field's default picture clause, Field_vald to record the field's validation criteria, and so on. This modified extended structure is clearly useful for documenting fields in a .dbf file and with additional work may be used as a core for building a passive data dictionary for an entire FoxPro application. In the following modified structure for Peoplex.dbf, we have added fields 5, 6, and 7. This file contains much more information about each field, but it can still be used to produce the structure of People.dbf.

```
Structure for database : PEOPLEX2.DBF
Number of data records : 5
Date of last update    : 2/10/90
Field  Field Name  Type        Width    Dec
    1  FIELD_NAME  Character      10
    2  FIELD_TYPE  Character       1
    3  FIELD_LEN   Numeric         3
```

```
    4  FIELD_DEC    Numeric       3
    5  FIELD_DESC   Character    65
    6  FIELD_PICT   Character    10
    7  FIELD_LOW    Character    10
** Total **                     103
```

A Functional FoxPro Data Dictionary System

A comprehensive data dictionary system that can serve the needs of an entire organization can be easily designed and implemented as a FoxPro application. We can make this dictionary much more useful than a regular passive one by including the following features:

- Each data element in the dictionary will have descriptive text of variable length that is implemented as a memo field. Then, in any application where a user is faced with a data entry or edit screen involving a given data element, the memo field data associated with that element can be made to pop up in a help window whenever the user presses the F1 key. This technique eliminates the need to create individual help screens for each field in each and every application. Moreover, any corporate policy changes that alter the definition or intent of the data element require changing only one source—the memo field data in the dictionary. Note that for the dictionary to be available in this way, the organization must adopt a standard that requires the dictionary .dbf to remain open in some agreed-on work area for all applications that require the services of the dictionary.
- The data dictionary is solely responsible for building .dbf files required by any or all applications. In effect, developers are not permitted to use the CREATE or MODIFY STRUCTURE commands in any application other than the dictionary system.
- Adding information such as field range values and edit or validation criteria for fields in the dictionary can be the basis for making the dictionary active at a later time by enforcing such rules in the application code.

Here are some of the steps we have followed to design and implement a corporate data dictionary:

1. Assemble a core group of people—a data dictionary committee—charged with the responsibility of defining all data elements required by the organization. This group should consist of representatives from

user and data processing organizations who have intimate knowledge of the organization's work processes, including data sources and paper forms. This group can also be very helpful in providing a first draft of the help text (memo field data) associated with a data element.

2. Define the structure of the data element dictionary. What information about data elements should be part of the dictionary? What other .dbf files should be part of the dictionary?
3. Adopt a field naming convention to ensure that a data element appears once and only once in the dictionary, and that we can easily tell from their names which nonkey fields belong to which .dbf files. Also, adopt a rule as to which work area, for example, FoxPro work area 25, to reserve for the dictionary in any application that requires its services.

One example of a field naming convention is that all nonkey fields must begin with the first three letters of the .dbf file to which they belong and that the fourth character in their names must be an underscore. For instance, Per_Dob, Per_City, and Per_State are nonkey fields in the Person.dbf file. Naturally, for this naming convention to work, no two data files in the system can have the same first three letters.

Since key fields may appear in multiple .dbf files (especially as foreign keys), they are not subject to the same rule. They may have an underscore in their names, but to minimize confusion, the organization should not allow it to be in the fourth position. Sample key field names are ProjectNo and Employ_Id.

Data Dictionary Files

To implement a FoxPro data dictionary system, we will probably require the following starter set of .dbf files:

- Fld_Dct.dbf
- Fil_Fld.dbf
- Dbf_Idx.dbf

Fld_Dct.dbf

This is the data element (field) dictionary. It includes all the attributes for each data element. We will discuss this file in more detail in the next section as it relates to the Fil_Fld.dbf data file.

Fil_Fld.dbf

This is a data file that associates which key fields belong to which .dbf file. It is used to create a .dbf file from its component fields. The files to which nonkey fields belong are already obvious from their names, so they don't have to be included here. The structure for this file is simply:

```
Structure for database : FIL_FLD.DBF
Number of data records : 5
Date of last update    : 2/20/90
Field  Field Name  Type        Width    Dec
    1  FILE_NAME   Character       8
    2  FIELD_NAME  Character      10
** Total **                       19
```

To build the required .dbf file (which happens to be the same as File_Name), we gather all the File_Name records from this file to capture all its key fields, and then we combine them with the nonkey fields obtained from Fld_Dct.dbf in an EXTENDED STRUCTURE ready to be CREATEd.

Listing 3-1 shows a sample routine to create a specified .dbf file from a data dictionary. The program first determines all the key fields in the .dbf as defined in the Fil_Fld.dbf file, and then looks up their attributes (for example, field_type) from Fld_Dct.dbf. Next, the program adds each key field as a record to Extend.dbf, which is just a file with an extended structure. The program then finds all of the file's nonkey fields from Fld_Dct, and once again adds each one as a record to Extend.dbf. Finally, the program creates the desired file with the single command:

```
CREATE (dbf) FROM Extend
```

The added advantage of creating .dbf structures this way is the ease with which we can enforce the rule that fields must appear in the structure in alphabetical order with key fields ahead of nonkey ones. This rule becomes very important with .dbf files that have many fields and at the early stages of data dictionary development when files are still in the process of being normalized. Arranging a long list of field names alphabetically clearly helps us locate a data element of interest even though the sequence of the fields is immaterial to FoxPro's CREATE command.

Listing 3-1. Procedure BuildDbf is a sample routine to create a .dbf file out of its key and nonkey fields defined in a data dictionary.

```
PROCEDURE BuildDbf
************************************************************
* Program ...: BuildDbf.prg
* Author ....: P. L. Olympia & Kathy Cea
* Purpose....: Sample procedure to create a database file from
*            : a data dictionary. Key fields are obtained from
*            : Fil_Fld.Dbf, nonkey fields and all key parameters
*            : are obtained from Fld_Dct.Dbf.  Extend.Dbf is
*            : just a STRUCTURE EXTENDED .dbf for use by CREATE
*            : FROM
* Syntax ....: DO BuildDbf with Dbf
*            :  where Dbf is the name of the file to create.
************************************************************
PARAMETER dbf   && name of dbf to build
SET SAFETY OFF
USE Fld_Dct in 1 INDEX Fld_Dct       && index on Field_name
USE Fil_Fld in 2
USE Extend in 3      && some extended structure to be zapped
SELE Extend
ZAP

*-- Pick up key field names of desired .dbf from Fil_Fld
SELECT Fil_Fld
SET RELATION TO Field_Name INTO Fld_Dct
SCAN FOR Fil_Fld->File_Name = dbf
  DO AddField
ENDSCAN
SET RELATION TO
*-- Pick up nonkey field names from Fld_Dct
SELE Fld_Dct
SCAN FOR SUBSTR(Fld_Dct->Field_Name,1,3) = SUBSTR(dbf,1,3)
  DO AddField
ENDSCAN
USE IN 3
CREATE (dbf) FROM Extend     && One command builds the file
RETURN
```

(continued)

Listing 3-1. Continued

```
PROCEDURE AddField
  SELECT Extend
  APPEND BLANK
  REPLACE Extend->Field_Name WITH Fld_Dct->Field_Name, ;
    Extend->Field_Type WITH Fld_Dct->Field_Type, ;
    Extend->Field_Len  WITH Fld_Dct->Field_Len,  ;
    Extend->Field_Dec  WITH Fld_Dct->Field_Dec
RETURN
```

Periodically we may want to use this same .dbf generation scheme to ensure that all .dbf files used by an application are consistent with the current dictionary and are neither obsolete nor have been improperly modified by a programmer.

Dbf_Idx.dbf

This data file defines the key expression of each index file as well as which index files belong to which .dbf files. It is useful not only as an integral part of the system documentation but also for ensuring that all system indexes can be rebuilt correctly should they become corrupt. Note that the REINDEX command is useless if the index file header containing the key expression is itself damaged.

At a minimum, this data file has the following structure:

```
Structure for database : FIL_FLD.DBF
Number of data records : 5
Date of last update    : 2/20/90
Field  Field Name  Type        Width    Dec
    1  FILE_NAME   Character       8
    2  INDEX_NAME  Character       8
    3  INDEX_EXPN  Character     100
** Total **                      117
```

In Chapter 12, we introduce a facility for storing the .dbf name in the index file header area. We also demonstrate a way of extracting the .dbf name and the index expression for any index file and storing this information in a Dbf_Idx.Dbf file. The structure of the Dbf_Idx file we used for the examples is displayed in that chapter. We can use the sample programs to build and maintain our Dbf_Idx.dbf database file. In addition, Chapter 14 provides code for using the Dbf_Idx.dbf file to ensure that all associated indexes are opened with a given data file. It also contains a program for rebuilding index files.

The Dbf_Idx.dbf file has the added benefit of guaranteeing that all index files associated with a .dbf file reflect current changes to the actual data file. Once an application opens a specified .dbf file, it looks to this file next to determine which index files should also be opened so they can be updated whenever necessary, ensuring that the index pointers always remain in sync with the data. In effect, such a procedure offers the same benefits provided by dBASE IV's multiple index (.mdx) facility, which ensures that multiple tags in the index file reflect current data updates.

The Data Element Dictionary

What fields should the data element dictionary contain beyond the usual Field_Name, Field_Type, Field_Len, and Field_Dec? Largely it depends on the organization's requirements. Several of the fields included in popular data dictionary systems such as those provided by Recital and Wallsoft's UI2 Programmer are presented here.

Field Description

The data element dictionary needs a description field, say, Field_Desc, not only to fully describe the field, but also to use in a help window when a user presses the F1 key during a data entry or edit operation. Given the limitations in many Dbase dialects, this field often has been implemented in the past either as a single 254-character field or a series of, say, five 75-character fields called Desc1 through Desc5. However, the very nature of the information kept in this field, which would be extensive for some but skimpy in others, along with FoxPro's versatile memo field facility dictate that this should be a memo field in a FoxPro data dictionary. The contents of this field may then be popped easily through a memo window to a user during data entry.

Picture Clause

This field defines the display format of the data element, for example, @R 999-99-9999 in the case of Social Security Number. Both UI2 and Recital can automatically include the picture clause in the @...GET statement for the field.

Valid Clause and Range

A field range may be considered a subset of the Valid clause, although many data dictionaries include both. The Valid clause may specify an expression or function that an @...GET statement can use to determine if the user-supplied value for the data element is valid. This field may be implemented as a string that would be part of a Boolean expression, for example, "$ABCD" to indicate that only codes A, B, C, or D are valid for the data element. If the Valid clause is complex, this field can be implemented simply as the name of a user-defined function that is responsible for validating the data element's value.

A Range clause, like the Valid clause, specifies the domain of acceptable values for the data element, particularly for numeric and date fields. You may choose to implement this as two separate values, high and low, defining the ceiling and floor of the field.

An alternative to the Valid or Range clause is a Lookup clause that can be used to specify the name of an indexed table of allowed values for the desired data element.

Required Field

You may choose to include a required field attribute in your field dictionary. This attribute determines whether a user will be allowed to exit a data entry screen without entering a value for the field.

Default or Initial Value

Some data element dictionaries specify the default or initial values assigned to the field until the user modifies them.

Data Source

If your organization requires that the origin of the data element be documented, a dictionary entry for the field's data source may be in order. Data sources may refer to some standard government forms or company paper forms, surveys, questionnaires, or similar instruments.

Cross-Reference Field

For organizations that exchange data with other companies that use different data dictionaries, a cross-reference field in the dictionary keeps track of both the name of the field in the foreign dictionary and the data source of the field in the foreign system.

Extending the Dictionary Concept

Based on the contents of a data element dictionary, it is clear that its two major functions are to clarify or enforce field validation rules and to document the field as fully as possible for all users of the dictionary. We can extend the concept of the dictionary further by keeping track of which application module in the organization initializes, modifies, or simply reads each field in the dictionary. Such information is useful for establishing module dependencies because a module that uses or reads a field cannot precede one that initializes it. It is also useful (in the case of a passive dictionary implementation) in determining which modules will be affected by policy changes that necessitate modifying the validation rules for a field.

Data Dictionary Implementation in the Dbase Family

Since a data dictionary facility is largely ignored in the Dbase family of products, except in Recital, its enforcement or implementation is left to third-party products such as Wallsoft's UI2 or Symmetry Software's Symmetry IV. Note that the data dictionary implementation in these products is much narrower in scope than the enterprise-wide dictionary concept we've discussed thus far.

UI2 is primarily a screen and code generator of Dbase programs that use modifiable code templates. It allows you to define field characteristics that can become global default definitions for the field, which can then be stored in a central data dictionary. UI2 uses any validation rules you define for the field as part of the @...GET routine in the code it generates. Thus, it automatically takes care of initial value, picture, and valid or range clauses you attach to the field definition, just like an active dictionary would do. It also allows you to specify a display formula for the field so a user can better understand the screen prompt for the field. UI2 permits you to define up to three template-specific field attributes (called slots) to supplement standard field properties.

Symmetry IV's approach to a data dictionary is primarily for documentation only, which is in line with its principal focus of being a documenting and debugging tool for Dbase-type applications. You tell Symmetry the name of your top-level (main) program and where your .dbf and index files are, and it proceeds to read your entire application to produce summary and detailed data dictionary reports. In these reports, you provide the descriptive text for fields, data files, and index files. The database dictionary summary report lists all the .dbf files that the application used, along with the descriptions you supply. The field dictionary summary report shows the structure of each .dbf file, along with your supplied description for each field in the file. The field dictionary detail report lists the field attributes, including alias and range of values.

The Recital Data Dictionary Facility

In Recital you immediately notice that something is different because the CREATE command gives you a 25-character column in which to enter the field description. This descriptive text may be displayed automatically as part of the prompt for the field in full-screen system-generated forms such as those produced by APPEND, EDIT, or CHANGE. The SET DESCRIPTIONS OFF command disables the display of the text as a field prompt.

Recital can create an optional data dictionary file with a file type of .dbd. Field attributes that can be defined as part of the data dictionary are picture clause, valid clause, range values for dates and numerics, default initial value, calculation formula, and the following additional properties.

Property	**Description**
Error	Specifies the error message to display if validation for the field fails.

Property	Description
Help	Specifies the Field prompt to display in the message line.
Choices	Defines a popup list of choices for the field when the user presses the Help key.
Required	Specifies if the user must enter a value for the field.
Recalculate	Serves as a trigger causing all calculated fields to be recalculated and displayed whenever this field is modified in a form.

Recital automatically uses the field definition properties in the dictionary during data entry. For example, it attaches the defined picture, valid, or range clause to an @...GET statement for the field.

The Recital @...GET statement has options or qualifiers that may override, or be invalidated by, similar field attributes in the dictionary. For instance, the CALCULATE option cannot be used if the dictionary already has the property defined for the field. Similarly, any picture clause defined for the field in the dictionary cannot be overridden by a picture option in the @...GET command. On the other hand, the CHOICELIST option of the @...GET statement can override any Choices attribute for the field defined in the dictionary. Similarly, the HELP/MESSAGE option or the RANGE option of the @...GET statement may override the corresponding definitions in the dictionary for the field.

Chapter Summary

A data dictionary is an organized system for defining and managing data elements. It is at once a tool for data resource management, data standardization, and system documentation. A data dictionary may be manual or automated, standalone or dependent, active or passive.

In this chapter, we discussed some of the advantages offered by a data dictionary. Among the Dbase family of products, only Recital provides a dictionary facility. However, a comprehensive dictionary system can be easily implemented as a FoxPro application. At a minimum, such a system requires a file of data elements, a file associating database names with key fields, and a third file establishing index and .dbf relationships. Any required .dbf file may be generated from an EXTENDED STRUCTURE file using CREATE FROM.

We discussed the field attributes that are commonly included in a data field dictionary including picture, valid, range, and default values as well as text for prompts, helps, and error messages. We pointed out the advantages of using a memo field for storing descriptive text about data elements in the dictionary.

Finally, we described the data dictionary facility offered by Recital and by third-party Dbase products such as UI2 Programmer and Symmetry IV.

Chapter 4

Designing and Customizing an Application

Good programming practices dictate a modular approach to system design. This includes identifying commonly used routines and organizing them into separate procedures. Then, rather than have the same program code appear in many places, you have one routine that application programs can call as needed. The advantage to this approach is obvious—it simplifies maintenance and debugging and reduces the amount of code in the system. Structured program modules are designed to perform just one basic function (for example, add a record, modify a record, validate a user entry, or generate a report). When you take this approach, the result is a set of relatively small, understandable, and easy-to-maintain program modules that constitute your application.

Calling Other Program Modules

Once you have determined the modules you need in your system and their purposes, you need to think about how the modules are to be called. This is dictated in part by the purpose (and return values) of the module and in part by the language in which you are writing. Most, if not all, of your modules in a FoxPro application are written using the FoxPro language. These modules are written as procedures or user-defined functions (UDFs). Occasionally there is a need to perform some operating system–specific or low-level function that cannot be accomplished with the FoxPro programming language. In these cases, you can write a program in assembly language or C and convert it to a .bin (binary) file, which may be LOADed and CALLed from a

FoxPro procedure. You also have the option to execute an external program with the RUN command.

FoxPro Procedures

A typical FoxPro application contains many separate procedures. A procedure is a program or subprogram consisting of any number of FoxPro statements. Optionally a procedure can be called with parameters using the following syntax:

```
DO <procedure> WITH <parameter list>
```

Parameters are passed to procedures either by reference or value. When parameters are passed by reference, changes made to a parameter in the called procedure change the value of the parameter in the calling program as well. When passing parameters by value, a change made to a parameter's value from within a called procedure is known only to that procedure—the value of the parameter remains unchanged in the calling program. By default, FoxPro passes parameters to a procedure by reference. However, if a parameter is enclosed in parentheses when passed to a procedure, it is passed by value.

Procedures do not return a specific value to a calling procedure, although they can change the value of any parameters passed by reference or of any global variable.

A procedure is identified with the PROCEDURE <procedure name> statement as the first executable statement, although, as will be discussed later, it may be called as either a procedure or a function.

User-Defined Functions (UDFs)

A UDF is similar to a procedure in that it consists of a number of FoxPro commands or statements. It is identified with the FUNCTION <function name> statement as the first executable statement. It differs from a procedure in its calling syntax, return values, and its default use of parameters, however. A function is called with the following syntax:

```
<Function> ([<parameter list>])
```

where the parameter list is optional. A function always returns a value to the calling program. By default, parameters passed to a function are passed by value. You can SET UDFPARMS TO REFERENCE if you wish to pass parameters to functions by reference instead. The following example illustrates the difference between passing by reference and passing by value:

```
FUNCTION ChgParam

PARAMETERS x
x = x * 100
RETURN x
```

Example 1:

```
* Set UDFPARMS is VALUE by default
STORE 1 TO a
?a
?ChgParam(a)
?a
```

The results are:

```
1
100
1
```

Example 2:

```
SET UDFPARMS TO REFERENCE
STORE 1 TO a
?a
?ChgParam(a)
?a
```

The results are:

```
1
100
100
```

As this example demonstrates, changes made to a parameter are permanent only if parameters are passed by reference. As with procedures, a parameter that is enclosed in parentheses is passed by value, regardless of SET

UDFPARMS. Since one set of parentheses is always required to call a function, an extra pair is needed for each parameter to be passed by value if SET UDFPARMS is REFERENCE. Again using the ChgParam function displayed in the preceding example, consider the following results:

```
SET UDFPARMS TO REFERENCE
STORE 1 TO a
?a
?ChgParam((a))
?a
```

The results are:

```
1
100
1
```

Although SET UDFPARMS is REFERENCE, the parameter *a* is passed by value since it is enclosed in parentheses.

Like a procedure, a UDF may be called as either a function or a procedure. If called as a procedure (with the DO <function> syntax), the function behaves like a procedure in that the return value is ignored and any parameters are passed by reference (unless enclosed in parentheses). Similarly, a procedure that is called as a function with the <procedure> ([<parameter list>]) syntax must return a value, and treats passed parameters according to the rules for functions. Thus the calling syntax actually determines whether a module is to behave like a procedure or a function.

Using LOAD, CALL, and RUN

For programs that are too difficult, too cumbersome, or altogether impossible to code in the FoxPro command language as procedures or UDFs, binary (.bin) files offer an attractive alternative. Binary routines are most often coded in assembly language or in C and called within a FoxPro application. FoxPro treats .bin routines as though they were built-in procedures or functions. Examples of such routines that are popular in a multiuser application include those that redirect output to a variety of network printers as well as those that take advantage of the resources offered by the LAN operating system, for instance, transaction processing.

How do you create and use a .bin file? Normally, you would write the routine in assembly language, compile it, link it, and then convert the resulting .exe to a .bin file using DOS's EXE2BIN program. To use the routine, you must first load it into memory with the LOAD command. For instance, the FoxPro command

```
LOAD tts
```

fetches the Tts.bin file from disk and loads it into memory. You only need to load the routine once, no matter how many times you use it in the application.

When the application needs to use the services of the .bin routine, you invoke it with the CALL command, for example,

```
CALL tts [WITH <memvar>]
```

where the optional parameter may be a character expression or memory variable that allows you to pass data to and from the routine. If you no longer need the routine, you should free up the memory space it takes with the RELEASE MODULE command. Thus

```
RELEASE MODULE tts
```

releases the space occupied by Tts.bin. FoxPro allows up to 16 .bin files to be in memory at one time, so it is always a good idea to release those that your application no longer needs.

Binary routines are subject to a few rules. For instance, they cannot be larger than 32,000 bytes, they must originate at an offset of zero rather than at 100h, and they must never alter the length of the memvar passed to them as a parameter.

If you cannot convert an executable file to a binary file, you may still be able to execute the program from within your application. The RUN or equivalent ! command can be used to execute an external program, including DOS internal commands like COPY. If the program requires more memory than is available, you can issue the RUN command as follows:

```
RUN /n <command>
```

where *n* is the number of kilobytes required by <command>. If *n* is greater than the number of remaining kilobytes, FoxPro invokes FOXSWAP, a program that frees as much memory as is required by swapping the contents of memory to disk. To optimize performance, *n* should be set to the smallest number required for successful program execution, minimizing the amount of memory to be swapped to disk. If *n* is set to 0, the entire contents of memory are swapped to disk. RUN /0 should be used only when necessary to avoid the overhead incurred when swapping all of memory to disk and back.

Establishing a Set of Library Routines

We recommend that you establish a central location, that is, a dedicated directory, for all your standard routines. This will become your library. You must make your programming team aware of the existence and purpose of your library routines and provide them with the calling syntax of each routine. You must then require that all application programs call the library routines rather than duplicate code for those functions available in your library. The routines thus become "black boxes"; they accept a set of parameters and perform a specified function, possibly returning a value to the calling program.

What types of routines are likely candidates for a library? Generally any procedure or function that is needed by more than one program, or even that is needed by just one program in several different places. If your application is not designed yet, establishing a set of library routines is easy. Simply identify commonly performed operations and create procedures and functions to meet these needs. If your application already exists, you will have to evaluate your existing code in order to determine where identical or similar code appears in several places. If several programs contain similar, but not identical, code for a given purpose, a standard method must be agreed upon and implemented. This is why it is easier to design your library before you start coding. However, even if your application is already written, it is probably well worth your time to develop a set of common routines and modify the existing programs in order to simplify future maintenance activities.

Some typical candidates for library routines are as follows:

- Online help facilities
- Standard screen displays (color settings and placement of borders, boxes, and windows)
- Message placement
- Printer selection and control
- Data validation
- Opening and closing database and index files
- Error processing
- Multiuser functions (such as record and file locking)

- Naming of temporary work files
- Standard security measures such as validation of user id and password

Sample code is provided in Chapter 14 for a library routine designed to open a .dbf with all its associated indexes. Listing 4-1 demonstrates a routine that standardizes the presentation of error messages for an application. This routine, L_Msg, is called with the error message, which may contain from one to three characters strings, each a maximum of 40 characters. Later in this chapter, we discuss and provide sample code for online help routines, data validation routines (and presentation of error messages), and error processing.

You also need to establish a naming convention for library routines. This way, you can easily identify the library routines in your application. It also ensures that the program names for your library routines do not conflict with the names of the other application programs. The naming convention we use is to prefix the library routine names with "L_". For example, a routine to handle printer selection might be named L_Print. One of our applications, which provides a system maintenance subsystem for the network administrator, applies a prefix of "M_" to the routines designated for the maintenance programs. For example, a reindex routine might be M_Reindx. If you wish to distinguish functions from procedures, you could assign a prefix of "F_" to library UDFs.

Performing Data Validation

One of the most time-consuming programming activities is the coding and testing of edit and validation procedures for each application module. Furthermore, modifying validation criteria may well be the most common maintenance activity in an application. A standard approach to data validation should help streamline these activities.

UDFs can be used in connection with the VALID option on an @...SAY/GET command to validate screen field entries. You can write a generic validation UDF to be used in connection with a .dbf containing your validation expressions, or you can write UDFs specific to each field. We provide examples of both in this chapter.

One way to standardize your validation procedures is to store your validation criteria in a .dbf. The .dbf contains one record for each field requiring validation. You can also store error messages in the validation .dbf. The advantage of this method is that a change in validation requirements (for example, a list of valid codes changes) does not require any program modifi-

Listing 4-1. L_Msg.prg, procedure to place a one- to three-line error message on the screen.

```
PROCEDURE L_Msg

********************************************************************
* Program: L_Msg.prg
* Author : P.L. Olympia & Kathy Cea
* Purpose: Standard library routine to place error messages on
*        : the screen.
*        :
* Syntax : L_MSG ("line1","line2", "line3")
*        : where each line may contain up to 40 characters.
*        : "line2" and "line3" are optional.
*        :
********************************************************************

PARAMETERS Msg1, Msg2, Msg3

mNumParm = PARAMETERS()

DEFINE WINDOW ErrMsg ;
        FROM 16,15 TO 23,65 ;
        TITLE "Error"

ACTIVATE WINDOW ErrMsg
mCnt = 1
DO WHILE mCnt <= mNumParm
        mCntStr = ALLTRIM(STR(mCnt))
        @(mCnt - 1),1 SAY PADC(Msg&mCntStr,WCOLS())
        mCnt = mCnt + 1
ENDDO
WAIT
DEACTIVATE WINDOW ErrMsg
```

cations. A sample .dbf structure containing field name, validation expression, and error message is shown in Figure 4-1. Note that the validation expression is limited to 254 characters since we are using a character field. If the

```
Structure for database: C:\VALID.DBF
Number of data records:       12
Date of last update    : 02/28/90
Field  Field Name  Type       Width    Dec
    1  SCRNFLD     Character     12
    2  VALID_EXPR  Character    254
    3  ERRORMSG    Character     72
** Total **                     339
```

Figure 4-1. Sample .dbf structure to store validation expressions and error messages for screen fields.

validation expression requires more space, a memo field could be used in place of the character field.

Listing 4-2 presents a program "shell" that we will use for many of our examples in the remainder of this chapter. This program is designed to perform a simple product entry procedure for an order processing system. We will be including code fragments specific to the function we are discussing; these code fragments work in connection with the program shown in Listing 4-2 to perform the product entry function.

You can perform the validation from a standard UDF, as shown in Listing 4-3. The F_Valid function uses the VARREAD( ) function, which returns the name of the screen field being entered during a READ operation. It then searches the Valid.dbf file (indexed on UPPER(Scrnfld)) for a record that matches the results of the VARREAD( ) function. If found, the validation expression is evaluated, and if false, the error message is displayed. Note that if the expression is false, we return a value of zero rather than .F. This is required in order to suppress the FoxPro error message. This method has the added advantage of allowing the application to define the placement of the error message on the screen.

If you implement your own context-sensitive help facility (rather than the FoxPro SET HELP TO option), you can store your data validation in the same .dbf file with your help text. This method requires only one work area for the .dbf containing validation and help information. We discuss a custom help function that incorporates validation criteria in the next section.

You can also use the VALID option of the @...SAY/GET command with a UDF, without the validation .dbf file. In this case, you write one field-specific UDF for each screen field requiring validation. This method does require code modification and recompilation if a validation requirement changes, but it still has an advantage over placing the validation code in the calling

Listing 4-2. AddProd.prg, program "shell" to be used with sample code fragments that follow.

```
PROCEDURE AddProd
*******************************************************************
* Program: AddProd.prg
* Author : P.L. Olympia & Kathy Cea
* Purpose: Add a new product
*        :
* Syntax : DO AddProd
*        :
* Notes  : This is a program shell to be used with other examples
*******************************************************************
CLEAR
SET ECHO OFF
SET TALK OFF

*Initialize screen field values
mProdNum = SPACE(12)
mPro_Name = SPACE(20)
mPro_Cost = 0
mSupplId = SPACE(5)

*|                                                      |*
*|   Insert the appropriate AddProd code fragment here  |*
*|                                                      |*

READ

* Do other processing
```

program. At least your code modifications are limited to your validation UDFs, limiting the impact on the rest of your application. Listing 4-4 demonstrates a program segment that uses UDFs for field validation.

There is an advantage to using a field-specific UDF over a generic function that reads a validation .dbf. The VALID clause provides an option to determine the next GET field based on a numeric value returned from the validating UDF. Thus, depending on the contents of the field, you can elect to return

Listing 4-3. F_Valid function to perform data validation from the Valid.dbf database.

```
*  AddProd.prg code fragment
*  This example uses the F_VALID() function to perform
*  screen field validation.

* Open the .dbf containing validation expressions
SELECT 25
USE Valid INDEX ScrnFld

* Define Error message window
DEFINE WINDOW ErrWind ;
        FROM 20,1 TO 23,78 ;
        TITLE "Invalid Product Entry"

* Display Add Product screen
@2,1 SAY PADC("-- Add Product Record --",WCOLS())
@3,1 TO 12,80 DOUBLE
@5,10 SAY "Product Number: " GET mProdNum VALID F_VALID()
@7,10 SAY "Product Name: " GET mPro_Name VALID F_VALID()
@9,10 SAY "Product Cost: " GET mPro_Cost;
       PICT "$99999.99" VALID F_VALID()
@9,45 SAY "Supplier Number: " GET mSupplId;
       PICT "@! ANNNN" VALID F_VALID()



FUNCTION F_VALID
*******************************************************************
* Program: F_Valid.prg
* Author : P.L. Olympia & Kathy Cea
* Purpose: Perform screen field validation, using Valid.dbf
*        :
* Syntax : VALID F_VALID()
*        : Returns .T. if user-entered data is valid
*        :
*******************************************************************

SELECT Valid
```

(continued)

Listing 4-3. Continued

```
* Assumes that the .dbf containing validation criteria, Valid,
* is already opened in a work area

* Determine screen field to be validated
SEEK VARREAD()

IF FOUND()
        Val_Expr = Valid->Valid_Expr
        IF EMPTY(Val_Expr)
                * If there is no validation clause, return .T.
                RETURN .T.
        ENDIF
        IF &Val_Expr
                RETURN .T.
        ELSE
                ACTIVATE WINDOW ErrWind
                @1,1 SAY ErrorMsg
                WAIT
                DEACTIVATE WINDOW ErrWind
                * Return 0 instead of .F. to suppress the
                * Standard FoxPro error message
                RETURN 0
        ENDIF
ELSE
        * If screen field is not found in .dbf, return .T.
        RETURN .T.
ENDIF
```

to a previous field or skip one or more fields. When the UDF returns a negative number, the READ command moves back that number of fields on the screen. If the number returned is positive, the READ moves forward the relative number of fields. Since the decision to move forward or backward normally depends on the field and its contents, you would not be able to use this feature in a generic validation UDF. We show an example of a UDF that returns a numeric value to determine the next GET field in Chapter 5 (Listing 5-9).

Listing 4-4. Program segment showing the use of field-specific UDF validation procedures.

```
*  AddProd.prg code fragment
*  This example uses UDFs specific to each screen field to
*  perform field validation.
*  Note that only the F_PRDNUM function is shown in this example

* Define Error message window
DEFINE WINDOW ErrWind ;
        FROM 20,1 TO 23,78 ;
        TITLE "Invalid Product Entry"

* Display Add Product screen
@2,1 SAY PADC("-- Add Product Record --",WCOLS())
@3,1 TO 12,80 DOUBLE
@5,10 SAY "Product Number: " GET mProdNum VALID F_PRDNUM()
@7,10 SAY "Product Name: " GET mPro_Name VALID F_PRDNAM()
@9,10 SAY "Product Cost: " GET mPro_Cost PICT "$99999.99";
       VALID F_PRDCST()
@9,45 SAY "Supplier Number: " GET mSupplId PICT "@! ANNNN";
       VALID F_SUPPID()


FUNCTION F_PRDNUM
*******************************************************************
* Program: F_PrdNum.prg
* Author : P.L. Olympia & Kathy Cea
* Purpose: Validate the Product Number screen field
*        :
* Syntax : VALID F_PRDNUM()
*        :
*******************************************************************

IF EMPTY(mProdNum)
     ACTIVATE WINDOW ErrWind
     @1,1 SAY "Product Number is required"
     WAIT
     DEACTIVATE WINDOW ErrWind
    * Return 0 instead of .F. to suppress the
```

(continued)

Listing 4-4. Continued

```
          * Standard FoxPro error message
           RETURN 0
     ELSE
           RETURN .T.
     ENDIF


     FUNCTION F_PRDNAM
     * Validate the mPro_Name field
     RETURN .T.

     FUNCTION F_PRDCST
     * Validate the mPro_Cost field
     RETURN .T.

     FUNCTION F_SUPPID
     * Validate the mSupplId field
     RETURN .T.
```

Implementing Your Own Help Facility

Using FoxPro's Built-in Help

FoxPro provides a complete online help facility. The help data is stored in the FoxHelp.dbf file and contains the most up-to-date information for each command and function. This help facility is designed more for the application developer than for the end user, however. When you install your own help system, you probably want to provide application-specific information rather than FoxPro-specific help. For this reason, FoxPro allows you to integrate your own help database with the built-in online system.

To customize the FoxPro help system with your own data, you first create a .dbf that conforms to the following rules:

1. The first field must be of type character. This field is used as the Topic field.
2. The second field must be a memo field. This field contains the help text.

You can name these fields anything you like. Also, you may have additional fields in the .dbf. Any additional fields are used only for selecting the appropriate record. They are not displayed to users. For example, you may add a field that contains the screen variable name corresponding to the particular data item so that you can present the associated help text when the user presses the F1 key from a data entry screen.

This built-in help system may be used in several different ways. First, you can implement a help facility similar to what FoxPro provides by simply defining your own .dbf and then issuing the SET HELP TO <your-own.dbf> command. Whenever the user types HELP or presses the F1 key, your list of topics is presented. The user selects the desired topic to view the help text. Although this is very easy to implement, it does not offer any context-sensitive help processing and probably will not be satisfactory in any but the most elementary systems.

To provide context-sensitive help, use the SET TOPIC TO <topic-name> command. This predefines the topic for which the help text will be displayed. The user no longer needs to select a topic from the list. For example, an order processing system may have data entry screens for Customer information, Sales Person information, Supplier information, Order information, and Product information. Upon entry to a particular data entry module, you can issue the appropriate SET TOPIC TO command; for example, when entering the Add Products module, you can SET TOPIC TO Product. This means that you must have a record with a Topic field (the first field in the .dbf) of Product. The memo field for the Product record will probably contain information such as how to enter new Product information to the system. This method has the advantage of preselecting the relevant help text for the user.

You can provide help information that is even more specific by relating the help topic to the particular data entry field from which help is requested. To implement such a context-sensitive help system, you need a field in your help database that corresponds to the data entry field names. You also need a separate help procedure to determine the field from which help was called. The sample program in Listing 4-5 demonstrates how you would implement such a facility. The SYS(18) (or equivalent VARREAD( )) function is used to determine the field being entered when the help key was pressed. These functions always return the field name in uppercase. This program assumes that we have a field called ScrnFld in the OurHelp.dbf file, containing the names of the screen fields.

Figure 4-2 shows the screen displayed when the F1 key is pressed over the Product Cost field. Note that if a record matching SET TOPIC TO <topic> is not found in the help database, the list of available topics is presented to the user.

Listing 4-5. A sample context-sensitive help facility using FoxPro's built-in help.

```
*  AddProd.prg code fragment
*  This example uses the FoxPro help system, called from L_Help

ON KEY = 315 DO L_Help

@2,1 SAY PADC("-- Add Product Record --",WCOLS())
@3,1 TO 12,80 DOUBLE
@5,10 SAY "Product Number: " GET mProdNum
@7,10 SAY "Product Name: " GET mPro_Name
@9,10 SAY "Product Cost: " GET mPro_Cost PICT "$9999.99"
@9,45 SAY "Supplier Number: " GET mSupplId PICT "@! ANNNN"


PROCEDURE L_HELP
*******************************************************************
* Program: L_Help.prg
* Author : P.L. Olympia & Kathy Cea
* Purpose: Display context-sensitive help using the FoxPro
*        : built-in help system and the OurHelp.dbf file
*        :
* Syntax : ON KEY = 315 DO L_Help
*        :
*******************************************************************

SET HELP TO OurHelp
SET TOPIC TO UPPER(ScrnFld) = SYS(18)
HELP
```

Advantages and Disadvantages of the FoxPro Help System Using FoxPro's help system that is customized with your own database is simple and effective. Even implementing a context-sensitive help function requires very little code, as we have demonstrated. In addition, it does not require you to use one of the 25 work areas for your help database since FoxPro opens the help database in a reserved area. With minimal work and little overhead, you can provide a fairly sophisticated facility.

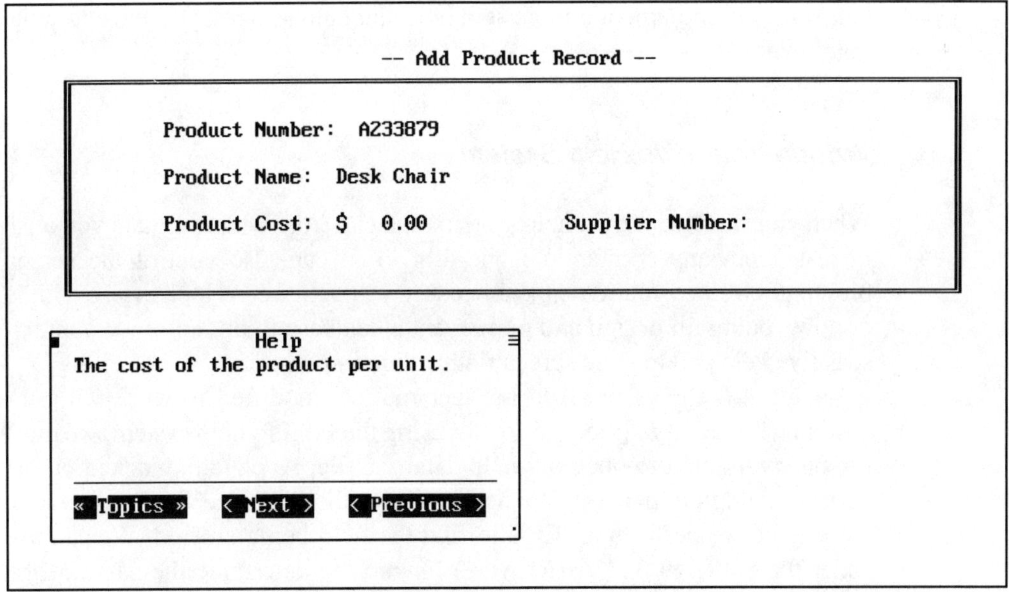

Figure 4-2. Screen display showing context-sensitive help for the Product Cost field, using the FoxPro help system.

When you use the SET TOPIC TO option, your user is not limited to just that one topic. This can be an advantage or disadvantage, depending on your application needs. If you want all of your users to be able to access all of your help database, this feature is a plus. Even though you present a help message related to the particular field or screen, the user can return to the Topics screen or scroll through the help records. However, if you need to limit the help records to which a user has access, you have a problem. You have no means of controlling which records a user can view from within the help system.

The cost associated with using FoxPro's built-in help facility is a loss of flexibility. Although you may define as many extra fields as you like in the help database, you can only use these fields for selecting the appropriate record to be displayed. You cannot, for example, have several different memo fields in one record that display varying levels of help depending on a user's clearance level, department, or level of expertise. Although you can use the database to store whatever related information you like, you cannot access the data directly from your application. This means that although it may make sense to store your help text and validation criteria together in one .dbf, you cannot use the validation data if the database is already in use as the help database. To implement a more sophisticated help system, you have to write your own.

Writing Your own Help System

When you write your own help system, you can store whatever data you wish in just about any format into one .dbf. You can also control the screen presentation since you write the procedure yourself. Let us look at an example of how you might design and implement a database to both provide context-sensitive help and to store screen field validation criteria.

Listing 4-6 shows the Add Product routine, modified to work with our custom help facility. Since we are not using the FoxPro help system, we must use one work area to open our help database file, ApplHelp, indexed on the ScrnFld field in uppercase. We no longer use the SET HELP TO command, but instead we perform a SEEK to find the field being entered. We can use either the SYS(18) or VARREAD( ) function to determine the name of the field currently being entered. We also define a window in which to perform the MODIFY MEMO. This allows us to control window placement, colors, title, and so on. Our help procedure places a standard message on the screen if there is no record in the database for the field being entered. Figure 4-3 shows the screen display when the user presses the F1 key over the Product Cost field.

Once we have implemented this feature, it is easy to extend its use to automated field validation. Listing 4-7 shows the Add Product routine with field validation performed from the VALID clause on the @...SAY/GET command. Every field calls the same generic validation function, F_VALID. This function determines the field being entered with the VARREAD( ) function and then performs a seek in the Help/Validation .dbf to find the associated screen field. If the field is not found or if the validation expression is blank, .T. is returned. Otherwise, the expression is evaluated, and, if the expression is invalid, the error message stored in the database is displayed. This function is essentially the same as the one presented in Listing 4-3, except that it now includes all our help and validation information in the same database. Figure 4-4 displays the .dbf structure we are using to store help text, data validation expressions, and error messages.

Error Handling

No matter how carefully you test and debug your code, at some time a user is going to try something with your application that you never thought of and an

Listing 4-6. Add Product routine modified to use our custom help facility, L_CusHlp.

```
*  AddProd.prg code fragment
*  This example uses our custom help system, called from L_CusHlp

* Open the custom help database in work area 25
SELECT 25
USE ApplHelp INDEX HelpScrn

* Define the help window
DEFINE WINDOW HelpWind ;
              FROM 18,40 TO 24,78 ;
              TITLE "Product Help"

ON KEY = 315 DO L_CusHlp

@2,1 SAY PADC("-- Add Product Record --",WCOLS())
@3,1 TO 12,80 DOUBLE
@5,10 SAY "Product Number: " GET mProdNum
@7,10 SAY "Product Name: " GET mPro_Name
@9,10 SAY "Product Cost: " GET mPro_Cost PICT "$99999.99"
@9,45 SAY "Supplier Number: " GET mSupplId PICT "@! ANNNN"


PROCEDURE L_CusHlp
******************************************************************
* Program: L_CusHlp.prg
* Author : P.L. Olympia & Kathy Cea
* Purpose: Custom help facility to display context-sensitive
*        : help from the ApplHelp.dbf file
*        :
* Syntax : ON KEY = 315 DO L_CusHlp
*        :
******************************************************************

SELECT ApplHelp

* Assumes the the Custom help file, ApplHelp, is already opened
* in a work area
```

(continued)

Listing 4-6. Continued

```
SEEK VARREAD()
ACTIVATE WINDOW HelpWind
IF FOUND()
        * Display help if record is found
        MODIFY MEMO HelpText NOEDIT WINDOW HelpWind
ELSE
        * Display message if there is no help
        @0,0 SAY "Sorry. There is no help available for this field."
        WAIT
ENDIF
DEACTIVATE WINDOW HelpWind
```

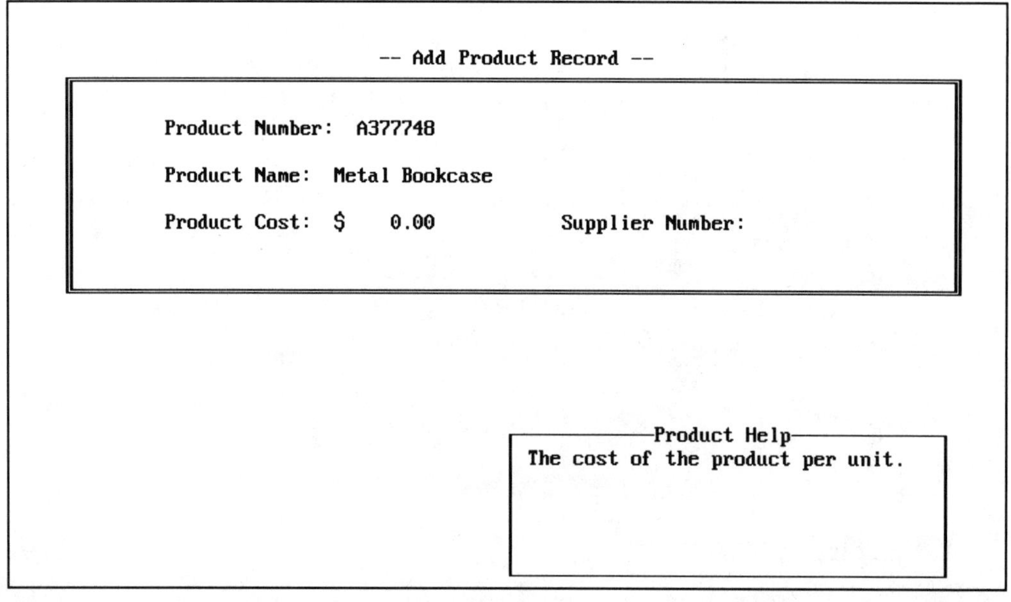

Figure 4-3. Screen display showing context-sensitive help for the Product Cost field, using our own help facility.

Listing 4-7. Add Product routine modified to perform custom help and data validation from the ApplHelp.dbf file.

```
*  AddProd.prg code fragment
*  This example uses our custom help system, called from L_CusHlp and
*  our generic data validation routine, F_Valid().

* Open the .dbf containing help and validation data
SELECT 25
USE ApplHelp INDEX HelpScrn

* Define the window for error messages
DEFINE WINDOW ErrWind ;
        FROM 20,1 TO 23,78 ;
        TITLE "Invalid Product Entry"

* Define the help window
DEFINE WINDOW HelpWind ;
              FROM 18,40 TO 24,78 ;
              TITLE "Product Help"

ON KEY = 315 DO L_CusHlp

@2,1 SAY PADC("-- Add Product Record --",WCOLS())
@3,1 TO 12,80 DOUBLE
@5,10 SAY "Product Number: " GET mProdNum VALID F_VALID()
@7,10 SAY "Product Name: " GET mPro_Name VALID F_VALID()
@9,10 SAY "Product Cost: " GET mPro_Cost PICT "$99999.99";
       VALID F_VALID()
@9,45 SAY "Supplier Number: " GET mSupplId PICT "! ANNNN";
       VALID F_VALID()


PROCEDURE L_CusHlp
*******************************************************************
* Program: L_CusHlp.prg
* Author : P.L. Olympia & Kathy Cea
* Purpose: Custom help facility to display context-sensitive
```

(continued)

Listing 4-7. Continued

```
*        : help from the ApplHelp.dbf file
*        :
* Syntax : ON KEY = 315 DO L_CusHlp
*        :
*********************************************************************

SELECT ApplHelp

* Assumes the the Custom help file, ApplHelp, is already opened
* in a work area

SEEK VARREAD()
ACTIVATE WINDOW HelpWind
IF FOUND()
        * Display help if record is found
        MODIFY MEMO HelpText NOEDIT WINDOW HelpWind
ELSE
        * Display message if there is no help
        @0,0 SAY "Sorry. There is no help available for this field."
        WAIT
ENDIF
DEACTIVATE WINDOW HelpWind

FUNCTION F_VALID
*********************************************************************
* Program: F_Valid.prg
* Author : P.L. Olympia & Kathy Cea
* Purpose: Perform screen field validation, using Valid.dbf
*        :
* Syntax : VALID F_VALID()
*        :
*********************************************************************

SELECT ApplHelp
* Assumes that the .dbf containing help & validation criteria,
* ApplHelp, is already opened in a work area
```

(continued)

Listing 4-7. Continued

```
* Determine screen field to be validated
SEEK VARREAD()

IF FOUND()
        Val_Expr = ApplHelp->Valid_Expr
        IF EMPTY(Val_Expr)
                * If there is no validation clause, return .T.
                RETURN .T.
        ENDIF
        IF &Val_Expr
                RETURN .T.
        ELSE
                ACTIVATE WINDOW ErrWind
                @1,1 SAY ErrorMsg
                WAIT
                DEACTIVATE WINDOW ErrWind
                * Return 0 instead of .F. to suppress the
                * Standard FoxPro error message
                RETURN 0
        ENDIF
ELSE
        * If screen field is not found in .dbf, return .T.
        RETURN .T.
ENDIF
```

error is going to be generated. The best you can do is to be prepared with a comprehensive error processing routine and error report. A good error routine should provide most or all of the information you need to re-create the error and diagnose it. With such a routine, a user need not remember and describe the specific circumstances under which the error occurred.

FoxPro's ON ERROR command allows you to pass control to a specific error handling routine whenever a system error is encountered. If you do not implement the ON ERROR process in your application, your users are presented a FoxPro error message that is likely to be meaningless to them. By trapping the error and redirecting control, you can determine what the users

```
Structure for database: C:\APPLHELP.DBF
Number of data records:       12
Date of last update   : 02/28/90
Field  Field Name  Type         Width    Dec
    1  HELPTOPIC   Character       12
    2  HELPTEXT    Memo            10
    3  SCRNFLD     Character       12
    4  VALID_EXPR  Character      254
    5  ERRORMSG    Character       40
** Total **                       329
```

Figure 4-4. Sample .dbf structure to store help text, validation expressions, and error messages.

see when an error occurs. Then you can take an appropriate course of action based on the error number and, if appropriate, generate a report that you can review later.

Table 4-1 lists useful commands and functions for an error processing routine. You may include any or all of these commands in your error trapping program. Listing 4-8 provides an example of an error processing routine that uses many of these commands and functions by writing the results to an error report. Note that it is important to turn off the error trapping facility from within your ON ERROR process to prevent an endless loop in the event that your ON ERROR process generates its own error.

Debugging Facilities

FoxPro provides a complete set of tools for debugging a program. Its Trace and Debug windows allow you to observe program execution line by line, to monitor specific program values, and to set program breakpoints. You can monitor or set a breakpoint for any expression that can be evaluated. You can also set breakpoints for specific lines of source code. Based on the nature of the error, you can decide which debugging tools to use.

Tracing Program Execution

If you wish to view your source code as it executes line by line, issue a SET ECHO ON command. Your source code appears in the Trace window for

Table 4-1. Useful Functions and Commands for an ON ERROR Process

Function	Return Value
DATE( )	Current system date.
TIME( )	Current system time.
ERROR( )	The number of the error causing the ON ERROR routine to be called.
MESSAGE( )	The error message string corresponding to the error causing the ON ERROR routine to be called.
MESSAGE(1)	The source code line causing the error condition. Note that this function is not available in the FoxPro Runtime version. If you execute it from within the Runtime environment, it returns the value of MESSAGE( ).
PROGRAM([n])	The name of the program executing when the error occurred. The optional *n* parameter indicates how many levels of nesting to go back. The *n* parameter can take a value from 1 through *N*, where *N* is the level of nesting to get to the currently executing program. A parameter of 0 or 1 returns the name of the master program, and *N* returns the name of the current program. PROGRAM( ) returns only the program name, without a path specification.
SYS(16[,n])	The name of the program being executed. As with the PROGRAM( ) function, the optional *n* parameter indicates how many levels of nesting to go back. SYS(16) returns the full path specification and program name, and also returns the name of the procedure file, if applicable. This function is most useful in a loop, as shown in Listing 4-8.
SYS(18) and VARREAD( )	The name of the field being entered.
VERSION( )	The FoxPro version number.

(continued)

Table 4-1. Continued

Command	Description
LIST STATUS	Describes the status of the FoxPro environment.
LIST MEMORY	Lists the currently active memory variables and arrays with their values.
RETRY	Returns control to the calling program and reexecutes the last line.
RETURN	Returns control to the calling program and executes the line following the last line.
RETURN TO MASTER	Returns control to the highest level calling program (normally the main routine).

each program as it executes. You can slow program execution to no more than four command statements per second by pressing the Ctrl or Shift key, or by clicking the mouse. Pressing any two of these together slows execution to no more than two statements per second. If you want only one statement to execute at a time, SET STEP ON. This suspends program execution after each statement.

To cancel or suspend the program at any time, press the Esc key. This temporarily halts execution (unless SET ESCAPE is OFF). You can select Suspend, Cancel, or Ignore. The Suspend option is useful if you wish to view and/or change environment settings or memory variable values before you RESUME program execution.

Monitoring Program Values

You can specify expressions to be monitored as your program executes. You do this in the Debug window, typing your variable names or expressions in the left side of the window. When your program executes, the value of each expression is displayed on the right side of the window. The Debug window can be accessed from the Window menu. Figure 4-5 displays the Debug window with several values set for monitoring.

Listing 4-8. L_Error.prg, sample ON ERROR procedure.

```
PROCEDURE L_Error
*****************************************************************
* Program: L_Error
* Author : P.L. Olympia & Kathy Cea
* Purpose: Error Processing routine
*        :
* Syntax : ON ERROR DO L_Error
*        :
*****************************************************************

PRIVATE mErrorNum,mFile,mCnt
SET TALK OFF

* Disable the ON ERROR routine to prevent recursive calls
ON ERROR

mErrorNum = ERROR()
mFile     = SPACE(1)
mCnt      = 0

* Define system error window
DEFINE WINDOW SysErr ;
        FROM 10,15 TO 18,65 ;
        TITLE "System Error"

ACTIVATE WINDOW SysErr

DO CASE

*Check for recoverable errors

CASE mErrorNum = 108  && File is in use
        * For Multi-user system only
        * Ask user whether he/she wants to retry locking file
CASE mErrorNum = 109  &&Record is locked by another
        * For Multi-user system only
```

(continued)

Listing 4-8. Continued

```
        * Ask user whether he/she wants to retry locking record
CASE mErrorNum = 125    && Printer not ready
        *Ask user to check printer status

* ...(Other application-specific error checks)

OTHERWISE    && Display message, print error report, return to main

   * Display error message to user
   @1,1 SAY PADC("A System Error has occurred.",50)
   @2,1 SAY PADC("Please contact your System Administrator.",50)
   @3,1 SAY PADC("Press any key to return to the Main Menu.",50)
   WAIT ""
   DEACTIVATE WINDOW SysErr

   * Determine output file name, write error report
   mFile = space(1)
   DO WHILE LEN(SYS( 2000, mFile )) > 0 .or. mCnt = 0
      mCnt  = mCnt + 1
      mFile = "ERRORS." + tran( mCnt,"9" )
      IF mCnt = 9
         EXIT
      ENDIF
   ENDDO
   SET CONSOLE OFF
   SET PRINTER ON
   SET PRINTER TO &mFile

   * Display header
   ? PADC('Order Processing System Error Report',78,'*')
   ? 'Date: ' + DTOC(DATE())
   ? 'Time: ' + TIME()
   ?

   * Loop through the FoxBASE SYS(16) function values.
   * displaying all of the procedures that were called when the
   * error occurred
```

(continued)

Listing 4-8. Continued

```
mCnt = 1
DO WHILE LEN( SYS( 16,mCnt ) ) <> 0
    IF mCnt = 1
        ? 'Master Prg: ' + SYS( 16,mCnt )
    ELSE
        ? SPACE( mCnt - 1 ) + 'Called to: ' + SYS( 16,mCnt )
    ENDIF
    mCnt = mCnt + 1
ENDDO

* Display error message, memory, etc.
?
? 'Line causing error: '
? MESSAGE(1)
?
? 'Error code is: ' + LTRIM(STR(mErrorNum))
? MESSAGE()
?
? 'FoxPro Version: '
? VERSION()
?
? 'Display of Status:'
LIST STAT
?
? 'Display of Memory:'
LIST MEMO
?


* Close output file
SET PRINTER TO
SET PRINTER OFF
SET CONSOLE ON

* Reset error trapping routine
ON ERROR DO L_Error
```

(continued)

Listing 4-8. Continued

```
        * Return to the main procedure
        RETURN TO MASTER

    ENDCASE
    RETURN
```

Setting Breakpoints

A breakpoint can be a line of code, a memory variable, a database field, or any valid expression. Program execution is suspended whenever the line of code is reached or the value of the variable or expression changes. There are two ways to set breakpoints:

1. To designate a source line of code as a breakpoint, press the Spacebar or click the mouse on the desired line of code while in the Trace window.
2. To identify a variable or expression as a breakpoint, list it in the Debug window and then press the Spacebar or click the mouse in the column separating the left side of the window from the right side.

The SET DOHISTORY Option

When SET DOHISTORY is ON, program statements that have been executed are placed in the Command window. This allows you to review the program flow and, if desired, reexecute one or more of the commands from the Command window. Although this tool can be valuable during the debugging process, it slows program execution considerably. It can also temporarily consume a large amount of disk space since it builds a temporary document that contains the executed source lines. Therefore, if you SET DOHISTORY ON while in the test and debugging stage, be certain to SET it OFF before going to production. Note that if you compile a program with the NODEBUG option, DOHISTORY is not available.

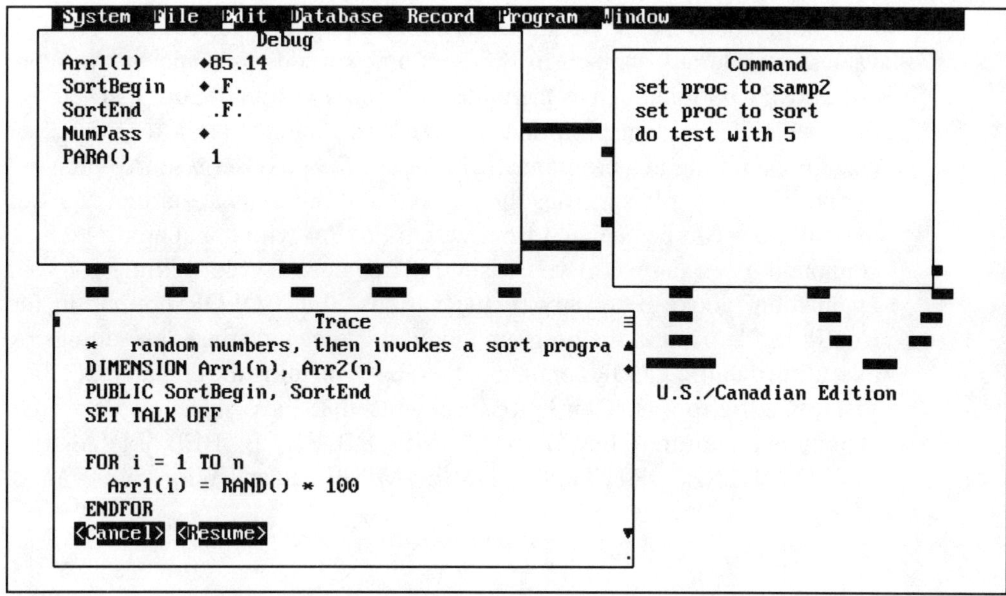

Figure 4-5. Sample screen showing the Debug window.

The LOGERRORS Setting

If you SET LOGERRORS ON (the default setting), an error log file will be written whenever you compile a program that contains errors. This file will have the same name as the program being compiled, but with an extension of .ERR. The error log file is a useful debugging tool because it identifies each source line in error and provides a diagnostic error message. If you SET LOGERRORS OFF, however, the error log file is not written.

Custom Configuration

Many FoxPro features can be customized for each user or application. This can be done by making entries in the Config.fp file or by issuing the appropriate SET commands in a program. A variety of SET commands are provided to control such configuration options as screen display, debugging facilities, memory allocation, date and time presentation, and output destination.

Appendix A lists the SET commands with descriptions, ranges of acceptable values, and default values. In this section, we address some of the more critical SET options such as the multiuser configuration options and settings that can affect system performance. We also demonstrate a technique for changing a setting in a program and introduce the FoxUser resource file.

The Config.fp file specifies the configuration options at startup. Most of these options can be changed from within FoxPro with the appropriate SET command. For example, if you wish to define default color settings for your application, you can set any of the various SET COLOR options in the Config.fp file. Any of the program modules can change the color settings by executing a SET COLOR command, thereby overriding the defaults specified in the Config.fp file. Config.fp statements that have no equivalent SET statements include COMMAND, EMS, INDEX, LABEL, MVARSIZ, MVCOUNT, REPORT, TEDIT, TIME, TMPFILES, and WP.

Multiuser Configuration Settings

In a multiuser environment (FoxPro/LAN), users can have their own Config.fp files. When FoxPro starts up, it searches the DOS path until it finds a Config.fp. To specify the location of the Config.fp to be used, a DOS environment variable may be set from the DOS command level as follows:

```
SET FOXPROCFG=<location of Config.fp>
```

For example, if user Molly stores her Config.fp in her network home directory, F:\USERS\MOLLY, the following statement may be added to her Autoexec.bat file:

```
SET FOXPROCFG=F:\USERS\MOLLY\CONFIG.FP
```

Alternatively, FoxPro can be started with the following syntax to specify the location of the Config.fp file:

```
FoxPro -C<location of Config.fp>
```

Some of the configuration settings can affect performance on a network. These are OVERLAY, EDITWORK, SORTWORK, PROGWORK, and

TMPFILES. These options specify alternate locations for the FoxPro overlay files and temporary files as follows:

Option	**Description**
OVERLAY	Specifies where FoxPro should place its overlay files.
EDITWORK	Specifies where FoxPro should place its text editor work files.
SORTWORK	Specifies where FoxPro should place its temporary work files for sorting and indexing.
PROGWORK	Specifies where the FoxPro cache file will be placed.
TMPFILES	Specifies a drive for EDITWORK, SORTWORK, and PROGWORK files if not otherwise specified.

Refer to Appendix A for more details. The usual advice is for you to consider assigning an alternate location for temporary files. For instance,

1. If you have more than one disk, you can improve performance by writing the temporary files to a disk other than the default drive.
2. When running on a network, you can improve performance by assigning a local drive for the alternate location of temporary files.

In some cases, you will encounter a fatal error if you run out of disk space when writing temporary files. For this reason, it is not advisable to assign a RAM disk for the alternate drive for EDITWORK, SORTWORK, or TMPFILES since temporary editor files and sort files can become quite large. It may be desirable to assign PROGWORK to a RAM disk, however, since the program cache file is generally smaller.

The SET EXCLUSIVE command is another important multiuser setting. This specifies whether files will be opened for EXCLUSIVE use by default. Generally it is preferable to SET EXCLUSIVE OFF to permit shared access to files. Note that even if SET EXCLUSIVE is OFF, files residing on a local drive will be opened EXCLUSIVEly, unless the DOS SHARE program has been loaded. You should not load SHARE unless your network requires it because local files will be opened for shared use (nonexclusively) by default.

The SET EMS Option

By default, FoxPro takes advantage of all expanded memory (EMS) it finds on your computer. FoxPro uses EMS to speed up all I/O operations such as sorting, indexing and other .dbf handling tasks. It also uses EMS for its overlay file. On computers with EMS that conform to LIM 4.0 specifications (or higher), FoxPro uses the first 64K of expanded memory as general purpose memory to manage Browse windows, memory variables, user-defined windows, menus, and programs.

Extended memory must be mapped to expanded memory in order for FoxPro to use it. Commercial products are available to convert extended memory to expanded memory. For example, QEMM and 386Max can map extended memory on 80386-based machines to expanded memory. The same software allows memory-resident programs, including network shells, to be loaded in High RAM (memory area between 640 KB and 1 MB), freeing up more general purpose memory for use by FoxPro.

You can limit the amount of expanded memory that FoxPro uses by placing the following statement in your Config.fp file:

```
EMS = <n>
```

where *n* is the number of kilobytes of expanded memory you are allowing FoxPro to use. To prevent FoxPro from using any expanded memory, include the line

```
EMS = OFF
```

in the Config.fp file. Alternatively, you can turn EMS usage off by invoking FoxPro with the command line parameter of -e.

Changing a Configuration Setting in a Program

As we mentioned earlier, many of the FoxPro configuration settings can be changed from within a procedure. When you change a setting, though, you must consider the impact this change will have on the other procedures in your application. Often you need to establish a setting for a particular procedure, then return the setting to what it was when your procedure was called. Since you do not necessarily know what the configuration settings are at the time a procedure is called, you need a technique for saving the old setting, assigning the setting you require, then returning the setting to its original state.

The following code fragment demonstrates how to do this with SET EXACT as an example:

```
OldExact = SET("Exact")
SET EXACT ON
* Do some processing
SET EXACT &OldExact
```

Note that in this example it is possible that SET EXACT is already ON when your procedure is called. If this is the case, it would appear that the preceeding code fragment is unnecessary. It is necessary, however, because you cannot be certain that a setting will be what you expect at all times. The code shown here ensures that you will return a setting to its original state before exiting your procedure.

The FoxUser Resource File

The FoxUser resource file stores specific resource information such as the position of various windows, color settings, diary data, and Browse window settings. Each time a user changes a resource setting (such as changing the position of the Command window or adding a diary entry), FoxPro updates the FoxUser file with the information required to restore the environment the next time the user runs FoxPro. Figure 4-6 displays the FoxUser.dbf structure.

The Type, Id, and Name fields are used to categorize the entries. ReadOnly is used to identify an entry as permanent (if its value is set to .T., as described later). FoxPro computes CkVal by calculating the CRC-16 value of the Data field to ensure that the record is not corrupted. If the CkVal contained in the record does not match the current value FoxPro computes, the record is ignored. The Data field contains the actual data for the record—depending upon the type of record, this may contain binary values. The Updated field is the date the record was last updated.

FoxPro creates a temporary index file, FoxUser.Idx, whenever it is invoked. FoxUser.Idx is indexed on Type, Id, and Name. It is deleted whenever the user executes an external command (with RUN or !) or whenever RESOURCE is SET OFF, and recreated when the user returns to FoxPro or RESOURCE is SET ON (respectively). The file is deleted when the user exits FoxPro. These precautions are taken to ensure that the index file is not accidentally deleted or corrupted from the DOS command line.

Two SET commands affect the resource file: SET RESOURCE ON/OFF and SET RESOURCE TO <alternate file>. SET RESOURCE OFF (it is ON

```
Structure for database: D:\FOXLAN\FOXUSER.DBF
Number of data records:       22
Date of last update   : 05/03/90
Field  Field Name  Type        Width    Dec
    1  TYPE        Character      12
    2  ID          Character      12
    3  NAME        Character      24
    4  READONLY    Logical         1
    5  CKVAL       Numeric         6
    6  DATA        Memo           10
    7  UPDATED     Date            8
** Total **                       74
```

Figure 4-6. The FoxUser.dbf structure.

by default) disables the resource file and displays the environment with its default settings. SET RESOURCE TO allows you to specify an alternate .dbf containing resource information.

You can make several types of modifications to the FoxUser file. You can establish a permanent setting by changing the ReadOnly field in the record to .T., you can delete any setting by deleting the corresponding record, and you can add application-specific records. To make any modifications, you must first disable the resource file with SET RESOURCE OFF. Then you USE FOXUSER to access the data stored in the file.

Using any of the FoxPro commands to edit a .dbf (such as BROWSE), you can change the ReadOnly field from .F. (default) to .T. for any record you wish to make a permanent setting. For example, if you have moved your Command window and you want to make the new location permanent, find the record where ID = "WindCmd" and change the ReadOnly value to .T. Then, even if you move the Command window to another location later, FoxPro will always start out with the window in the position stored in the .dbf.

You can also delete any of the records in the FoxUser file. If you do delete one or more record, you should also PACK the file. In the absence of a record specifying a particular setting, FoxPro presents a resource in its default configuration (location, color, and so on).

In addition, an application may add its own records to the FoxUser file. This is handy whenever a user-specific piece of information is required, since the application can rely on the fact that the FoxUser.dbf file is always there for each user. A good example of a record an application could add to each user's FoxUser.dbf file is a system password. If you add records to the FoxUser file, be sure to compute the CkVal value of the Data field using the SYS(2007) function.

When you are finished modifying resource information, close the FoxUser file and SET RESOURCE ON.

In a multiuser environment, users must have their own resource file. Since the file is used EXCLUSIVEly, the first user to access any given resource file will be the only user to whom it is available. You should ensure that a resource file is available to each user by either running the AddUser program for each user or by placing a resource file in each user's home directory on the network. You can specify the location of the resource file at startup with the following setting in the Config.fp file:

```
RESOURCE = <pathname>
```

Chapter Summary

A modular approach to system design improves your application by making it easier to understand, debug, and maintain. There are a number of ways to create and call separate program modules in FoxPro. These separate program modules can be FoxPro functions or procedures, programs written in assembly language or C and converted to .bin files, or external programs or commands that are invoked with the RUN command. Whatever your set consists of, it is important to maintain a set of library routines for use by your entire application. In this chapter we presented a number of sample library programs that you can use in your application.

FoxPro provides a built-in help facility that can be integrated with an application. We discussed the advantages and disadvantages of using this facility, and presented an alternative for implementing a custom help system. We also introduced several options for performing data validation, including the use of a .dbf containing all screen field validation expressions, and we demonstrated the various techniques with sample programs.

Error trapping and processing is an important issue that must be addressed in order to maintain and support an application. We summarized useful commands and functions for diagnosing errors and provided a program designed to trap errors, present a consistent message to the user, and generate a comprehensive error report. We also briefly summarized the FoxPro trace and debug facilities.

Finally, we reviewed customization options available in the Config.fp file and the FoxUser resource file. We discussed the highlights of these options and emphasized their use in a multiuser environment.

Chapter 5

The User Interface

Among FoxPro's outstanding features are its facilities for defining a sophisticated end-user interface. With little effort, developers can design an elegant system interface that includes pop-up windows, different types of menus, picklists, and custom color setups. In this chapter, we define these concepts and present techniques for designing and enhancing the user interface.

User-Defined Windows

A window is an area of the screen to which output may be specifically directed. It can be of any size up to the size of the entire screen and, while active, essentially acts as the screen. In addition, windows can be sized, zoomed, moved, closed, and placed inside other windows. Windows allow us to place related data or messages in one self-contained area. An application can use windows to catch the user's attention, for example, when it presents an error message or help text.

Defining Windows

A window must be DEFINEd before it can be ACTIVATEd. A window name and the screen coordinates must be supplied. Optional clauses specify a title, border type, shadow, colors, and the availability of CLOSE, FLOAT, GROW, and ZOOM options. A window's definition remains in memory until specifically RELEASEd or CLEARed. A window may be temporarily hidden with the HIDE WINDOW command. A hidden window remains active, which means that you may continue to direct output to it. When you redisplay it with the SHOW WINDOW command, it redisplays the data it contained when hidden. You can erase the window from the screen with the DEACTIVATE WINDOW command, and although its contents are lost, its definition remains in memory.

A screen is activated with the ACTIVATE WINDOW command. This displays it on the screen and directs all output to it. All screen positions are relative to the window's position. Thus the following command places the text on the top line of the window, regardless of where the window is placed on the screen:

```
@0,0 SAY "Top Line of Window"
```

Multiple windows may be defined and activated at the same time. The number of windows that can be defined and displayed is limited only by available memory and the FILES = parameter. However, output is directed only to the most recently activated window. When a window is DEACTIVATEd, the previously ACTIVATEd window becomes active. The code fragment in Listing 5-1 defines and activates three windows, each designed to hold related data items. Note that, although output goes only to the active window, all windows remain on the screen unless specifically removed.

The ACTIVATE SCREEN command may be issued at any time to direct output to the screen. Text placed in an area on the screen where a window is positioned is hidden from view unless the window is moved.

A number of commands support the [IN [WINDOW] <window name> | IN SCREEN] clause, allowing windows to be defined within other windows. If this clause is used, a "child/parent" relationship is established between the windows, with the inner window being the "child," and the outer window being the "parent." A child window may be moved only within the bounds of the parent window, and cannot be larger than the parent window. Whenever the parent window is moved, the child window automatically moves with it. If you close the parent window or release it from memory, its child window is also closed. Similarly if you DEACTIVATE the parent, the child is also DEACTIVATEd; if you HIDE the parent, the child too is hidden.

Table 5-1 displays the commands and functions relating to user-defined windows.

Listing 5-1. A code fragment that shows the use of three different windows.

```
*******************************************************************
* Program: ChgPass.prg
* Author : P.L. Olympia & Kathy Cea
* Purpose: Code fragment to demonstrate use of multiple windows
*        :
* Syntax : DO ChgPass
*******************************************************************

* Define color schemes
SET COLOR OF SCHEME 17 TO SCHEME 1
SET COLOR OF SCHEME 18 TO SCHEME 2

* Define windows
DEFINE WINDOW UserId FROM 10,10 TO 15,40 ;
        TITLE "Change Password" DOUBLE ;
        COLOR SCHEME 17

DEFINE WINDOW Retype FROM 14,20 TO 17,70 ;
        TITLE "Retype Password" DOUBLE ;
        COLOR SCHEME 18

DEFINE WINDOW MisType FROM 12,15 TO 17,60 ;
        TITLE "ERROR" PANEL ;
        COLOR SCHEME 7

* Prompt user for id and new password
DO WHILE .T.
        mInit = SPACE(3)
        mPass = SPACE(5)
        mRePass = SPACE(5)
        ACTIVATE WINDOW UserId
        @1,1 SAY "User ID" GET mInit
        * COLOR ,X blanks field
        @2,1 SAY "Enter a new password" GET mPass COLOR ,X
        READ
```

(continued)

Listing 5-1. Continued

```
        ACTIVATE WINDOW Retype
        @1,1 SAY "Please retype your password" GET mRePass COLOR , X
        READ

        IF mPass <> mRePass
                ACTIVATE WINDOW MisType
                @1,1 SAY PADC("You have mistyped your password",;
                          WCOLS())
                @2,1 SAY PADC("Please try again",WCOLS())
                WAIT
                DEACTIVATE WINDOW MisType
                HIDE WINDOW ReType
        ELSE
                EXIT
        ENDIF
ENDDO

* Deactivate windows
DEACTIVATE WINDOW UserId
DEACTIVATE WINDOW Retype
```

Table 5-1. Window Commands and Functions

Command/Function	Description
@...CLEAR	Clears an area of the screen or window.
ACTIVATE SCREEN	Directs output to the screen.
ACTIVATE WINDOW	Directs output to the window.
CLEAR	Erases the screen or current window.
CLEAR WINDOWS	Erases all user-defined windows and removes them from memory.
DEACTIVATE WINDOW	Removes window from the screen, but leaves window definition in memory. Contents of the window are lost.

(continued)

Table 5-1. Continued

Command/Function	Description
DEFINE WINDOW	Describes a window and its attributes.
HIDE WINDOW	Removes a window from the screen but not from memory. Contents of the window are saved.
MOVE WINDOW	Changes a window's screen location.
RELEASE WINDOWS	Erases named windows from screen and releases them from memory.
RESTORE SCREEN	Restores contents of a screen from a buffer or memory variable.
RESTORE WINDOW	Restores window definition from disk file or memo field.
SAVE SCREEN	Copies contents of screen to a buffer or memory variable.
SET BORDER TO	Defines the default border string for boxes, menus, popups, and windows.
SET WINDOW OF MEMO	Defines a window for editing a memo field.
SHOW WINDOW	Places a window on the screen or in a window.
COL( )	Returns the cursor's current column position on the screen. If output is being directed to a window, the column position is relative to the upper left corner of the window.
ROW( )	Returns the cursor's current row position on the screen. If output is being directed to a window, the row position is relative to the upper left corner of the window.
SCOLS( )	Returns the number of columns available on the screen.
SROWS( )	Returns the number of rows available on the screen.
WCOLS( )	Returns the number of columns available on the window.

(continued)

Table 5-1. Continued

Command/Function	Description
WEXIST( )	Returns a logical value indicating whether the window has been defined.
WLCOL( )	Returns the window's column position on the screen.
WLROW( )	Returns the window's row position on the screen.
WONTOP( )	Returns a logical value indicating whether the window is frontmost if a window name is passed to it; otherwise, returns the name of the frontmost window. The frontmost window is the most recently activated window that has not been hidden.
WOUTPUT( )	Returns a logical value indicating whether output is currently being directed to the window.
WROWS( )	Returns the number of rows available in a window.
WVISIBLE( )	Returns a logical value indicating whether the window is active (has been activated and is not hidden).

Saving and Restoring Windows

FoxPro has a set of commands for saving the contents of a window to a file or a memo field and restoring it at a later time. The command to save a window is as follows:

```
SAVE WINDOW <window list> | ALL
          TO <file> | TO MEMO <memo field>
```

To restore a previously saved window, issue the following command:

```
RESTORE WINDOW <window list> | ALL
        FROM <file> | FROM MEMO <memo field>
```

This feature is useful for diagnosing errors, for example, as part of an error processing routine. It is also useful when standard screen displays are incorporated into an application for viewing at specific times. For example, an opening screen display may be defined once, SAVEd to disk, and then RESTOREd each time the application is started.

Setting Colors

FoxPro offers almost unlimited color customization options. Yet the tradeoff is a somewhat complex set of features for defining the color setup. FoxPro has introduced many new terms for defining color combinations and has included a number of new commands and functions for manipulating color presentations. In this section we describe these new features and compare them with the familiar FoxBase+ color options.

Three concepts are central to the color system: color pairs, color schemes, and color sets. The concept of color pairs should be familiar to anyone who has programmed in FoxBase+; however, color schemes and color sets are new in FoxPro and are often confusing.

Colors may be defined for both color monitors and monochrome monitors. On monochrome monitors, the various color options control the intensity of the contrast of the screen display. If you are developing an application for use on both color and monochrome monitors, check the screen presentation on both types of monitors to be sure that it displays correctly.

Color Pairs

A color pair defines the foreground and background colors for an individual screen attribute. Examples of screen attributes are normal text, text box, and border. Retained from FoxBase+, the command

```
SET COLOR TO [[<standard>] [,/[<enhanced>] [,[<border>] [,[<back-
ground>]]]]]
```

allows you to define foreground and background colors for the standard and enhanced display, and to define a color for the border.

The "standard" screen element is the area where your text will appear, such as @<row>,<col> SAY text. The "enhanced" elements are the data entry fields, such as are defined by your GET statements. Border is simply the screen border.

Colors are defined with the following codes:

Color	Code	Color	Code
Black	N	Green	G
Blank	X	Magenta	RB
Blue	B	Red	R
Brown	GR	White	W
Cyan	BG	Yellow	GR+

An asterisk (*) is used to indicate blinking (if SET BLINK is ON) or bright. A plus sign (+) indicates high intensity. On monochrome monitors, the only colors available are:

Black (N)
Inverse video (I)
Underlined (U)
White (W)

Color Schemes

A color scheme is a set of up to ten color pairs, with each pair defining a screen attribute and each scheme defining the colors for related attributes. Examples of schemes are windows, menu popups, and the Browse window. A total of 24 schemes are available. FoxPro uses Schemes 1 through 11 as shown in Table 5-2. Schemes 12 through 16, although theoretically available, are reserved for future use, so you should resist using these schemes in an application. Schemes 17 through 24 are designated specifically for application customization, although actually any of the schemes may be redefined.

Although as many as ten color pairs may be assigned to each scheme, some schemes, such as the Menu Bar scheme, have considerably fewer than ten color pairs. For example, the Windows scheme (Scheme 8) has color pairs assigned for the following screen attributes:

Normal text
Text box
Border
Active title
Idle title
Selected text
Hot keys
Shadow
Enabled control
Disabled control

Table 5-2. FoxPro Color Schemes

Scheme	**Description**
1	User windows
2	User menus
3	System menu bar
4	Menu popups
5	Dialogs and system messages
6	Scrollable lists and menu popups within dialogs
7	Alerts
8	System windows (e.g., Command window, Debug)
9	Window popups
10	Browse window
11	Report layout
12–16	Reserved (use colors of Scheme 1 by default)
17–24	For application use (use colors of Scheme 1 by default)

The Menu Bar scheme (Scheme 3) has color pairs designated for the following screen attributes:

Disabled pads
Enabled pads
Selected pads
Hot keys

Appendix B defines the color pairs used for each scheme.

Color Sets

A color set is a group of 24 color schemes. It defines colors for virtually every screen attribute available. Fortunately FoxPro comes preconfigured with a large selection of color sets. You can easily select a predefined color set with the SET COLOR SET TO [<ColorSetName>] command, or in the Config.fp file with the COLOR SET = <ColorSetName> statement. You can also define your own color set in the Color Picker dialog, discussed in the next section. When you define your own color set, you can assemble a group of predefined color schemes, define your own color schemes, or use a combination of both.

In summary, a color set can be defined as follows:

1 Color Set = 24 Color Schemes
1 Color Scheme = (Up to) 10 Color Pairs
1 Color Pair = 1 Foreground + 1 Background Color Code

The Color Picker

The Color Picker dialog is a completely integrated facility for defining color schemes and color sets. It is available from the Window menu. It allows you to view existing color combinations and change various color pairs for any of the color schemes. It also gives you the ability to assemble your own color set, and to try out a different color set by “loading” it for experimentation. The best way to define a set of custom colors is to define the desired combinations in the Color Picker, try them out, and make any necessary modifications. Then, when you are satisfied, you can save your changes for use within your application.

To define your own color settings, select the scheme to be modified by selecting the pop-up control in the upper right corner of the screen. You are presented a list of schemes from which to choose. When you have selected a scheme, each screen attribute associated with the scheme will be listed on a "radio button," a set of parentheses followed by text that describes the attribute. Only one radio button may be selected at a time. To change the colors for a particular attribute (for the selected scheme), select the appropriate radio button. All available color pairs are presented in the lower left corner of the screen. The X indicates the foreground color, and the box behind it shows the background color.

You can continue defining color pairs for each radio button for as many schemes as you like. When you are finished, you can test out your color selections by selecting "Load." Once you are happy with the color set, save the set by selecting "Save." It is a good idea to save a custom color set under a new name, rather than overwriting an existing color set, so just type a name for the color set you have defined. You can use the color set in an application by either issuing a SET COLOR SET TO command or including a COLOR SET = statement in the Config.fp file. Remember that changes made in the Color Picker dialog are lost unless you save them to a particular color set.

Using Colors in Applications

Although the Color Picker dialog is very effective for defining colors interactively, an application developer often needs to be able to control color presentation programmatically. Many commands contain an optional clause for defining color pairs or selecting a color scheme. In addition, a number of commands and functions are available for specifying color defaults within an application.

Color pairs or colors schemes may be specified as an optional clause with the following commands:

@...SAY/GET
@...FILL
@...TO
BROWSE
CHANGE
DEFINE POPUP
DEFINE WINDOW
EDIT

Colors can be controlled with the following commands and functions:

Command/Function	Description
ISCOLOR( )	Returns a logical value indicating whether a color monitor is being used.
SCHEME( )	Returns a color pair or color pair list for the specified scheme.
SET BLINK	Determines whether screen attributes can be made to blink on EGA and VGA monitors.
SET COLOR OF	Sets colors for specific screen attributes of Schemes 1 and 2.
SET COLOR OF SCHEME	Assigns a color pair list to a particular color scheme.
SET COLOR SET	Loads the specified color set.
SET COLOR TO	Specifies the colors for user-defined menus and windows. This command is compatible with the FoxBase+ SET COLOR TO command.
SET DISPLAY	Specifies the monitor display mode.
SYS(2006)	Returns the type of graphics card and monitor in use.

Listing 5-2 displays a code fragment designed to set up colors for a particular module. It demonstrates the use of many color commands.

Designing Menus

Menus play an important role in defining a friendly, easy-to-use application. A well-designed menu interface can reduce end-user training time and result in a higher level of user satisfaction. Menus provide an event-driven interface in that users can easily select a desired option and execute the associated action.

FoxPro supports many different styles of menus. In this section, we explore the various types of menus and the commands and functions that support each menu type. We also present sample code to demonstrate the use of many of these menu types.

A menu system is typically made up of one or more of the following components:

Listing 5-2. Colors.prg, a program fragment that demonstrates several of the color commands that may be used within an application.

```
*********************************************************************
* Program: Colors.prg
* Author : P.L. Olympia & Kathy Cea
* Purpose: Program to demonstrate use of color commands
*        :
* Syntax : DO Colors
*********************************************************************

SET TALK OFF

* Select the Spring Color Set (available in FoxPro version 1.01)
SET COLOR SET TO E_SPRING

*Assign default colors of Scheme 9 to Scheme 17
SET COLOR OF SCHEME 17 TO SCHEME 9

* Assign individual colors pairs, 1 through 10
FOR clnum = 1 TO 10
        clpr = ALLTRIM(STR(clnum))
        color&clpr = SCHEME(17,clnum)
ENDFOR

*Customize a few screen attribute colors
color1 = "W+/B"   && @SAY Fields.  Default is RB/BG
color2 = "GR+/R"  && @GET Fields.  Default is B+/BG*

* Create a color pair list
colorlist = color1
FOR clnum = 2 TO 10
        clpr = ALLTRIM(STR(clnum))
        colorlist = colorlist + "," + color&clpr
ENDFOR

* Assign our customized color pair list to Scheme 17
SET COLOR OF SCHEME 17 TO &colorlist
```

(continued)

Listing 5-2. Continued

```
* Show our colors
DEFINE WINDOW ShowColors FROM 5,20 TO 15,60 ;
        TITLE "Demonstrate Custom Colors" ;
        DOUBLE SHADOW ;
        COLOR SCHEME 17

ACTIVATE WINDOW ShowColors

mColor2 = SPACE(2)
@1,1 SAY "Color Pair 1" GET mColor2
READ

DEACTIVATE WINDOW ShowColors
```

Component	Description
Menu Bar	A bar that displays the names of available menus.
Menu Pad	A one- or two-word menu name that appears on a menu bar.
Menu Popup	A menu that appears with a list of options when a menu pad is selected.
Menu Option	A selectable item on a menu popup.

Figure 5-1 displays a menu made up of each of these components. The menu styles supported by the FoxPro language are:

Bar menus
Pop-up menus
Light-Bar menus
Component-style menus (also called Pull-down menus)

Some of these menus can be implemented in several different ways. More than thirty FoxPro commands and functions support user-defined menus.

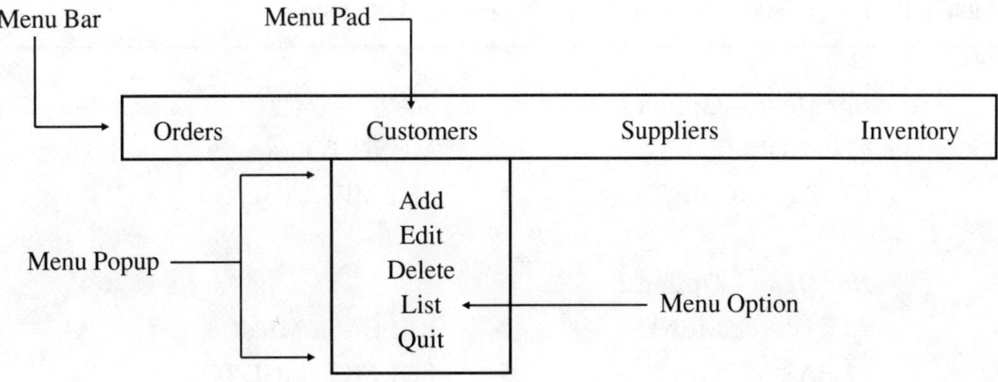

Figure 5-1. Sample menu components.

Table 5-3 lists related menu commands and functions by category. Commands that support more than one style of menu appear in multiple categories.

Bar Menus

Bar menus are most often used in connection with pop-up menus to create a component-style, or pull-down, menu. However, these commands can also be used to create a standalone bar menu. This is useful when presenting a user with a list of three or four choices, such as a list of available output destinations within a reporting module. Listing 5-3(a) shows a code fragment designed to put up such a bar menu using the @...PROMPT and related commands. Listing 5-3(b) demonstrates the use of the DEFINE MENU, DEFINE PAD, and related commands to achieve a similar effect.

Pop-up Menus

Pop-up menus are popular for presenting a set of related options. As with bar menus, popups are frequently found within component-style menus. However, these too are used as standalone menus. Listing 5-4(a) shows a program to display a set of options for processing orders, using the @...MENU and READ MENU TO commands. Listing 5-4(b) shows a similar program that uses the DEFINE POPUP, DEFINE BAR, and related commands.

Table 5-3. FoxPro Menu Commands and Functions, By Category

***Bar Menu*—Option 1**	
@...PROMPT	MENU TO
CLEAR PROMPT	SET MESSAGE TO
***Bar Menu*—Option 2**	
ACTIVATE MENU	RELEASE MENUS
CLEAR MENUS	SET MESSAGE TO*
DEACTIVATE MENU	SHOW MENU
DEFINE MENU	MENU( )
DEFINE PAD	PAD( )
HIDE MENU	PROMPT( )
ON SELECTION PAD	
***Pop-up Menu*—Option 1**	
@...MENU	READ MENU TO
***Pop-up Menu*—Option 2**	
ACTIVATE POPUP	RELEASE POPUPS
CLEAR POPUPS	SET MESSAGE TO*
DEACTIVATE POPUP	SHOW POPUP
DEFINE BAR	BAR( )
DEFINE POPUP	POPUP( )
HIDE POPUP	PROMPT( )
ON SELECTION POPUP	
Light-Bar Menu	
@...PROMPT	MENU TO
CLEAR PROMPT	SET MESSAGE TO

(continued)

Table 5-3. Continued

Component-style Menu—**Option 1**	
ACTIVATE MENU	ON SELECTION POPUP
CLEAR MENUS	RELEASE MENUS
CLEAR POPUPS	RELEASE POPUPS
DEACTIVATE MENU	SET MESSAGE TO*
DEACTIVATE POPUP	SHOW MENU
DEFINE BAR	SHOW POPUP
DEFINE MENU	BAR( )
DEFINE PAD	MENU( )
DEFINE POPUP [ACTIVATE POPUP]	PAD( )
HIDE MENU	POPUP( )
HIDE POPUP	PROMPT( )
ON PAD	

Component-style Menu—**Option 2**	
MENU	READ MENU BAR TO
MENU BAR	SET MESSAGE TO*

*Although these menu options can use the SET MESSAGE TO command for selecting a line number for messages, they do not recognize the LEFT | CENTER | RIGHT clause.

If you decide to include pop-up menus in your application, you should include code to handle the situation where a user presses the left or right arrow key. If you use the @...MENU and READ MENU TO commands, pressing the right or left arrow key will exit the user from the menu and return the immediately preceding option. If you use the DEFINE POPUP and related

Listing 5-3(a). A bar menu defined with the @...PROMPT command.

```
********************************************************************
* Program: Bar1.prg
* Author : P.L. Olympia & Kathy Cea
* Purpose: Bar menu to select report output destination
*        :
* Syntax : DO Bar1
********************************************************************

* Set up environment
SET TALK OFF

* Define Bar menu
@22,10 PROMPT "To Screen" MESSAGE "Send Report to Screen"
@22,20  PROMPT "Local Printer" MESSAGE "Send Report to Local Printer"
@22,34  PROMPT "Network Printer";
    MESSAGE "Send Report to Network Printer"
@22,50  PROMPT "To File" MESSAGE "Send Report to File"
@22,58  PROMPT "Cancel" MESSAGE "Cancel Report"

* Select message placement
SET MESSAGE TO 24 CENTER
MENU TO Choice

* Process based on user's selection
DO CASE
        CASE Choice = 1
                DO ToScreen
        CASE Choice = 2
                DO PrintRep WITH "Local"
        CASE Choice = 3
                DO PrintRep WITH "Net"
        CASE Choice = 4
                DO ToFile
        CASE Choice = 5
                RETURN
ENDCASE
```

(continued)

Listing 5-3(a). Continued

```
PROCEDURE ToScreen
@22,1 CLEAR TO 22,78
* Send report to screen
RETURN

PROCEDURE PrintRep
PARAMETERS Printer
@22,1 CLEAR TO 22,78
* Send report to selected printer
RETURN

PROCEDURE ToFile
@22,1 CLEAR TO 22,78
* Send report to file
RETURN
```

Listing 5-3(b). A bar menu defined with the DEFINE MENU command.

```
*******************************************************************
* Program: Bar2.prg
* Author : P.L. Olympia & Kathy Cea
* Purpose: Bar menu to select report output destination
*        :
* Syntax : DO Bar2
*******************************************************************

* Set up environment
SET TALK OFF

* Define Bar menu

DEFINE MENU OutPut
```

(continued)

Listing 5-3(b). Continued

```
DEFINE PAD Screen of OutPut PROMPT "To Screen" AT 22,10 ;
        MESSAGE "Send Report to Screen"
DEFINE PAD LocalP of OutPut PROMPT "Local Printer";
        MESSAGE "Send Report to Local Printer"
DEFINE PAD NetWorkP of OutPut PROMPT "NetWork Printer" ;
        MESSAGE "Send Report to Network Printer"
DEFINE PAD File of OutPut PROMPT "To File" ;
       MESSAGE "Send Report to File"
DEFINE PAD Cancel of OutPut PROMPT "Cancel" ;
       MESSAGE "Cancel Report"

* Define actions to take based on selection
ON SELECTION PAD Screen OF OutPut Do ToScreen
ON SELECTION PAD LocalP OF OutPut DO PrintRep WITH "Local"
ON SELECTION PAD NetWorkP OF OutPut DO PrintRep WITH "Net"
ON SELECTION PAD File OF OutPut DO ToFile
ON SELECTION PAD Cancel OF OutPut DEACTIVATE MENU OutPut

* Select message placement
SET MESSAGE TO 23

ACTIVATE MENU OutPut

PROCEDURE ToScreen
* Send report to screen
DEACTIVATE MENU Output
RETURN

PROCEDURE PrintRep
PARAMETERS Printer
* Send report to selected printer
DEACTIVATE MENU Output
RETURN

PROCEDURE ToFile
* Send report to file
DEACTIVATE MENU Output
RETURN
```

Listing 5-4(a). A pop-up menu defined with the @...MENU command.

```
*******************************************************************
* Program: Pop1.prg
* Author : P.L. Olympia & Kathy Cea
* Purpose: Popup menu for order processing system
*        :
* Syntax : DO Pop1
*******************************************************************

* Set up environment
CLEAR
SET TALK OFF

* Define array with menu options
DIMENSION OrdMenu[5]
OrdMenu(1) = "Add"
OrdMenu(2) = "Edit"
OrdMenu(3) = "Delete"
OrdMenu(4) = "List"
OrdMenu(5) = "Quit"

* Activate menu and get user's selection
@5,10 MENU OrdMenu,5 TITLE "Order Processing Options"
READ MENU TO Choice

* Process based on user's selection
DO CASE
        CASE Choice = 1
                DO AddOrd
        CASE Choice = 2
                DO ModOrd
        CASE Choice = 3
                DO DelOrd
        CASE Choice = 4
                DO ListOrd
        CASE Choice = 5
                CLEAR
                RETURN
```

(continued)

Listing 5-4(a). Continued

```
ENDCASE

PROCEDURE AddOrd
CLEAR
* Add Order Processing
RETURN

PROCEDURE ModOrd
CLEAR
* Modify Order Processing
RETURN

PROCEDURE DelOrd
CLEAR
* Delete Order Processing
RETURN

PROCEDURE ListOrd
CLEAR
* List Order Processing
RETURN
```

commands and a user presses the right or left arrow key, he or she will be exited from the menu with no option selected.

Light-Bar Menus

Light-bar menus can be viewed as a cross between bar menus and pop-up menus. They present options on separate "bars"; however, the options are listed vertically rather than horizontally. The code is essentially the same as for a bar menu using the @...PROMPT and related commands, except that the prompts are placed on different lines. Listing 5-5 demonstrates an order processing menu using the light-bar menu approach.

Listing 5-4(b). A pop-up menu defined with the DEFINE POPUP command.

```
*******************************************************************
* Program: Pop2.prg
* Author : P.L. Olympia & Kathy Cea
* Purpose: Popup menu for order processing system
*        :
* Syntax : DO Pop2
*******************************************************************

* Set up environment
CLEAR
SET TALK OFF

* Define menu popup
DEFINE POPUP Ord ;
        FROM 5,10 TO 11,25 ;
        MESSAGE "Order Processing Options" ;
        SHADOW ;
        COLOR SCHEME 3

DEFINE BAR 1 OF Ord PROMPT "Add"
DEFINE BAR 2 OF Ord PROMPT "Edit"
DEFINE BAR 3 OF Ord PROMPT "Delete"
DEFINE BAR 4 OF Ord PROMPT "List"
DEFINE BAR 5 OF Ord PROMPT "Quit"

* Define action to take once selection is made
ON SELECTION POPUP Ord DO Ordproc WITH BAR()

* Activate popup menu
ACTIVATE POPUP Ord

PROCEDURE Ordproc
PARAMETERS Choice
* Choice contains the value of BAR(), which is the number
*  corresponding to the BAR selected
```

(continued)

Listing 5-4(b). Continued

```
DO CASE
        CASE Choice = 1
                DO AddOrd
        CASE Choice = 2
                DO ModOrd
        CASE Choice = 3
                DO DelOrd
        CASE Choice = 4
                DO ListOrd
        CASE Choice = 5
                RETURN
ENDCASE

* Deactivate Popup only after other processing is complete
PROCEDURE AddOrd
* Add Order Processing
DEACTIVATE POPUP Ord
RETURN

PROCEDURE ModOrd
* Modify Order Processing
DEACTIVATE POPUP Ord
RETURN

PROCEDURE DelOrd
* Delete Order Processing
DEACTIVATE POPUP Ord
RETURN

PROCEDURE ListOrd
* List Order Processing
DEACTIVATE POPUP Ord
RETURN
```

Listing 5-5. A light-bar menu.

```
*******************************************************************
* Program: LBMenu.prg
* Author : P.L. Olympia & Kathy Cea
* Purpose: Light-bar menu for order processing system
*        :
* Syntax : DO LBMenu
*******************************************************************

* Set up environment
CLEAR
SET TALK OFF

* Select message placement
SET MESSAGE TO 20 CENTER

* Define menu options
@3,10 PROMPT "Add" MESSAGE "Add Order Records"
@5,10 PROMPT "Edit" MESSAGE "Edit Order Records"
@7,10 PROMPT "Delete" MESSAGE "Delete Order Records"
@9,10 PROMPT "List" MESSAGE "List Order Records"
@11,10 PROMPT "Quit"

* Activate menu
MENU TO Choice

* Process based on user's selection
DO CASE
        CASE Choice = 1
                DO AddOrd
        CASE Choice = 2
                DO ModOrd
        CASE Choice = 3
                DO DelOrd
        CASE Choice = 4
                DO ListOrd
```

(continued)

Listing 5-5. Continued

```
        CASE Choice = 5
                RETURN
ENDCASE

PROCEDURE AddOrd
* Add Order Processing
DEACTIVATE POPUP Ord
RETURN

PROCEDURE ModOrd
* Modify Order Processing
DEACTIVATE POPUP Ord
RETURN

PROCEDURE DelOrd
* Delete Order Processing
DEACTIVATE POPUP Ord
RETURN

PROCEDURE ListOrd
* List Order Processing
DEACTIVATE POPUP Ord
RETURN
```

Component-style (Pull-down) Menus

Component-style menus are a combination of bar menus and pop-up menus. The menu pads on the bar each correspond to a menu popup, which is displayed when the pad is selected. The FoxPro System Menu is a good example of a component-style menu. As shown in Table 5-3, there are two sets of commands designed to create component-style menus. The DEFINE MENU, DEFINE PAD, DEFINE POPUP, and related commands offer a very rich set of capabilities; the MENU BAR, MENU, and READ MENU BAR TO commands are simpler yet more limited in functionality. Listing 5-6(a) shows a component-style menu using such commands as DEFINE MENU and DEFINE PAD.

Listing 5-6(a). A component-style menu defined with the DEFINE MENU command.

```
*******************************************************************
* Program: CMenu1.prg
* Author : P.L. Olympia & Kathy Cea
* Purpose: Component-style menu for a complete system
*         :
* Syntax : DO CMenu1
*******************************************************************

* Set up environment
CLEAR
SET TALK OFF

* Define Menu Bar & Pads
DEFINE MENU Options

DEFINE PAD Ord OF Options PROMPT "Orders" ;
        MESSAGE 'Add, Edit, Delete, or List Customer Orders'
DEFINE PAD Cust OF Options PROMPT "Customers" ;
        MESSAGE 'Add, Edit, Delete, or List Customer information'
DEFINE PAD Suppl OF Options PROMPT "Suppliers" ;
        MESSAGE 'Add, Edit, Delete, or List Supplier information'
DEFINE PAD Inv OF Options PROMPT "Inventory" ;
        MESSAGE 'Add, Edit, Delete, or List Inventory information'
DEFINE PAD Quit of Options PROMPT "Exit"

* Define popups to correspond to pad selections
ON PAD Ord OF Options ACTIVATE POPUP Ord
ON PAD Cust OF Options ACTIVATE POPUP Cust
ON PAD Suppl OF Options ACTIVATE POPUP Suppl
ON PAD Inv OF Options ACTIVATE POPUP Inv
ON SELECTION PAD Quit OF Options DEACTIVATE MENU Options

* Define Menu Popups and Options
DEFINE POPUP Ord ;
        FROM 1,0
DEFINE BAR 1 OF Ord PROMPT "Add"
DEFINE BAR 2 OF Ord PROMPT "Edit"
```

(continued)

Listing 5-6(a). Continued

```
DEFINE BAR 3 OF Ord PROMPT "Delete"
DEFINE BAR 4 OF Ord PROMPT "List"
DEFINE BAR 5 OF Ord PROMPT "Quit"
ON SELECTION POPUP Ord DO ProcOpt WITH POPUP(), BAR()

DEFINE POPUP Cust ;
       FROM 1,9
DEFINE BAR 1 OF Cust PROMPT "Add"
DEFINE BAR 2 OF Cust PROMPT "Edit"
DEFINE BAR 3 OF Cust PROMPT "Delete"
DEFINE BAR 4 OF Cust PROMPT "List"
DEFINE BAR 5 OF Cust PROMPT "Quit"
ON SELECTION POPUP Cust DO ProcOpt WITH POPUP(), BAR()

DEFINE POPUP Suppl ;
       FROM 1,21
DEFINE BAR 1 OF Suppl PROMPT "Add"
DEFINE BAR 2 OF Suppl PROMPT "Edit"
DEFINE BAR 3 OF Suppl PROMPT "Delete"
DEFINE BAR 4 OF Suppl PROMPT "List"
DEFINE BAR 5 OF Suppl PROMPT "Quit"
ON SELECTION POPUP Suppl DO ProcOpt WITH POPUP(), BAR()

DEFINE POPUP Inv ;
       FROM 1,33
DEFINE BAR 1 OF Inv PROMPT "Add"
DEFINE BAR 2 OF Inv PROMPT "Edit"
DEFINE BAR 3 OF Inv PROMPT "Delete"
DEFINE BAR 4 OF Inv PROMPT "List"
DEFINE BAR 5 OF Inv PROMPT "Quit"
ON SELECTION POPUP Inv DO ProcOpt WITH POPUP(),BAR()

ACTIVATE MENU Options

* Process based on user's selections
PROCEDURE ProcOpt
```

(continued)

Listing 5-6(a). Continued

```
PARAMETERS mPopup, mBar
* mPopup contains the name of the PAD selected
* mBar contains the BAR number selected on the popup
* PROMPT() could be passed instead of BAR() to obtain
*  the prompt name in place of number
DEACTIVATE MENU Options
RETURN
```

Listing 5-6(b) shows a similar menu defined using the MENU commands. Note that the MENU command works in connection with a 2-dimensional array that defines the menu prompts and messages. Element (n, 1) defines the nth prompt, and element (n, 2) defines the message corresponding to the nth option. Although messages are optional in all the menu systems, the (n, 2) array elements must be initialized to at least a null character string to avoid generating an error when the READ MENU BAR TO command is invoked. As shown in Listing 5-6, this can be done by equating the array to a null string, provided that SET COMPATIBLE is OFF.

Controlling Menu Options

Three facilities are available for controlling menu options. The following characters may be placed in the prompt string of the menu option:

Character	Description
\<	May be placed anywhere in the prompt string to specify a hot key. The letter immediately following the \< is the hot key.
\	When placed at the front of the string, makes the option unselectable.
\-	When placed at the front of the string, draws a horizontal line where the option would go.

Listing 5-6(b). A component-style menu defined with the MENU commands.

```
*********************************************************************
* Program: CMenu2.prg
* Author : P.L. Olympia & Kathy Cea
* Purpose: Component-style menu for a complete system
*        :
* Syntax : DO CMenu2
*********************************************************************

* Set up environment
CLEAR
SET TALK OFF

NumPads = 5
NumChoice = 2
NumOpt = 5

* Initialize array to contain menu choices
*  We initialize all elements to a null string
*  to ensure that each element contains a character value
DIMENSION Options[NumPads,NumChoice]
Options = ""

* Define Menu Bar & Pads
Options(1,1) = 'Orders'
Options(1,2) = 'Add, Edit, Delete, or List Customer Orders'
Options(2,1) = 'Customers'
Options(2,2) = 'Add, Edit, Delete, or List Customer information'
Options(3,1) = 'Suppliers'
Options(3,2) = 'Add, Edit, Delete, or List Supplier information'
Options(4,1) = 'Inventory'
Options(4,2) = 'Add, Edit, Delete, or List Inventory information'
Options(5,1) = 'Exit'

* Define each menu popup
DIMENSION OrdOpt[NumOpt]
OrdOpt(1) = 'Add'
```

(continued)

Listing 5-6(b). Continued

```
OrdOpt(2) = 'Edit'
OrdOpt(3) = 'Delete'
OrdOpt(4) = 'List'
OrdOpt(5) = 'Quit'

DIMENSION CustOpt[NumOpt]
CustOpt(1) = 'Add'
CustOpt(2) = 'Edit'
CustOpt(3) = 'Delete'
CustOpt(4) = 'List'
CustOpt(5) = 'Quit'

DIMENSION SuppOpt[NumOpt]
SuppOpt(1) = 'Add'
SuppOpt(2) = 'Edit'
SuppOpt(3) = 'Delete'
SuppOpt(4) = 'List'
SuppOpt(5) = 'Quit'

DIMENSION InvOpt[NumOpt]
InvOpt(1) = 'Add'
InvOpt(2) = 'Edit'
InvOpt(3) = 'Delete'
InvOpt(4) = 'List'
InvOpt(5) = 'Quit'

MENU BAR Options,NumPads
MENU 1,OrdOpt,NumOpt
MENU 2,CustOpt,NumOpt
MENU 3,SuppOpt,NumOpt
MENU 4,InvOpt,NumOpt

PadSel = 1
OptSel = 1

* Activate menu
READ MENU BAR TO PadSel,OptSel
```

(continued)

Listing 5-6(b). Continued

```
* Process option selected
* PadSel contains a number corresponding to PAD selected
* OptSel contains a number corresponding to the option selected
*  on the menu popup
```

Listing 5-7 demonstrates a sample program that is called with a Security parameter. If Security is 5 or higher, all of the menu options are available. Otherwise, the Edit and Delete options are made unselectable. This program also demonstrates the use of the \- option to place a horizontal line between the program options and the exit option; it also uses the \< option to designate menu hot keys.

Deactivating Menus and Popups

Each of the menu types that requires an ACTIVATE MENU or ACTIVATE POPUP command to place the menu on the screen has a corresponding DEACTIVATE command to erase the menu from the screen. Whenever a DEACTIVE (MENU or POPUP) command is issued, program control returns to *the line immediately following the line that activated the menu.* This can lead to unexpected results if you do not properly position the DEACTIVATE command in your program. Consider the following example:

```
DEFINE MENU Test

DEFINE PAD P1 of Test PROMPT "Pad 1" AT 5,10
DEFINE PAD P2 of Test PROMPT "Pad 2" AT 7,10

ON SELECTION PAD P1 OF Test Do ProcPad
ON SELECTION PAD P2 OF Test DO ProcPad

ACTIVATE MENU Test
?"Line after Activate"
```

Listing 5-7. A sample program demonstrating use of the \ , \ -, and \ < options.

```
*******************************************************************
* Program: ProcRec
* Author : P.L. Olympia & Kathy Cea
* Purpose: Generic menu to process records.  Disables
*        :  Edit and Delete options if user security is < 5
*        : This example also shows how to designate hotkeys
*        :  and how to draw a line between options
*        :
* Syntax : DO ProcRec WITH <Security>
*        :  where <Security> is a numeric value indicating
*        :  level of user
*******************************************************************
PARAMETERS Security

* Set up environment
CLEAR
SET TALK OFF

* Define array with menu options
DIMENSION Menu1[6]
Menu1(1) = "\<Add Records"      && Hotkey is "A"
Menu1(2) = "\<Edit Record"      && Hotkey is "E"
Menu1(3) = "\<Delete Record"    && Hotkey is "D"
Menu1(4) = "\<List Records"     && Hotkey is "L"
Menu1(5) = "\-"                 && Draw a line
Menu1(6) = "\<Exit"             && Hotkey is "E"

* Disable the Edit and Delete options if security level is too low
IF Security < 5
        Menu1(2) = '\' + SUBSTR(Menu1(2),3)
        Menu1(3) = '\' + SUBSTR(Menu1(3),3)
ENDIF

* Activate menu
@0,0 MENU Menu1,6
READ MENU TO Choice
```

(continued)

Listing 5-7. Continued

```
* Process based on user's selection
DO CASE
        CASE Choice = 1
                DO AddOrd
        CASE Choice = 2
                DO ModOrd
        CASE Choice = 3
                DO DelOrd
        CASE Choice = 4
                DO ListOrd
        CASE Choice = 6
                CLEAR
                RETURN
ENDCASE

PROCEDURE AddOrd
CLEAR
* Add Order Processing
RETURN

PROCEDURE ModOrd
CLEAR
* Modify Order Processing
RETURN

PROCEDURE DelOrd
CLEAR
* Delete Order Processing
RETURN

PROCEDURE ListOrd
CLEAR
* List Order Processing
RETURN
```

```
PROCEDURE ProcPad
* Dummy procedure to show DEACTIVATE
DEACTIVATE MENU Output
* Do some processing
?"Line After Deactivate"
RETURN
```

When a pad is selected from this light-bar menu, program control passes to the ProcPad procedure. However, once the DEACTIVATE MENU command is executed, control returns to the line following the ACTIVATE MENU command in the main routine. Thus the ProcPad processing is never executed, meaning that the "Line After Deactive" message is never displayed. If you run this program, the following message displays on the screen when you select a menu pad:

```
Line after Activate
```

This program can be modified as follows to continue processing in the ProcPad procedure:

```
DEFINE MENU Test

DEFINE PAD P1 of Test PROMPT "Pad 1" AT 5,10
DEFINE PAD P2 of Test PROMPT "Pad 2" AT 7,10

ON SELECTION PAD P1 OF Test Do ProcPad
ON SELECTION PAD P2 OF Test DO ProcPad

ACTIVATE MENU Test
?"Line after Activate"

PROCEDURE ProcPad
* Dummy procedure to show DEACTIVATE
* Do some processing
?"Line before Deactivate"
DEACTIVATE MENU Output
RETURN
```

In this case, we perform all processing prior to issuing the DEACTIVATE MENU command. Running this program produces the following messages when a pad is selected:

```
Line before Deactivate
Line after Activate
```

Why So Many Options?

The availability of so many menu options offers much flexibility in programming an application, but it can also be confusing. The justification for the various sets of commands that produce the same results is simple—compatibility. Some commands are provided to maintain compatibility with FoxBase+ applications, some are compatible with dBASE IV commands and functions, and others offer compatibility with Clipper. If you are starting from scratch, with no concern for compatibility with existing code, you can select whichever approach you prefer. Table 5-3 can help you determine the relationships between the many menu commands and the various ways of producing the same result.

Picklists

A picklist is a pop-up menu that returns a value that the user has selected. The DEFINE POPUP command allows for three types of picklists: field values, field names, and filenames. With these options, the definition and use of a picklist is simple.

A typical picklist presents users with a list of field values from which they select one. This is handy when used in connection with an @...SAY/GET to prompt the user for a value that may not be easily remembered. A simple example of a picklist designed to prompt for a state abbreviation is as follows:

```
DEFINE POPUP StateCd FROM 5,1 TO 15,50 ;
        PROMPT FIELD States->StateName
ON SELECTION POPUP StateCd ?"State Code is ",States->StateCd
ACTIVATE POPUP StateCd
```

In this example, the user is presented with a list of full state names, and the state abbreviation is displayed. A States.dbf file is required, with at least

StateName and StateCd fields. Users can keep selecting states until they press the <Esc> key to terminate the display.

If there are more values than will fit in the defined area, FoxPro allows you to scroll through the options. Also, when the first letter of one of the options is typed, the cursor is positioned at the first option starting with that letter. If the letter is typed again, the cursor is positioned on the next option starting with that letter.

The PROMPT( ) function returns a character string containing the selected option, in uppercase letters. The following example allows a user to select a program file (*.prg) and prints the selected option on the screen.

```
DEFINE POPUP Progs FROM 5,1 TO 15,50 ;
        PROMPT FILES LIKE *.PRG
ON SELECTION POPUP Progs ?PROMPT()
ACTIVATE POPUP Progs
```

Again, users may keep selecting options until they press the <Esc> key. If you want to limit the users to exactly one selection, you could modify the code as follows:

```
DEFINE POPUP Progs FROM 5,1 TO 15,50 ;
        PROMPT FILES LIKE *.PRG
ON SELECTION POPUP Progs DO PrintProg
ACTIVATE POPUP Progs

PROCEDURE PrintProg
?PROMPT()
DEACTIVATE POPUP Progs
RETURN
```

This example could easily be expanded to perform additional processing once the filename is selected. For example, the program file could be edited or compiled from within the PrintProg procedure.

Another type of picklist supported by the DEFINE POPUP command is a list of database fields. The PROMPT STRUCTURE clause on the DEFINE POPUP command presents a list of field names for selection. For example, the following code fragment prompts the user for a field from the Customer.dbf file:

```
DEFINE POPUP CustFields FROM 5,10 TO 15,65;
     PROMPT STRUCTURE
```

```
ON SELECTION POPUP CustFields DO ProcFlds
ACTIVATE POPUP CustFields

PROCEDURE ProcFlds
* Do something with the selected field
DEACTIVATE POPUP CustFields
```

Listing 5-8 is a program designed to process a parts order. It demonstrates the use of a field value picklist, in this case, a list of all valid part names. When the user selects a part name, the corresponding part number is entered into the appropriate field. Note that the picklist is activated under two different circumstances: if the user leaves the part number field blank or if the user presses <F2> while editing the part number field. The program requires the Parts.dbf file, with at least PartName and PartNum fields.

The @...SAY/GET Command

One of the most powerful data entry facilities is the @...SAY/GET command. This command can place text on the screen or window, prompt for user input, and edit values input by the user. It can format data being input and output, validate user entries, display appropriate error messages, define default values when appending records, and define a memo editing window. In this section, we summarize the formatting options and discuss the important data validation options.

Pictures and Functions

PICTURE and FUNCTION are optional clauses applied to SAY and GET commands to format data for display and editing. These powerful options can eliminate a lot of unnecessary edit and validation code by allowing the user to input only certain types of data. The PICTURE clause defines the format and allowable character types (if used with GET) for each character position. For example, the following statement prompts for a five-digit value that must consist of two alphabetic characters followed by three numeric digits:

```
mValue = SPACE(5)
@5,10 GET mValue PICTURE "AA999"
READ
```

Listing 5-8. A parts order program that uses a picklist to select the part number.

```
******************************************************************
* Program: OrdPart.prg
* Author : P.L. Olympia & Kathy Cea
* Purpose: Gather data to order parts.  Uses a picklist for the
*        :  part number field.
*        :
* Syntax : DO OrdPart
******************************************************************

* Set up environment
SET TALK OFF
CLEAR

* Define window
DEFINE WINDOW AddOrder FROM 2,1 TO 22,78 ;
        TITLE "Order Parts" DOUBLE;
        SHADOW;
        COLOR SCHEME 8

mSuppId = SPACE(8)
mOrdId = SPACE(10)
mPartNum = SPACE(6)
mQuantity = 0
mOrdDt = DATE()

ACTIVATE WINDOW AddOrder

* Loop until user either saves or abandons
DO WHILE .T.
        @18,1 CLEAR TO 18,78
   * Present picklist if F2 is pressed while on the Part Number field
        ON KEY LABEL F2 DO V_Parts WITH "Edit"
        @1,1 SAY "Supplier ID: " GET mSuppId
        @3,1 SAY "Order ID: " GET mOrdId
        @5,1 SAY "Date of Order: " GET mOrdDt PICTURE "99/99/99"
    * Validate part number from V_Parts
```

(continued)

Listing 5-8. Continued

```
        @7,1 SAY "Part Number: " GET mPartNum VALID V_Parts()
        @9,1 SAY "Quantity: " GET mQuantity PICTURE "9999"
        READ
        ON KEY LABEL F2

    * Put up bar menu to save, edit, or abandon record
        @18,1 PROMPT "Save Record"
        @18,25 PROMPT "Edit Record"
        @18,50 PROMPT "Abandon Record";
            MESSAGE "WARNING - All changes will be lost!"
        Continue = 1
        MENU TO Continue
        DO CASE
                CASE Continue = 1
                        DO AddRec
                        EXIT
                CASE Continue = 2
                        LOOP
                CASE Continue = 3
                        EXIT
        ENDCASE
ENDDO While .T.

DEACTIVATE WINDOW AddOrder
RETURN


FUNCTION V_PARTS
* Function to validate Parts number field. If field is blank, or
*  if user pressed F2, present picklist.

PARAMETERS Mode
mNumParm = PARAMETERS()
ON KEY LABEL F2

* If user pressed F2 from any other field, just return
```

(continued)

Listing 5-8. Continued

```
IF VARREAD() <> "MPARTNUM"
        ON KEY LABEL F2 DO V_PARTS WITH "Edit"
        RETURN
ENDIF

DEFINE POPUP Parts FROM 7,5 TO 16,25 ;
        PROMPT FIELD Parts->PartName ;
        COLOR SCHEME 1

SELECT 1
USE Parts

IF EMPTY(mPartNum) .OR. (mNumParm = 1)
        ON SELECTION POPUP Parts DO ShowPart
        ACTIVATE POPUP Parts
        ON KEY LABEL F2 DO V_Parts WITH "Edit"
        RETURN .T.
ELSE
        * IF the user-supplied part number is valid
                ON KEY LABEL F2 DO V_Parts WITH "Edit"
                RETURN .T.
        * ELSE part number invalid
                ON KEY LABEL F2 DO V_Parts WITH "Edit"
                RETURN .F.
        * ENDIF
ENDIF

PROCEDURE ShowPart
mPartNum = PartNum
@7,15 GET mPartNum
CLEAR GETS
DEACTIVATE POPUP Parts
RETURN

PROCEDURE AddRec
* Code to append new record and update from memory variables
RETURN
```

The FUNCTION clause defines the format and allowable characters for the entire input field rather than character by character. Function codes may be included within the PICTURE clause as long as they are preceded by an @ and appear before the picture codes, or they may be explicitly defined with the FUNCTION keyword. If in the preceding example the first two digits of mValue must be uppercase alphabetic characters, we must use a function code and a PICTURE clause as follows:

```
mValue = SPACE(5)
@5,10 GET mValue PICTURE "@! AA999"
READ
```

Some of the function codes are very powerful. Data can be left or right justified or centered with the B, J, and I codes, respectively. Leading and trailing blanks can be removed with the T option. In the picture code you can embed characters that will display on the screen but will not be stored in the variable named in the GET field with the R function code. For example, the following code prompts for a social security number, but only stores the digits to the mSSN field:

```
mSSN = SPACE(9)
@5,10 SAY "Enter Social security number:" ;
     GET mSSN PICTURE "@R 999-99-9999"
```

The M <list> option allows the user to enter only choices specified in <list>. The <list> choices must be separated by commas. The user can scroll through the available choices by pressing the Spacebar or by typing the first letter of a valid choice. The following code allows a user to select a state code of MD, PA, DE, or NY only:

```
mStateCd = SPACE(2)
@5,10 SAY "Enter State Code:" ;
     GET mStateCd FUNCTION "M MD,PA,DE,NY"
READ
```

Note that since the mStateCd field does not contain a value from <list> when the READ is executed, it is prefilled with MD, the first value in the list.

Appendix C contains the complete list of picture and function codes for the @...SAY/GET command.

VALID and WHEN Clauses

The VALID clause lets you validate data while still in the READ. This means that you can prevent a user from exiting a GET field if the field contents fail the validation criteria. The format of the VALID clause is as follows:

```
VALID <expL1> | <expN1>
```

The VALID expression (often a UDF) must return either a logical value or a number. If .T. is returned, the user may proceed to the next field; if .F. is returned, an error message is displayed and the user remains in the GET field. A zero may be returned instead of .F. to suppress the system-displayed error message. This is convenient if your validation UDF handles the error message display itself. Listing 5-8 showed the use of the VALID clause in connection with a UDF (V_Parts). Although the use of a UDF is much more powerful, there may be times when a simple expression will do the job. For example, the following code fragment requires that the mZip field be filled in:

```
mZip = SPACE(9)
@5,10 SAY "ZIP Code:" GET mZip PICTURE "@R 99999-9999" ;
            VALID (.NOT. EMPTY(mZip));
            ERROR "Zip Code is required"
READ
```

The optional ERROR clause lets you define custom error messages when the VALID clause returns .F. If you do not define an ERROR message, FoxPro displays an "Invalid Input" message.

If a numeric expression is returned rather than a logical expression, the number indicates the number of GET fields to move forward or backward on the screen. A positive number indicates the number of fields to move forward on the screen and a negative number indicates the number of fields to move backward. This is particularly useful when your screen contains interfield dependencies. Listing 5-9 demonstrates a program that uses the VALID clause with a UDF that returns a numeric value. Note that the system does not display messages if a number is returned from a VALID clause, so you have to handle error messages yourself.

The VALID clause is evaluated when the GET field is exited during the full-screen READ operation. As discussed in Chapter 4, the VALID clause

Listing 5-9. A program that uses the VALID clause to return a numeric value.

```
********************************************************************
* Program: Payment.prg
* Author : P.L. Olympia & Kathy Cea
* Purpose: Process incoming payments.  Demonstrate the use of a
*        :  VALID clause that returns a number.
*        :
* Syntax : DO Payment
********************************************************************

* Set up environment
CLEAR
SET TALK OFF

DEFINE WINDOW ProcPay FROM 5,1 TO 18,60 ;
        TITLE "Process Order Payment" PANEL ;
        SHADOW ;
        COLOR SCHEME 3

mOrdId = SPACE(6)
mCusId = SPACE(8)
mBal = 100.00
mCash = 0
mCharge = 0

ACTIVATE WINDOW ProcPay
@2,1 SAY "Order Number:" GET mOrdId PICTURE "@! AA9999"
@4,1 SAY "Customer ID:" GET mCusId PICTURE "@R 999-99999"
@5,15 SAY "Total Due:     "
@5,30 SAY mBal PICTURE "$9999.99"
@6,15 SAY "Cash Received: " GET mCash PICTURE "9999.99"
@7,15 SAY "Paid by Charge:" GET mCharge PICTURE "9999.99" ;
                VALID L_Charge()
READ

* Process record

DEACTIVATE WINDOW ProcPay
```

(continued)

Listing 5-9. Continued

```
FUNCTION L_Charge
* Make sure that mCharge + mCash = the total due
*  If not, return to mCash field

DEFINE WINDOW Err FROM 16,10 TO 20,50 ;
        TITLE "Data Entry Error" DOUBLE ;
        SHADOW ;
        COLOR SCHEME 4

IF mCharge + mCash <> mBal
* Must define our own error message since system error
*  message is suppressed if numeric value is returned
        ACTIVATE WINDOW Err
        @0,0 SAY PADC("Cash + Charge must = Total Due",WCOLS())
        WAIT
        DEACTIVATE WINDOW Err
        RETURN -1
ELSE
        RETURN .T.
ENDIF
```

can be used very effectively with the VARREAD( ) function to perform several types of field-by-field validation.

The WHEN clause is similar to the VALID clause except that it is evaluated when the user enters the GET field. This feature is useful if you want to conditionally execute a GET based on, for example, other values input during the READ operation, a user's security level, or some calculated value. Listing 5-10 shows a program segment that is designed to add employee records. If the employee is an outside consultant, the Employee ID and Date of Hire fields are skipped. Also, if the employee is a U.S. citizen, the Social Security Number is available and the Alien Registration number field is skipped; otherwise, the Alien Registration number field is accessible and the Social Security number is skipped.

Listing 5-10. A program demonstrating the use of the WHEN clause.

```
*******************************************************************
* Program: AddEmp.prg
* Author : P.L. Olympia & Kathy Cea
* Purpose: Add Employee record.  Demonstrate use of WHEN clause.
*        :
* Syntax : DO AddEmp
*******************************************************************

* Set up environment
SET TALK OFF
CLEAR

DEFINE WINDOW AddEmp FROM 5,1 TO 18,60 ;
        TITLE "Add Employee Record" ;
        SHADOW

mEmpFName = SPACE(10)
mEmpLName = SPACE(15)
mConsult = .F.
mEmpId = SPACE(6)
mUS = .T.
mHireDt = {"  /  /  "}
mAlienNum = SPACE(9)
mSSN = SPACE(9)

ACTIVATE WINDOW AddEmp
@2,1 SAY "First Name:" GET mEmpFName PICTURE "@!A"
@2,25 SAY "Last Name:" GET mEmpLName PICTURE "@!A"
@3,5 SAY "Outside Consultant?" GET mConsult PICTURE "Y"
* Request Employee ID and Hire Date only if not Outside consultant
@4,1 SAY "Employee ID:" GET mEmpId PICTURE "A99999";
      WHEN .NOT. mConsult
@4,20 SAY "Hire Date:" GET mHireDt WHEN .NOT. mConsult
@5,5 SAY "U.S. Citizen?" GET mUS PICTURE "Y"
* If U.S. Citizen, get SSN.  Otherwise get Alien Registration number
@6,1 SAY "Social Security Number:" GET mSSN PICTURE "@R 999-99-9999" ;
                WHEN mUS
```

(continued)

Listing 5-10. Continued

```
@7,1 SAY "Alien Registration Number:" GET mAlienNum;
      PICTURE "A99999999" WHEN .NOT. mUS
READ

* Process record
DEACTIVATE WINDOW AddEmp
```

Trapping Keystrokes

In an application you sometimes need to know if the user pressed a particular key. The ON ESCAPE, ON KEY, ON KEY =, and ON KEY LABEL commands allow you to trap for specific keypresses and perform alternative actions based on those keystrokes.

The ON ESCAPE command can be used to initiate an application-defined routine whenever the <Esc> key is pressed during program execution. Many operations are automatically aborted if you have not defined an ON ESCAPE routine and a user presses the <Esc> key. An ON ESCAPE routine can protect your user from losing data if he or she accidentally presses the <Esc> key. The following code segment places a standard message on the screen to ensure that the user really wants to abort an operation whenever <Esc> is pressed:

```
SET ESCAPE ON
ON ESCAPE DO L_Escape

* Program code goes here

PROCEDURE L_Escape
ON ESCAPE   && Disable recursive calls

DIMENSION EscMenu[2]
EscMenu(1) = "Abandon Operation"
EscMenu(2) = "Resume Operation "
@5,10 MENU EscMenu,2 TITLE "Escape Key Pressed"
* Set default to Resume option
Choice = 2
```

```
READ MENU TO Choice
ON ESCAPE DO L_Escape
DO CASE
       CASE Choice = 1
               * Perform any program clean-up here
               * Exit routine, possibly with a RETURN TO MASTER
        CASE Choice = 2
                RETRY
ENDCASE
RETURN
```

Note that the ON ESCAPE routine will not be called if the <Esc> key is pressed while waiting for user input. For example, ON ESCAPE is ignored during a READ or while waiting for the user to make a menu selection. If SET ESCAPE is OFF, the ON ESCAPE routine is ignored.

The ON KEY = command is used to trap for specific keystrokes during a READ operation. Only one ON KEY = command routine may be active at a time. If you wish to perform the preceding L_Escape routine whenever the <Esc> key is pressed during a READ, include the following statement in your program prior to issuing the READ statement:

```
ON KEY = 27 DO L_Escape
```

The ON KEY command traps for any keystroke. It does not distinguish among keys—any key pressed activates the ON KEY command. This is useful when waiting for user input since you can pass program control to a named routine upon accepting a keystroke. Only one ON KEY routine is active at a time.

The ON KEY LABEL command is perhaps the most versatile of the group. Multiple ON KEY LABEL commands may be active, and keystrokes will be trapped during READ, BROWSE, EDIT, and CHANGE operations, in addition to user-defined menus and popups. It also traps keystrokes pressed between program statements.

Browse

The BROWSE command has been greatly enhanced in FoxPro. In FoxBase+, it was not generally thought of as an application tool. It was usually reserved for developers who needed to quickly view or change some records in a database file. With its new optional clauses and flexible interface, it can now be incorporated into applications and save programming time. This section summarizes the Browse enhancements that are most significant in a programming environment.

With the FIELDS clause, you can specify the fields that are to be displayed, and the order in which they are to appear. In addition, calculated fields can be specified. Data validation can be performed, error messages can be defined, PICTUREs can be included, and valid ranges can be specified. A field can be designated as read-only, and its width on the screen can be defined.

With the FORMAT option, you can name a format file to control the screen display and validation options.

With the KEY option, you can limit the records to be displayed to those that fall within a given range by specifying an index key value or range of key values.

The NOAPPEND option prevents records from being added.

The NODELETE option prevents records from being marked for deletion.

The NOEDIT/NOMODIFY option prevents changes from being made to the database records.

In addition, a number of clauses are available for defining the presentation of the Browse window such as colors, title, and placement in a user-defined window. Up to 25 Browse windows may be opened simultaneously, provided there is sufficient memory.

Chapter Summary

In this chapter, we covered the important commands and functions used to enhance the user interface. We discussed the use of windows in an application and defined the many commands associated with them. We discussed in detail the color customization options, including the interactive Color Picker dialog and the many color options available from within an application. We defined color pairs, color schemes, and color sets, and we provided sample code that demonstrated a number of the color commands defined to work in connection with these concepts.

We reviewed the basic menu components and the numerous options for defining FoxPro menus. We categorized associated menu commands and provided sample programs for each type of menu available. We then discussed picklists, which are essentially a specialized type of menu that returns values. We showed code fragments for several picklists defined with the DEFINE POPUP command.

We reviewed the powerful @...SAY/GET command and summarized important PICTURE and FUNCTION clause options. We discussed the WHEN and VALID clauses and showed program code that used these options. We also summarized the four commands for trapping user keystrokes.

Finally, we looked briefly at the BROWSE command and summarized the major enhancements that make this command useful within an application.

Chapter 6

Handling Date and Time Data

The ease of unit conversion is clearly one of the advantages of the metric system over the English system of measurement. In the metric system, just about every conversion constant, regardless of the physical property being measured, is a multiple of 10; for example, there are 10 deciliters to a liter, 100 centigrams to a gram, and 1000 millimeters to a meter. On the other hand, it is difficult to keep track of the many conversion constants in the English system; for example, there are 12 inches to a foot, 3 feet to a yard, 16 ounces to a pound, and 4 quarts to a gallon.

Unfortunately our calendar system is worse than the English system of measurement where the uninitiated almost always need to carry a quick reference card to be reminded that although there are 12 months to a year, the number of days in a month may be any number from 28 through 31, depending on the month and year. As if that were not enough, people from different parts of the world cannot even agree on a standard date format. So, although Americans consider 07/04/11 to be the 135th anniversary of the Declaration of Independence, the Japanese know that date as April 11, 1907, and the French recognize it as April 7, 1911.

Imagine how much computer code could be saved if only we had a calendar system where every month had 30 days and everyone were satisfied with a single date format like YYYY/MM/DD. As it is, a typical computer program includes so much code just to do such things as date validation. Luckily FoxPro spares us much of the drudgery by providing us with date-smart facilities. For example, the @D PICTURE format of @...SAY/GET command, as in

```
@ 10,12 SAY "Enter Date of Birth: " GET dob PICTURE '@D'
```

validates the user-supplied value for the date variable, taking into account the current SETting of the date format (American, Japanese, and so on). Thus we need not write a separate procedure to break the entered data into month, day, and year. We also need not ensure that each date component falls within proper bounds, for example, the day cannot be larger than 28 if the month is February unless the year is a leap year.

Of course, we could easily write a customized date validation routine using FoxPro's date functions such as DTOC( ). For instance, a clever technique for ensuring that a user-supplied character string represents a valid date is to convert it to a date variable using the CTOD( ) function, then convert it back to characters using DTOC( ), and finally compare the result with the original, user-supplied value. If the input variable is DOB, the following code fragment illustrates the technique:

```
dob = ALLTRIM(dob)              && trim leading & trailing blanks
IF DTOC(CTOD(dob)) = dob
   * input value is valid date
   * proceed with the rest of the program
ELSE
   * invalid date input
   * process error
ENDIF
```

The technique works because FoxPro returns a blank date when CTOD( ) is invoked with a character string that translates to an invalid date, for example, 02/29/91. In that case, converting the result back to a string by way of the DTOC( ) function results in a value that is different from the original string. On the other hand, DTOC(CTOD(expC)) returns expC again if it translates to a valid date, for instance, 02/28/91. Obviously, the IF statement in the preceding code fragment could be replaced by a statement such as

```
IF EMPTY(CTOD(dob))
```

but this works only in FoxPro, whereas the earlier code works in dBASE III PLUS, dBASE IV, FoxBASE+, and others.

Table 6-1 summarizes the FoxPro functions for handling date and time data.

Table 6-1. Summary of FoxPro Time and Date Functions

Function	Description
{mm/dd/yy}	Converts the literal mm/dd/yy to date. See also CTOD( ). *Example:* {02/20/90}
BETWEEN(d1,d2,d3)	Returns .T. if d1 is a date that falls between the two dates d2 and d3. This function accepts date, numeric, or character arguments so long as all three parameters are of the same type. *Example:* ? BETWEEN({01/15/90}, {12/25/89},{02/20/90}) .T.
CDOW(d)	Returns the name of the weekday corresponding to date, d. *Example:* ? CDOW({02/20/90}) Tuesday
CMONTH(d)	Returns the name of the month of date, d. *Example:* ? CMONTH({12/25/90}) December
CTOD(s)	Converts character string, s, to a date variable. The format of the string depends on the current setting of SET DATE and SET CENTURY. See also {mm/dd/yy}.
DATE( )	Returns the system date. Default format is MM/DD/YY.
DAY(d)	Returns a number corresponding to the day of date, d. *Example:* ? DAY({02/20/90}) 20
DMY(d)	Returns the date in the format DD Month YY (or DD Month YYYY if SET CENTURY is on). *Example:* ? DMY({12/25/90}) 25 December 90

(continued)

Table 6-1. Continued

Function	Description
DOW(d)	Returns a number, 1–7, corresponding to the day of the week of date, d. Sunday is 1, Saturday is 7. *Example:* isweekend = MOD(DOW(date_var)-1,6) <>0 returns .T. if a date falls on a weekend.
DTOC(d,[1])	Converts date, d, to a character string. Useful for concatenating dates with character variables and literals, and for comparing two dates. The optional second parameter, 1, returns the date string in YYYYMMDD just like the DTOS function does. *Example:* ? DTOC(DATE( )) > DTOC(Today) .F. *Example:* ? DTOC({02/20/91},1) 19910220
DTOS(d)	Converts date, d, to a character string of the form YYYYMMDD regardless of the setting of SET CENTURY and SET DATE. Useful in indexing on date expressions. *Example:* INDEX ON DTOS(hiredate) TO EmpHire
EMPTY(d)	Returns .T. if date, d, is null. This function also works with arguments of character, numeric, logical, and memo data types. *Example:* IF EMPTY(HireDate) ? 'HireDate should not be blank' ENDIF
GOMONTH(d,n)	Returns the date that is n months after or before date, d. *Example:* ? GOMONTH({02/20/90},3) 05/20/90 *Example:* ? GOMONTH({02/20/90},-3) 11/20/89

(continued)

Table 6-1. Continued

Function	Description
INLIST(d1,d2,d3...)	Returns .T. if date d1 is included in the list d2,,d3... . This can be used for validating a date. INLIST( ), like BETWEEN( ), is not specific to dates per se, but can be used also for other data types such as character; the only restriction is that all arguments must be of the same data type. *Example:* IF INLIST(DATE( ),hol1,hol2,hol3) ? 'Today is one of 3 holidays' ENDIF
MDY(d)	Returns the date in the format Month DD, YY (or Month DD, YYYY, if SET CENTURY is on). *Example:* SET CENTURY ON ? MDY({12/25/90}) December 25, 1990
MONTH(d)	Returns a number representing the month of date, d. *Example:* ? MONTH({12/25/99}) 12
SECONDS( )	Returns the number of seconds since midnight with a resolution of one millisecond. This is the same value produced by the SYS(2) function except that SECONDS( ) returns the value as a number in seconds.thousandths format, whereas SYS(2) returns the value as a whole number expressed in a character string. *Example:* ? SECONDS( ) 7345.678
SYS(1)	Returns a character string representing the Julian period number of the current system date. *Example:* ? SYS(1) 2447943

(continued)

Table 6-1. Continued

Function	Description
SYS(2)	Returns a character string representing the number of seconds since midnight. This function differs from SECONDS( ) in that it returns the number as an integer and in character form, whereas SECONDS( ) returns the same value as a numeric with millisecond level precision. *Example:* ? SYS(2) 7346
SYS(10,n)	Converts the Julian period number, n, to the equivalent Gregorian date expressed as a character string. *Example:* ? SYS(10, 2447943) 02/20/90
SYS(11,d_c)	Converts a date expression or a character string in date format to the corresponding Julian number expressed as a character string. If the date parameter is the system date, this function returns the same value as the SYS(1) function. *Example:* ? SYS(11, DATE( )) 2447943
TIME( )	Returns the system time as a character string in the 24-hour format HH:MM:SS, for example, 13:55:10. *Example:* t = IIF(VAL(t)<12,t+ 'am',IIF(VAL(t)=12,t + 'pm', STR(VAL(t)-12,2)+SUBS(t,3)+'pm')) converts time, t, to standard 12-hour format.
YEAR(d)	Returns a four-digit number representing the year of date, d. *Example:* ? YEAR({12/25/90}) 1990

Summary of Important FoxPro Date/Time Features

In FoxBASE+, as in dBASE III PLUS, a character string can be converted to a date value using the CTOD( ) function. FoxPro, like dBASE IV, has a more convenient alternative to the function—the curly brackets can be used to convert a string literal to date values. Thus the following commands give the same result:

```
? DTOC("02/20/90")
? {02/20/90}
```

FoxPro has all the new date functions of dBASE IV, including MDY( ) and DMY( ) to print date values in familiar formats as well as DTOS( ) to facilitate using dates in index expressions. FoxPro has other unique commands and functions. For instance, GOMONTH( ) returns a date that is a specified number of months from a given date. The SYS(11) function, which returns the Julian date, is a great timesaver in date arithmetic operations.

In dBASE III PLUS and FoxBASE+, subtracting the base date from a date variable yields the proper numeric value. The base date is the date the world began according to dBASE. In FoxPro, as in dBASE IV, subtracting the base date from a date variable yields only zero. One important difference between FoxPro and dBASE IV is that although dBASE IV can report and process any dates after 1 A.D., FoxPro can only process dates beginning with October 15, 1582; dates before this are treated as blank (null) dates and will yield a Julian equivalent of zero. Chronology buffs will recall that Friday, October 15, 1582, was the start of the Gregorian calendar and was the day after October 4, 1582, decreed by Pope Gregory as the last day of the Julian calendar; the transition resulted in ten "lost" days between the two dates.

Date Operations

FoxPro treats dates as special types of numbers that can be used in some arithmetic operations, for example:

```
datevl - datev2 =  number        && gives elapsed days
datevl + number =  datev3        && new date later than datevl
datevl - number =  datev4        && new date earlier than datel.
```

The first expression results in a positive or negative number depending on whether Datev1 is earlier or later than Datev2.

On the other hand, subtracting a date from a number or adding two dates together would not make sense, so the two commands

```
? 12345  - datev1
? datev2 + datev3
```

produce the error message "Operator/Operand type mismatch."

In a typical business application, date arithmetic operations such as those shown here ease the computation of elapsed days or of dates for making critical business decisions. FoxPro handles the chore of figuring out how many days are in each of the months involved in the computation.

dBASE IV and FoxPro have an important incompatibility related to date values and date calculations. In FoxPro any date conversion that yields an invalid date always yields an empty date. For example,

```
? {01/32/91}          && No such date
   /  /
```

In dBASE IV, there really are no invalid dates. dBASE IV automatically performs the implied arithmetic in a date that appears invalid in order to yield a valid date. For example,

```
? {01/32/91}          && Seems invalid but dBASE IV
 02/01/91             && translates to next day
```

dBASE IV's undocumented ability to perform the date arithmetic implied in a seemingly invalid date value can be put to good use for determining past and future dates with shorthand notation. For instance, if the date format is American and today's date is 02/20/90, and we want to know what date is 214 days from today, we can always say

```
? DATE() + 214, or
? {02/20/90} + 214
```

but it is much easier to say

```
? {02/234/90}          && Just add 214 to the day
```

Date Comparisons

Relational operators may be used on dates, as well as on numeric or character variables, to yield a logical (.T. or .F.) result. For instance,

```
. ? date1 >= date2
  .T.
. ? date3 = date4
  .F.
```

Use the EMPTY( ) function to test whether or not a date variable is blank, or whether or not a date literal is invalid.

```
. ? EMPTY({})
  .T.
. ? EMPTY({12/32/90})
  .T.
```

Time data may be packed with dates, so the safest way to test whether two dates are identical is to first convert them to character strings before making the comparison, for example,

```
. ? DTOC(datev1) = DTOC(datev2)
  .F.
```

Date Formats

FoxPro has the same set of display formats for dates as dBASE IV. Changing the display format does not alter the date field or the variable itself. The default format is American, but it may be overridden either by adding a line such as

```
DATE = JAPAN
```

to the CONFIG.FP file or by issuing the command

```
SET DATE <date-format>
```

in the command window or in a program, where the permissible <date-format> keywords and their display forms are as follows:

Date Format	**Display**
AMERICAN	MM/DD/YY
ANSI	YY.MM.DD
BRITISH	DD/MM/YY
FRENCH	DD/MM/YY
GERMAN	DD.MM.YY
JAPAN	YY/MM/DD
USA	MM-DD-YY
MDY	MM/DD/YY
DMY	DD/MM/YY
YMD	YY/MM/DD

Note that the French, British and DMY formats are the same; the Japan format is the same as YMD, and the American format is the same as MDY.

In dBASE IV, but not in FoxPro, you have to be wary of changing display formats while performing date arithmetic that involves date literals. As we have seen previously, dBASE IV automatically performs the date arithmetic implied in a date value. Therefore, values of date constants expressed as literals depend on the display format that is in effect, whereas the values of date fields or memory variables do not change with a change in date formats. Thus, if the currently active format is JAPAN, dBASE translates the date {02/20/90} to October 31, 1903, whereas FoxPro translates it to an empty date (since 20 is an invalid month).

If the SET CENTURY ON command is in effect, the year displays as a four-digit number, for instance, 1990. Otherwise, FoxPro defaults to SET CENTURY OFF, which assumes that the year is in the twentieth century, and only displays the last two digits of the year.

The function MDY( ), which should not be confused with the SET DATE format MDY, prints the date in the familiar display format: Month DD, YY, which comes in handy in applications that write mailmerge letters, for example,

```
. SET CENTURY ON
. ? MDY({02/20/90})
   February 20, 1990
```

Similarly, the function DMY( ) displays the preceding date in the format 20 February 1990.

Null Date

A date field in a database record that has not been initialized (to a valid date value) is a null date field. The statement

```
nulldate = {}
```

also creates a null date, which FoxPro displays as an empty (blank) date.

In FoxPro (as in FoxBASE+ and dBASE III PLUS or IV), any arithmetic operation involving a null date and a valued date field or variable always yields zero:

```
  today = DATE()
02/20/90
  ? nulldate - today
        0
  ? today - nulldate
        0
```

Similarly, all arithmetic operations involving a null date and a number always yield a null date:

```
? nulldate + 98765
/  /
? nulldate - 98765
/  /
```

In dBASE IV, comparing a null date variable to a valued (nonblank) one for inequality erroneously returns false:

```
? today <> nulldate
.F.
```

Here the dates had to be converted first to character in order to get the correct result.

```
? DTOC(today) <> DTOC(nulldate)
.T.
```

This is not a problem in FoxPro, where all comparisons with a null date always yield the correct value.

To test whether a date variable is null, use either of the following alternative IF clauses:

```
IF {} = datevar
IF EMPTY(datevar)
```

To understand why operations with null dates behave as they do, we need to know how FoxPro stores dates.

Date Storage Format

In a .dbf file, database records are stored as text. The values of numeric fields are stored as text, complete with any decimal points. Likewise, values of date fields are stored as text in the format YYYYMMDD, for example, 19901225 for December 25, 1990. On the other hand, FoxPro, like FoxBASE+ and dBASE, stores dates in memory and in .mem files not as text data, but as 8-byte numbers in IEEE (Institute of Electrical and Electronic Engineers) format consisting of an exponent, a significand, and a sign bit.

To confirm that FoxPro treats dates as numbers and stores them as such in a .mem file, all we need to do is define one date variable, save it to a .mem file, and inspect the result with DEBUG or similar utility, for example, Microsoft's symbolic debugger, SYMDEB.

```
  today = DATE()
  02/20/90
  display memory
  TODAY        pub   D  02/20/90
  save to test
  !symdeb test.mem
  -d100 12f
7D3A:0100  54 4F 44 41 59 00 00 00-00 00 00 44 00 00 00 00  TODAY......D....
7D3A:0110  00 00 00 00 00 00 00 00-00 00 00 00 00 00 00 00  ................
7D3A:0120  00 00 00 80 23 AD 42 41-1A FF 89 F0 BA 02 00 EB  ....#-  BA...p:..k
  -d1120
7D3A:0120  00 00 00 80 23 AD 42 41  +0.2447943E+7           <---- Today
```

From the 44h byte at location 010B (corresponding to the solitary "D" on the right) we know that TODAY is a date variable—44h translates to the

ASCII character "D." We can tell also that FoxPro "knows" the date 02/20/90 as the number (Julian period) 2447943.

One way to confirm that the date 02/20/90 is the same as the number 2447943 as far as FoxPro is concerned is to change the 44h byte to 4Eh (converting "D" to "N"), then restore the .mem file in FoxPro, and see what happens to the TODAY variable.

```
  -e10b 4e                      <--- change 44 to 4E
  -d100 10f
7D3A:0100  54 4F 44 41 59 00 00 00-00 00 00 4E 00 00 00 00  TODAY......N....
  -w                            <--- write the change back to file
   Writing 0029 bytes
  -q                            <--- quit Symdeb
. restore from test
. display memory
  TODAY        pub   N      2447943  (2447943.000000000000)
```

So, FoxPro now thinks TODAY is a numeric variable with the value that we expected. That confirms the notion that dates are just special types of numbers in FoxPro.

Listing 6-1 displays the Julian period corresponding to a given date, or the date corresponding to a given Julian period. The program uses as a reference date the beginning of the Gregorian calendar, namely, October 15, 1582, although any arbitrary date after this date can be used also. This program produces the same results as the SYS(10) and SYS(11) functions.

FoxPro Base Date

We can now answer the question, "What does FoxPro consider as its base date, that is, date zero?" Since we now know that 02/20/90 is the same as the number 2447943, subtracting the latter from the former should tell us the base date.

```
. base = today - 2447943
  /  /
```

As you can see, FoxPro does not provide the information. Instead, it displays a null date, which is consistent with the observation that FoxPro displays any date earlier than 10/15/1582 as null. Let's check to see if it is

Listing 6-1. F_Jul.prg, date, and Julian period converter function.

```
FUNCTION F_Jul
**********************************************************************
* Program :  F_Jul.prg
* Author :   P. L. Olympia and Kathy Cea
* Purpose :  Returns either Julian number or Gregorian date depending
*         :  whether the passed parameter is date or numeric.
*         :
* Syntax  :  x = F_Jul(date_num)
*         :  where date_num may be date or numeric. If date, the
*         :  function returns the Julian number just like SYS(11).
*         :  If date_num is numeric, the function returns the
*         :  Gregorian date, similar to that returned by the SYS(10)
*         :  function.
**********************************************************************
PARAMETER DateOrNum
Private dateref, julref, Jul_Greg
CentSet = SET("CENTURY")
SET CENTURY ON
*  Use some reference dates, e.g., the earliest date in
*  the FoxPro calendar
dateref = {10/15/1582}
julref  = 2299161                && Julian period for 10/15/1582
*  Determine the result depending on type of parameter passed
IF TYPE("DateOrNum") = "D"
   Jul_Greg = (DateOrNum - dateref) + julref
ELSE
   IF TYPE("DateOrNum") = "N"
      Jul_Greg = (DateOrNum - julref) + dateref
   ELSE
      Jul_Greg = "Invalid"
   ENDIF
ENDIF
* Reset CENTURY setting
SET CENTURY &CentSet
RETURN (Jul_Greg)
```

really null, and then determine what number corresponds to a null date according to FoxPro.

```
  nulldate={}
  / /
  ? base = nulldate
  .T.                          && looks like base date is null
  save to test2
  !symdeb e:test2.mem
-d100 17f
891E:0100  54 4F 44 41 59 00 00 00-00 00 00 44 00 00 00 00  TODAY......D....
891E:0110  00 00 00 00 00 00 00 00-00 00 00 00 00 00 00 00  ................
891E:0120  00 00 00 80 23 AD 42 41-42 41 53 45 00 00 00 00  ....#-BABASE....
891E:0130  00 00 00 44 00 00 00 00-00 00 00 00 00 00 00 00  ...D............
891E:0140  00 00 00 00 00 00 00 00-00 00 00 00 00 00 00 00  ................
891E:0150  4E 55 4C 4C 44 41 54 45-00 00 00 44 00 00 00 00  NULLDATE...D....
891E:0160  00 00 00 00 00 00 00 00-00 00 00 00 00 00 00 00  ................
891E:0170  00 00 00 00 00 00 00 00-1A 03 2E 04 4F 04 00 00  ............O...
-dl148
891E:0148  00 00 00 00 00 00 00 00   +0.0E+0            <---  Base
-dl170
891E:0170  00 00 00 00 00 00 00 00   +0.0E+0            <---  Nulldate
```

The results show that indeed FoxPro considers its base date as a null date, and that the null date is zero. In contrast, dBASE IV considers null date as a large number (one googol), whereas dBASE III PLUS considers null date as infinity (a number divided by zero). In PLUS, the base date can be used in date calculations. For example,

```
.jul = DATE() - base
```

gives the correct numeric value, whereas the same expression gives zero in both FoxPro and dBASE IV.

We can easily deduce what date FoxPro considers as its base date. Using the function F_Jul.Prg in Listing 6-1 or the FoxPro SYS(11) function, we know that 12/31/90 is the 2448257th day in the FoxPro calendar. Therefore,

```
2448257 days ÷ 365.2425 days/year = 6703.10 years
```

have elapsed since the base date. Thus, the number of years B.C. is

```
6703.10 - 1990 = 4713.10.
```

If we can ignore the fractional part of 4713.10, the FoxPro base date must be January 1, 4713 B.C. This is the same date that astronomers consider to be the base date in the Julian calendar as devised by Joseph Scaliger in the sixteenth century. Although day 0 in the FoxPro (and dBASE) calendar is January 1, 4713 B.C., FoxPro can only display or correctly use in calculations dates beginning with the start of the Gregorian calendar, namely, October 15, 1582 A.D. By contrast, dBASE IV can display and handle dates up to 1 A.D.

Note that knowing FoxPro's base date, or the base date of any software for that matter, is more of an academic, rather than practical interest. It really doesn't matter which base date one chooses—it could be someone's birthday, for instance. A base date simply serves as a reference point for performing date arithmetic.

Packing Date and Time

We just saw that FoxPro stores dates in memory and in .mem files as numbers. These numbers need not be integers—they may contain a fractional component, which in this case would be time. For example (Schulman, 1987),

```
today = DATE()
02/20/90
today_noon = today + .5
02/20/90
tomorrow = today_noon + .5
02/21/90
```

We learn two lessons from this example. First, FoxPro stores date fractions. Second, precisely because of that, date comparisons such as

```
? today = today_noon
.F.
```

would seem to be inconsistent with the displayed values of the two variables. Thus the safe way to compare the two variables is to convert them first to character values:

```
? DTOC(today) = DTOC(today_noon)
.T.
```

Being able to pack date and time into one variable saves memory variable space and ensures that the two are always together. However, note that just as the DTOC( ) function strips away the fractional component of the date, time data packed with dates are lost when the date is stored in a .dbf file since, unlike dates in a .mem file, dates in a .dbf file are stored as text in the form YYYYMMDD.

Although FoxPro version 1.02 can pack time data into dates just like dBASE, it does not allow you to extract the fractional part of the date (that is, time data) since it insists on converting the value to an integer regardless of how SET FIXED and SET DECIMALS are defined.

Random Numbers and the System Clock

A few of FoxPro's built-in functions depend on the time kept by the system clock. For instance, the random number generator function RAND( ), when invoked with a negative number as a parameter, uses a seed value derived from the system clock. If FoxPro did not include a RAND( ) function, we could define our own equivalent function using other FoxPro functions such as SECONDS( ), which returns the number of seconds since midnight to the thousandth digit.

The FoxPro manuals do not document the fact that the popular SYS(3) function also is based on the system clock. This function is often used to generate a unique DOS filename for temporary files. Developers of multiuser applications that depend on this function for names of temporary files should be forewarned that two users on the network could easily produce duplicate filenames if their workstation clocks show identical times when the function is invoked. It is easy enough to show that SYS(3) depends on the system clock and that duplicate names could be generated by the function. The following short program, when run a few times, shows the problem:

```
* TESTSYS3.PRG -- Demonstrates that SYS(3) depends on the system
*                 clock and can generate non-unique DOS filenames
SET TALK OFF
FOR i = 1 TO 3             && Try 3 runs
    ?
    ! TIME 11:00:00        && Set the clock to a fixed time
```

```
    FOR j = 1 TO 10        && Let's generate 10 filenames
        ? SYS(3)
    ENDFOR   && j
ENDFOR       && i
SET TALK ON
```

Averaging Dates

To compute the average value of a date field in a database, we need a reference point for computing elapsed days. This reference point could be the base date or some other date. In the following example, we compute the average of a date field, DOB, using the date 01/01/80 as a reference.

```
refdate = {01/01/80}
AVERAGE ON (hiredate - refdate) TO ave_days
ave_hire = refdate + ave_days
```

Indexing on Dates

A date field may be used directly in an index expression to index a database in chronological order. For instance,

```
INDEX ON HireDate to EmpNdx.
```

If the index expression requires the concatenation of a date field and a character expression, use the CTOS( ) function to convert the date to character data in the form YYYYMMDD, regardless of the current setting of SET DATE and SET CENTURY. Alternatively, you may use the CTOD( ) function with the second parameter of 1, for example, CTOD(Date_Fld,1).

FoxPro version 1.02 does not have the multiple index (.mdx) file facility of dBASE IV, and so, like FoxBASE+ and dBASE III PLUS, it does not have built-in support for indexes in descending order. To index a file in reverse chronological order, we can use a scheme where the date field is subtracted from a reference date that is early in the FoxPro calendar. For example,

```
startdate = {10/15/1582}
INDEX ON startdate  - <date_fld> TO <idxfile>
```

Listing 6-2. IsLeap user-defined function returns .T. if a year is a leap year.

```
FUNCTION isleap
*********************************************************************
* Program :  IsLeap.prg
* Purpose :  Returns .T. if year is a leap year
*         :
* Syntax  :  YesNo = IsLeap(yy)
*********************************************************************
PARAMETER yy
* yy may be 2-digit or 4-digit numeric. Returns .T. if leap year
yy = INT(yy)
yy = IIF(yy < 100, 1900+yy, yy)     && assume 20th century year
                                    && if only two digits
yesno = (MOD(yy,4)=0 .AND. MOD(yy,100)<>0) ;
          .OR. mod(y,400)=0
RETURN(yesno)
```

Is It a Leap Year?

A leap year is a year that is divisible by 400 or by 4 depending on whether it is, respectively, a centennial year or not. Thus 1992 (divisible by 4) is a leap year, but 1990 is not. Similarly, 1900 was not a leap year (not divisible by 400), although the year 2000 will be. The function IsLeap in Listing 6-2 uses that definition and returns .T. if the year passed to the function is a leap year.

However, an easier way to tell whether a year is a leap year is to take advantage of FoxPro's knowledge of dates. Recall that FoxPro returns an empty date when it is asked to perform a string-to-date conversion that leads to an invalid date, for example, {12/32/90}. So, if we ask FoxPro to convert a string such as 02/29/90 to a date, it returns an empty date if 1990 is not a leap year, and a nonblank value otherwise. Thus our ISLEAP function could be coded using just one line:

```
isleap = !EMPTY({02/29/&yy})
```

where *yy* is a character variable representing the desired year and assuming a date format of American.

Note that this function does not work in dBASE IV. As we have already seen, dBASE IV does not return an empty date when given a string that represents an obviously invalid date since it automatically performs the implied arithmetic that will result in a valid date. We can use this dBASE IV feature to arrive at an equivalent function. Clearly, if 02/29 of a given year is the same as 03/01, the year is not a leap year; otherwise, it is. The equivalent dBASE IV function is then:

```
isleap = {02/29/&yy} < {03/01/&yy}.
```

How Many Days Remain in a Month or Year?

Given a date, say, Date_Fld, how many days remain in the month? The exercise is trivial once we know the last day of the month. To compute this for any month other than December, we first determine the first day of the following month and then subtract one from it.

```
last_day = CTOD(STR(MONTH(date_fld)+1) +
"/01/"+STR(YEAR(date_fld))) - 1
```

So,

```
days_left = last_day - date_fld
```

If the month is December, Days_Left is the same as the number of days that remain in a year. This number is much easier to determine since we always know the last day of the year:

```
dl_in_yr = CTOD("12/31/"+STR(YEAR(date_fld))) - date_fld
```

Computing the Number of Workdays

Many business applications require knowing the number of workdays between two dates, for example, applications that require tickler reports or reminder letters. Other applications may require knowing a future, promised date that is some number of workdays from a given start date.

Clearly the number of workdays between two dates is simply the number of elapsed days less weekends and holidays. We can always tell the weekends using the FoxPro DOW( ) function—Sundays yield 1 and Saturdays yield 7. Thus, the expression

```
isweekend = MOD(DOW(date_fld)-1,6) <>0
```

is true whenever DATE_FLD falls on a weekend.

To account for the holidays, we have a choice of either setting up a data file of holiday dates or constructing a long string of holidays that is hardcoded in the program. In general, we should avoid hardcoding constants in a program; setting up a data file of holidays gives us much more flexibility and is the preferred method, even though it requires another work area.

The user-defined function F_WRKDAY.PRG, shown in Listing 6-3, can be invoked in either of two ways:

```
Workdays = F_WRKDAY(begdate, enddate)
Fut_Date = F_WRKDAY(begdate, num_workdays)
```

The first syntax returns the number of workdays between the two specified dates. The second syntax returns a future date that is <num_workdays> days from <begdate>.

The program borrows some clever code from the Weekday.prg program (White, 1987). In particular, the line:

```
begdate = begdate + VAL(SUBSTR("1000002"),DOW(begdate),1))
```

ensures that <begdate> does not fall on a weekend by advancing the date to the next Monday whenever the date falls on a Sunday (adds 1 to <begdate>) or Saturday (adds 2 to <begdate>).

Before using the program, you should create the data file Holiday.dbf and load it with all the dates your business considers as holidays. The file may span a period of any number of years. Its structure consists of the following single date field:

```
HOLIDAY, D, 8.
```

The file may contain holidays, spanning multiple years if you wish, to compute the number of workdays between those years.

Listing 6-3. F_Wrkday.prg, returns number of workdays or future date.

```
FUNCTION F_WrkDay
**********************************************************************
* Program :  F_WrkDay.prg
* Author  :  P. L. Olympia and Kathy Cea
* Purpose :  Compute the number of workdays between 2 dates or
*         :  a future date from a given number of workdays from
*         :  a specified start date
*         :
* Syntax  :  workdays = F_WrkDay(begdate, enddate)  -or-
*         :  fut_date = F_WrkDay(begdate, num_workdays)
*         :
*         :  The first computes the # of workdays between the 2 dates
*         :  The 2nd computes a future date <num_workdays> from
*         :  <begdate>
**********************************************************************
PARAMETERS begdate,datenum
*       datenum = either enddate or number of workdays from begdate
*       Make sure begdate falls on a weekday
begdate = begdate + VAL(SUBSTR("1000002",DOW(begdate),1))
IF TYPE("datenum")="D"
   enddate = datenum - VAL(SUBSTR("2000001",DOW(datenum),1))
   elapsed = enddate - begdate + 1
   *       Subtract weekends
   workdays = elapsed - INT(elapsed/7) * 2
ELSE         && datenum = num of workdays
   workdays = datenum
   *       Add weekends
   elapsed = workdays + INT(workdays/5) * 2
ENDIF
USE holiday
COUNT TO numholi FOR holiday >= begdate;
      .AND. holiday <= begdate + elapsed - 1;
      .AND. MOD(DOW(holiday)-1,6) <>0
IF TYPE("datenum")="D"
   workdays = workdays - numholi
   RETURN(workdays)
```

(continued)

Listing 6-3. Continued

```
ELSE
   elapsed = elapsed + numholi
   enddate = begdate + elapsed - 1
   enddate = enddate - VAL(SUBSTR("2000001",DOW(enddate),1))
   RETURN(enddate)
ENDIF
*                -EOP, F_Wrkday.Prg-
```

Chapter Summary

FoxPro treats dates as special types of numbers that can be used in some arithmetic operations. It supports a variety of formats for displaying dates. Changing display formats changes the results of arithmetic operations involving date literals.

Any arithmetic involving a null date and a valued date field or variable always yields zero. All arithmetic operations involving a null date and a number always yield a null date. Unlike dBASE IV, FoxPro produces the expected result when a null date is compared to a valued (nonblank) one. Whereas the dBASE IV null date translates to a very large number, the FoxPro null date has a numeric equivalent of zero.

FoxPro stores date values in .dbf files as text data, but stores them in memory and in .mem files as 8-byte numbers in IEEE format. The numbers are stored with fractional components, representing time values, so the safest way to check for date equality is to first convert dates to characters, using the DTOC( ) function, for example, prior to comparing them.

The FoxPro base date appears to be January 1, 4713 B.C., the same date that astronomers consider to be the base date in Joseph Scaliger's Julian Period system. However, FoxPro does not properly display any date earlier than October 15, 1582—the beginning of the Gregorian calendar. Consequently any date arithmetic that requires a reference date cannot have this date be any earlier than 10/15/1582.

The chapter presents simple commands to average dates, index on dates, identify a leap year, and compute the number of days remaining in a month or year. It also shows a program that computes the number of workdays between two dates and a future date that is a given number of workdays from a start date.

Chapter 7

Memo Field Techniques

Memo fields are blocks of data normally used to store descriptive information about a database record. Unlike other FoxPro data types such as character or numeric, memo fields do not have predefined lengths—the space they occupy varies from record to record. Memo fields allow us to store and display large amounts of free-form text about the record, for example, a student's education and aptitude history, reviews of a given videotape movie by selected critics, or the text of a piece of legislation.

Why Use Memo Fields?

Most fields in a typical database (.dbf) are of type character. The perennial problem in designing a structure for a database that consists of character fields is determining the optimal length to assign to a field, given that all Dbase products preallocate the space whether or not the field contains data. For example, many applications require a REMARKS field for recording user comments about a database record. How do you arrive at the best length to assign to this field? Often, users cannot agree on the optimal length of this field. You may eventually decide on the maximum 254-character length, or even create multiple fields such as REMARK1, REMARK2, and so on, knowing that these fields could well be only partly filled for many records, thereby wasting precious disk space.

Memo fields are the way out of this dilemma for several reasons. They have variable length, the space they occupy is a function of their length, and memo fields that have not been assigned any values do not occupy any space. In the past, application users and developers avoided memo fields because they were extremely cumbersome to use and the software offered precious few commands and functions to manipulate them. These restrictions are gone in FoxPro, which treats memo fields like ordinary character fields, meaning that the rich set of functions for handling character data can be used to manipulate memo field data as well.

FoxPro's ability to store binary data in addition to text data in a memo field opens up a host of applications that truly are limited only by our imagination. For instance, graphics files or scanned images can be stored in FoxPro memo fields. Consequently we can easily develop a database of, say, WordPerfect art (.wpg files) or scanned photographs of houses for a real estate application. Given the proper hardware and sufficient memory, we could display the appropriate graphics stored in memo fields as a user browses through the database.

Another powerful way that takes advantage of memo fields' ability to contain any type of data is to use them for storing scanned letters and other correspondence in native word processing format for a correspondence control application. In Chapter 11, we will discuss how to use memo fields for producing user-revisable mailmerge letters without the aid of word processing software.

Summary of Memo Field Enhancements in FoxPro

FoxPro offers significant enhancements over FoxBASE+, dBASE IV, dBASE III PLUS, and compatible products in the use of memo fields. Some of the most important enhancements are summarized below and discussed in detail in subsequent sections.

- FoxPro allows text and binary data in a memo field including the null (ASCII decimal 0) and Ctrl-Z (ASCII decimal 26) characters. In contrast, dBASE IV memo field data terminates at the first occurrence of Ctrl-Z. Of course, FoxBASE+ and dBASE III PLUS only allow text data.
- FoxPro memo field blocksize can be as small as 33 bytes and as large as 16,384 bytes, with the default at 64 bytes. dBASE IV's blocksize ranges from 512 through 16,384 bytes, in increments of 512, with the default at 512 bytes. Consequently FoxPro's memo files tend to occupy less space than those of dBASE IV. Note that the blocksize of FoxBASE+ and dBASE III PLUS memo fields is fixed at 512 bytes.

- Unlike dBASE IV, FoxPro has built-in commands that support storing varied types of data in a memo field, including memory variables, macros, and windows. It also has the complement commands to restore those saved values. FoxPro's ability to store memory variables in a memo field allows us to use it as a space-saving file cabinet to store such things as printer control codes for a variety of printers supported by an application to replace multiple .mem files normally used for that purpose.
- Memo field data can be imported from, or exported to, an external file under program control, as in dBASE IV.
- In FoxPro, memo fields can be treated like character fields. It has many more functions for string manipulation of memo fields than dBASE IV.
- Memo field data can be accessed under program control. It can be viewed and edited using a predefined window. The MODIFY MEMO command (unavailable in dBASE IV) permits the display and edit of multiple memo fields from any open work area in their own editing windows.
- Entry and reporting of memo fields are simple tasks in FoxPro. They can be entered, edited, or displayed in their own windows, which can be manipulated just like all other FoxPro windows.

FoxPro can read the database and memo files of all Dbase family members without first converting them with a special utility program. dBASE IV memo files are converted to FoxPro .fpt format, but they may be rewritten in dBASE III PLUS-style .dbt format with the command

```
COPY TO <dbfname> TYPE FOXPLUS
```

Once the file is converted, FoxPro can write directly to the file without first having to convert it to .fpt format. For the files to remain completely readable by other members of the Dbase family such as FoxBASE+, the memo fields should be edited in FoxPro so they do not contain binary data, particularly the Ctrl-Z character. The TYPE FOXPLUS option of the COPY command does not convert any fields of type F to the usual numeric N type. Therefore, if the .dbf structure is modified to contain a floating-point field, only dBASE IV can read the converted file since FoxBASE+ and compatible software do not support fields of type F. To export data from such a .dbf to FoxBASE+, either change the structure so it contains only N types for numeric data, or unload the data using the SDF or DELIMITED option of the COPY command and then import it to a FoxBASE+ file with a similar .dbf structure using the APPEND FROM command.

Table 7-1 summarizes the FoxPro commands and functions that involve memo fields or memo files. Commands that are specific to memo fields and files are so indicated. If a command has several forms, only the variant syntax pertinent to memo fields is listed.

Creating and Accessing Memo Fields

We define memo fields when we CREATE a .dbf file. In principle, the maximum number of memo fields in a FoxPro file is 255, which is the maximum number of fields that FoxPro allows.

In Edit/Browse mode, a memo field normally displays as a "memo marker"—the word "memo" either in all lowercase letters or with the first letter in uppercase. If the memo field contains data, the marker displays as the word "Memo," with the first letter capitalized. In dBASE IV, the equivalent memo marker shows the word "MEMO" in all uppercase letters. In an Edit screen, a memo field may also appear in a memo window. A memo window is a predefined box that displays the contents of the memo field. Memo windows may be designed as part of a custom screen format for use in data entry, edit, or view operations.

FoxPro's SET WINDOW OF MEMO TO <window name> command allows editing of memo fields within the named window whose location and other attributes are specified with the DEFINE WINDOW command. This user-defined window may be opened with APPEND, BROWSE, CHANGE, EDIT, GET/READ, or MODIFY MEMO commands. The following code fragment shows one way to view and edit a memo field under program control using a memo window.

```
DEFINE WINDOW mwind FROM 1,4 TO 16,70 TITLE "Ctrl-W to save/exit"
SET WINDOW OF MEMO TO mwind
@ 3,0 GET memofld WINDOW mwind
READ
*--- Press <Ctrl-Home> to access the memo window
```

The TITLE option of the DEFINE WINDOW command reminds the user of the keypress required to save the data and exit the window. Since the FoxPro GET/READ command has the OPEN WINDOW option, SET WINDOW is not needed. In either case, the user needs to press <Ctrl-Home>, <Ctrl-PgDn>, or <Ctrl-PgUp> to get into the window to edit the memo field.

Table 7-1. Summary of FoxPro Commands and Functions Involving Memo Fields and Memo Files

<table>
<tr><th>FoxPro
Command/Function</th><th>Syntax and Description</th></tr>
<tr><td>$</td><td><expC1> $ <memfld>
Returns .T. if <expC1> is contained in memo field <memfld>.</td></tr>
<tr><td>@...SAY/GET</td><td>@ <row>, <col>
SAY <expr> [PICTURE <p1>] [FUNCTION <fcode1>]
GET <var> [PICTURE <p2>] [FUNCTION <fcode2>]
[RANGE <expN1>[,<expN2]] [VALID <expL1> |
<expN3>] [ERROR <expC3>] [WHEN
<expL2>] [DEFAULT
<expr2>] [MESSAGE <expC4>] [[OPEN]
WINDOW <win name>] [COLOR ...]
Displays formatted output to screen, window, or printer. The WINDOW clause allows editing of a memo field in a window defined previously with the DEFINE WINDOW command. The OPEN option automatically opens the editing window.</td></tr>
<tr><td>APPEND</td><td>APPEND [BLANK]
The BLANK option leaves memo fields empty.</td></tr>
<tr><td>APPEND MEMO*</td><td>APPEND MEMO <memfld> FROM <file> [OVERWRITE]
Imports data from <file> to <memfld> memo field of the current record, optionally overwriting existing data.</td></tr>
<tr><td>AT</td><td>AT(<expC1>, <memfld> [, <expN>]
Returns an integer representing the byte position of <expC1> in <memfld>. If <expN> is specified, the <expN>th occurrence of <expC1> is searched. Returns 0 if string is not found.</td></tr>
</table>

(continued)

Table 7-1. Continued

FoxPro Command/Function	Syntax and Description
ATC	ATC(<expC1>, <memfld> [, <expN>] Same as AT( ) but without regard to upper- or lower-case.
ATCLINE	ATCLINE(<expC1>, <memfld>) Returns an integer (or 0 if not found) representing the line number in <memfld> where <expC1> appears. The search is case insensitive. Dependent on MEMOWIDTH.
ATLINE	ATLINE(<expC1>, <memfld>) Same as ATCLINE( ), but search is case sensitive.
BROWSE CHANGE EDIT	Memo fields may be displayed or edited in BROWSE, CHANGE, or EDIT.
CLEAR ALL	Closes memo files along with other files.
CLOSE MEMO*	CLOSE MEMO <memfld1> [, <memfld2> ...] | ALL Closes any memo window(s) opened with MODIFY MEMO or BROWSE.
COPY MEMO*	COPY MEMO <memfld> TO <file> [ADDITIVE] Copies the contents of <memfld> of the current record to the file, appending to old data if the ADDITIVE option is specified.
COPY TO	COPY TO <file> ... TYPE FOXPLUS ... Copies memo files to FoxBASE+ compatible format.
DISPLAY/LIST	DISPLAY/LIST [<field list>] ... Does not display memo field data unless the memo field name is specified in the field list. DISPLAY/LIST STATUS Shows currently active memo files, blocksize, and memowidth setting.

(continued)

Table 7-1. Continued

FoxPro Command/Function	Syntax and Description
EMPTY	EMPTY(<memfld>) Returns .T. if <memfld> has no data.
INDEX	INDEX ON <expr> TO <file> [FOR <expL> [UNIQUE] Memo fields may not be used in index expressions.
LEFT	LEFT(<memfld>, <expN>) Returns <expN> number of characters beginning with the first character of <memfld>.
LEN	LEN(<memfld>) Returns the length of <memfld>.
MEMLINES*	MEMLINES(<memfld>) Returns the number of lines in <memfld>. Dependent on MEMOWIDTH.
MLINE*	MLINE(<memfld>, <expN>) Returns the <expN>th line in <memfld>. Dependent on MEMOWIDTH.
MODIFY MEMO*	MODIFY MEMO <memfld1> [, <memfld2> ...] [NOEDIT] [NOWAIT] [RANGE <expN1>, <expN2>] [WINDOW win1>] [SAVE] [IN [WINDOW] <win2>]] Opens editing windows for memo fields of databases open in any work area. NOEDIT allows only viewing of text. NOWAIT is available in a program and continues execution after opening the window. RANGE opens the window with the specified range of bytes in the memo field already selected (highlighted). SAVE keeps the window on the screen if you move to another window.
RAT	RAT(<expC1>, <memfld> [, <expN>] Searches <memfld> for <expC1> starting from the right and returns the position where <expC1> was found.

(continued)

Table 7-1. Continued

FoxPro Command/Function	Syntax and Description
RATLINE	RATLINE(<expC1>, <memfld>) Searches <memfld> for the last occurrence of <expC1> and returns the line number where <expC1> was found.
REPLACE	REPLACE [<scope>] [FOR <expL1>] [WHILE <expL2>]<memfld 1> WITH <expr1> [ADDITIVE] [, <memfld2> WITH <expr2> [ADDITIVE] ...] Replaces the values of memo fields with the indicated expression values. The ADDITIVE option is for memo fields only and causes new data to be appended to data already in the memo fields.
RESTORE FROM	RESTORE FROM MEMO <memfld> [ADDITIVE] Variant of the RESTORE FROM command which restores memory variables and arrays previously SAVEd to <memfld>. ADDITIVE does not remove memvars and arrays currently defined.
RESTORE MACROS	RESTORE MACROS FROM MEMO <memfld> Variant of the RESTORE MACROS command that restores keyboard macros previously SAVEd to <memfld>, adding the macros to those already defined.
RESTORE WINDOW	RESTORE WINDOW <window list> | ALL FROM MEMO <memfld> Variant of the RESTORE WINDOW command that restores windows specified in the list (or all windows if ALL is specified instead) that were previously SAVEd to <memfld>.

(continued)

Table 7-1. Continued

<table>
<tr><th>FoxPro
Command/Function</th><th>Syntax and Description</th></tr>
<tr><td>RIGHT</td><td>RIGHT(<memfld>, <expN>)
Returns the rightmost <expN> characters of <memfld>.</td></tr>
<tr><td>SAVE MACROS</td><td>SAVE MACROS TO MEMO <memfld>
Variant of the SAVE MACROS command that stores keyboard macros to <memfld>.</td></tr>
<tr><td>SAVE TO</td><td>SAVE TO MEMO <memfld> [ALL LIKE <skel> | ALL EXCEPT <skel>]
Variant of the command that stores memory variables and arrays to <memfld>.</td></tr>
<tr><td>SAVE WINDOW</td><td>SAVE WINDOW <window list> | ALL TO MEMO <memfld>
Variant of the command that stores current window definitions to <memfld>.</td></tr>
<tr><td>SET BLOCKSIZE*</td><td>SET BLOCKSIZE TO <expN>
Defines the size in bytes of memo file block size. If <expN> is between 1 and 32, <expN> × 512 bytes are allocated. Default is 64.</td></tr>
<tr><td>SET MEMOWIDTH*</td><td>SET MEMOWIDTH TO <expN>
Specifies the width of memo field output. Default is 50.</td></tr>
<tr><td>SET WINDOW*</td><td>SET WINDOW OF MEMO TO <win>
Specifies a previously defined user-defined window for editing a memo field.</td></tr>
<tr><td>SUBSTR</td><td>SUBSTR(<memfld>, <expN1> [, <expN2>]
Returns a substring of <memfld> beginning with the <expN1>th character to the end or containing <expN2> number of characters.</td></tr>
</table>

* Specific to memo fields/files.

Since these are nonintuitive keypresses for those who are not Dbase-literate, one technique we can use is to stuff the keyboard with the required keypress once the cursor moves to the memo marker. Another technique is to adopt an application-wide standard such that a given function key, for example, F9 (Zoom in dBASE IV), is always used to get at the window's data.

In dBASE IV, if we want users to have automatic access to the memo window without requiring them to press <Ctrl-Home> (incidentally, <Ctrl-PgDn> is not an alternative in dBASE IV), we would define a keyboard macro that executes a <Ctrl-Home> when the cursor moves to the memo marker. Since a keyboard macro is activated only by a program request for keyboard input, the program must have the PLAY MACRO command before a READ. Also, the memo field must have its own READ command in order for the macro to affect only the memo field, rather than all the GET fields on the screen.

This technique can be used also in FoxPro. The PLAY MACRO command can be included in the WHEN clause of the @...GET command. For example,

```
@...GET <field> WHEN temp()
```

where the temp( ) function is

```
FUNCTION temp()
PLAY MACRO CtrlHome
RETURN .t.
```

Additionally, FoxPro's KEYBOARD and MODIFY MEMO commands provide better alternatives. The MODIFY MEMO command (see Table 7-1) opens a window and automatically places the user in the window to edit the data without requiring a preliminary keypress. The command opens one edit window for each memo field listed. The CLOSE MEMO command can be used to terminate editing and close the window. The NOWAIT option is available only in a program and has the effect of continuing program execution without waiting for a CLOSE MEMO command or keypresses such as <Ctrl-W> to end the editing session. This option, like the NOEDIT option, can be used to display multiple memo fields in separate windows without allowing users to edit any of them.

Other Ways to Display Memo Fields

Memo field data may also be displayed with the DISPLAY, LIST, ?/??, REPORT FORM, and LABEL FORM commands. The output of these commands may be directed to the screen, printer, or file. Directing the results to a file facilitates further processing of the data by, say, desktop publishing software. Note that the @...SAY command does not display memo field data.

The memo field name must be specified in the DISPLAY/LIST commands, or else only the memo marker shows instead of the memo field data. The display width of the memo field is dictated by the current setting of the MEMOWIDTH parameter. FoxPro's default value for this is 50. The parameter may be changed with the SET command, for example,

```
SET MEMOWIDTH TO 72
```

or by including a line in the Config.fp file such as,

```
MEMOWIDTH = 72
```

If you intend to change the MEMOWIDTH value in an application, it is a good idea to store the current value to a memory variable before you change it, and then restore the parameter to its original value when you are done. The following code fragment shows how you would do this using the SET function:

```
old_width =  SET("MEMOWIDTH")        && Store original value
SET MEMOWIDTH TO new_width           && change to new value
... rest of code goes here ...
SET MEMOWIDTH TO old_width           && restore value
```

The MEMOWIDTH setting is important, not only because it dictates how the field will be displayed or printed, but also because it affects the values returned by the ATLINE( ), ATCLINE( ), RATLINE( ), MEMLINES( ), and MLINE( ) functions. Memo field data display correctly according to the MEMOWIDTH setting if they were entered with the FoxPro editor. If they were created elsewhere with hard carriage returns and imported into the memo field, some of the lines display short of the MEMOWIDTH margins.

Probably the most versatile way of reporting memo field data is through FoxReport, invoked with the REPORT command using report definition files created by the CREATE/MODIFY REPORT command. FoxReport paginates correctly even when printing memo fields. When designing memo fields in a report, you should check the "Stretch Vertically" and "Float as the Band Stretches" options to ensure that the report zone containing the memo field stretches vertically and horizontally to accommodate the varying length of the memo field.

Memo field data may also be included in a label designed with the CREATE/MODIFY LABEL command, but the facility has little practical value. By definition, a label has limited dimensions and a memo field is meant to contain long text. The amount of memo field data that can be printed on a label is restricted by the label's skimpy dimensions.

Memo Field Length

In dBASE III PLUS, the length of a memo field is limited only by available disk space or by the maximum size of a file imposed by the operating system. However, any memo field that is edited using the dBASE III PLUS built-in editor cannot be longer than approximately 5000 bytes because that is the maximum size that the editor can handle. In dBASE IV, the maximum length of a memo field is 64K bytes. The dBASE IV text editor can handle a maximum of 32,000 lines of up to 1024 characters each, effectively limiting the length of a memo field to 32K bytes. In FoxPro, a memo field can be any size, limited only by available disk space or by restrictions imposed by the operating system on file sizes. The FoxPro editor also does not set any bounds on the size of a file, so it does not impose any artificial constraint on the length of a memo field.

Memo fields and memory variable strings can be used interchangeably; indeed, one can be assigned the value of the other. However, note that a FoxPro memory variable string cannot be longer than 65,504 bytes and FoxPro has the additional limitation that the total size of all strings stored in memory variables cannot exceed the size of the string pool as defined by the MVARSIZ value in Config.fp, which itself is limited to 64K bytes. In contrast, dBASE IV allows a memory variable string to be assigned a memo field value, but the value is truncated after the first 254 bytes.

.dbf and .fpt Files

A FoxPro database without a memo field (and without a floating field) is virtually indistinguishable from a database created by FoxBASE+ and dBASE. Such a file contains the hexadecimal value of 03H in byte 0 (the "signature" byte) of the .dbf header. On the other hand, the signature byte differs among the products for a database with memo fields, as Table 7-2 shows.

A FoxPro database with memo fields really consists of two files: the usual .dbf file and a .fpt file where the actual memo field data is stored. Each memo

Table 7-2. Signature Byte of Dbase Family Products' .dbf with Memo Fields

Product	Signature Byte
FoxBASE+, Clipper, dBASE III PLUS, dBXL/Quicksilver	83H
dBASE IV	8BH (no SQL)
FoxPro	F5H

field occupies only 10 bytes in the .dbf file; these bytes are used to store the block number in the corresponding .fpt file where the memo field value is stored.

The FoxPro .dbf File Structure

A FoxPro .dbf file consists of a header record and data records. The header record contains identifying information about the file (such as the date of last update and the number of database records) in the first 32 bytes, followed by field subrecords. Each field subrecord is 32 bytes long and contains information about database fields such as field names and field types. Clearly, there are as many field subrecords as there are database fields, so the length of the header record depends on the number of fields in the database. Table 7-3 shows the structure of a .dbf file header record, and Table 7-4 shows the structure of a field subrecord.

Each .dbf data record begins with a delete flag byte which is either a space (ASCII decimal 32) if the record is not deleted, or an asterisk (ASCII decimal 42) if the record is deleted. Following the delete flag are the field data without any separator among the fields.

The FoxPro .fpt File Structure

A FoxPro memo file consists of a header record and one or more memo blocks. The header record is 512 bytes long and contains the location of the next available block and the blocksize in the file. A block consists of a block

Table 7-3. The Structure of a FoxPro .dbf Header Record

Byte	Description
00	Signature byte. Contains 03H if the database has no memo fields, and F5H otherwise
01–03	Date of last update (YYMMDD)
04–07	Number of records in the database
08–09	Length of the header record
10–11	Length of a data record including the delete flag
12–31	Reserved
32–*n*	Field subrecords
n + 1	Header record terminator. Contains 0DH

header (containing the block signature and the length of the memo field data) followed by the actual memo text. All memo blocks start at even block boundary addresses. Table 7-5 shows the structure of a FoxPro memo file.

As we have seen, memo field data in the .fpt file is stored in blocks after the header block. In FoxBASE+ and dBASE III PLUS, the blocksize is fixed at

Table 7-4. The Structure of a Field Subrecord

Byte	Description
00–10	Field name
11	Field data type. Contains one of the following; C, D, F, L, M, N
12–15	Displacement of field in the record
16	Field length
17	Number of decimal places in the field
18–31	Reserved

Table 7-5. The Structure of a FoxPro .fpt File

Byte	Description
A. Memo Header Block	
00–03	Location of next available block
04–05	Reserved
06–07	Blocksize (bytes per block)
08–511	Reserved
B. Memo Block	
00–03	Block signature. Contains 0 for picture, and 1 for text.
04–07	Length of memo (in bytes)
08–*n*	Memo text (*n* = length). Data spills over consecutive blocks.

512 bytes. dBASE IV has the same default blocksize, but its blocksize can be changed, beginning with 512, in increments of 512 bytes up to 32 x 512 (16,384 bytes). FoxPro supports a blocksize smaller than 512 bytes (in fact, as small as 32 bytes) up to a maximum of 16,384 bytes, with the default set at 64 bytes. The command to change the blocksize is

```
SET BLOCKSIZE TO <expN>
```

where <expN> is the desired number of bytes, except that if it is an integer from 1 through 32, memo field storage is allocated in blocks of <expN> x 512 bytes. Thus SET BLOCKSIZE TO 64 defines a blocksize of 64 bytes, but SET BLOCKSIZE TO 32 defines a blocksize of 32 x 512, or 16,384, bytes. The COPY TO command must be issued thereafter in order for the software to re-create the .fpt file with the new blocksize. Of course, the COPY TO command also packs the .fpt file by recycling the space used by obsolete data. The current setting of BLOCKSIZE may be obtained either by using the DISPLAY/LIST STATUS command or the SET("BLOCKSIZE") function.

Choosing the Optimum Blocksize

What is the optimum blocksize to use? It depends on the anticipated average length of memo field data. To understand this, let's look at how FoxPro stores information in both .dbf and .fpt files. For our purposes, assume that the blocksize is set at 64 bytes.

FoxPro, like FoxBASE+ and dBASE, does not preallocate any space in the .fpt (.dbt) file for memo fields in each .dbf record. Rather, only those memo fields with actual data occupy space in the .fpt file. Like dBASE, FoxPro stores memo field data in the .fpt file in the order they are entered, not in the order of record number in the .dbf file. When a database with a memo field is CREATEd, the .fpt file consists of only the header block. The header block is 512 bytes long, independent of the setting of the blocksize, and it contains the address of the first empty block (the next available block for storing memo field data) which, in this case, would be 1.

Assume we have a .dbf file with one record and one memo field containing, say, 32 bytes of data. Disregarding any constraints on minimum file sizes that may be imposed by the operating system, the .fpt file should contain only one 64-byte data block, sufficient to contain the 32 bytes of actual data. Clearly, except for a few bytes of pointer information, the remainder of the 64-byte block is empty. If we now edit this field to add more information such that the length of the field is now 65 bytes, FoxPro allocates a second data block to contain data that exceeds the blocksize. This second data block will be mostly empty because not much data spilled over from the first block. The location of the first block containing the memo field data for a given .dbf record is stored in the 10 bytes allocated in the .dbf file for each memo field. To retrieve the value for a given memo field in a specified record, FoxPro reads these 10 bytes, which direct it to the appropriate block in the .fpt file. FoxPro then continues to read data for the same memo field that goes on for two or more blocks.

From this example it is easy to see that choosing the right blocksize often requires a tradeoff between speed of I/O processing and conservation of disk space. Small blocksizes are best for relatively short memo field data. Choose larger blocksizes for storing large amounts of memo field information.

Managing Memo Field Space

One of the deficiencies of dBASE III PLUS pertains to the way it manages memo field space. It rewrites an entire block of memo field data to the next available block at the end of the .dbt file even if a user changed only a single byte in the data. This causes the file to grow rapidly and be filled with obsolete data that simply wastes disk space. FoxPro, like dBASE IV, is more intelligent in managing .fpt (.dbt) file space. When SET EXCLUSIVE is ON, it does not rewrite a block after an edit as long as the edit does not result in the addition of text that exceeds the length of the block. This approach has the additional advantage of minimizing I/O activity because the memo field pointer in the .dbf file need not be updated.

However, dBASE IV is better than FoxPro in recycling space containing obsolete memo field data. When dBASE IV rewrites a block to the end of the .dbt file because new edits have caused an overflow in the current block space, the block number occupied by the original data is pointed to in the header record as the next available block. Thus it first tries to recycle newly vacated space to keep the .dbt file size from growing unnecessarily. FoxPro does not appear to recycle unused space as dBASE IV does.

Importing and Exporting Memo Field Data

In FoxBASE+ and dBASE III PLUS, data for memo fields may only be entered, exported, or imported in interactive mode while we are in the memo field editor. Were we to import data to, or export data from, a large number of database records, this procedure would quickly become cumbersome. FoxPro, like dBASE IV, permits importing and exporting memo field data both interactively under the memo field editor, and in unattended mode, with a command, under program control. Selected portions of the data, rather than the entire contents of the memo field, can be exported consistent with the block operations (marking, moving, and copying) of the editor.

Exporting Memo Field Data With a Command

Memo fields may be written to an external file from the command windows or under control of a program with the COPY MEMO command. The following command writes the contents of the Notes memo field in the current record to the Notes.out file on the A: drive.

```
COPY MEMO Notes TO a:Notes.out ADDITIVE
```

The optional ADDITIVE clause appends the memo field contents to the data already in the file; otherwise, information already in the file is overwritten without further warning unless SET SAFETY is ON. The clause implies that the target file already exists; otherwise, FoxPro generates an error message. Note that if you do not specify the target file's extension, FoxPro assumes a file extension of .txt. Data written to the file is in the same raw format with which it was created, independent of the current setting of MEMOWIDTH. The COPY MEMO command may be used to export text as well as binary data. Along with the APPEND MEMO command, it is very useful in applications such as a program version control system that maintains and tracks application programs and executables.

Suppose we have a customized help file similar to Foxhelp.dbf that contains the Details memo field. We want to copy the contents of Details for selected database records, where the field has values, into one text file for use in preparing the application's documentation. The DumpMemo procedure, which exports the data using the COPY MEMO command, can be used to do this. The program is shown in Listing 7-1. The procedure uses several commands new to FoxBASE+ users. For example, SCAN/ENDSCAN is a looping construct that is easier and more efficient than DO WHILE/ENDDO with a SKIP. The program also uses filename substitution, for example,

```
USE (DbfName)
SET ALTERNATE TO (outfile)
```

instead of using macros, as in USE &dbf. In FoxPro, as in dBASE IV, filename substitution may be used in place of macros parsing to a valid filename. It is also more efficient. Note that since the ADDITIVE clause of the COPY MEMO command generates an error if the target file does not previously exist, we use the SET ALTERNATE command to force the system to create the file if it does not exist.

Importing Memo Field Data With a Command

Text or binary data from an external file may be loaded into a memo field from the command window or under control of a program with the APPEND MEMO command. For instance, the command

```
APPEND MEMO Notes FROM Notes.txt OVERWRITE
```

imports all data from the Notes.txt file to the Notes memo field of the current database record. The OVERWRITE option erases the contents of the memo

Listing 7-1. DumpMemo.prg, a procedure to export memo field contents of selected records to a target file.

```
PROCEDURE DumpMemo
***************************************************************
* Program :  DumpMemo.Prg
* Author  :  P. L. Olympia & Kathy Cea
* Purpose :  Copies contents of selected records of a specified
*         :  memo field to a target file.
* Syntax  :  DO DumpMemo WITH DbfName, MemFld, RecBeg, RecEnd,
*         :      OutFile
*         :    RecBeg and RecEnd define the beginning and ending
*         :    record numbers to copy. Outfile is the target
*         :    file.  DbfName is the .dbf file. MemFld is the
*         :    memo field.
* Note    :  Error trapping excluded from code.
***************************************************************
PARAMETER DbfName, MemFld, RecBeg, RecEnd, Outfile
*-- Store, then change,  environment
 SafeSW = SET("SAFETY")
 SET SAFETY OFF

 rec_str   = STR(RecBeg,4)       && for use as macro

*-- We need the following two statements to make sure OutFile is
*-- created if not already present
 SET ALTERNATE TO (OutFile)      && Note filename substitution
 CLOSE ALTERNATE

 USE (DbfName)
 &rec_str                        &&  move pointer to start

 SCAN  WHILE (recno() >= RecBeg .AND. recno() <= RecEnd ;
        .AND. !(EMPTY(MemFld)))
    COPY MEMO &MemFld TO (OutFile) ADDITIVE  && Exports memo
 ENDSCAN
 SET SAFETY &SafeSW
 RETURN
**==============================================================
```

field before the data transfer is performed. If the option is omitted, information from the external file is appended to the current memo field data.

Note that APPEND MEMO is intended for data transfer between one memo field and one external file at a time. Nonetheless, this command has a host of uses, especially when coupled with FoxPro's facility for treating memo fields just as though they were character fields. For example, the FindStr.prg procedure in Listing 7-2 uses properties of a FoxPro memo field to search a text file for the desired *N*th occurrence of a specified string. It uses APPEND MEMO to load the file to a memo field, and then uses the ATC( ) function to perform a case-insensitive search of the string. To highlight the string just located, it uses the RANGE option of the MODIFY MEMO command. You can easily modify this program to find all occurrences of the specified string by invoking ATC( ) in a loop where the Noccur parameter changes each time. If you need to extract every line containing the string for printing or for appending to an open .dbf file, set MEMOWIDTH to 80 or a large enough number, and then use MLINE( ) to return the desired line.

The same memo field handling facility used in FindStr.prg can be used to determine if two DOS files are identical. Here all we need to do is use APPEND MEMO to import one file to one memo field and import the other file to a second field, and then compare the two. Also, with just a little bit more work, we can expand upon FindStr.prg and exploit FoxPro's versatile memo field handling facility to write a program that builds an Index of terms and phrases for a given manuscript or document. If the electronic form of the document contains the page number in the header or footer, we can easily determine the page number(s) in the document where the desired word or phrase can be found.

Importing/Exporting Memo Field Data From and To Character Fields

Like other Dbase family products, FoxPro does not allow a memo field to appear in an index expression. However, with some advanced planning we can get around this limitation. If we are careful to reserve the first line of a memo field's value so it contains identifying information suitable for indexing (for example, Social Security number, date of birth, and part number), we can equate a character field in the file to the contents of the memo field's first line and sort the records based on the value of the character field. The following code copies the first line of the ClientHist memo field to a character field called ClientName and then indexes the database based on ClientName:

Listing 7-2. The FindStr.prg procedure finds and highlights the *n*th occurrence of a specified string in a given text file using memo field commands and functions.

```
PROCEDURE FindStr.prg
*********************************************************
* Program ...: FindStr.prg
* Author     :  P. L. Olympia & Kathy Cea
* Purpose....: Searches a text file for the Nth occurrence of
*            : a specified string using FoxPro memo field
*            : commands/functions
* Syntax ....: DO FindStr WITH <string>, <txtfile>, <Noccur>
* Notes .....: Assumes .dbf in current area has memo field
*            :  called MemFld
*********************************************************
PARAMETERS string, txtfile, Noccur

*-- Make sure file exists

IF !FILE((txtfile))
   ? "Can't seem to find " + txtfile
   RETURN
ENDIF

Noccur = IIF(Noccur < 1, 1, Noccur)    && Can't be less than 1

*-- Load the file to the memo field
APPEND MEMO memfld FROM (txtfile) OVERWRITE

*-- Search the memo field for the string
start = ATC(string, memfld, Noccur)
IF start = 0
   ? string + 'not found'
ELSE
   *  Display string highlighted in window
   long = start + LEN(string)
   MODIFY MEMO memfld NOEDIT RANGE start, long
ENDIF
RETURN
```

```
REPLACE ALL ClientName WITH MLINE(ClientHist,1)
INDEX ON ClientName TO <newindex>
```

To load a memo field with data from a character field, memory variable, or string, use the REPLACE command. Although REPLACE requires that the field to be replaced and its replacement have the same data type, memo fields may be replaced by any character expression. FoxPro's REPLACE command, like that of dBASE IV, includes the ADDITIVE option to enable memo fields to be loaded incrementally from various character expressions. This option is valid only for memo fields. We can take advantage of the ADDITIVE option by using a memo field to hold historical information of various character fields in the record. For instance, we can easily build a program library system for a complete application that, like a simple program version control system, tracks the modification history for any program in the application, and also uses a memo field to store the most current version of the program. Assume that the database has the following fields:

Field Name	**Field Type**	**Width**	**Description**
PgmName	C	12	Program name
PgmRevNo	C	5	Revision number
PgmRevDate	D	8	Revision date
PgmRevNote	C	254	What's new in this version
PgmRevHist	M	10	Revision history
PgmSrc	M	10	Current program copy

Every time we generate a new version of the program, we need to move the data from the other fields to the PgmRevHist memo field, which maintains the modifications history, before the other fields are overwritten with new data. We use the REPLACE command with the ADDITIVE option to accumulate historical data, and APPEND MEMO to replace the copy of the program in the second memo field:

```
REPLACE PgmHist WITH PgmRevNo + ", " + DTOC(PgmRevDate) + ;
   CHR(13) + CHR(10) + PgmRevNote  ADDITIVE
APPEND MEMO PgmSrc FROM <new pgm version>
```

Note that this technique offers the facility for moving data from a hierarchical database system to a relational type of system such as FoxPro. Entire nodes or repeating groups can be stored and manipulated as memo fields.

Memo Fields as Filing Cabinets

One of the most outstanding enhancements in FoxPro, and surely one of the least documented, pertains to the use of memo fields as repositories of information, much like an application's massive file cabinet. As Table 7-1 shows, FoxPro's enhancements to the various "flavors" of the SAVE and RESTORE commands enable us to store memory variables, memory variable arrays, window definitions, and keyboard macros to memo fields. Immediately this saves us from having to create a multitude of DOS files with the attendant problems not only of maintaining them, but even of just coming up with unique filenames in a multiuser environment. In essence, this facility lets us capture the entire environment of an application, including its keyboard macros, windows, and memory variables, and lets us restore that environment simply with a RESTORE from a given memo field.

All we need for each application is one data file containing at least three memo fields, one for storing values of memory variables and arrays, a second for keyboard macros, and a third for windows. With the SAVE ... MEMO <memfld> command, one .dbf/.fpt file set stores the same information that would require separate .mem, .win, and .fky files. Users may still define their keyboard macros or windows and have them available alongside the application's standard values as long as the organization adopts a naming convention that eliminates the possibility that a user-defined keyboard macro or window name will conflict with those used by the standard application.

The ability of FoxPro to save and restore memory variables and arrays from a memo field takes on special significance. This facility can be put to good use in the following applications.

Saving and Restoring Screens

Suppose we want to maintain a copy of an application screen or output window image so it can be reused in other modules of the application without us having to redraw the screen each time. We can do this by saving the screen to a memory buffer, or better yet, to a memory variable. Storing the screen to a memory variable and then saving that variable to permanent storage means that the screen never has to be redrawn again. Normally you would save memory variables to .mem files, but saving them to a memo field has the advantage that you won't need to create and track many small files. The sequence of commands for saving and restoring screens to a memo field is as follows:

```
SAVE SCREEN TO scr1          && scr1 is a memvar
SAVE TO MEMO Memfld          && scr1 and other memvars saved
RESTORE FROM MEMO Memfld     && Later restores scr1 and others
RESTORE SCREEN FROM scr1     && restores screen scr1
```

Tracking Changes to a Record

A popular way to copy a record of one database to another uses FoxPro's versatile SCATTER and GATHER commands. SCATTER copies a record to an array, creating the array as needed, with each array element containing the value of the corresponding field in the record. This procedure is useful in multiuser applications where we may want to maintain snapshots of the record at various times to determine whether or not the record has changed between the time we started editing it and the time we finished. We can save the array to a memo field to guard against system failure before we can use it. With the MEMO clause of the SAVE and RESTORE commands, we can store multiple records of one or more databases and use only those that we need at one time to conserve string or memory variable space.

Accommodating Different Printers

In the Dbase world, a widely accepted tenet is never to hardcode any output with printer-specific codes, for example,

```
@ 1, 0 SAY CHR(15) + title + CHR(18).
```

This is good advice because a program containing such code quickly becomes obsolete with a change of printers. Before the advent of printer drivers, application developers like to define a set of memory variables such as BoldOn or BoldOff so that output destined for a printer can have some semblance of printer independence. For instance, the statement

```
@ 1, 0 SAY BoldOn + title + BoldOff
```

should work for any printer as long as the memory variables have been assigned the proper control sequence.

The usual way to implement this approach is to define a set of identically named memory variables for each printer and store those to separate memory variable files, for example, Epson.mem, Hp.mem, and Okidata.mem. Then, depending on the printer currently in use, the appropriate .mem file can be used to restore the correct set of printer control codes. This procedure works well except that the proliferation of small .mem files, one for each supported printer, eventually presents a maintenance nightmare.

Again, this is not a problem with memo fields. All we need to do is define a simple .dbf consisting of as many memo fields as there are printers to support. With SAVE TO MEMO, we can save to each one a set of memory variables for a given printer. Memory variables stored in each memo field will have identical names, but they will usually have different values. This solution requires one .dbf/.fpt file set compared to a large number of .mem files.

Chapter Summary

Memo fields are useful for storing and displaying varied and vast amounts of information associated with a database record. Unlike other data types, memo fields have lengths that may vary from record to record. This makes memo fields very useful along with the desirable attribute that unlike other data types, memo fields do not occupy disk space unless they have assigned values. Memo fields can be used to hold historical information for one or more fields in the data file and, more importantly, can be used as an infinitely expanding file cabinet for storing memory variables, arrays, printer definitions, screens, keyboard macros, and windows for an entire application.

The length of FoxPro's memo fields is limited only by available disk space. Memo fields may contain any type of data, text as well as binary, including pictures, sound, graphics, and executable programs. In FoxPro, anything you can do with a string you should also be able to do with memo fields. FoxPro provides a host of commands and functions, discussed in this chapter, to permit manipulating memo fields as though they were character fields.

Memo field data can be imported and exported interactively under the memo field editor or in unattended (batch) mode under program control. Thus data created from other software can be loaded easily into memo fields. Conversely, memo field data can be exported easily to another environment.

In this chapter, we discussed the structure of a FoxPro .fpt file. We discussed how FoxPro manages memo field space and how the BLOCKSIZE setting affects disk space and data retrieval speed. We also discussed techniques that take advantage of the facilities offered by memo fields, including the use of memo fields to accumulate historical data about the record, to locate strings in a DOS text file, or to determine if two files are the same.

Chapter 8

Handling String and Character Data

In FoxPro, as in most other database management systems, character data is the data type processed by most applications. Given that memo fields and character strings also consist of character data, it is easy to see why the FoxPro language has an extensive set of commands and functions to manipulate, format, and transform character data. Most Dbase language novices make the mistake of defining fields such as employee number or social security number as numeric rather than character fields. In general, even fields that are expected to contain numbers should be defined as character fields, unless they are to be used in computations. For example, fields such as document number that may consist partly of characters and partly of numbers that are intended to be incremented serially can be safely defined as character fields.

This chapter examines the various FoxPro facilities for manipulating character data, beyond those already discussed in Chapter 7. It discusses practical applications of commands and functions that support character data and describes generically useful string-handling UDFs.

Data Type Conversion

Table 8-1 summarizes the FoxPro commands and functions to convert numeric, date, logical and memo data types to and from character type.

Note that the numeric values returned by the VAL( ) function are dependent on the current setting of SET DECIMALS. A few nonnumeric characters

Table 8-1. FoxPro Functions and Commands To Convert Various Data Types To and From Character.

Conversion	Function/Command
Numeric to Character	STR(<expN1> [,<expN2>] [,<expN3>]]) ? STR(576) 576 ? STR(576.12, 8, 3) 576.120 && 8 chars long, 3 dec.
Character to Numeric	VAL(<expC>) ? SET("DECIMALS") 2 ? VAL("-254.1") 254.10 ? VAL("3.75E4") 37500.00 ? VAL("X123") 0.00
Character to Date	CTOD(<expC>), or {<expC>} ? CTOD("10/03/91") 10/03/91
Date to Character	DTOC(<expD> [,1]) DTOS(<expD>) ? DTOC({10/03/91} + 2, 1) 19911005
Logical to Character	IIF(<expL>, <expr1>, <expr2>) ? IIF(isopen, "Open", "Closed") Open
Character to/from Memo	REPLACE <field1> WITH <expr1> [<scope>] [ADDITIVE] [, <field2> WITH <expr2> ...] [FOR <expL1>] [WHILE <expL2>]

such as E, used in exponential notation, and the minus sign are valid characters in the VAL( ) argument field. If the argument begins with a character that is not a digit, the VAL( ) function returns zero; in that sense, it serves as an alternative to the ISDIGIT( ) function.

To copy memo field data to a character field, use the REPLACE command. The same command, of course, can be used to copy the value of a character field to a memo field. In this case, the ADDITIVE option of the command does not overwrite any previous data in the memo field.

The IIF( ) function's facility to convert logicals to character values is useful in creating an index with a compound key expression. The function allows a logical field to be concatenated with a character field, for example,

```
INDEX ON IIF(IsMember, "Y", "N") + Name TO MemName
```

Some applications, for example, a correspondence control system, use a system-generated record id number as a key. Often this number is a composite that includes such things as document type in combination with today's date and a serial number maintained by the system. The DTOC( ) and DTOS( ) functions, which we have already seen to be useful in index key expressions involving dates, can be used for the date-dependent portion of the record id number.

At the beginning of this chapter, we mentioned that unless a field is to be used in computations, the field is best defined as character rather than numeric. Any requirement to increment a portion of the field serially, for example, to produce the next record id in the series, is easily satisfied. For instance, suppose that the record id has a format of IDnnnn, where *nnnn* is to be incremented from one record to the next. The following command generates the next ID in the series:

```
next_id = LEFT(rec_id,2) +  STR(VAL(RIGHT(rec_id,4)) + 1, 4, 0)
```

Searching Character Strings

FoxPro has a number of functions designed to help search a string for a character or another string. These are shown in Table 8-2.

With one or more of these functions, it is relatively easy to write a FoxPro program similar to the UNIX utility Fgrep to search all the text files in a subdirectory for a desired string. Such a program would use FoxPro's low-level file I/O functions as well. Alternatively we can read the file's data into a memo field and search the memo field for the desired string. The following code fragment shows how this is done:

```
* Assume a .dbf with memo field Notes in the active select area
* "Substring" is the string to find
```

Table 8-2. FoxPro Functions to Search Characters or Strings

Function	Summary
$	Returns .T. if a substring is contained in a string or memo field.
AT( )	Returns an integer representing the position of the first occurrence of a substring in a string or memo field.
ATC( )	Like AT( ) but is *not* case sensitive.
ATCLINE( )	Returns an integer representing the line number where a substring first occurs within a string or memo field. Matching proceeds without regard to case.
ATLINE( )	Same as ATCLINE( ) but matching is case sensitive.
BETWEEN( )	Returns .T. if an expression lies between two other expressions.
DIFFERENCE( )	Returns a number from 0 through 4 representing the relative phonetic difference between two strings.
INLIST( )	Returns .T. if a character expression is contained in a series (list) of expressions.
LIKE( )	Returns .T. if a character expression, which may include wildcard characters, is contained in another character expression.
OCCURS( )	Returns the number of times that a substring appears in a string or memo field. This is a case-sensitive function.
RAT( )	Returns an integer representing the position where a substring last appears in a string or memo field. This is a case-sensitive function.
RATLINE( )	Returns an integer representing the line where a substring last appears in a string or memo field.

(continued)

Table 8-2. Continued

Function	Summary
SOUNDEX( )	Returns the phonetic code of a character expression, useful in comparing two or more strings.

```
APPEND MEMO Notes FROM <filename> OVERWRITE
SET MEMOWIDTH TO 80
FOR i = 1 TO MEMLINES(Notes)
  line = MLINE(Notes, i)
  IF ATC(substring, line) > 0
     ? line
  ENDIF
ENDFOR
```

With very little effort, we can make the program even more versatile by allowing wildcards in the target substring. In this case, all we need to do is replace ATC( ) with the LIKE( ) function. So the IF statement now reads

```
IF LIKE("*" + substring + "*", line)
```

Unlike ATC( ), LIKE( ) performs a case-sensitive match except that both wildcard characters (* and ?) will match both lowercase and uppercase letters. If it is important to have the search remain case-insensitive, apply the UPPER( ) function to both arguments of LIKE( ).

A similar technique can be used to quickly count the number of times a given word or string appears in a document or text file. In this case, use APPEND MEMO to load the file to a memo field, and then use the OCCURS( ) function to report the desired count. For example,

```
? 'The word ' + word + ' appears ', OCCURS(word, Notes), ' times.'
```

Remember that OCCURS( ) is a case-sensitive function.

The RAT( ) function is particularly useful for tasks such as word wrapping, which is described in the next section. It is also handy for such things as removing path and subdirectory prefixes from a fully qualified filename. For instance, if the filename is something like C:\DOS\UTILITY\-WP\LJ\WHATSUP.DOC, stripping the prefix usually entails going through a loop to look for the \ character and stripping the appropriate substring. With RAT( ), the filename can be extracted with one command:

```
FileName = SUBSTR(FileName, RAT("\", FileName) + 1).
```

Word Wrapping in a Character Field During Data Entry

Due to serious limitations in memo field handling in most Dbase family products prior to FoxPro, many developers have resorted to holding text information in multiple character fields rather than in a single memo field. For instance, a travel tracking system might include four long character fields, say, Justif1 through Justif4, to record the travel justification narrative. One disadvantage of such a structure, of course, is that most records probably will not have data in all four of these fields, so the structure unnecessarily wastes disk space. Another disadvantage is that although the user has the benefit of word wrap during memo field entry, such a facility is never built into data entry involving character fields.

On the other hand, we can use one of FoxPro's many character handling functions to provide the necessary word wrap capability as users enter narrative text into contiguous character fields or memory variables. The technique consists of extracting the spillover (last) word on a line, using RAT( ), and then stacking the keyboard buffer with the word using the KEYBOARD command. That way, the spillover word wraps to the next character field. Listing 8-1 shows how this is done in the Wrapit user-defined function. As usual, we take advantage of the VALID clause of the @...GET command to force the Wrapit UDF to be invoked. The function uses VARREAD( ) to identify the currently active GET field or memvar. Note that the VALID clause is omitted in the GET statement for the last character field because word wrapping ceases on that field.

Comparing Strings

FoxPro's equal sign operator is commonly used to test if two values of the same type (character, numeric, date, or logical) are the same. When used to test the equality of two character expressions, this operator begins by comparing the strings character for character from left to right until it encounters the

Listing 8-1. Wrapit user-defined function and driver program. The function shows a technique for enforcing word wrap during data entry on contiguous character fields or memory variables.

```
*-- This is a sample driver program for the Wrapit UDF
*-- to show word wrap during data entry on contiguous
*-- character fields or memvars

SET TALK OFF
STORE SPACE(50) TO note1, note2, note3, note4

@ 10,10 GET note1 VALID wrapit()
@ 11,10 GET note2 VALID wrapit()
@ 12,10 GET note3 VALID wrapit()
@ 13,10 GET note4        && No VALID here since there
                         && is no place to word wrap
READ

SET TALK ON
RETURN

FUNCTION Wrapit
***************************************************************
* Program ...: Wrapit.prg
* Author ....: P. L. Olympia & Kathy Cea
* Purpose....: Performs word wrap during data entry on
*            : contiguous character fields. Uses RAT() to
*            : find the last (spillover) word.
* Syntax ....: @ row, col GET <charfield> VALID Wrapit()
* Notes .....: Adapted from a public domain program by G. Neill
***************************************************************

*-- Use VARREAD() to save field or memvar name
fld = VARREAD()
long = LEN(&fld)

*-- Don't need word wrap if trimmed(fld) < long
IF LEN(TRIM(&fld)) < long
   RETURN (.T.)             && just return true
```

(continued)

Listing 8-1. Continued

```
ELSE
*-- Save spillover word and strip it from current field
   LastWord = SUBSTR(&fld, RAT(' ', &fld) + 1)
   &fld = STUFF(&fld,RAT(' ',&fld)+1,LEN(LastWord), ;
          SPACE(LEN(LastWord)))
ENDIF

*-- Stuff the keyboard with the last word
KEYBOARD LastWord
RETURN(.T.)
```

first inequality between the two strings. The result of the operation also depends on the value of SET EXACT.

With SET EXACT OFF, the operation ceases as soon as the characters of the string to the right of the equal sign are exhausted. Thus, the command

```
? "123.4" = "123"
```

yields .T., but the command

```
? "123" = "123.4"
```

yields .F.

Clearly any string comparison involving a null string to the right of the equal sign, for example,

```
? "123" = ""
```

always yields .T. with SET EXACT OFF.

With SET EXACT ON, the comparison operation continues through to the end of the two strings. The operation ignores trailing blanks, so the following commands both yield .T.

```
? "123" = "123 "
? "123 " = "123"
```

Table 8-3. FoxPro Functions for Replacing Characters and Strings

Function	Summary
CHRTRAN( )	Translates the characters of a string using translation tables defined by two other strings.
STRTRAN( )	Searches a string for a specified substring, and then replaces it with another substring.
STUFF( )	Returns a string resulting from the insertion, deletion, or replacement of a component substring.
SYS(15)	Translates the characters of a string using a character expression as a translation table.

From this example it is clear that SET EXACT ON does not guarantee complete equality between the two strings before the operation yields .T. If you need to compare two strings for exact equality, use the double sign operator. This operator yields .T. if, and only if, the two strings contain exactly the same sequence of characters including the same number of trailing blanks. Regardless of the setting of SET EXACT, the following commands all yield .F.

```
? "123" == "123 " && Trailing blanks not ignored
? "123" == ""
? "123" == "123.4"
```

Replacing Characters and Strings

FoxPro also has powerful functions designed to search and replace a character or a string with another character or string. These are summarized in Table 8-3.

Traditionally Dbase developers employ two general procedures for replacing one character with another in a string:

1. Using AT( ) and SUBSTR( ) (or its variant LEFT( ) and RIGHT( )).
2. Using AT( ) and STUFF( ).

For example, if Memvar = "Radar" and we want to replace the first "a" with "i", the following statements demonstrate the two methods:

1. Using SUBSTR( ) and AT( ).

```
Memvar = IIF("a" $ Memvar, SUBSTR(Memvar, 1, AT("a", Memvar) ;
 - 1) + "i" + SUBSTR(Memvar, AT("a", Memvar) + 1), Memvar)
```

2. Using STUFF( ) and AT( ).

```
Memvar = IIF("a" $ Memvar, STUFF(Memvar, AT("a", Memvar), 1, ;
"i"), Memvar)
```

To replace both occurrences of "a" in the string, we need a loop. Ordinarily we have no choice but to write a program. However, FoxPro's CHRTRAN( ) can make the global replacement with one statement:

```
? CHRTRAN(Memvar, "a","i")
```

Both CHRTRAN( ) and STRTRAN( ) are extremely useful for replacing substrings in database fields. Suppose we want to replace all occurrences of "%" with "#" in a database field called CharFld for all records in the database. In dBASE III Plus, we would need a program with a clever twist, for example,

```
*-- dBASE III Plus program to replace all occurrences of one
*-- character with another. Adapted from a program by H. Vega.
DO WHILE .NOT. EOF()
   REPLACE CharFld WITH IIF("%" $ CharFld, STUFF(CharFld, ;
     AT("%", CharFld), 1, "#"), CharFld)
*-- Note the following technique to decide what to do next
   next_cmd = IIF("%" $ CharFld, "LOOP", "SKIP")
   &next_cmd
ENDDO
```

With CHRTRAN( ) the entire preceding program is reduced to one command:

```
REPLACE ALL CharFld WITH CHRTRAN(CharFld, "%", "#")
```

Now, suppose we need to update a mailing list database because the zip code 12345 is no longer valid, having been replaced by the code 34567. This still remains a trivial exercise in FoxPro:

```
REPLACE ALL zipcode WITH STRTRAN(zipcode, "12345", "34567")
```

Both STRTRAN( ) and CHRTRAN( ) are useful for removing unwanted characters from a file, for instance, null characters sent out by a mainframe during a communication session that had been captured to a file. User manuals that describe the use of the PC function keys often have a problem printing on devices such as the Hewlett-Packard LaserJet printers because the ASCII character representing the keyboard's right arrow key is really ASCII decimal 26, the end of-file character. Consequently the printer stops printing as soon as it encounters the right arrow key character. To counter this, use CHRTRAN( ) to replace the character with a printable one, and then restore it after the file is printed.

dBASE III Plus had a little-known bug where the APPEND FROM SDF or APPEND FROM DELIMITED command caused database corruption if the SDF or delimited file contained ASCII decimals 138 and 141 (soft linefeed and carriage return). Such a file could originate as a WordStar document. Because the dBASE III APPEND command strips the high bit off the ASCII character, CHR(138) becomes CHR(10), the linefeed character, and CHR(141) becomes CHR(13), the carriage return character. It appears that dBASE III was treating these characters as record terminators, causing it to truncate the data. One fix, of course, is to use CHRTRAN( ) to substitute another character before the APPEND and restore the characters later.

Soft spaces, soft hyphens, and soft carriage returns that have the high bit set may present problems in searching for substrings. For instance, if we were looking for the substring "Hot Dog", we may not find the string if CHR(141) is between the two words. In this case, we can just substitute a space for every occurrence of CHR(141) between the two words. The FoxPro SYS(15) function is designed primarily for European users whose character sets have the high bit set. With the European memory variable as a translation table (the variable is supplied in the European.mem distribution file), characters with diacritical marks are translated into corresponding characters with the high bit set off. In essence, SYS(15) in conjunction with the European memvar performs the same function as utility programs that convert a WordStar document to non-document mode. However, SYS(15) is slightly more versatile than most WordStar conversion programs because with it we can define the translation table in such a way that the conversion preserves the IBM box drawing symbols.

Encrypting and Decrypting Strings

Many applications institute a password system to control access to various system functions. Usually the security system is set up for multilevel access so that some users can perform only certain select functions, but the application administrator or "super-user" has access to all facilities, including maintenance functions such as deleting records and rebuilding indexes.

Password systems generally rely on the encryption of character strings. FoxPro's character functions make elaborate string encryption a simple task. Although most people have their own favorite encoding scheme, the scheme shown in Encrypt.prg (Listing 8-2) provides enough security to make the enrypted string difficult to decode. The encryption algorithm is in just one line. In essence, each character of the string is first converted to its ASCII decimal equivalent with the ASC( ) function. The program then adds to that value the character's position in the string and also the length of the string. This helps ensure that the same letter or number in the string or a similar string is encrypted differently. Finally, the resulting ASCII code is converted back to character using the CHR( ) function.

To use the function to encrypt a user-supplied password, you should take steps to keep the password from being echoed as it is being typed. You don't need an elaborate routine to accomplish this. The following code fragment shows how this can be done easily with FoxPro:

```
oldcolor = SET ("COLOR")        && save color setting
SET COLOR TO ,X                 && make GET data entry invisible
@...GET <password>              && get password
READ
SET COLOR TO &oldcolor          && restore old color
```

Note that the SET COLOR TO ,X command makes the password invisible during data entry.

Listing 8-2 also shows Decrypt.prg, a function that decodes the string encrypted by Encrypt.prg. Clearly the decoding scheme uses the same functions used to encode the string.

Listing 8-2. UDFs to encrypt and decrypt a string.

```
FUNCTION Encrypt
***********************************************************
* Program ...: Encrypt.prg
* Author ....: P. L. Olympia & Kathy Cea
* Purpose....: Encrypt a string (for example a password)
* Syntax ....: Encoded = Encrypt(string)
*            :   String is the string to be encrypted
*            :   Returns the encoded string
***********************************************************
PARAMETERS string
estring = ""
long = LEN(string)
FOR i = 1 TO long
 estring = estring + CHR(ASC(SUBSTR(string,i,1)) + i + long)
ENDFOR
RETURN estring


FUNCTION Decrypt
***********************************************************
* Program ...: Decrypt.prg
* Author ....: P. L. Olympia & Kathy Cea
* Purpose....: Decrypt a string (for example a password)
* Syntax ....: Decoded = Decrypt(string)
*            :   String is the string to be decrypted
*            :   Returns the decoded string
***********************************************************
PARAMETERS string
estring = ""
long = LEN(string)
FOR i = 1 TO long
 estring = estring + CHR(ASC(SUBSTR(string,i,1)) - i - long)
ENDFOR
RETURN estring
```

String Animation

One way to attract a user's attention in an application and focus it on an important screen message is to use string animation. For instance, we can have an application welcome message move slowly across the screen, perhaps inside a graphics box such as a drawing of a computer monitor.

The user-defined function, Animate1.prg, shown in Listing 8-3 is one of the shortest animation programs you can write to move a specified string from right to left across the screen. For instance, the command:

```
= Animate1("Welcome to the LRAP System", 11, 16, 15)
```

moves the quoted string from right to left at screen row 12 (remember that the screen home position is 0, 0). The string begins to fade at column 17. The string moves in an area that is 15 characters wide.

FoxPro is so fast at running this function that in order to see the animation, you'll need to put in a delay loop just before the ENDFOR statement. A delay loop could be something as simple as

```
FOR j = 1 TO 200
ENDFOR
```

You may wish to add more pizzazz to the animation by changing the text color of the string using commands such as @...FILL.

Listing 8-4 is a slightly more elaborate animation program. It moves two strings—first vertically on each side of the screen and then horizontally toward each other at a specified row—until they come together at the center.

The REPLICATE( ) Function

After converting a number to character using STR( ), you may want to replace the leading blanks in the resulting string with zeros. One way to accomplish this is to use STUFF( ) along with REPLICATE( ). Assuming that the string is *s*, the desired statement becomes simply

```
s = STUFF(s, 1, LEN(s) - LEN(LTRIM(s)), REPLICATE("0", ;
    LEN(s) - LEN(LTRIM(s))))
```

One of the most popular uses of REPLICATE( ) is in drawing extended IBM graphic character symbols as in a bar chart. Figure 8-1 shows a chart

Listing 8-3. Animate1.prg, a simple string animation function.

```
FUNCTION Animate1
*************************************************************
* Program ...: Animate1.prg
* Author ....: P. L. Olympia & Kathy Cea
* Purpose....: Animate a string by moving it from right to left
*            : at screen row Nrow, fading at column Ncol.
*            : Animation area is Nwide characters long.
* Syntax ....: = Animate1(string, Nrow, Ncol, Nwide)
*************************************************************
PARAMETERS message, nrow, ncol, nwide
FOR i = 1 TO LEN(message) - nwide + 1
   @ nrow, ncol SAY SUBSTR(message , i, nwide)
ENDFOR
RETURN ""
```

Listing 8-4. Animate2.prg, an animation function that moves two strings on either side of the screen and then joins them at the center of a specified row.

```
FUNCTION Animate2
*************************************************************
* Program ...: Animate2.prg
* Author ....: P. L. Olympia & Kathy Cea
* Purpose....: Animate two strings (Lstring and Rstring) by
*            : moving them vertically (ending at row Erow)
*            : on either side of the screen then joining them at
*            : the center.
* Syntax ....: = Animate2(Lstring, Rstring, Erow, Width
*            :  Width = screen area where animation occurs, usually
*            :  80.
*************************************************************
PARAMETERS Lstring, Rstring, Erow, Width
```

(continued)

Listing 8-4. Continued

```
LenLeft=LEN(lstring)
LenRight=LEN(rstring)

FOR i = 1 TO Erow - 1
   @ i,1 SAY SPACE(LenLeft)
   @ i,width-LenRight SAY SPACE(LenRight)
   @ i+1,1 SAY lstring
   @ i+1,width-LenRight SAY rstring
   * Delay to slowdown FoxPro a bit
     FOR j = 1 to 200
     ENDFOR
ENDFOR

lstop=(width-LenLeft+LenRight+1)/2
lstop=lstop-10
rstop=lstop+LenLeft

moveit = IIF(lstop > (width - rstop), lstop, width - rstop)

FOR i = 1 TO moveit
   IF i <= lstop
      @ Erow, i SAY lstring
   ENDIF

   IF width-(LenRight-1+i) >= rstop
      @ Erow, width-(LenRight-1+i) SAY rstring
   ENDIF
 ENDFOR

FOR i = 1 TO moveit
   IF i <= lstop-1
      @ Erow, i SAY " "
   ENDIF

   IF width-i >= rstop+LenRight
      @ Erow, width-i SAY " "
   ENDIF
ENDFOR
RETURN ""
```

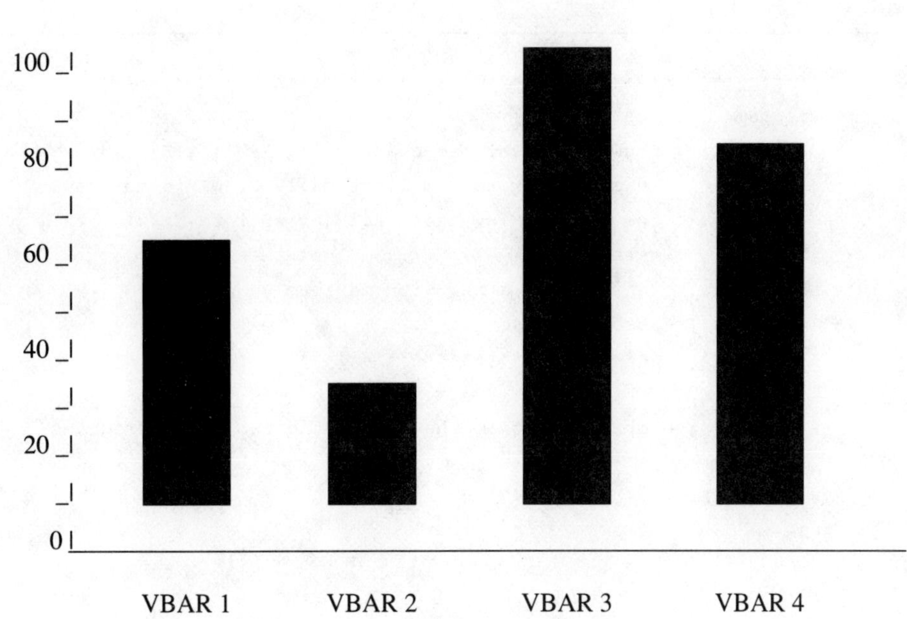

Figure 8-1. Vertical bar chart drawn by Vbar.prg using REPLICATE().

with four vertical bars drawn by the Vbar.prg program. The program is shown in Listing 8-5. The graph is drawn by calling two procedures. The first procedure, DrawAxis, draws the graph axis (using REPLICATE( )), prints a graph title, labels the vertical axis, and prints the axis tick marks. Note that this procedure uses the FoxPro PADC( ) function to print a centered string.

The second procedure, DrawBar, draws the actual bar chart in the specified screen column position. As implemented, the program is set to chart data values less than or equal to 100, with a resolution of about 5. A desirable enhancement you may pursue is to make the programs generic so they can handle any data values with appropriate scaling.

Chapter Summary

Character data is the predominant data type in typical database applications. FoxPro has an extensive set of commands and functions for manipulating character string data. In this chapter, we discussed how to convert various

Listing 8-5. Driver program and procedures for drawing bar charts using the REPLICATE() function.

```
***********************************************************
* Program ...: Vbar.prg
* Purpose....: Draws vertical bar chart using REPLICATE()
*            : This driver program first calls DrawAxis to draw
*            : the graph axis, then calls DrawBar to draw a
*            : vertical bar
* Notes .....: Set to draw a bar with maximum value of 100,
*            : Resolution set at 5.
***********************************************************

*-- This is the driver program that calls the two graph programs

SET TALK OFF
CLEAR

PUBLIC ymax, ymin, yincr, row0
*-- Define bounds
ymax = 100
ymin = 0
yincr = 20

DO DrawAxis WITH 16, 4, "g+", "w+", "* Graph Sample *"
DO DrawBar WITH 60, 6, 17, 16, "VBAR 1", "r"
DO DrawBar WITH 32, 6, 17, 30, "VBAR 2", "g"
DO DrawBar WITH 100, 6, 17, 44, "VBAR 3", "g+"
DO DrawBar WITH 82,  6, 17, 58, "VBAR 4", "r+"

SET TALK ON
RETURN

PROCEDURE DrawAxis
***********************************************************
* Program ...: DrawAxis.prg
* Purpose....: Draws the graph axes including labels and
*            : tick marks. Also prints a centered title.
* Syntax ....: DO DrawAxis with x_row, t_row, ax_color,
```

(continued)

Listing 8-5. Continued

```
*              :    ti_color, title
*              : x_row = row where the x-axis is drawn
*              : t_row = row where the title is drawn
*              : ax_color = color of axis
*              : ti_color = color of title
*              : title = graph title
* Notes .....: Adapted from a program by Jon Wind.
************************************************************
PARAMETERS  x_row, t_row, ax_color, ti_color, title

SET COLOR TO &ti_color
@ t_row, 0 SAY PADC(title, 80)          && Note PADC to center
SET COLOR TO &ax_color

@ x_row-10,10 TO x_row,10               && draw y axis
@ x_row,10 SAY CHR(192)                 && draw corner
@ x_row,11 TO x_row,70                  && draw x axis

row0 =x_row - 1
FOR i = ymin TO ymax+1 STEP yincr
  @ x_row,5   SAY STR(i,3)+IIF(i > ymin," _","")  && Label
  @ x_row-1,9 SAY IIF(i < ymax,"_","")             && tick marks
  x_row=x_row-2
ENDFOR
RETURN


PROCEDURE DrawBar
************************************************************
* Program ...: DrawBar.prg
* Purpose....: Draws a vertical bar given a value
* Syntax ....: DO DrawBar with value, barwidth, g_row, g_col
*              :  g_label, bar_color
*              : Value = numeric value to graph
*              : barwidth = width of bar (in chars) to draw
*              : g_row = start row where bar is drawn
*              : g_col = column where bar is drawn
*              : g_label = bar label (limit to barwidth)
```

(continued)

Listing 8-5. Continued

```
*           : bar_color = color of bar
* Notes .....: Based on a program by Jon Wind
*******************************************************
PARAMETERS value, barwidth, g_row, g_col, g_label, bar_color

row = row0
gyval = 2.5
resol = 5
ntick = 10

SET COLOR TO &bar_color
@ g_row,g_col + barwidth/2)-(LEN(g_label)/2) SAY g_label

DO WHILE gyval <= ymax  .AND. gyval <= value
  IF value >= gyval + resol
    @ row, g_col SAY REPLICATE(CHR(219),barwidth)  && long vert bar
ELSE

    IF value >= gyval
      @row, g_col SAY REPLICATE(CHR(220),barwidth)  && short Vbar
    ENDIF
  ENDIF
  gyval = gyval + ntick
  row = row-1
ENDDO
SET COLOR TO
RETURN
```

data types to character and some of the practical advantages defining database fields as character.

We discussed the FoxPro functions for searching strings and memo fields for a character or substring with or without regard to case. We showed a code fragment to search a text file for a desired substring, with or without wildcard characters, by first loading it into a memo field and performing the search there with one FoxPro function. The chapter describes how to use the RAT( )

function, along with the KEYBOARD command, to allow word wrapping during data entry on character fields or memory variables.

We also discussed functions such as CHRTRAN( ) and STRTRAN( ), which are designed to replace characters and strings, including removing unwanted characters from DOS files. Both functions solve the problem of removing or replacing characters with the high bit set so that string matches can proceed as expected.

The chapter provided examples of procedures and user-defined functions that demonstrate character data handling. These include functions to encrypt and decrypt a user-supplied password, functions to animate a string to focus users' attention to the message, and functions to draw a vertical bar chart based on user-supplied values.

Chapter 9

Array Techniques

Arrays in FoxPro

Arrays have varied uses in a typical application. For example, they provide the facility for building and displaying menus, implementing table lookups, and allowing direct edits on database records without necessarily compromising the integrity of the data. FoxPro memory variable arrays may be either one- or two-dimensional. Some FoxPro commands, SCATTER, for example, can create arrays automatically, whereas others such as COPY TO ARRAY require that arrays be defined previously. Arrays may be defined with the DECLARE, DIMENSION, or PUBLIC commands. The following statements all create a one-dimensional array of ten elements and a two-dimensional array with two rows and three columns:

```
DIMENSION ArrayA(10), ArrayB[2,3]
DECLARE   ArrayA[10], ArrayB(2,3)
PUBLIC ARRAY ArrayA(10), ArrayB(2,3)
PUBLIC ArrayA[10], ArrayB[2,3]
```

Note that FoxPro recognizes both the parentheses (used by FoxBASE+) and the square brackets (used by Clipper and dBASE IV) to reference array elements. The size of an array may be declared using a numeric expression. For instance, the statement

```
DIMENSION B[FCOUNT()]
```

defines a one-dimensional array with as many elements as there are fields in the currently active .dbf file. An array may also be redimensioned at will, but the values of its elements are reinitialized to the default logical .F. values each time.

Arrays created by a program are normally private or local—available only to the program that created them and its subprograms. However, arrays defined with the PUBLIC command are available throughout the application just like regular memory variables.

A FoxPro array uses only one memory variable from the memory variable pool, MVCOUNT, regardless of the size of the array. Recall that MVCOUNT can be set to a maximum of 3600 in Config.fp. The maximum number of elements in an array is 3600, and the maximum number of arrays active at one time is also 3600.

Array Element Addressing

Unlike arrays in C, which are zero-based, FoxPro arrays are one-based—array subscripts begin with 1. A two-dimensional array may be accessed with a single subscript, because, in fact, declaring a two-dimensional array of *r* rows and *c* columns simply allocates storage for a one-dimensional array of $r * c$ elements. FoxPro and languages like Basic that support two-dimensional arrays really just provide the facility for referencing a desired element using a row-column index address. This built-in facility is missing in the Summer '87 version of Clipper, so it does not appear to support two-dimensional arrays explictly. However, it is easy enough to write UDFs to translate two-dimensional index addresses to one-dimensional addresses. Function Index1, discussed later in this chapter, does just that.

FoxPro arrays are stored in row-major order and single subscript addressing is based on this storage order. For example, Figure 9-1 shows the single subscript address of an array with two rows and three columns.

Note that the array element B(2,1) may also be referenced with B(4). The single subscript address of an element in a two-dimensional array located at row *r* and column *c* is defined by the formula

```
Index1 = (r - 1) * numcols + c
```

where numcols is the number of columns in the array.

Row	Column 1	Column 2	Column 3
1	1	2	3
2	4	5	6

Figure 9-1. Single subscript address of a 2 x 3 array.

Listing 9-1 shows three UDFs for converting array element addresses, including Index1. The RowNum function returns the row number and the ColNum function returns the column number in a two-dimensional array where the specified single subscript address lies.

Listing 9-1. User-defined functions to help translate index addresses in one- and two-dimensional arrays.

```
FUNCTION Index1
PARAMETERS r, c, numcol
* Returns one-dimensional index address given row and column
* position of a two-dimensional array of NumCol columns
RETURN ((r - 1) * numcol + c)

FUNCTION RowNum
PARAMETERS addr1, numcol
* Returns row number of 2-D array element given the element's
* one-dimensional index address & num columns in the 2-D array
RETURN INT((addr1 - 1) / numcol) + 1

FUNCTION ColNum
PARAMETERS addr1, numcol
* Returns column number of 2-D array element given the element's *
one-dimensional index address & num columns in the 2-D array
RETURN MOD((addr1 - 1), numcol) + 1
```

```
DIMENSION ArrayA(3)
ArrayA(2) = DATE()
ArrayA(3) = "Sneakers"
DISPLAY MEMORY LIKE ARRA*

  ARRAYA      Pub    A
       (   1)      L   .F.
       (   2)      D   02/20/90
       (   3)      C   "Sneakers"
   1 variables defined,       15 bytes used
 255 variables available,   5985 bytes available
```

Figure 9-2. Defining and initializing an array. Note that the array elements may be of different data types.

Initializing Arrays

Elements of the same array need not be of the same data type. One element may contain character data and another may contain numeric or date data. However, an array element cannot be used to contain memo field information.

When an array is first defined, all its elements are initialized as logical data types with values of .F. They retain those values until they are changed with the assignment statement or with commands such as COPY TO ARRAY. Figure 9-2 shows a series of commands that first defines an array of three elements and then stores a date value to the second element and a character value to the third element. The DISPLAY MEMORY command shows the result.

As discussed in Chapter 1, the effect of an assignment statement in initializing an array depends on the setting of the COMPATIBLE switch. With the default setting of SET COMPATIBLE FOXPLUS, the assignment statement

```
ArrayB = SPACE(1)
```

changes all elements of ArrayB to type character and each element of the array is initialized to one space. If the same command had been issued with SET COMPATIBLE DB4, the memory variable array would be replaced by a scalar variable of the same name initialized to a single space. In effect, the array is erased.

FoxPro Arrays versus Clipper Arrays

As we mentioned before, the Summer 87 release of Clipper supports only one-dimensional arrays. However, it is possible, via a scheme similar to the single subscript formula described earlier, to refer to a specific element as though it were part of a two-dimensional array.

FoxPro, like Clipper, allocates array memory dynamically. A pointer is set from the memory variable area to a chunk of memory where reference to array elements is kept. This array area is 18 bytes wide (Clipper's is 22 bytes wide) and its length is equal to the dimension of the array. Numeric values of array elements are stored in the 18-byte area for the element. If the element is of type character, the 18-byte area contains a pointer to a contiguous area of memory where the actual value for the element is stored.

In Clipper, the TYPE( ) function returns "A" for an array. FoxPro's TYPE( ) function does not return the same result. Instead, it returns the type of the first element of the array. For instance,

```
DECLARE ArrayA[3]
? TYPE("ArrayA")
  L                      && Array type is Logical, initial
                         && default

ArrayA[1] = "Molly"
? TYPE("ArrayA")
  C                      && Array type is now Character.
```

FoxPro's TYPE( ) function correctly returns the data type of a specified array element. For example,

```
ArrayA[5] = 12
ArrayA[6] = "Donnie"
? TYPE("ArrayA[5]")
  N                  && Type is Numeric
? TYPE("ArrayA[6]")
  C                  && Type is Character
```

In Clipper, the TYPE( ) function returns "U" (for undefined) if provided a specific array element such as ArrayA[6]. For it to behave like FoxPro's function, we must first assign a memory variable to the array element and then use that memory variable name as the argument to the function.

Clipper has one other deficiency concerning arrays—it returns a runtime error message when an attempt is made to perform a GET directly into an array element. To work around this problem, Clipper developers have had to first assign the array element to a memory variable and then perform a GET on that variable. FoxPro does not have this problem, so the following commands work as expected in FoxPro:

```
@ 7, 11 GET ArrayA[12]
READ
```

How do we tell the current dimension of an array? In Clipper, all we do is pass the array name to the LEN( ) function. FoxPro's LEN( ) function does not return the array dimension but we can work around this deficiency by writing a UDF. Note that FoxPro's TYPE( ) function returns "U" if provided an array element whose subscript exceeds the dimension of the array. Therefore, all our UDF needs to do is increment the subscript until the function returns a "U." Listing 9-2 shows the A_LEN( ) function, which returns the current dimension of a specified array.

To call this function, you can supply the name of the array as a literal, that is, enclosed in quotes or square brackets. You can also invoke the function with the name of a memory variable that has been assigned previously to the name of the array, for example,

```
ArrayName = "Arry"
LenArray = A_LEN(ArrayName)
```

These are the usual ways to pass the name of an array to a function or procedure. You cannot simply supply the name of the array in the argument list. Of course, with public arrays, you won't need to pass the array name. If the called procedure in turn passes the name of the array to a subprocedure, it does so without bothering to pass the name as a literal string.

You don't need a separate A_Len( ) function to determine the dimensions of a two-dimensional array since, as we pointed out earlier, the only real distinction between a one- and two-dimensional array in most languages is the way in which the index addresses are referenced. However, the results produced by a few FoxPro commands depend on the dimension of the affected array.

Listing 9-2. User-defined function A_Len returns the current dimension of a specified array.

```
FUNCTION A_Len
PARAMETERS Arr

*--  FoxPro UDF that returns the current dimension of Array, Arr
*--  Similar to Clipper's LEN() for arrays
*--  Calling syntax:  LenArray = A_LEN("Arry")

FOR i = 1 TO 3600        && max dimension is 3600 in FoxPro
  IF TYPE("&Arr[i]") = "U"
     RETURN i-1
  ENDIF
ENDFOR
RETURN 3600
```

FoxPro UDFs of Clipper Built-in Array Functions

Clipper has built-in functions that either use arrays or make array manipulation easy. These functions are summarized in Table 9-1.

Clipper developers who are interested in porting their applications to FoxPro will find that equivalent UDFs can be developed easily using FoxPro's command language. For instance, a UDF equivalent of ACHOICE( ) can be coded in a few lines because FoxPro's MENU command is its functional equivalent. Programmers who normally favor the combination of Clipper's ADIR( ) and ACHOICE( ) functions to present a menu of filenames to users will find a vastly superior alternative to these in FoxPro's FILER command. Thus, the command

```
FILER LIKE *.prg
```

produces a pop-up menu of all filenames with the .prg extension.

Note, however, that the FILER command is unavailable in FoxPro Runtime. The ADIR( ) function can be coded using FoxPro's SYS(2000) func-

Table 9-1. Built-in Array Functions in Clipper That Are Not in FoxPro

Function	Description
ACHOICE( )	Executes a pop-up menu using an array of character strings as menu items.
ACOPY( )	Copies the elements of one array to another.
ADEL( )	Deletes an array element moving up all elements below it by one.
ADIR( )	Fills a series of arrays with directory information and/or returns the number of files matching a skeleton.
AFIELDS( )	Fills a series of arrays with the structure information of the current database.
AFILL( )	Fills an array with a specified value.
AINS( )	Inserts an element into an array, pushing down by one all elements below it, and discarding the last element.
ASCAN( )	Searches an array for a specified value.
ASORT( )	Sorts an array in ascending order.

tion, which returns the name of files that match a character expression, including wildcard characters. Later in this chapter, we present various alternatives to the ASORT( ) function.

Listing 9-3 shows a series of FoxPro UDFs to implement some of the built-in array functions in Clipper. It is intended to show you examples of how to use arrays and how to ease the transition from one Dbase-compatible product to another using UDFs. You are encouraged to look over the examples and to code the rest of the functions described in Table 9-1.

Note that the AFields( ) UDF implements Clipper's AFIELDS( ) function using the COPY STRUCTURE EXTENDED command to access all the field attributes of the .dbf in the current select area. The FoxPro FIELDS( ) and TYPE( ) functions can be used if all we're interested in are the .dbf field names and field types.

Listing 9-3. FoxPro user-defined functions to emulate some of Clipper's built-in array functions.

```
FUNCTION ACopy
************************************************************
* Program ...: ACopy.prg
* Purpose....: FoxPro equivalent of Clipper's function to copy
*            : elements of one array to another
* Syntax ....: =ACopy(ArSrc, ArTgt[, ElBeg[, ElEnd [, ElBegTgt]]])
*            :  ArSrc = Source array
*            :  ArTgt = Target array
*            :  ElBeg = optional start element in source array
*            :  ElEnd = optional end element in source array
*            :  ElEnd = optional start element in target array
* Returns    : Nothing
* Note ......: Uses A_Len to find array dimension, see Listing 9-2
************************************************************
PARAMETERS ArSrc, ArTgt, ElBeg, ElEnd, ElBegTgt
NumParms = PARAMETERS()

DimSrc = A_Len(ArSrc)
DimTgt = A_Len(ArTgt)
MinDim = MIN(DimSrc, DimTgt)

IF NumParms = 2       && copy all elements
   FOR i = 1 TO MinDim
       &ArTgt(i) = &ArSrc(i)
   ENDFOR
   RETURN ""
ENDIF

sBeg = IIF( TYPE("ElBeg") = "N", MAX(1, Elbeg), 1)
sEnd = IIF( TYPE("ElEnd") = "N", MIN(ElEnd, DimSrc), DimSrc)
tBeg = IIF( TYPE("ElBegTgt")  = "N", MAX(1, ElBegTgt), 1)
Num2Copy = MIN(sEnd - sBeg, DimTgt - tBeg) + 1

FOR i = 0 TO Num2Copy - 1
    &ArTgt(tBeg + i) = &ArSrc(sBeg + i)
ENDFOR
RETURN ""
```

(continued)

Listing 9-3. Continued

```
FUNCTION ADel
************************************************************
* Program ...: ADel.prg
* Purpose....: FoxPro equivalent of Clipper's function to delete
*            : an element of an array, moving everything below up one
* Syntax ....: Success =ADel(Arr, Element)
*            :  Arr = Array
*            :  Element number to delete
* Returns    : .T. if operation is successful, .F., otherwise
* Note ......: Uses A_Len to find array dimension
*            : Last element set to .F.
************************************************************
PARAMETERS Arr, Element

LenArr = A_Len(Arr)
If Element < 1 .OR. ELEMENT > LenArr
   RETURN .F.
ENDIF
DO WHILE Element < LenArr
   &Arr(Element) = &Arr(Element + 1)
   Element = Element + 1
ENDDO
&Arr(LenArr) = .F.
RETURN .T.


FUNCTION AIns
************************************************************
* Program ...: AIns.prg
* Purpose....: FoxPro equivalent of Clipper's function to insert an
*            : element of an array, moving everything below down one
* Syntax ....: Success =AIns(Arr, Element)
*            :  Arr = Array
*            :  Element = Element number to insert
* Returns    : .T. if operation is successful, .F., otherwise
* Note ......: Uses A_Len to find array dimension
*            : Last element in old array is lost
************************************************************
```

(continued)

Listing 9-3. Continued

```
PARAMETERS Arr, Element

LenArr = A_Len(Arr)
If Element < 1 .OR. ELEMENT > LenArr
   RETURN .F.
ENDIF
FOR i = LenArr TO Element STEP -1
   &Arr(i) = &Arr(i - 1)
ENDFOR
&Arr(Element) = .F.
RETURN .T.


FUNCTION AFill
************************************************************
* Program ...: AFill.prg
* Purpose....: FoxPro equivalent of Clipper's function to fill
*            : array elements with a specified expression
* Syntax ....: =AFill(Arr, Exp [, ElBeg[, NumEl]])
*            :  Arr = Array
*            :  Exp = Expression
*            :  ElBeg = optional start element to fill (default 1)
*            :  NumEl = optional number of elements to fill (default
*            :  all)
* Returns    : Nothing
* Note ......: Uses A_Len to find array dimension
************************************************************
PARAMETERS Arr, Exp, ElBeg, NumEl
DimArr = A_Len(Arr)

sBeg = IIF( TYPE("ElBeg") = "N", MAX(1, Elbeg), 1)
sEnd = IIF( TYPE("NumEl") = "N",;
       MIN(NumEl + sBeg - 1, DimArr), DimArr)

FOR i = sBeg TO sEnd
    &Arr(i) = Exp
ENDFOR
RETURN ""
```

(continued)

Listing 9-3. Continued

```
FUNCTION AFields
************************************************************
* Program ...: AFields.prg
* Copyright..: (c) 1990, P. L. Olympia & Kathy Cea
* Purpose....: FoxPro equivalent of Clipper's function to fill
*            : passed arrays with the Field Names, Field Types,
*            : Field Widths, Field Decimals of the .dbf in the
*            : current work area.
* Syntax ....: =AFields(AName [,AType [,AWidth [,ADec]]]
*            :  AName  = Array to fill with Field Name
*            :  AType  = Optional Array to fill with Field Type
*            :  ALen   = Optional Array to fill with Field Width
*            :  ADec   = Optional Array to fill with Field decimals
* Returns    : Number of fields or 0 if no .dbf in use
* Note ......: Uses A_Len to find array dimension
*            : Make sure passed arrays are large enough to hold
*            : all field values. No error checking done for that.
************************************************************
PARAMETERS AName, AType, ALen, ADec
NumParm = PARAMETERS()

IF "" = DBF()
   RETURN 0      && No .dbf in use
ENDIF

COPY STRUCTURE EXTENDED TO temp$    && heart of the routine

Compat = SET("Compatible")
SET COMPATIBLE FOXPLUS       && need to know what Select area we're in
orig_area = STR(SELECT(), 2)
SET COMPATIBLE TO DB4        && we need to find vacant Select area
vac_area = STR(SELECT(), 2)

*--  Move to vacant area
SELECT &vac_area
USE temp$
```

(continued)

Listing 9-3. Continued

```
numrec = RECCOUNT()

FOR i = 1 TO numrec
  &AName(i) = Field_Name
  IF NumParm > 1
     &AType(i) = Field_Type
  ENDIF
  IF NumParm > 2
     &ALen(i) = Field_Len
  ENDIF
  IF NumParm > 3
     &ADec(i) = Field_Dec
  ENDIF

  SKIP
ENDFOR

USE
DELETE FILE temp$.dbf

SET COMPATIBLE &Compat
SELECT &orig_area
RETURN numrec
```

FoxPro Commands and Functions Involving Arrays

As we have seen, FoxPro arrays are usually created using the DIMENSION, DECLARE, or PUBLIC commands, although a few commands such as SCATTER will also create arrays as required. The memory space occupied by arrays is released with the RELEASE, CLEAR MEMORY, or CLEAR ALL commands. Since RELEASE supports an optional clause such as LIKE <skel> or EXCEPT <skel>, it can be used to release a given set of arrays whose names match or do not match the specified name skeleton.

Arrays, like ordinary memory variables, may be saved to a .mem file or memo field with the SAVE TO command and restored with the RESTORE FROM command. If you issue the RESTORE FROM command in the command window, the arrays are restored as public variables. Issuing the command from a program restores the arrays as private variables.

FoxPro's command system uses arrays in various ways, for example,

- To move database fields to arrays.
- To move array data to database fields.
- To store results of computations.
- To store screens or window images.
- To use as an integral part of the FoxPro menu facility.

Table 9-2 summarizes the FoxPro commands that support these functions. For the sake of completeness, the table also includes the commands to define, initialize, save, release, and restore arrays.

Moving Data to/from Arrays and Database Fields

FoxPro's set of commands that include SCATTER, GATHER, COPY TO ARRAY and APPEND FROM ARRAY facilitate a number of database operations by reducing entire subroutines into a few lines of code. We discuss the use of these commands in greater detail in Chapters 13 and 14.

One of the most popular uses of the SCATTER and GATHER commands is to allow application users to edit a database record directly, instead of having to first copy the field values to corresponding memory variables. In this technique, SCATTER is used to store the contents of the current record to an array. The user is then free to edit the current record directly. If the user decides later to discard the edits, the record is restored to its original state with the GATHER command. The same set of commands is useful also in copying the contents of one record to another or in blanking a record. Blanking a record is another popular technique for recycling a record instead of deleting it and later getting rid of it permanently by packing the database. Packing a database not only requires exclusive use of the file, thereby making it temporarily unavailable to others, but also entails extensive and unnecessary disk I/O activity.

An important database operation that benefits from the use of arrays is table lookup, which searches a sorted array for a key, returning one or more column values from the table or array. This operation executes faster when implemented using arrays rather than related data files because all searches use only

Table 9-2. Summary of FoxPro Commands That Use Arrays

Commands to Move Database Fields to Arrays	
`COPY TO ARRAY <array> [FIELDS <field list>] [<scope>] [FOR <expL>] [WHILE <expL2>]`	Copies data from one or more records of the currently selected database to an array. Each record becomes a row in the array. The command ignores memo fields.
`SCATTER [FIELDS <field list>] TO <array> | TO <array> BLANK | MEMVAR | MEMVAR BLANK`	Moves data from the current record of the selected database to an array or a set of memory variables (with the same name as database fields). The BLANK option leaves the array or memory variables empty. The command ignores memo fields.
Commands to Move Array Data to Database Fields	
`APPEND FROM ARRAY <array> [FOR <expL>]`	Adds one or more records to the currently selected database from data stored in an array. Each row of the array becomes a record in the database. The command ignores memo fields.
`GATHER MEMVAR | FROM <array> [FIELDS <field list>]`	Transfers data from an array or a set of memory variables (with the same names as database fields) into the current record of the selected database. The command ignores memo fields.
Commands to Store Computation Results to Arrays	
`AVERAGE [<expr list>] [<scope>] [FOR <expL1>] [WHILE <expL2>] [TO <memvar list> | TO ARRAY <array>]`	Computes the arithmetic mean of numeric fields in the database and optionally stores the results to a one-dimensional array or a set of memory variables.

(continued)

Table 9-2. Continued

Command	Description
CALCULATE <expr list> [<scope>] [FOR <expL1>] [WHILE <expL2>] [TO <memvar list> | ARRAY <array>]	Computes various statistical and financial measures involving database fields and stores the results to a one-dimensional array or a set of memory variables. The quantities computed include average, count, maximum value, minimum value, net present value, standard deviation, sum, and variance.
SUM [<expr list>] [<scope>] [FOR <expL1>] [WHILE <expL2>] [TO <memvar list> | TO ARRAY <array>]	Computes the totals of one or more numeric fields in the database and stores the results to a one-dimensional array or a set of memory variables.

Commands to Store Screens or Window Images

Command	Description
SAVE SCREEN [TO <memvar>]	Saves the current screen or output window image to a buffer, memory variable, or array element. The memory variable or array element has a data type of "S."
RESTORE SCREEN [FROM <memvar>]	Restores a screen or window image, previously stored by the SAVE SCREEN command, from a buffer, memory variable, or array element.

Commands to Use Arrays in FoxPro Menus

Command	Description
@ <row, col> MENU <array>, <expN1> [, <expN2>] [TITLE <expC>] [SHADOW]	Creates a menu popup, activated by the READ MENU command. Options that appear on the menu popup are stored previously in a one-dimensional character array with elements no longer than 76 characters.

(continued)

Table 9-2. Continued

Command	Description
`MENU BAR <array1>, <expN1>` `MENU <expN2>, <array2>, <expN3> [, <expN4>]`	Along with the READ MENUBAR TO command that activates them, these two commands constitute FoxPro's menu creation facility. MENU BAR installs <array1> into the menu bar. The array is a two-dimensional character array, the first column of which constitutes the menu pads. If defined, elements in the second column of the array appear in the SET MESSAGE location as additional message. MENU installs a menu popup into a menu bar. The menu options are stored in the one-dimensional character array <array2>.
Commands to Define and Initialize Arrays	

`DIMENSION <array1> (<expN1> [, <expN2>]) [<array2> ...]`
`DECLARE <array1> (<expN1> [, <expN2>]) [<array2> ...]`
`PUBLIC [ARRAY] <array1> (<expN1> [, <expN2>]) [<array2> ...]`
	Create one or more memory variable arrays of one or two dimensions.

`STORE <expr> TO <memvar list> | TO <array>`	Like the assignment statement (for example, A = 1), stores data to a memory variable, array, or array element. The SET COMPATIBLE switch determines whether the entire array can be initialized by a single STORE command.

(continued)

Table 9-3. Continued

Commands to Release Memory Space Occupied by Arrays	

`CLEAR MEMORY`
`CLEAR ALL`
`RELEASE ALL [LIKE <skel> | EXCEPT <skel>]`
	Frees up memory occupied by arrays or memory variables with names that match the pattern defined by <skel>.

Commands to Save/Restore Arrays	
`SAVE TO <file> | TO MEMO <memfield> [ALL LIKE <skel> | ALL EXCEPT <skel>`	Saves arrays and memory variables to a .mem file or memo field.
`RESTORE FROM <file> | FROM MEMO <memfield> [ADDITIVE]`	Restores arrays and memory variables previously saved in a .mem file or memo field.

random access memory. It has the added advantage of saving a file handle and a work area in which to open another database, an important consideration in applications that require a large number of databases to be open at one time.

In implementing table lookup using arrays, we normally have the data stored permanently in a .dbf file. The application opens this file, copies its contents to an array, and then closes the file. The amount of coding, along with the usual overhead associated with copying the .dbf records to the array, is reduced drastically because it takes just one COPY TO ARRAY command to load the array. The only serious limitation to this approach is the finite size of the array, which in FoxPro cannot exceed 3600 elements.

In moving database field values to and from arrays, remember that the operation always ignores memo fields, and that the data transfer occurs in one-to-one correspondence between fields and array elements. Thus, if there are more array elements than there are fields in the database, the values of the extra elements remain unchanged by the SCATTER or COPY TO ARRAY command. Conversely, if there are more fields than there are array elements, the values of the extra fields are not copied.

Assume that we have a database consisting of four fields, the third of which is a memo field. Issuing the command

```
SCATTER TO x
```

where *x* is an undefined memory variable creates *x* as a one-dimensional array of three elements because the command ignores the memo field. The first two elements have the data type and values of the first two fields of the current record, and the third array element has the data type and value of the fourth field, not the third field, which is of type memo. If *x* is a predefined one-dimensional array of four elements, the SCATTER command leaves the value of the fourth element unchanged and, as expected, stores the value of the fourth field to the third array element. Since all operations that transfer data to and from fields and arrays ignore memo fields, we can save array memory space by defining array sizes that do not take memo fields into account.

We have repeatedly made the point that in most languages the only real distinction between one- and two-dimensional arrays is the manner in which the index address is referenced. This is not exactly correct in FoxPro because the results of the COPY TO ARRAY and APPEND FROM ARRAY commands depend on the dimension of the specified array. Recall that these commands can copy data to and from multiple records. The command

```
COPY TO ARRAY x
```

where *x* is a one-dimensional array copies only the values of the fields in the current record even though *x* has a size that can accommodate field values from several records. On the other hand, if *x* is a two-dimensional array, this command copies the field values from the current record to as many records as there are rows in the array. Naturally we can limit the range of records that the command transfers by using a scope specification such as NEXT 3.

SCATTER/GATHER versus COPY/APPEND Commands

SCATTER and COPY TO ARRAY both copy database fields to arrays, but they differ in two important ways. SCATTER does not require the target array to be previously defined because it creates the array as needed. In contrast, COPY TO ARRAY requires the array to be predefined. SCATTER copies database field values from the current record to a one-dimensional array. On the other hand, COPY TO ARRAY can copy field values from one or more database records, depending on the dimension of the array and the scope specified in the command.

GATHER and APPEND FROM ARRAY are the complement commands of SCATTER and COPY TO ARRAY, respectively. They differ in the same ways that their complement commands differ. Thus, APPEND FROM ARRAY can create multiple records, but GATHER is confined to only one record.

Sorting Data

Sorting data is one of the most commonly used operations in computer applications. FoxPro, like other members of the Dbase family, provides a convenient way of sorting data. For instance, assume that we want to sort a table of survey results in ASCII that may have been downloaded from a mainframe or produced by an optical scanner. We can simply create a database structure that matches the table and then write a sorted file back to disk with the following commands:

```
USE <dbfname>
APPEND FROM <tablefile> SDF
INDEX ON <sortfield>
COPY TO <sortedfile> SDF
```

Array Sorting Techniques

Lookup procedures that are implemented using arrays clearly require the arrays to be sorted. There are a number of sorting algorithms we can use. Our choice is usually governed by efficiency considerations: the time required to code the program, the machine time required to execute the sort, and the amount of memory or disk space that the program needs.

The optimal sort algorithm is one in which the sort time is always of the order of the item count, that is, $O(n)$, independent of whether the input data is already almost sorted or not. Unfortunately such an algorithm does not exist. Sort time is most commonly a function of the original sequence of data. For most algorithms, sort time is $O(n)$ if the items are almost sorted, and $O(n*n)$ if the items are in completely reversed order. If we have no advanced knowledge of the original sequence of data, we may want to select the sort strategy that can handle the average case in $O(n \log n)$. Such an algorithm increases sort time by less than 3000 for every 1000-fold increase in the number of items to sort compared to a million-fold increase in a method where the sort time is $O(n*n)$.

However, note that when n is small, an $O(n*n)$ sort may still be preferable to an $O(n \log n)$ sort because the former is usually much easier to program and has little overhead since most of the operations are comparisons and replacements during each pass through the data.

Let's look at some common sort methods—their strengths and weaknesses and how we would code them as FoxPro procedures.

Bubble Sort

The Bubble sort, so called because each item slowly "bubbles" to its proper position, is the easiest sort technique to code but is probably the most inefficient. Thus it is most suited for sorting a short list of items or records in a small file. Its efficiency is usually $O(n*n)$, but this improves considerably up to $O(n)$ for a list that is almost sorted.

This method requires passing through the array items several times. Each pass consists of comparing each element to its successor and exchanging the two if they are not in proper order. Since each iteration places a new element in its proper position, the procedure requires no more than $n - 1$ iterations to sort an array of n items. After k iterations, elements in positons $(n - k + 1)$ and greater will be in their proper order and need not be compared in succeeding iterations. We can speed up the procedure by recognizing if the array is already sorted after less than $n - 1$ iterations. Clearly the array is completely sorted as soon as no element interchange occurs in any one pass.

Listing 9-4 is a FoxPro procedure that sorts an array using the Bubble technique. A sample invocation syntax is shown in the code.

Shell Sort

The Shell (or Diminishing Increment) sort orders separate subarrays of the original array. The subarrays contain every mth element (the increment) of the original. For instance, if m is 7, the elements A[1], A[8], A[15], ... are sorted first. Seven subarrays, each containing one-seventh of the original array elements, are sorted this way. After the first m subarrays are sorted, a new smaller value of m is chosen and the array is partitioned into a new set of subarrays. Eventually m is set to 1 and the entire array is sorted.

Listing 9-4. A FoxPro program that sorts an array using the Bubble sort technique.

```
PROCEDURE Bubble.prg
************************************************************
* Program ...: Bubble.prg
* Copyright..: (c) 1990, P. L. Olympia & Kathy Cea
* Purpose....: Sorts an array using the Bubble technique
* Syntax ....: DO Bubble WITH "Arr", n
*            :  Arr = Array, n = elements
************************************************************
PARAMETERS Arr, n

   IntChange = .T.
   NumPass = 1
   DO WHILE NumPass <= n-1 .AND. IntChange
      IntChange = .F.
      FOR j = 1 TO n - NumPass
          IF &Arr(j + 1) < &Arr(j)  && Out of order, so interchange
             Temp = &Arr(j)
             &Arr(j) = &Arr(j+1)
             &Arr(j+1) = Temp
             IntChange = .T.
          ENDIF
      ENDFOR   && j
      NumPass = NumPass + 1
   ENDDO
RETURN
```

The Shell method is ideal for moderately sized arrays of a few hundred elements. Its efficiency is influenced by the value of the increment and approaches $O(n (\log n)(\log n))$ when an appropriate set of increments is used. In the Shell sort, partial sorts on a subarray do not disturb subarrays that have already been sorted earlier using a larger increment value.

Listing 9-5 shows a FoxPro procedure that implements the technique.

Listing 9-5. A FoxPro program that sorts an array using the Shell sort technique.

```
PROCEDURE Shelsort.prg
***********************************************************
* Program ...: Shelsort.prg
* Copyright..: (c) 1990, P. L. Olympia & Kathy Cea
* Purpose....: Sorts an array using the Shell sort technique
* Syntax ....: DO ShelSort WITH "Arr", n
*            :  Arr = Array, n = elements
***********************************************************
PARAMETERS Arr, n

midl = INT(n/2)
DO WHILE midl > 0
      i =  midl + 1
      DO WHILE i <= n
            j = i - midl
            DO WHILE ((j >= 1) .AND. (&Arr[j] > &Arr[j+midl]))
                  hold = &Arr[j]
                  &Arr[j] = &Arr[j+midl]
                  &Arr[j+midl] = hold
                  j = j - midl
            ENDDO
            i = i + 1
      ENDDO
      midl = INT(midl / 2)
ENDDO
RETURN
```

Quicksort

Quicksort (or Partition Exchange sort) is a recursive procedure. It rearranges the keys and partitions the array into two subsections such that all keys in the first subsection are smaller than all keys in the second subsection. The two subsections are then sorted recursively, after which the array is completely sorted.

Quicksort's efficiency is of the range $O(n \log n)$ through $O(n*n)$, depending on the input data and the size of the array. The unmodified Quicksort algorithm ironically works best for items that are completely unsorted and worst for those that are already almost sorted. Quicksort is also much better for medium to large arrays than for very small ones.

Listing 9-6 shows a FoxPro procedure that implements the Quicksort technique.

Note that the procedure uses recursive function calls to QSortSub. Without the ability to make recursive calls, this procedure would be difficult to code. The following code fragment demonstrates a very simple use of recursive function calls—it computes the factorial of the parameter x. Bear in mind that the use of a recursive procedure in this example is very inefficient; it is shown merely to demonstrate the capability.

```
PROCEDURE recurse
PARAMETERS x
* Demonstrate recursive capability by
* computing x! (factorial)
Factrl = 1
=factor(x)
? Factrl
FUNCTION factor
PARAMETERS x
IF x > 2
     =factor(x-1)
ENDIF
Factrl = Factrl * x
RETURN .T.
```

The recursive capability works regardless of whether the parameters are passed by value or by reference. Generally it is advisable to use recursion only when absolutely necessary (such as in our Quicksort example). This is because the recursive function must place a copy of all parameters on a stack for each separate call, usually slowing execution and consuming additional system resources. Note also that recursion in FoxPro has one major limitation: recursion that results in a <program> nesting which is more than 32 levels deep produces a runtime error.

The Quicksort procedure in Listing 9-6 sets element partitioning such that all elements below a given pivot point are less than or equal to the value of the pivot, and all elements above are greater than or equal to the pivot point value. The pivot point is simply an arbitrary element of the array. In our example, we

Listing 9-6. A FoxPro program that sorts an array using the Quicksort technique.

```
PROCEDURE QSort.prg
************************************************************
* Program ...: Qsort.prg
* Copyright..: (c) 1990, P. L. Olympia & Kathy Cea
* Purpose....: Sorts an array using the Quicksort technique
* Syntax ....: DO Qsort WITH "Arr", n
*            :  Arr = Array, n = elements
* Calls .....: QSortSub which calls PART and recursively calls
*            : itself.
************************************************************
PARAMETERS Arr, n

PUBLIC pivot
=QSortSub(arr,1,n)
RETURN

FUNCTION QSortSub
PARAMETERS arr,low,high
IF low < high
        DO PART WITH arr,low,high
        =QSortSub(arr,low,pivot-1)
        =QSortSub(arr,pivot+1, high)
ENDIF
RETURN .T.

PROCEDURE Part
PARAMETERS arr, startlow, starthigh
pos = &arr(startlow)
high = starthigh
low = startlow
DO WHILE low < high
        DO WHILE (&arr(low) <= pos) .AND. (low < starthigh)
                low = low + 1
        ENDDO
        DO WHILE (&arr(high) > pos)
                high = high - 1
        ENDDO
```

(continued)

Listing 9-6. Continued

```
        IF low < high
                temp = &arr(low)
                &arr(low) = &arr(high)
                &arr(high) = temp
        ENDIF
ENDDO
&arr(startlow) = &arr(high)
&arr(high) = pos
pivot = high

RETURN
```

select the first element of each partition to act as the pivot point. Once we have separated our initial array into two partitions, we treat each partition separately, again selecting a pivot element and rearranging elements so that they meet the preceding criteria. We continue partitioning and rearranging elements until the entire array is sorted. Again, this technique cannot be used if the recursion results in program nesting that is more than 32 levels deep.

Heapsort

The Heapsort technique uses a data structure that is essentially a binary tree with some of its rightmost leaf nodes removed. The structure may be defined as a descending heap or an ascending heap. A descending heap with *n* elements is an almost complete binary tree with *n* nodes; the content of each node is less than or equal to the content of its father node. Conversely, an ascending heap is an almost complete binary tree with the contents of each node greater than or equal to the contents of its father node. In this example we will be using a descending heap.

Heapsort processing consists of two parts. In the first part, we build the heap from the unordered array. We do this by traversing the tree from the bottom up for each element of the array, seeking the first element greater than or equal to the element we wish to insert. When an element is inserted, the nodes it has passed are shifted down. This is called a shiftup operation.

The second part of the process uses a siftdown operation to delete nodes from the heap in descending order and place them in their proper position in the array. The result is a sorted array.

In a heap, both insertion and deletion can be done in $O(\log n)$ operations, and the sorting can be done in place with no additional space requirements except for program variables. Thus the Heapsort algorithm is an in-place sort with an efficiency of $O(n \log n)$, even in the worst case. It is not very efficient for small n because of the overhead associated with constructing the heap.

Listing 9-7 shows a FoxPro procedure that implements the Heapsort technique.

Chapter Summary

FoxPro supports one- or two-dimensional arrays of up to 3600 elements. Its array subscript notation is compatible with those of FoxBASE+, Clipper, and dBASE IV. An array can contain elements of varying data types except memo. When provided a literal with the name of an array, FoxPro's TYPE( ) function returns the data type of the first array element.

FoxPro uses arrays extensively in its own command language. Array usage in FoxPro falls into the following categories:

- To move database fields to arrays.
- To move array data to database fields.
- To store computation results to arrays.
- To store screens or window images.
- To use as an integral part of the FoxPro menu facility.

We discussed how some of the array-related commands can be used to allow direct edits on database records without compromising the integrity of the data, and how they can be used for table lookups. We also discussed the primary differences between SCATTER and COPY TO ARRAY, and between GATHER and APPEND FROM ARRAY.

In this chapter we discussed the differences in FoxPro and Clipper arrays. We showed a FoxPro UDF that returns the dimension of an array similar to Clipper's LEN( ) function. We also provided a set of FoxPro UDFs that

Listing 9-7. A FoxPro program that sorts an array using the Heapsort technique.

```
PROCEDURE HeapSort.prg
************************************************************
* Program ...: HeapSort.prg
* Copyright..: (c) 1990, P. L. Olympia & Kathy Cea
* Purpose....: Sorts an array using the Heapsort technique
* Syntax ....: DO HeapSort WITH "Arr", n
*            :  Arr = Array, n = elements
************************************************************
PARAMETERS Arr, n

* Build the heap
FOR i = 2 TO n
        element = &arr(i)
        son = i
        father = INT(son/2)
        DO WHILE (son > 1) .AND. (&arr(father) < element)
                &arr(son) = &arr(father)
                son = father
                father = IIF((son > 1), INT(son/2),1)
        ENDDO
        &arr(son) = element
ENDFOR

maxint = 9999999   && assign to # larger than any element
* Sort the Heap
FOR i = n TO 2 STEP -1
        lastval = &arr(i)
        &arr(i) = &arr(1)
        father = 1
        son = IIF((i = 2),0,2)
        FOR j = 3 TO (n - 1)
                IF ( i > j) .AND. (&arr(j) > &arr(j-1))
                        son = j
                ELSE
                        EXIT
                ENDIF
        ENDFOR
```

(continued)

Listing 9-7. Continued

```
          newval = IIF ((son > 0), &arr(son),0)
          DO WHILE (son > 0) .AND. (lastval < newval)
                  &arr(father) = &arr(son)
                  father = son
                  son = 2 * father
                  IF ((son + 1) <= (i - 1)) .AND. ;
                     (&arr(son) < &arr(son + 1))
                          son = son + 1
                  ENDIF
                  IF son < i
                          newval = &arr(son)
                  ELSE
                          son = 0
                          newval = maxint
                  ENDIF
          ENDDO
          &arr(father) = lastval
  ENDFOR

  RETURN
```

emulate Clipper's built-in array handling functions to help port Clipper applications to FoxPro.

The chapter concluded with an extensive discussion of array sorting algorithms including Bubble sort, Quicksort, Shell sort, and Heapsort. We discussed the general principle involved in each technique, along with its efficiency and the circumstances under which each one is suited. We also presented FoxPro programs to show how each sort algorithm is implemented.

Chapter 10

Indexing and Sorting

Database management systems allow us to store and quickly retrieve data items. Indexing and sorting are the two methods for manipulating a database file to facilitate searches and to report in a prescribed order. In this chapter we examine both methods, including their strengths and weaknesses, and the circumstances under which each is more appropriate.

Sorting

A database may be physically reordered with the SORT command. This command creates a new .dbf in the order specified by the SORT statement. The SORT command's options allow you to sort on any number of database fields, in ascending or descending order. Additionally the FIELDS option allows you to include in the sorted file any or all of the fields in the original database file. You can use a FOR or WHILE clause to limit the records included in the sorted file.

You can SORT only on database fields. FoxPro does not allow sorting on expressions of any type, memory variables, or calculated values. Thus you cannot include an expression such as TRIM(UPPER(LName)) in the ON clause.

A sorted database is most often created for temporary purposes such as to output a report in a given order. It is a temporary solution since the sorted file is out of date as soon as the original file is modified. The SORT command also consumes a great deal of disk space, sometimes as much as three to four times as much space as the original .dbf occupies. Before performing a SORT, you should verify that you have sufficient disk space. You can use the FoxPro functions DISKSPACE( ), HEADER( ), RECCOUNT( ), and RECSIZE( ) to compute the available or required disk space.

You can also produce a sorted file by opening a database file with an index, or creating an index (where the index expression matches the expression you wish to sort on), and then COPYing the file. This results in a new .dbf file in sorted order. Although this approach requires less available disk space, we found it to be slower during our testing. In tests involving a sample database with 10,000 records of randomly generated numbers, a SORT took an average of 21 seconds, whereas an INDEX ON and COPY sequence required a total of 54 seconds (18 and 36 seconds, respectively). This means that even if the index had already existed, the SORT was faster than the COPY.

Searches are not usually performed on a sorted database because FoxPro offers a rich and powerful set of searching commands for indexed databases. However, as discussed later in this chapter, you can design your own algorithm to speed up searches in a sorted database, if necessary.

Sorting is also slow, especially when a large file is involved. Often it is too slow to be acceptable in an interactive environment and is reserved only for overnight batch report runs.

Indexing

The alternative to sorting a database is to create index files. An index file has one record for each corresponding database record. This record consists of the value of the key expression and a pointer to the record in the .dbf. An index logically reorders the database without affecting the physical order of the records. It is useful for reporting data in a given order, for quickly searching for a key expression, and for relating databases with primary and secondary keys using the SET RELATION command.

Any number of index files may be created for each database file. However, in FoxPro, a maximum of 25 index files can be open at one time in an application. Once you reach the limit of 25 open index files, you are unable to open additional index files, meaning that you may be left with out-of-date indexes. Because of this limit, it becomes impractical to create too many indexes, since an index that is not opened with a database file during an update cycle will have to be rebuilt to keep it synchronized with the .dbf file.

Open indexes add processing overhead when database records are being added, deleted, or modified because each index must be examined to determine the impact of the changes. The processing overhead is particularly noticeable with large files. For this reason, you should create and maintain an index only if the key is frequently searched, if the resulting order is commonly used for reporting purposes, and/or if the file will be related to other database files with the SET RELATION command. You can create temporary index files or sorted files for reports that require infrequently used sort orders.

Indexing Options

The INDEX command in FoxPro contains two very important optional clauses. The command syntax is as follows:

```
INDEX ON <expr> TO <file>
     [FOR <expL>] [UNIQUE]
```

The FOR option allows you to specify a condition for including records in the index; any record not meeting the condition <expL> is excluded from the index file (although not from the .dbf). The UNIQUE clause specifies that only the first record containing any particular key value will be included in the index file. Note that if SET UNIQUE is ON, an index is created with the UNIQUE option even if it is not specified in the command. SET UNIQUE's default setting is OFF.

Index File Format

Index files consist of one header record and one or more node records in a tree structure. The header record contains information pertaining to the entire file such as the file size and index key expression. Table 10-1 displays the index file header format. For more information about the index file format, refer to Appendix E.

Nodes are categorized as index, root, or leaf. The root node is the top node in the tree, where a search always begins. Leaf nodes are the bottom nodes of the tree and point to database records. Index nodes are indexes into other nodes; they narrow down the set of nodes to be searched as they are traversed. Figure 10-1 shows the structure of the index tree.

The key value in the search expression is compared to the values stored in the root node to determine the direction to search in the tree. A path is determined from root node to leaf node, based on the comparisons of the search value against the key values stored in each node traversed. Nodes are

Table 10-1. Index File Header Format

Byte	Description
00–03	Pointer to root node
04–07	Pointer to free node list (-1 if not present)
08–11	Pointer to end of file (file size)
12–13	Length of key
14	Index options (may be one of the following, neither, or the sum of both): 1 A UNIQUE index 8 FOR clause used
15	Index signature (reserved for future use)
16–235	Key expression (uncompiled)
236–455	FOR expression (uncompiled, ends with null byte)
456–511	Unused

traversed until the leaf node is reached; the leaf node points to the desired database record. This structure is a very fast, efficient search mechanism.

Database Searches

As stated earlier, one of the primary goals of a database application is to be able to locate specific data items quickly. Depending on whether your database is sorted, indexed, or unordered, there are several ways to search for a particular record. In this section, we look at options for searching an indexed database, a sorted database, and an unordered database.

Indexed Databases

If your database is indexed on the key value you wish to search for, you can use the FIND or SEEK commands, or the SEEK( ) function. The command syntax for each of these is as follows:

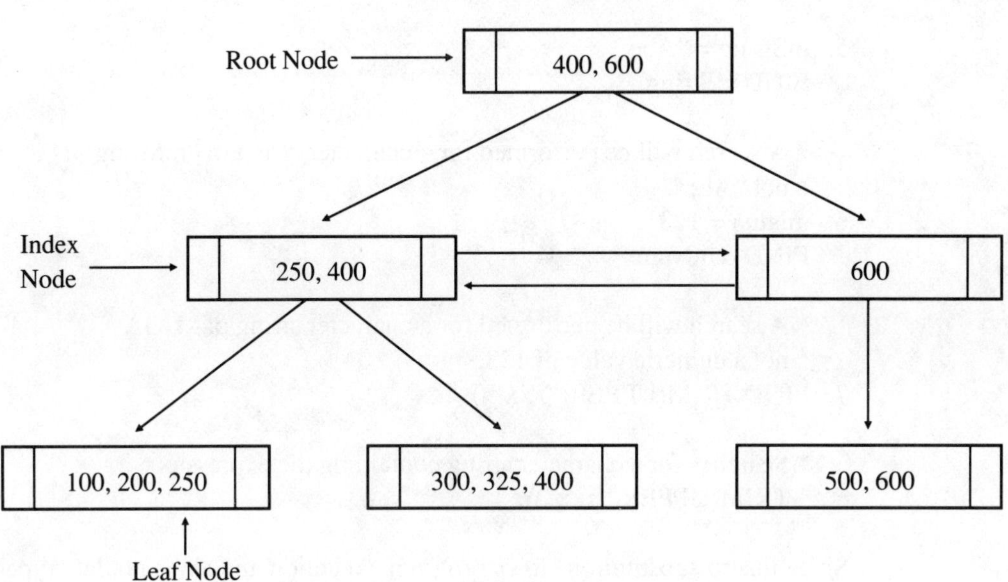

Figure 10-1. An index tree structure.

```
FIND <char string>
SEEK <expr>
SEEK(<expr>[,<alias>])
```

The FIND commands accepts only a character string and moves the record pointer to the first record whose key matches the string. The character string must be passed as a literal; if you wish to FIND a memory variable that contains a character expression, precede the variable with the & function. A literal may be passed with or without quotes. The following examples are valid statements:

1. FIND "Abc"
2. FIND Abc
3. mString = "Abc"
   FIND &mString
4. mExpr = TRIM(UPPER("xxx"))
   FIND &mExpr

However, the following examples are invalid. Even though they do not generate a syntax error, they will not produce the desired results.

5. mString = "Abc"
   FIND mString

   * A search will be performed for a character string of "mString",
   * not "Abc".
6. mNum = 123
   FIND &mNum

   * A search will be performed for a character string of "123",
   * not a numeric value of 123.
7. FIND TRIM(UPPER("xxx"))

   * Searches for a character string containing the expression
   * TRIM(UPPER("xxx")).

Since macro substitution slows program execution and since no data type other than character can be used, the SEEK command is preferred to FIND. SEEK can be used with any valid expression, and it works with memory variables without requiring macro substitution. As with the FIND command, SEEK moves the record pointer to the first record whose key matches <expr>. The equivalent commands that use SEEK for the preceding examples are as follows:

1. SEEK "Abc"
2. SEEK "Abc"
3. mString = "Abc"
   SEEK mString
4. mExpr = TRIM(UPPER("xxx"))
   SEEK mExpr
5. mString = "Abc"
   SEEK mString
6. mNum = 123
   SEEK mNum
7. SEEK TRIM(UPPER("xxx"))

The SEEK( ) function is more powerful than even the SEEK command. This function combines the SEEK command with the FOUND( ) function, returning .T. if a match is found, and .F. if not. In addition to eliminating one line of program code for each SEEK( ), an optional parameter may be passed to indicate the work area (alias) in which the search is to be performed. FIND and SEEK both work only in the current work area. Unless compatibility with an existing system is an issue, you should use SEEK( ) in place of SEEK or FIND. If you must maintain compatibility with a system that does not support the SEEK( ) function, you are better off using the SEEK command than FIND, for the reasons discussed earlier.

The Effect of SET NEAR and SET EXACT With FIND or SEEK, the record pointer moves to the bottom of the file if a matching record is not found in the database, unless SET NEAR is ON. If SET NEAR is ON, the pointer is moved to the record whose key value immediately follows the value sought.

Both FIND and SEEK return a value of true (.T.) for FOUND( ) if a matching record is found, and a value of false (.F.) otherwise. However, the return value for EOF( ) varies depending on the SET NEAR setting. If SET NEAR is OFF (the default), a value of .F. is returned for EOF( ) if the record is found, a value of .T. is returned otherwise. If SET NEAR is ON, a value of .F. is always returned for EOF( ) unless the search fails and the closest matching record happens to be the last record in the file. Since .F. is usually returned for EOF( ) with SET NEAR ON even if the match fails, it is better to check the value of FOUND( ) when determining whether a match was found.

If SET EXACT is ON, FIND and SEEK will match two character strings only if they are of equal length. If SET EXACT is OFF, a match will be found if the leftmost part of the record key matches the string being searched for. This is described in greater detail later in this chapter.

Searching for Multiple Records If you are going to search for multiple occurrences of a specified key, you should perform a SEEK( ) (or SEEK or FIND) to position the record pointer to the first matching record. The most efficient means of processing at that point is to use the SCAN...ENDSCAN structure. For example, to find all Customer records with a Last Name of "Smith" on a database file indexed on Last Name, your program code might look as follows:

```
mLName = UPPER(TRIM("Smith"))
IF SEEK(mLName)
  SCAN WHILE UPPER(TRIM(Cust->LName)) = mLName
    * process record
  ENDSCAN
ELSE
    * No matching records found
ENDIF
```

Searching a Sorted Database

As we previously discussed, a database is normally sorted only for temporary reporting purposes. However, if you happen to have a sorted database from which you need to extract a particular data item, how do you search it? You can't use the SEEK, FIND, or SEEK( ) commands designed for indexed databases because your database is not indexed, and you surely do not want to use LOCATE to perform a record-by-record search when you know that the records are in order. What you need is a search algorithm designed specifically for a set of sorted records.

The binary search is one such algorithm. It starts its search in the middle of the set (in our case, at the record in the middle of the .dbf) and determines whether the value in that record is equal to, greater than, or less than the search key. If they are equal, we've found the record and processing is complete. Otherwise, if the record value is less than the search key, the algorithm finds the record halfway between the current record and the end of the file; if the record is greater than the search value, it finds the record halfway between the top of the file and the current record. This logic continues until either the desired item is found or there are no additional records to search.

Listing 10-1 demonstrates a program, BinSrch, to perform a binary search on a sorted database. It requires two parameters: the name of the field to be searched and the field value to be found. The .dbf to be searched must already be open in the current work area. The program verifies that the field exists in the database and that the data type of the field matches the data type of the key value. Then it performs the search algorithm.

Since each pass reduces the number of records to be compared by a factor of 2, the maximum number of comparisons required is log n. Compare this to a sequential search, where the maximum number of comparisons is n. Although not usually as fast as a SEEK on an indexed database, the BinSrch program does perform reasonably well. In tests run on a sample database of 10,000 records, a SEEK typically required less than 1 second, and the binary search required about 1 second.

Note that the BinSrch program could be modified slightly to perform a binary search on a sorted array. (We discuss array sort techniques in Chapter 9.)

As with an indexed file, if multiple records containing the same key are to be processed, a SCAN...ENDSCAN structure with the WHILE clause is useful once the first matching record is located.

Listing 10-1. BinSrch.prg, a binary search program.

```
*****************************************************************
* Program: BinSrch.prg
* Author : P.L. Olympia & Kathy Cea
* Purpose: Performs a binary search on the open sorted .dbf
*        :  in order to locate a value of FldVal for field
*        :  FldName.
*        :
* Syntax : BinSrch(<FldName>,<FldVal>)
*        : where <FldName> is the field to be searched and
*        : <FldVal> is the value to be searched for
*****************************************************************

FUNCTION BinSrch
PARAMETERS FldName, FldVal

* Make sure there is a field FldName
mNumFlds = FCOUNT()
i = 0
FoundFld = .F.
DO WHILE (i <= mNumFlds) .AND. (!FoundFld)
     i = i + 1
    IF TRIM(UPPER(FldName)) = FIELD(i)
       FoundFld = .T.
    ENDIF
ENDDO

IF !FoundFld
* If there is no FldName Field in the database, Return .F.
   RETURN .F.
ENDIF

* Make sure the FldName TYPE matches the Field TYPE
IF TYPE("FldVal") <> TYPE(FIELD(i))
     RETURN .F.
ENDIF
```

(continued)

Listing 10-1. Continued

```
SET TALK OFF
FoundRec = .F.
Low = 1
High = RECCOUNT()

DO WHILE ( Low <= High) .AND. (.NOT. FoundRec)
        Mid = INT((Low + High) / 2)
        GOTO RECORD Mid
        IF (&FldName = FldVal)
                FoundRec = .T.
        ELSE
                IF FldVal < &FldName
                        High = Mid - 1
                ELSE
                        Low = Mid + 1
                ENDIF
        ENDIF
ENDDO

RETURN FoundRec
* If found, returns .T. and the .dbf pointer is set to matching record
*  Otherwise, returns .F. and the .dbf pointer location is random
```

Searching an Unordered File

If you need to find a record in a database that is not indexed on the expression you want to search for and the database is not sorted on your expression, you have several options. You can create a temporary index, with or without the FOR and UNIQUE clauses. You can also sort the file to a temporary file, which you delete upon completion of your processing. Or you can leave the file unordered and perform a sequential search.

An indexed file can be searched very quickly. Using the FOR clause with the INDEX command creates a smaller index to be searched, speeding things up even more. Although the search is very fast, you must consider the time required to create the index and the extra disk space required.

Similarly, a database may be SORTed to a temporary file. Again, extra time and much more additional disk space are required to perform the sort. Then, once your file is in sorted order, the efficiency of the search depends on your search algorithm. Since an indexed file can be searched faster than a sorted file, this option is not practical unless you also need the sorted file for reporting purposes.

If you opt not to temporarily index or sort your file, you still have several ways to find a record. The SET FILTER command is available, although it is not usually recommended. This command limits all access to the .dbf to those records that meet your specified condition. The operation of the filter is very slow because each record is read to determine whether or not it will be included in the accessible set. Unless most of your records meet the filter condition, you should not use the SET FILTER command.

The LOCATE command is similar to the FIND and SEEK commands in that it searches for a record matching the expression you supply. However, it is considerably slower because it operates on an unindexed database file and therefore must read the database file sequentially. It is best used for an occasional search of a nonkey value. The CONTINUE command may be used in conjunction with the LOCATE command to continue searching for records that satisfy the LOCATE criteria.

The SCAN...ENDSCAN command, described earlier, can also be used to search an unordered database. The FOR clause is particularly useful when searching for multiple records that meet a particular condition.

If you use the SET FILTER, LOCATE, or SCAN commands, be sure to turn off any active index. An active (but unrelated) index serves only to slow processing when performing sequential searches, for example, with the SET FILTER and LOCATE commands. To ensure that your indexes are kept updated but inactive, you may issue the SET ORDER TO 0 command.

Formulating Index Expressions

Creating indexes is critical to the efficiency of your entire application. To build efficient and useful indexes, you need to understand how to formulate the index expression.

Indexes may be created on any combination of numeric, character, logical, or date fields, although the entire expression must evaluate to just one data type. Special consideration must be given to character type indexes and to indexes made up of multiple data types.

Indexing on a Character Expression

A character field type can contain values in a number of different ways. Consider, for example, a code field containing two character positions. If left unedited during data entry, a user can elect to enter a code of 2 as " 2", "2 ", or "02". A search for " 2" will not find "2 " or "02". In addition, consider the set of codes as follows: 2, 4, 5, 6, 9, 12, 14, 21, 23, 26, 30, 35. If you index on this field, the result is as follows:

12
14
2
21
23
26
30
35
4
5
6
9

This is probably not the result you want. There are several ways to get around this problem. One way is to format the character field during the data entry process so that the string is right justified and padded with zeros. In this case, your values would look like: 02, 04, 05, 06, 09, 12, 14, 21, 23, 26, 30, 35. Thus they would sort in the order you expect.

If this requirement is too burdensome, you also have the option of converting the character string to a numeric value with the VAL( ) function. You can index on the numeric value and achieve the correct result, for example, INDEX ON VAL(Code) TO <IdxName>.

Indexing on Mixed Data Types

Although you can include different data types in your index expression, the entire expression must evaluate to just one data type. FoxPro offers a number of data conversion functions that make this task easier (see Chapter 8).

Example 1: Indexing on Date and Character Fields Consider an order database that should be indexed on Date of Order + Customer number. Date of Order is a date field type, and Customer number is a character field. The DTOS function (or equivalent DTOC(<expD>,1)) returns the date as an eight-digit character field, in the format YYYYMMDD, which is useful for indexing. Thus the index expression for the order database might be

```
DTOS(Order_Dt) + Cus_Id
```

Example 2: Indexing on Date and Numeric Fields Let's look at another date example where, instead of combining the date with a character expression, we want to combine it with a numeric expression. For example, an Accounts Overdue file might need to be ordered on Date_Billed + Days_Overdue, where Date_Billed is a date field and Days_Overdue is a numeric calculated field. Assume we have the following values in one of our records:

```
Date_Billed:     01/01/90
Days_OverDue:    95
```

If we index on Date_Billed + Days_Overdue, our key value for the preceding record would evaluate to 04/06/90. FoxPro actually adds the number of days to the date, and the result is a new, valid date. Although this can be a useful feature at times, it is hardly what we want when we index this file. Therefore, the correct expression would be

```
DTOS(Date_Billed) + STR(Days_Overdue,4)
```

This converts each value to a character string and concatenates them. Note that we included the ",4" in our STR function. Although any number can be used, this option should be specified whenever converting a numeric field to character for indexing purposes. This is because a variable length index can yield unpredictable results.

Example 3: Indexing on Logical and Character Fields Suppose we have a database in which we wish to index a logical field and a character field. For example, a department store's customer file includes a logical field for credit customers (Credit_Cus) and a Customer id character field. If we want to index on Credit_Cus and Customer id, we can write the following expression:

```
INDEX ON IIF(Credit_Cus,"1","0") + TRIM(Cus_Id)
```

This places the Credit_Cus = .F. records before the Credit_Cus = .T. records, the same order FoxPro uses if we index on just a logical field. Of course, you can always reverse this to suit your needs by simply modifying the IIF to

```
IIF(Credit_Cus,"0","1").
```

Conditional Indexes

The IIF( ) function is also useful for indexing on a field conditionally. For example, if you want to index on the first five digits of a company's phone number if it exists or on the first five digits of their zip code if the phone number does not exist, you could issue the command

```
INDEX ON IIF(EMPTY(Co_Phone),SUBSTR(Co_Zip,1,5),
  SUBSTR(Co_Phone,1,5))
```

Descending Indexes

FoxPro does not provide a built-in option for indexing in descending order (although the SORT command does have a DESCENDING clause). Fortunately you can easily write an expression to produce an index in descending order. Note that a descending option may become available when FoxPro supports multiple index (.mdx) files like dBASE IV.

If you want to index on a numeric field in descending order, simply subtract the field from a very large number. The following example indexes in descending order on a numeric field called Cus_Bal:

```
INDEX ON (99999999 - Cus_Bal) TO ...
```

This, of course, assumes that the Cus_Bal field will never contain a value as large as 99999999. If you want to avoid the assumption of the maximum expected number altogether, you can index on a numeric field in descending order by simply multiplying it by -1, for example,

```
INDEX ON (-1 * Cus_Bal) TO ...
```

A date field may be subtracted from a very early date or a very late date to achieve a descending index order. In this example, we use 10/15/1582 (the earliest date FoxPro recognizes) and subtract a date field called Overdue_Dt from it:

```
INDEX ON ({10/15/1582} - Overdue_Dt) TO ...
```

To index a database on a character field in descending order, we can take advantage of the facilities offered by the SYS(15) function. Note that this function was originally designed to preserve normal alphabetic order in European languages with letters that contain diacritical marks. On the FoxPro (and FoxBASE+) distribution disk is a file called European.mem. The file contains a character memory variable named European that, with SYS(15), can be used to translate a letter with a diacritical mark to the corresponding letter without the diacritical mark, thus preserving normal alphabetic order.

To index on a character field in descending order, all we need to do is construct a string similar to European that SYS(15) can use as a translation table. Clearly the only requirement for this string is that all ASCII characters appear in reverse order; that is, CHR(255) appears first in the string, followed by CHR(254), then by CHR(253), and so on. The following code fragment builds the desired string and then indexes the database in descending order of a character field called Grade:

```
*     Build a string of ASCII characters in reverse order
      stringrev = ""
      FOR i = 1 TO 255
           stringrev = stringrev + CHR(256 - i)
      ENDFOR
*     Save stringrev memvar to a .mem file for future use
      SAVE TO strrev ALL LIKE stringrev
*     Index using SYS(15) with the string we just built
      INDEX ON SYS(15,stringrev,Grade) TO RevGrade
```

Since the stringrev variable is actually part of the index expression, it must be known to FoxPro before you attempt to open the index file (RevGrade, in this case). Therefore, as part of your application initialization, before you open your .dbf and index files, you should issue the following command:

```
RESTORE FROM strrev ADDITIVE
```

This restores your stringrev memory variable, allowing you to open any index files that use it to establish descending order.

Index Expression Length

Although the maximum allowable length for an index expression is 220 characters, the expression must evaluate to no more than 100 characters. Also, as we indicated earlier, when converting a numeric expression to a character expression for indexing, you should always include the optional parameter to specify the length of the field. This ensures a fixed-length index expression. A variable-length index expression can lead to unpredictable results.

It is also a good idea, when indexing on a long character string, to use the SUBSTR function to limit the size of the index expression, if possible. This conserves disk space and also speeds up the search.

Opening Indexes and Index Order

When you open a database file, you should open all of its associated index files at the same time. Although opening all the files could require additional time and it does slow the processing of new records, we recommend this approach to ensure that all your indexes are kept up to date. Some applications open only the index needed to establish record order (the master index) and those that will be affected by data modifications. This approach has two problems. First, future program modifications that change the open index requirements could easily be missed. Second, as you move from program module to program module, you may have to open and close different sets of index files. This could increase delays in your system because opening and closing files (especially large ones) can be very time consuming.

As we indicated earlier, commands that process records sequentially are actually hindered by the presence of an active index. In these situations, issue a SET ORDER TO 0 command. This leaves all your indexes open for updating without activating any index for the purpose of determining record order.

The SET ORDER TO command is very useful in other situations as well. This command specifies the index in a list of indexes to be the master (controlling) index. The following code fragment demonstrates the use of this command:

```
USE Customer INDEX Cus_Id, Cus_Zip, Cus_Bal
SET ORDER TO 2
```

In this case, the Cus_Zip index is designated as the master index because it is the second index in the list. When you need to temporarily change your index order and then restore it to the original, you can include the following lines:

```
OldOrder = SYS(21)          && Store value of current index order
SET ORDER TO 4              && Set new order to 4 (or whatever)
* Do some processing
SET ORDER TO &OldOrder      && Restore original index order
```

As demonstrated in this code fragment, SYS(21) returns the currently active index order number. SYS(21) returns a null string if no indexes are open.

Other useful functions in determining current index status are the SYS(14) and equivalent KEY( ) functions. These functions return the index expression for the index in the position specified. Combining the SYS(21) and SYS(14) functions, you can obtain the index expression of the currently active (master) index as follows:

```
mOrder = SYS(21)              &&Store current index order in mOrder
mCurrExpr = SYS(14,&mOrder)   &&Ask for expression of current index
?mCurrExpr                    &&Display expression
```

The NDX( ) function is similar to the SYS(14) and KEY( ) functions except that it returns the name of the index file, rather than the index expression, for the index opened in order <expN>. ORDER( ) returns the name of the master index file, which is useful if you do not know the order of your master index file.

The SET INDEX command closes all active index files and opens those listed in the file list, opening the first index file in the list as the master index file. SET INDEX is not an efficient means of changing the master index file. The SET ORDER command is a better choice to designate a new master index. However, if additional or different index files need to be opened with the currently open database file, SET INDEX is preferred to reissuing the USE <dbfname> INDEX <index file list> command.

Reindexing

It is not difficult for an index file to become outdated. If a record is added, deleted, or modified in such a way that the key field is changed and the index file is not open at the time, the database file and the index file will no longer be synchronized. When this happens, the index file must be rebuilt.

FoxPro's two facilities for rebuilding a corrupted index are REINDEX and INDEX ON. The REINDEX command rebuilds each currently active index, using the index expression that was defined when the index was first created. The REINDEX command also recognizes the FOR criteria, if any, and the UNIQUE option. Although this command is useful if the file is simply out of date, it cannot restore the index if the file has become physically damaged (for example, if the header was corrupted). Therefore, we recommend that whenever you need to reindex in your application, you rebuild your indexes with the INDEX ON command rather than the REINDEX command. This way, a new file is built, and you will have recovered from both a synchronization problem and any physical file damage.

Of course, when you issue the INDEX ON command, you must supply the index expression and the FOR and UNIQUE options, if they are applicable. In Chapter 12 we provide sample code for maintaining a .dbf of all your application database files and associated index files. In Chapter 14, we show a sample program for using such a .dbf to rebuild all your indexes, without having to remember the original index expression. The example in Chapter 14 does not, however, handle FOR or UNIQUE options. It could be expanded to include these options with similar logic. Remember that, with the low-level file functions, you can obtain the FOR clause from the index header by reading the 220 bytes starting at byte offset 236. Similarly, you can determine whether or not the UNIQUE option was included by reading byte offset 14 (a value of 1 or 9 indicates that the UNIQUE option was used).

Indexing in a Multiuser Environment

In a multiuser environment, when you create (or rebuild) an index, or when you sort a database file, you must consider the implications of file availability. FoxPro does not require any lock when creating an index with the INDEX ON command or when creating a sorted file with the SORT command. However, if users are modifying the database file while an index or sorted file is being built, an invalid or inconsistent file could result. Thus, although not required by FoxPro, you should lock the .dbf with the FLOCK( ) function prior to issuing an INDEX ON or SORT command.

Searching for Close Matches

When we discussed the FIND and SEEK commands earlier in this chapter, we mentioned the effect of SET NEAR and SET EXACT on the placement of the record pointer and the result of comparing strings of different lengths. In this section, we look at how to use these settings as well as some additional functions for locating records that are close but not identical to the key being searched. Table 10-2 summarizes the commands and functions that assist you in finding close matches.

When SET EXACT is OFF (the default), the FIND and SEEK commands may find a match even if the key value is of different length than the string being searched for. For example, SEEK "ABC" can find any of the following strings: ABC, ABCDE, or ABCDEFGHIJ. This can be useful when searching for a string whose exact contents are not known. For instance, if a user is trying to locate a manufacturer in a specific city and remembers only that the city begins with "Fa," a SEEK "Fa" could be issued to find any of the following: Fairbanks, Fairfax, Falls River, or Fayette. If SET EXACT is ON, however, only strings that match exactly will qualify for the SEEK and FIND commands.

The SET NEAR command is also useful when looking for close matches. If SET NEAR is ON and a FIND or SEEK fails to find a matching record, the record pointer is moved to the record immediately following the location where a matching record would have been. This lets you show the user the value that comes closest to matching the requested key value.

Another means of looking up a key value when you are not sure of the exact spelling is to use the SOUNDEX( ) function. This function returns a four-character string that contains the first letter of the string and a three-number substring that represents the phonetic sound of the string. This is particularly useful in locating strings that sound the same but may be spelled differently. For example "HEAL" and "HEEL" both return a value of H400. However, this does not work in all cases; for example, "RAIN" returns a value of R500 and "REIGN" returns R250.

The DIFFERENCE( ) function is useful in determining how similar two character strings are. DIFFERENCE( ) returns a value from 0 through 4, with 4 meaning identical or very similar and 0 meaning very little is in common. For example, DIFFERENCE("HEAL","HEEL") returns 4, DIFFERENCE("RAIN","REIGN") returns 3, and DIFFERENCE("DAY","EVENING") returns 0.

Finally, the LIKE( ) function returns a logical value indicating whether a string matches a given character pattern. The format of this command is:

```
LIKE(<expC1>,<expC2>)
```

and the * and ? wildcard characters may be used in <expC1>. A value of .T. is returned if <expC1> is contained in <expC2>. The * wildcard character

Table 10-2. Commands and Functions For Finding Close Matches

Command/Function	Description
SET EXACT	Specifies whether an exact match in the length of two strings is required.
SET NEAR	Specifies the location of the record pointer after an unsuccessful search.
SOUNDEX( )	Returns a four-character string containing the phonetic representation of the string supplied.
DIFFERENCE( )	Returns a value from 0 through 4 representing the relative phonetic difference between two character expressions.
LIKE( )	Returns a logical value indicating whether a character string matches a given pattern.

replaces any number of characters, and the ? character substitutes for exactly one character. The following examples demonstrate the use of LIKE( ):

```
?LIKE("TIG??","TIGER")
.T.
?LIKE("T*","TIGER")
.T.
?LIKE("T*","CAT")
.F.
```

This, too, can be useful when searching for strings whose exact content is unknown.

Chapter Summary

Indexing and sorting are two alternative means of establishing a particular record order. Sorting physically rearranges the file to a new file and is most useful for reporting output in a given order. A sorted file becomes outdated as soon as the original database is modified. Sorting can be slow and can consume a large amount of disk space.

Indexes are files containing pointers into a database file. They are used to logically reorder a database, to facilitate fast searching, and for relating databases with the SET RELATION TO command. FoxPro keeps indexes up to date provided that they are opened with the associated .dbf. No more than 25 indexes may be open (for all open .dbf files) at any one time.

Indexed databases can be searched very quickly with the FIND, SEEK, and SEEK( ) commands. Although databases are not usually sorted to perform a search, you can develop your own search algorithm for a sorted database. We presented a binary search program in this chapter.

Unordered database files can also be searched, although the search time is typically longer. The SET FILTER, SCAN, and LOCATE commands can be used with unordered files.

The formulation of an index expression can be tricky, especially if mixing data types or trying to index in descending order. We presented techniques for handling these situations. We also discussed some important considerations when indexing on character fields.

A variety of FoxPro commands and functions are available for opening indexes, changing index order, and querying index order and index filenames. There are also two methods of rebuilding an out-of-date index file: the REINDEX command and the INDEX ON command. We reviewed the use of these commands and discussed the impact of indexing and reindexing in the multiuser environment.

Finally, we examined several approaches to searching for database records that are similar to but not exactly matching a given key value. We looked at options for finding related records and determining how similar two values really are.

Chapter 11

Report and Printing Techniques

In FoxBASE+ you've always been able to create reports with or without writing a program. For instance, its built-in report writer, activated by way of the CREATE/MODIFY REPORT command, lets you create simple reports interactively without requiring you to know any additional FoxBASE+ commands. On the other hand, if you want to create more complex reports that require more precise control of where on the page data should print, you had to write a program using the ?/ ?? and @...SAY commands to control the output.

FoxPro's Report Writing Facilities

FoxPro's report writing facilities are similar to those of dBASE IV's and are a vast improvement over those of FoxBASE+. The following list summarizes the new FoxPro report and print capabilities:

- To help you create intricate reports, FoxReport, the built-in report writer, provides a work surface with report bands that can be "painted" with database fields, text, lines, boxes, and user-defined functions. FoxReport stores the report specifications in a .frx file (equivalent to FoxBASE+'s .frm) which it reads internally to produce the report. Unlike dBASE IV, FoxPro does not translate the .frx file into a user-modifiable program (.prg), nor does it have dBASE IV's template language facility to control how the report program is translated. FoxReport can read and use FoxBASE+'s .frm file.

- To manage the printed page, FoxPro has system memory variables similar to those of dBASE IV. System memory variables define such things as page margins, page indents, text alignment, number of copies and whether automatic word-wrapping of text is in effect.
- To control text alignment, the @...SAY command has new picture functions such as I and J.
- To define the start of the output column, the ?/ ?? command has the new AT clause. The command now also also supports PICTURE and FUNCTION clauses. FoxPro version 1.02 does not support printer drivers as dBASE IV does. Consequently, FoxPro's ?/ ?? command does not include dBASE IV's STYLE clause.
- To print data in a column using a fixed number of (horizontal) character positions, the ?/ ?? command has a vertical stretch function.
- To write directly to the printer, FoxPro, like dBASE IV, has the new ??? command. You can use this command to send any control character, including the null byte, to the printer.
- To initialize the printer and define system memory variables (for example, the number of copies) that affect printed output, FoxPro has the PRINTJOB-ENDPRINTJOB command similar to dBASE IV's.
- To facilitate the handling of page breaks, footers, and headers, FoxPro has the ON PAGE command. The command is used to specify what action to take when a given line number is reached during report generation or when an EJECT PAGE command is issued. The page handler is also available in dBASE IV.
- To control the print destination including a file, local printer, or network printer, FoxPro has the SET PRINTER TO command. Additionally, the SET DEVICE TO command now redirects @...SAY output to a file.

Summary of FoxReport Features

FoxReport uses a what-you-see-is-what-you-get work surface (report layout window) on which you can place any report object virtually anywhere. Report objects include database fields, calculated fields, text, and boxes. The layout window is divided into report bands, which include the Title, Page Header, Group Header, Detail (Report Body), Group Footer, Page Footer, and Summary bands. A band may consist of any number of lines subject to the constraint that the maximum number of lines in the report definition is 255. The maximum width of a report is 255 columns, but FoxReport allows the fields in the Detail band to be stretched vertically so that the field data can be printed within a fixed number of columns. The maximum number of Group levels in a report is 20.

To speed up the process of designing reports, FoxReport includes a Quick Report facility when nothing has yet been defined in the Detail band. The two report layouts supported are Column and Form (dBASE IV has a third layout, MailMerge, that is not supported by FoxPro). Column layout is similar to the result of FoxBASE's REPORT FORM command, where fields are arranged in tabular form. Here, the field names act as column headings and are placed in the Page Header band. Fields that overflow the dimensions of the report are not included. Form Layout resembles the format of the FoxPro Edit screen, where each field is in a row preceded by the field name.

The Report Expression Dialog (shown in Figure 11-1) can be used to help define how you want a report field to display on the report. For instance, you can define the field's format or total option (such as count, sum, average, lowest, or highest). Choosing the <Expr...> button brings up the Expression Builder (Figure 11-2) to help you formulate the desired field expression. The expression can consist of one or more database fields; the appropriate math, string, logical, or date functions; as well as user-defined functions. By checking the Verify box, you can ask FoxReport to confirm that the report expression you just built is correct.

Including Percentages in a Report

Suppose your report includes a column for a numeric field, say, Salary, and you want to print alongside it another column that shows each record's salary value as a percentage of the total. You can easily do this in FoxReport. First, you'll need to compute the total value for the field and then store it in some memory variable, say, TotSalary. The SUM command that does that for you is as follows:

```
SUM salary TO TotSalary.
```

Next, include in the detail band of the report, a calculated field with the expression (Salary / TotSalary) * 100. The report column with the desired percentages now prints every time you invoke the report with the REPORT FORM command.

So that you don't forget to issue the SUM command before calling up the report form, you might want to write a two-line program that includes the SUM and REPORT FORM commands one after the other.

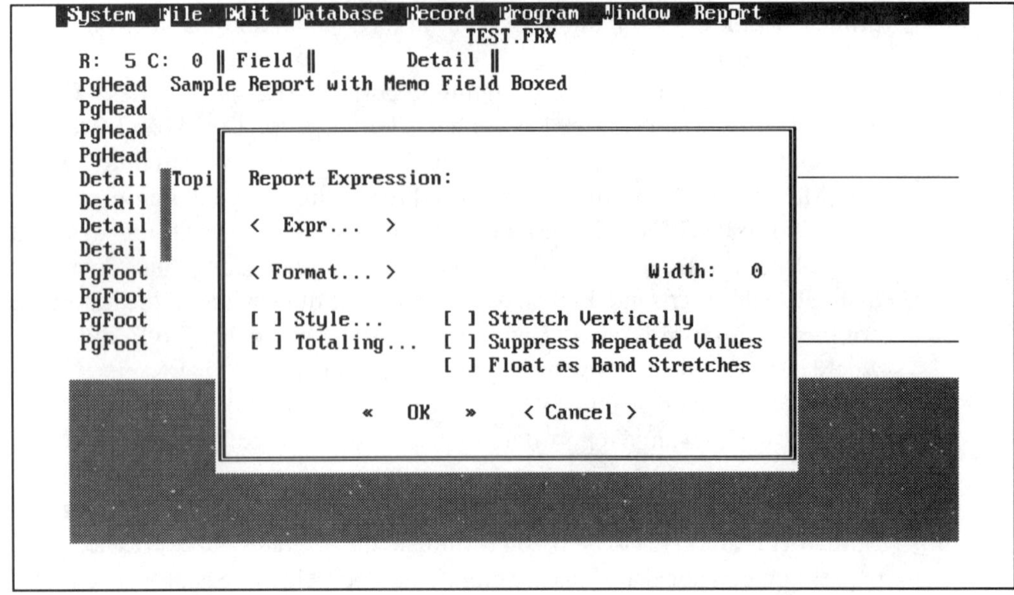

Figure 11-1. The FoxReport Expression Dialog screen.

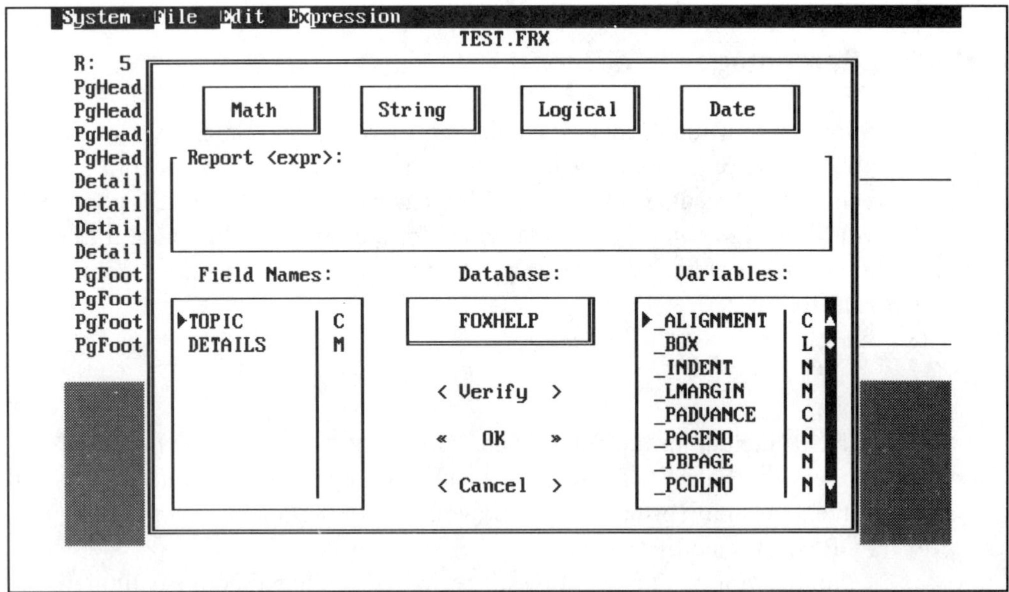

Figure 11-2. The FoxReport Expression Builder.

The FoxPro Report Form File

When you compose a report using the CREATE REPORT <RptName> command, FoxPro creates a report form file with the name <RptName>.frx, which contains the report layout and data that you defined. FoxPro uses the information stored in this file to produce the report when you issue the REPORT FORM <RptName> command. Unlike dBASE IV, FoxPro 1.02 does not translate the file into a program that it can then execute. Thus, although dBASE IV lets you further customize the translated program (.frg file) according to your needs (just like any other program) or even use it as a learning tool, FoxPro does not provide you with the same facility. However, a dBASE IV .frg file can be run using FoxPro with minor modifications.

Even though FoxPro does not automatically produce the equivalent of dBASE IV's .frg file, you can write a utility program that will if you know the format of a FoxPro .frx file. You and others can then customize the program as needed. This section describes the format of a .frx file.

All the information in a FoxPro .frx file is represented with ASCII characters. The file consists of a collection of Object records. There are five types of Object records in a FoxPro report, and each has a unique Object identifier. The Object types are shown in Table 11-1.

Unlike the format (.frm) file of dBASE III Plus and compatibles, which has a fixed record length of 1990 bytes, the .frx file has variable length. There are two reasons for this. First, the number of Object records in the file depends on how many objects were defined during CREATE/MODIFY REPORT—the .frx file contains one record for every report object defined. Second, the nature (and length) of the data contained in an object depends on the Object type, so the length of the record also varies depending on the Object type.

What constitutes an Object record? A record consists of fields. Each record, regardless of Object type, consists of 25 fields (although some are unused), but the type of fields contained in an Object record depends on the object. For instance, a Text object contains a field defining the actual text and its length, a Report Field object has a field containing the field expression, and a Band Information object contains a field defining the type of band.

Each field is delimited by the tab character (09h), and each record is terminated by a carriage return (0Dh) and linefeed (0Ah) character. Figure 11-3 shows an annotated hexadecimal dump of a portion of a .frx file that contains a report field object record. The report field shown is the database field Custdemo->Cust_Id. Note that the record begins with the Object type identifier, which is 17 in this case because it is a report field record. The figure shows the various fields in the Object record, including the field expression

Table 11-1. Object Types in a FoxPro Report

Object Id	Object Type
1	Screen
5	Text
7	Box
17	Report Field
18	Band Information

(custdemo->cust_id), the field type ("C"), the vertical and horizontal position of the field on the report, as well as its height and width. Note that the record ends with the 0Dh, 0Ah sequence.

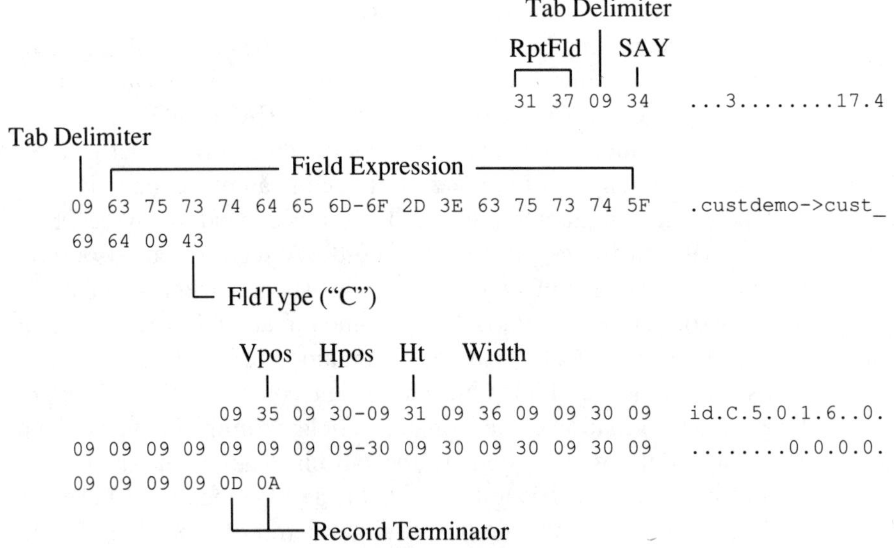

Figure 11-3. The anatomy of a report field object record.

Table 11-2. Fields of a Screen Object Record

Field #	Field	Field Value
0	Screen	1
1	Version	ASCII 1100 for char-based reports
2	Resource FileName	
3	Heading	
4	Vertical Position	
5	Horizontal Position	
6	Height	
7	Width	
8	Font Name	
9	Printer Offset	
10 –16	Reserved	
17–20	Null	
21	View File Info	

Tables 11-2, 11-3, 11- 4, 11-5, and 11-6 show the fields contained in a Screen, Text, Box, Report Field, and Band Information Object record, respectively. All records have the same types of data in the last three fields, so these fields are omitted from the tables. The omitted fields and the data they contain are as follows:

Field #	Field/Contents
22	Null
23	User comments
24	User data

Table 11-3. Fields of a Text Object Record

Field #	Field	Field Value
0	Text	5
1	SAY	Single-line box = 30h Double-line box = 31h GET (Input) = 32h SAY (Output) = 34h
2	Actual Text	
3	Null	
4	Vertical Position	
5	Horizontal Position	
6	Height	
7	Width of actual text	
8	Null	
9 –16	Reserved	
17–18	Null	
19	Top/Float	Top = 30h Stretch = 31h Float = 33h Float & Stretch = 34h
20–21	Null	

Only a position holder is present in a null field; there are no characters between the tab delimiters. Similarly, when a field is marked Reserved (for future use), only a tab delimiter appears in the field's position.

Listing 11-1 shows ReadFrx.c, a C language program that can be run from the DOS command line to list all the report fields specified in a .frx file. It is intended to show how you might begin to develop a DOS utility program that reads the report definition encoded in a .frx file and translates it into a FoxPro program similar to dBASE IV's report program (.frg) file. ReadFrx.c relies on the structure of the report form file described in this section.

Table 11-4. Fields of a Box Object Record

Field #	Field	Field Value
0	Box	7
1	Box Type	Single-line box = 30h Double-line box = 31h Character Line box = 32h
2–3	Null	
4	Vertical Position	
5	Horizontal Position	
6	Height	
7	Width	
8	Null	
9	Font Size	Single/double-line box = 30h For character box, the binary value of the character used is shifted 8 bits to the left and its value placed in the field as base 10-ASCII characters.
10 –16	Reserved	
17	Null	
18	Reserved	
19	Top/Float	Top = 30h Stretch = 31h Float = 33h Float & Stretch = 34h
20 –21	Null	

Printing Memo Fields

Memo fields included in a REPORT FORM print as expected, wrapping within the print columns assigned to them and printing correctly during page breaks. If you want a report where a memo field prints inside a box, you

Table 11-5. Fields of a Report Field Object Record

Field #	Field	Field Value
0	Report Field	17
1	SAY	Single-line box = 30h Double-line box = 31h GET (Input) = 32h SAY (Output) = 34h
2	Field Expression	
3	Field Type	C, D, L, M, N
4	Vertical Position	
5	Horizontal Position	
6	Height	
7	Width	
8	Null	
9 –17	Reserved	
18	Once/NoDup	Once = 30h No Duplicate = 31h
19	Top/Float	Top = 30h Stretch = 31h Float = 33h Float & Stretch = 34h
20	Total Type	No total = 0 Count = 1 Sum Total = 2 Average = 3 Minimum = 4 Maximum = 5
21	Reset Total	Report end = 0 Page end = 1 Column end = 2 Group end = 3 - 22

Table 11-6. Fields of a Band Information Object Record

Field #	Field	Field Value
0	Band Information	18
1	Band Type	Title = 030h Page header = 31h Group header = 33h Detail = 34h Group footer = 35h Page footer = 36h Summary = 37h
2	Group Expression	
3	Null	
4	Page Break	Group Hdr, Page Brk off = 0 Group Hdr, Page Brk on = 1 Null in all other cases
5	Reserved	
6	Height	
7	Reserved	
8	Null	
9	Swap Header	
10	Swap Footer	
11–21	Null	

should define the box, place the memo field at the appropriate column inside the box, and check the options Stretch Vertically and Float as Band Stretches in the Report Expression Dialog screen.

On a custom report, you can still display a memo field inside a box by setting the dimensions of the box slightly larger than the MEMOWIDTH setting and the number of lines in the memo field. The PrtMemo.prg proce-

Listing 11-1. ReadFrx.c, a C language program that reads a FoxPro .frx file and lists all the report fields defined in the file.

```
/*****************************************************************
 * Program: ReadFrx.C
 * Author : P.L. Olympia & Kathy Cea
 * Purpose: Reads a FoxPro .frx file, extracts the report field
 *        :  data, and display the contents on the screen.
 *        :
 * Syntax : ReadFrx <file name>
 *        :  where <file name> is the .frx file
 *        :  If no extension is provided for <file name>, .frx
 *        :  is assumed.
 *        :
 *        : Compile in Turbo C, version 2.0
 *****************************************************************/

#include <stdio.h>
#include <string.h>

#define MAXPROG     24
#define TAB         0x09
#define MAXLINE 1000  /* Arbitrarily assign max line length of 1000
bytes */
#define NUMFIELDS 22  /* Number of fields defined in report field re-
cord */
#define MAXFIELD 256  /* Maximum width of any field in record */

FILE *fp;
char frxfile[MAXPROG];
char rec_buffer[MAXLINE];
char field[NUMFIELDS][MAXFIELD];
char fieldexpr[MAXFIELD];
int foundend,
    fieldid,
    startpos,
    endpos,
    i;
```

(continued)

Listing 11-1. Continued

```
/* Define the field order in the report field record */
/* We define only those we are interested in */
int fldexpr = 3,
    vertpos = 5,
    horzpos = 6,
    width = 8;

main(int argc, char *argv[])
{
    /* Display program syntax if no file name supplied */
    if(argc < 2) {
        printf("ReadFrx - program to list .frx file report fields\n");
        printf("Usage is:   ReadFrx  <file-name>\n");
        printf("            where <file-name> is the .frx file\n");
        exit(1);
    }
    strcpy(frxfile,argv[1]);
    /* Assume extension of .frx if none supplied */
    if (strstr(frxfile,".") == NULL)
        strcat(frxfile,".frx");

    if ((fp=fopen(frxfile, "rt"))==NULL) {
        printf ("\nERROR: Unable to open %s", frxfile);
        exit(1);
    }
    foundend = 0;
    fgets(rec_buffer,MAXLINE,fp);
    do
    {
        /*Each field on each line is separated by a TAB character */
        /* Search for TABs to define start & end of fields */
        startpos = 0;
        endpos = findtab(rec_buffer,startpos);
        strncpy(field[1], &rec_buffer[startpos],(endpos - startpos));
        field[1][(endpos - startpos)] = '\0';
        fieldid = atoi(field[1]);
```

(continued)

Listing 11-1. Continued

```
        /* ID of 17 used for report fields */
        if (fieldid == 17) {
            for (i = 2;i <= NUMFIELDS;i++) {
            /* Read field values into array */
                startpos = endpos + 1;
                endpos = findtab(rec_buffer,startpos);
                strncpy(field[i], &rec_buffer[startpos], (endpos -
startpos));
                /* Make sure array element is null-terminated */
                field[i][(endpos - startpos)] = '\0';
            }
            /* Display selected fields to screen */
            printf("\nField: ");
            printf("%s\n",field[fldexpr]);
            printf("Vertical: %d\t",atoi(field[vertpos]));
            printf("Horizontal: %d\t",atoi(field[horzpos]));
            printf("Width: %d\n",atoi(field[width]));
        }
        if (fgets(rec_buffer,MAXLINE,fp) == NULL)
            foundend = 1;
    }
    while (!foundend);
}
int findtab(char *rec_buffer, int startpos)
/* Finds position of next tab, end-of-line, or EOF in rec_buffer */
{
    int foundtab,
        i;

    foundtab = 0;
    if (!rec_buffer[startpos])
        return (startpos);
    for (i = startpos;rec_buffer[i] && !foundtab;i++)
    {
        if ((rec_buffer[i] == TAB) ||
            (rec_buffer[i] == '\n') ||
```

(continued)

Listing 11-1. Continued

```
                (rec_buffer[i] == EOF))
                foundtab = 1;
        }
        return(i-1);
    }
```

dure, shown in Listing 11-2, prints a memo field beginning at a specified column inside a box. The procedure uses MEMLINES( ) to determine the number of lines in the memo field and assigns the height of the box to be 2 larger than MEMLINES( ) to account for the box characters. Similarly the procedure assigns the box width to be 2 larger than the MEMOWIDTH setting. Note that the system memvar _box must be .T. in order for the box to print. The procedure determines the number of print positions in the line using the two system memvars _rmargin and _lmargin. The procedure defines the number of print positions to be the MEMOWIDTH setting if it is less than the specified print width.

A memo field may also be printed at precise locations on a page without regard to the MEMOWIDTH setting. For instance, the command

```
?? memofld FUNCTION "J;V45" AT 10
```

prints the field centered between columns 10 and 55, wrapping the field in a column width of 45.

System Memory Variables

FoxPro automatically maintains a set of system memory variables to control the nature and appearance of printer and screen output. These memory variables are initialized with default values on startup. They are unaffected by the RELEASE or CLEAR MEMORY commands, although their values may be changed at any time. Appendix D briefly describes each system memvar.

System memvars such as _wrap that control the appearance of a paragraph have rendered FoxBASE+ or dBASE III programs that allow wordwrapping

Listing 11-2. PrtMemo.prg prints a memo field inside a box.

```
PROCEDURE PrtMemo
************************************************************
* Program ...: PrtMemo.prg
* Author ....: P. L. Olympia and Kathy Cea
* Purpose....: Prints specified memo field inside a box of
*            : given width beginning at specified column
* Syntax ....: DO PrtMemo WITH <memofld>, <col>, <width>
* Notes .....: Actual print width is either the specified
*            : width or number of print positions in the line
*            : whichever is less
************************************************************
PARAMETERS memofld, col, width

OldWidth = SET("MEMO")
Memwidth = MIN(_rmargin - _lmargin,  width)
SET MEMOWIDTH TO Memwidth
DEFINE BOX FROM col-1 TO (col+Memwidth+1);
    HEIGHT MEMLINES(&memofld) + 2
_box = .T.        && Must be True for box to print
?
?? &memofld AT col
?
?
_box  = .F.
SET MEMOWIDTH TO Oldwidth
RETURN
```

of long text obsolete. Thus, to print a mailmerge letter, all you need to do is set the memvar _wrap to .T.; define the application's alignment, indent, and margins; and then print the text using the ?/ ?? command. For instance,

```
_wrap = .T.
_indent = 5           && indentation of paragraph's 1st line
_lmargin = 10         && left margin
_rmargin = 70         && right margin
```

```
_alignment = [LEFT]    && left justify
? details              && print the text
```

Note that paragraph-specific memvars such as alignment and margins have no effect on the output unless _wrap is set to TRUE. If the text to be printed is a memo field, the resulting output is affected by the values of the system memvars as well as by the current setting of MEMOWIDTH.

With some system memvars you do not have to remember and issue control characters to the printer to achieve a desired result. For example, if you want to change the form (page) size, you can simply assign the appropriate value to the memvar _plength. Also, FoxPro keeps track of where you are on the page through the _plineno variable.

Page Handler

Remember the old days when you had to keep track of the number of lines that had been printed on a report so you would know when to write the report footer, issue a page break, and call the report's page header routine? With FoxPro, you won't have to work so hard to handle page breaks and the like. First, the system memvar _plineno automatically keeps track of the number of lines that have been printed on the page. Second, FoxPro's ON PAGE command provides a convenient way of handling end-of-page processing. With it you define what action to take during report generation when the output line reaches a specified line on the current page, for example,

```
ON PAGE [AT LINE <expN> <command>]
```

where <command> is usually a page break procedure.

The ON PAGE command is activated by EJECT PAGE or when the current line number reaches the number specified in the AT LINE clause. It is also activated automatically by the REPORT FORM command for reports that contain headers and footers. Invoking ON PAGE without the AT LINE clause disables the page handler.

Listing 11-3 shows a sample program that uses the page handler. It defines the trigger line number (AT LINE number) differently, depending on whether or not the report is single spaced. The page header routine writes the report title centered on the page. Above that, the routine writes the page number beginning with page 2. The page footer routine merely writes the revision date.

Listing 11-3. OnPage.prg, sample page handler.

```
PROCEDURE OnPage
************************************************************
* Program ...: OnPage.prg
* Author ....: P. L. Olympia and Kathy Cea
* Purpose....: Sample procedure to demonstrate FoxPro's
*            : ON PAGE command
* Syntax ....: DO OnPage
* Notes .....: Calls Pg_Brk, Pg_foot and Pg_Head
************************************************************
SET PRINT ON
Title = "My Report Title"

* Define OnPage AT Line depending on report spacing
OnPageLine = IIF(_pspacing > 1, _plength - (2 * _pspacing +1), ;
                               _plength - 6)

ON PAGE AT LINE OnPageLine DO Pg_Brk

DO Pg_head                          && Print page 1 header
SCAN ALL
   ? Field_1, Field_2               && Print fields
ENDSCAN
ON PAGE                             && disable PAGE handler
FOR i = _plineno TO OnPageLine STEP _pspacing
  ?
ENDFOR
DO Pg_foot
SET PRINT OFF
RETURN

PROCEDURE Pg_Brk
  DO Pg_foot
  DO Pg_head
RETURN

PROCEDURE Pg_foot
  ? 'Revised on ', DATE()
```

(continued)

Listing 11-3. Continued

```
  EJECT PAGE
RETURN

PROCEDURE Pg_head
  ?
  IF _pageno <> 1
     ? 'Page ' AT 65, LTRIM(STR(_pageno,4))
  ENDIF
  ?
  ? PADC(Title, _rmargin - _lmargin)
  ?
RETURN
```

Mailmerge Reports

Mailmerge reporting produces what may look like a custom letter by inserting information from a database record into a form letter template. In the past, this activity was handled by exporting the necessary data file from database management systems to full-featured word processing packages. For instance, we can use WordPerfect to produce mailmerge letters to a set of addressees from a FoxPro database. To do this, we would generate the required WordPerfect secondary merge files using the FoxPro COPY TO <txtfile> DELIMITED command. Much of the reluctance on the part of many to use Dbase or compatible software for mailmerge reports stems from the difficulty or tedium of exercising precise control over the printed page, including wordwrap. As we shall see, all that has changed with FoxPro. Indeed, a FoxPro mailmerge program, which has access to all of FoxPro's commands and functions, has numerous advantages over word processing software.

Simple mailmerge letters that do not require the insertion of database fields or functions in the body of the letter can be composed easily in any of the Dbase-compatible products. Here, we could just embed the letter inside a TEXT-ENDTEXT block and use the ?/ ?? commands to print the rest of the letter, including addressee information. Alternatively, we could store the letter as a memo field and print it with the ?/ ?? command.

Mailmerge letters that do require inserting database fields or functions in the body of the letter traditionally have been cumbersome to produce because of the excessive processing overhead associated with handling wordwrap correctly. In FoxPro, the system memvar _wrap and functions like RAT( ) greatly simplify coding a wordwrap routine.

Designing a Generalized FoxPro Mailmerge System

A generalized mailmerge system should be able to handle variable formatting requirements such as margin changes, hanging indents, and text alignment. It should also be able to use information from multiple data files and suppress segments of the letter for which the current database record has no information. For instance, it would be inappropriate to include in a letter to pet owners a paragraph expounding on the wonders of the company's new dog food product when the addressee is a cat owner.

A generalized mailmerge reporting system consists of three parts:

1. Letter template
2. Generic mailmerge routine
3. Mailmerge driver program that manages the first two.

To understand how the components fit together, consider a sample letter (Figure 11- 4) produced by such a system.

The Letter Template

The letter template that produced the letter in Figure 11- 4 is shown in Figure 11-5. Note that the template consists of fixed text and variable data. Variable data are bounded by delimiters. You are free to use any set of delimiters you want as long as they are consistent and will not appear in the letter in another context, for example, as a literal string. The sample presented in Figure 11-5 uses the following four types of delimiters:

1. The /* */ delimiter pair is used for comments. The generic mailmerge routine ignores comments.
2. The << >> delimiter pair is used for page format directives or processing directives. Examples of format directives include:

<<LM 5>>	Sets left margin to 5.
<<TS 5, 10>>	Sets tab stops to 5 and 10.

```
May 28, 1990

Mr. J. K. Jones
123 Main Street
Buffalo, NY 14022

Dear Mr. Jones:

     Thank you for your recent inquiry about our new product, For-
ever, the indestructible roofing material, Part Number TK3457.  En-
closed is the complete literature on this exciting product.

     The following are homeowners in your neighborhood who will be
able to provide you with testimonials about Forever's staying
power.

Emily Leak     555-3456
Earl Spout     555-4257

     If we can be of further assistance, please call our tollfree
number at 800-555-5432.

Sincerely,


Jim Roof
Accounts Manager
```

Figure 11-4. Sample letter produced by a mailmerge reporting system.

<<TAB>>	Executes a TAB command.
<<CR>>	Forces a hard carriage return.
<<IB>>	Begins indent.
<<RJ>>	Begins right justify.
<<WB>>	Begins wordwrap.
<<WE>>	Ends wordwrap.

Processing directives include looping constructs such as <<WHILE-ENDWHILE>> designed to retrieve database records that meet specific criteria.

```
/* Define page settings */
<<LM 5>>
<<RM 65>>
<<TS 5, 10, 15, 20>>

/* Define date format */
[[SET DATE MDY]]
{{DATE}}

{{TRIM(Customer->Cus_Title)}} {{TRIM(Customer->Cus_Fname)}}
  {{TRIM(Customer->Cus_Lname)}}
{{TRIM(Customer->Cus_Street)}}
{{TRIM(Customer->Cus_City)}} {{Customer->Cus_State}}
  {{Customer->Cus_Zip}}

Dear {{TRIM(Customer->Cus_Title)}} {{TRIM(Customer->Cus_Lname)}}

<<TAB>>Thank you for your recent inquiry about our new product,
{{TRIM(Product->Pro_Name)}}, {{TRIM(Product->Pro_Slogan)}},
{{TRIM(Product->Pro_PartN)}}. Enclosed is the complete literature
on this exciting product.

/* Include the next paragraph if there are testimonials */
<<IF SEEK(Customer->Cus_Zip, "Testimon")>>
The following are homeowners in your neighborhood who will be able
to provide you with testimonials about Forever's staying power.
<<WHILE Testimon->Tes_Zip = Customer->Cus_Zip>>
 {{TRIM(Testimon->Tes_Name)}} <<TAB>> {{Testimon->Tes_Phone}}
 [[SKIP IN Testimon]]
<<ENDWHILE>>
<<ENDIF>>

<<TAB>>If we can be of further assistance, please call our
tollfree number at 800-555-5432.

Sincerely, <<CR>><<CR>><<CR>>
Jim Roof
Accounts Manager
```

Figure 11-5. Sample letter template.

3. The {{ }} delimiter pair is used for FoxPro functions, variable names, field names, and expressions. For example, {{DATE( )}} prints today's date in the currently active date format.
4. The [[ ]] delimiter pair is used for FoxPro commands. For example, [[SET DATE MDY]] simply defines the date format to be MDY.

For maximum flexibility, you should store letter templates in a memo field of a letters database rather than storing them individually in small text files or hardcoding them in any program. Letter templates that are stored as memo fields can be easily retrieved and manipulated in FoxPro. If users need additional letters, you can simply provide them with another template in a different record rather than provide them with a completely different program. Users who are familiar with the database fields often become adept at creating additional letter templates of their own by copying and modifying those that they already use.

The Generic Mailmerge Routine

The generic mailmerge routine processes the letter template stored in a memo field by scanning the template for the four delimiter pairs and taking the appropriate action. For instance, it sets the relevant system memory variable when it encounters a format directive. Thus it issues the command

```
_rmargin = 65
```

when it encounters the directive <<RM 65>>, and it issues the command

```
_wrap = .T.
```

when it encounters the directive <<WB>>.

If the delimited string is a FoxPro command or function, the generic routine simply casts the string as a macro and then executes it. The routine also ensures that the letter template uses the delimiters correctly; for example, the delimiters should always appear in matching pairs.

The Mailmerge Driver Program

The driver program is responsible for setting the environment for the generic mailmerge routine. It opens the appropriate databases with their required

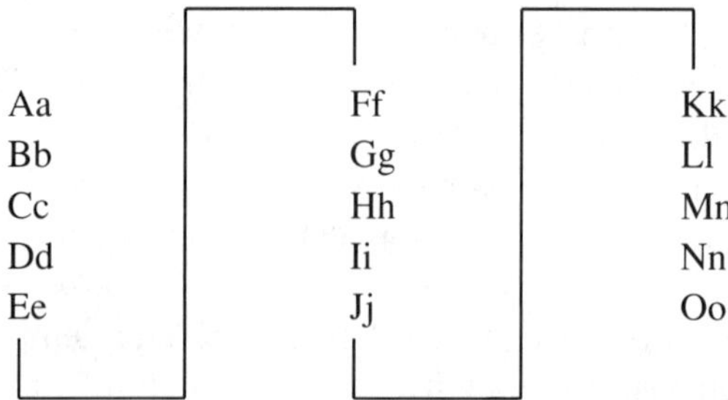

Figure 11-6. Snaked column schematic.

indexes, sets any required database relations, or, using the SEEK( ) function, positions the pointers of all databases to related records.

The program can include a user dialog to prompt the user for the desired letter template. The program then retrieves the appropriate template from the letters database and executes the generic mailmerge routine.

Snaked Column Reports

A snaked column report is a multicolumn report that resembles the format of a newspaper or telephone directory page. Entries on a page are arranged such that the item at the bottom of a given column is followed by the item at the top of the next column, rather than by the item to the right of it in the next column. Basically, in a snaked column report, order exists within a column, but not across columns. The schematic in Figure 11-6 shows a snaked column sequence typical of a telephone directory.

If the items to be included in a snaked column report will fit on a single line, for instance,

```
Name ........... Phone
```

the simplest way to handle the report is to use arrays. In the preceding example, you would loop through the indexed database, concatenating Name, the series of dots, and the phone number, and then assigning the whole string to an array element. Of course, the array solution assumes that no more than 3600 array elements are needed at one time. Assuming that the report only needs two columns and that the maximum number of items in a column is MaxPerCol, the code fragment that prints the report is simply

```
FOR i = 1 TO MaxPerCol
  ? item(i) AT 1, item(i+MaxPerCol) AT 41
ENDFOR
```

What happens if the items to be reported consist of multiple lines, for instance, a set of names and addresses similar to those in a mailing label? As you may suspect, the FoxPro mail label generator is a natural for the job because it allows multiple labels across a row. The trick is to index the database in such a way that the records appear in the order of the snaked column. Consider a report that requires 4 rows and 3 columns. The required index is one such that record 1, then record 5, and then record 9 are printed in the first row as shown here:

```
1   5   9
2   6   10
3   7   11
4   8   12
```

The following expression (Russell, 1989) gives the desired index.

```
INT(( RECNO() - 1/Recs_on_Page) * 1000 + ;  && accounts for page
  INT( MOD( RECNO() - 1), Recs_on_Page) / Num_rows + ; && rows
  MOD( RECNO() - 1), Num_Rows) * Num_Cols.             && cols
```

The snaked column report is then produced with the single command

```
LABEL FORM <LblName> NEXT Recs_on_Page TO PRINT.
```

Note that to maintain the proper snaked column format in the report's last page, there should be enough database records to produce Recs_on_Page number of entries. If there are not, you should append enough blank records to the database to fill the last page of the report.

The Structure of a Label (.LBX) File

When you define a label with the CREATE/MODIFY LABEL <LblName> command, FoxPro creates a file with the name <LblName>.lbx containing the label format and data you specified. The first 75 bytes of the file contain information pertaining to label dimensions and format. After that, the file contains the data (label expression) that will be printed on the label. Each

Table 11-7. The Structure of a Foxpro .lbx File

Byte	Contents
0	Version: 03 (FoxPro label)
01–60	Remarks
61–62	Number of lines in label
63–64	Column number of the left margin
65–66	Label width
67–68	Number of labels across row
69–70	Number of spaces between labels
71–72	Number of lines between labels
73–74	Length of expression contents
75–*n*	Label expression contents, separated by 0Dh.

label expression is terminated with a carriage return character, 0Dh. Table 11-7 summarizes the format of a FoxPro label file.

Listing 11- 4, ReadLbx.c, shows a C language utility program that reads a FoxPro mail label file and displays label format specifications and the field expressions contained in the label. The program demonstrates how you might use the structure information described in Table 11-7 to access or manipulate a mail label file.

Sending Commands Directly to the Printer

A control code sequence to take advantage of a specific printer capability (for example, go into landscape mode) may be issued directly to the printer using FoxPro's ??? command. The command leaves the printer row and column position unchanged. Thus it has the advantage over the usual FoxBASE+ (or dBASE III) command sequence such as

```
@ 2, 0 SAY CHR(27)+"G"    && Epson double strike mode
@ 2,20 SAY "Title"        && this prints beginning at 18, not 20
```

Listing 11-4. ReadLbx.c reads a FoxPro mail label file from the DOS command line and displays its contents on the screen.

```
/*****************************************************************
 * Program: ReadLbx.C
 * Author : P.L. Olympia & Kathy Cea
 * Purpose: Reads a .lbx file and extracts the format information
 *        :  and contents of label expressions,
 *        :  displaying the contents on the screen.
 *        :
 * Syntax : ReadLbx <file name>
 *        :  where <file name> is the .lbx file
 *        :  If no extension is provided for <file name>, .lbx
 *        :  is assumed.
 *        :
 *        : Compile in Turbo C, version 2.0
 *****************************************************************/
#include <stdio.h>
#include <string.h>

#define MAXPROG 24
#define FLDSEP 0x0d  /* Field Separator */
#define MAXLINE 1000 /* Maximum number of characters per line */
#define MAXEXPR 1000 /* Maximum length of label expression */
#define STARTEXPR 75 /* Start of field expression contents */

main(int argc, char *argv[])

{
char  vers;
char  remarks[61];
int   numlines,
      lmarg,
      width,
      labrow,
      numspc,
      numline,
      contlen;
```

(continued)

Listing 11-4. Continued

```
char expr[MAXEXPR];

/* Define starting positions (offsets) */
int versofs = 0,
    remofs = 1,
    numlnofs = 61,
    lmargofs = 63,
    widthofs = 65,
    labrowofs = 67,
    numspcofs = 69,
    numlineofs = 71,
    contlenofs = 73,
    exprofs = STARTEXPR;

FILE *fp;
char lbxfile[MAXPROG];
char rec_buffer[MAXLINE];
int foundend,
    startpos,
    endpos;

/* Display program syntax if no file name supplied */
    if(argc < 2) {
        printf("Readlbx - program to display .lbx file report
fields\n");
        printf("Usage is:   Readlbx  <file-name>\n");
        printf("            where <file-name> is the mail label
file\n");
        exit(1);
    }

    strcpy(lbxfile,argv[1]);
/* Assume extension of .lbx if none supplied */
    if (strstr(lbxfile,".") == NULL)
        strcat(lbxfile,".lbx");

/* Open in binary mode to preserve the carriage returns */
```

(continued)

Listing 11-4. Continued

```
        if ((fp=fopen(lbxfile, "rb"))==NULL) {
            printf ("\nERROR: Unable to open %s", lbxfile);
            exit(1);
        }

    /* All the data is stored in one record, so perform
       just one fget */
        fgets(rec_buffer,MAXLINE,fp);

    /* Get information in header area */
        vers = rec_buffer[versofs];
        strncpy(remarks,&rec_buffer[remofs],(numlnofs - remofs));
        remarks[(numlnofs - remofs)] = '\0';
        numlines = todec(&rec_buffer[numlnofs]);
        lmarg = todec(&rec_buffer[lmargofs]);
        width = todec(&rec_buffer[widthofs]);
        labrow = todec(&rec_buffer[labrowofs]);
        numspc = todec(&rec_buffer[numspcofs]);
        numline = todec(&rec_buffer[numlnofs]);
        contlen = todec(&rec_buffer[contlenofs]);

    /* Print the information we are interested in */
        printf("Label Information: \n");
        printf("\tNumber of lines in label: %d\n",numlines);
        printf("\tNumber of labels across row: %d\n", labrow);
        printf("\tNumber of lines between labels: %d\n", numline);
        printf("\t%s\n",remarks);
        printf("\nLabel Expression Contents:\n");

        startpos = exprofs;
        foundend = 0;
    /* Find each label expression, separated by carriage returns */
        do {
            endpos = nextdelim(rec_buffer,startpos,contlen);
            if (endpos == startpos)
                foundend = 1;
```

(continued)

Listing 11-4. Continued

```
            else {
                strncpy(expr,&rec_buffer[startpos],(endpos - startpos));
                expr[(endpos - startpos)] = '\0';
                printf("\t%s\n",expr);
                startpos = endpos + 1;
                if (startpos >= (STARTEXPR + contlen - 1))
                    foundend = 1;
            }
        }
        while (!foundend);
    }

    int todec(char *ascstr)
    /* Convert the ASCII 2-byte string to decimal value */
    {
        return(ascstr[0] + (ascstr[1] * 256));
    }

    int nextdelim (char *rec_buffer, int startpos, int contlen)
    /* Finds position of next carriage return character or EOF in
    rec_buffer*/
    {
        int foundcr,
            i;

        foundcr = 0;
        if ((!rec_buffer[startpos]) || (rec_buffer[startpos] == EOF))
            return (startpos);
        for (i = startpos; !foundcr && i <= (STARTEXPR + contlen); i++)
        {
            if ((rec_buffer[i] == FLDSEP) ||
                (rec_buffer[i] == EOF))
                foundcr = 1;
        }
        return(i-1);
    }
```

where the two control codes to put the printer in double strike mode count as characters even though they do not print and thus do not move the printhead. The result is that the word "Title" begins printing at column 18, not 20. To get around this problem, the usual technique is to pad the first command with as many spaces as there are control codes in the command stream, for instance,

```
@ 2, 0 SAY CHR(15)+"G"+SPACE(2)
```

Both printable and nonprintable ASCII characters may be sent directly to the printer. Nonprintable characters may be referred to in a variety of ways, including the CHR( ) function, the ASCII digit enclosed in curly braces, and control character specifiers. Thus, noting that {ESC} is the control specifier for the <Escape> character (which also has the ASCII decimal code of 27), the following commands are all equivalent:

```
??? CHR(27)+"G"
??? "{ESC}G"
??? "{27}G"
??? "{27}{71}"          && "G" is ASCII decimal 71
```

The control character specifiers for ASCII code 1 through 26 are simply {CTRL-A} through {CTRL-Z}. FoxPro also recognizes the usual "names" for the common control codes, for example, {RETURN} for {CTRL-M} and {TAB} for {CTRL-I}.

In FoxPro, the control character specifier is not case sensitive as it is in dBASE IV. For instance, the following commands are all equivalent in FoxPro and will ring the printer bell.

```
??? "{CTRL-G}"
??? "{ctrl-G}"
??? "{ctrl-g}"
```

In dBASE IV, the last command has no effect on the printer because all it does is send the small letter "g" to the printer.

Sending Nulls to a Printer

Some printers require the null character (ASCII decimal 0, or CHR(0)) to be part of a command. For instance, the command to change the form length to 3 inches in an Epson LQ printer is

```
CHR(27) + "C" +  CHR(0) + CHR(3)
```

This has been a constant source of frustration to dBASE III PLUS and FoxBASE+ users. Neither program is unable to send the null byte because they use CHR(0) internally to mark the end of strings. Thus, if you want to print the letter "P" and you give the command:

```
?? CHR(80)
```

what you are really printing are two bytes, namely, the letter "P" followed by the null byte, which terminates the string. Similarly, the command

```
?? CHR(0)
```

should print two null bytes. However, the first null byte effectively terminates the string and the printer "sees" nothing.

Fortunately there are workarounds to the problem. First, you can write a .bin routine to send a null byte to a printer (see Listing 11-5 and the following discussion). The .bin routine can then be LOADed and later CALLed in any Dbase program. Second, some printers have alternative commands to those that involve the null byte, so those should be used instead. Third, printers such as those from the Okidata line ignore the eighth bit of the ASCII code, so the character CHR(128) may be used in place of CHR(0). Fourth, printers such as those from the Epson line have a command to turn off the eighth bit, so to send a null byte to a printer you would turn off the eighth bit, send CHR(128), and then turn on the eighth bit again.

For instance, suppose that you want to print addresses on 3-inch mailing labels using an Epson LQ printer. The FoxBASE+ code to change the form length to 3 inches is

```
SET PRINT ON
?? CHR(27) + "="                      && turn off eighth bit
?? CHR(27) + "C" + CHR(128) + CHR(4)  && form length to 3"
?? CHR(27) + ">"                      && turn on eighth bit
```

With FoxPro you no longer have to go through this roundabout procedure because the software can send the null byte to a printer without any problems. Thus the FoxPro equivalent to the preceding code is simply

```
??? "{ESC}C{NULL}{CTRL-C}"
```

where, again, codes such as {ESC} and {CTRL-C} are FoxPro control character specifiers. It appears that such codes are really one-byte characters and not null-terminated strings.

The ability of FoxPro to avoid the use of the null byte to terminate a string and determine its length has important ramifications. For instance, Russ Freeland (Freeland, 1989) has shown that the ??? command, with output redirected to a file, can be used to create small .bin, .com, or .exe files. Consider the assembly language program, PrtNull.asm, in Listing 11-5.

It is a utility that allows nulls to be sent to a printer from dBASE III or FoxBASE programs that cannot do it otherwise. Before you can use the utility, you must first assemble it, link it, and then use EXE2BIN to convert it to a .bin file. Alternatively, you can just write a three-line FoxPro program that does the same thing. The program is as follows:

```
SET PRINTER TO FILE prtnull.bin
???"PR1{210}{184}{0}{5}{205}!ZX{203}"
SET PRINTER TO
```

Redirecting Printer Output to a File

One of the most vexing deficiencies of dBASE III PLUS is its inability to redirect printer output produced by the @...SAY command to a file. This limitation is gone in FoxPro, which has a built-in facility to capture @...SAY command output to a file by way of the command

```
SET DEVICE TO FILE <filename>
```

Additionally, FoxPro streaming output, including that produced by the ??? command, can be directed to a file using the command

```
SET PRINTER TO FILE <filename>
```

followed by

```
SET PRINTER ON
```

Redirecting printer output to a file has several uses. One, it is useful for trapping an application system's reports for inclusion in the system documentation. Two, it is an indispensable tool for diagnosing program or printer

Listing 11-5. PrtNull.asm can be turned into a .bin file to allow Dbase programs to send nulls to a printer.

```
; PrtNull.asm
;

CODESEG SEGMENT PARA 'CODE'
        ASSUME CS:CODESEG

PRTNULL  PROC  FAR
         PUSH  AX
         PUSH  DX
         XOR   DX, DX
         MOV   AX, 0500H
         INT   21H
         POP   DX
         POP   AX
EXIT:
         RET
PRTNULL  ENDP
CODESEG  ENDS
         END   PRTNULL
```

problems. When a printer does not appear to respond correctly to commands being issued to it by a program, redirecting the output to a file permits closer examination of exactly what codes, if any, the printer is receiving from the program. Having seen too many networked printers, under the misguided direction of a run-away Dbase program, spew forth mountains of paper containing nothing but garbage, we can attest to the utility of redirecting printer output to a file if nothing else but to save the nation's trees.

Finally, redirecting printer output to a file permits testing of a program even when a printer is unavailable. The FoxPro PRINTSTATUS( ) or SYS(13) function may be used to determine if the printer is ready to accept output. However, if a print spooler is active, the PRINTSTATUS( ) function returns a logical true (.T.), and SYS(13) returns "ONLINE" regardless of the printer's actual status. Therefore, the presence of a print spooler also permits testing of a report-producing program even when a printer is unavailable.

Printing on a Network

Surely one of the rewards of networking is the facility for sharing expensive print devices such as laser printers. The traditional problem with printing on a network is that between the time an application system generates its report and the time the report actually prints, someone else on the network may have changed fonts or paper orientation. Sooner or later, you could wind up with a report printed sideways even if you had not intended it to be.

FoxPro/LAN has facilities that help manage printing on a network. For instance, the SET PRINTER TO command allows redirection of printer output to a local printer, a network printer, or a file. The network SET PRINTER TO command has two alternative forms. One form is

```
SET PRINTER TO [\\<machinename> \<printername> = <dest>]
```

which spools printer output to the network printer assigned the name <printername>. <machinename> is a unique name assigned to your workstation and <dest> may be LPT1, LPT2, or LPT3.

On a Novell network, the command can take the form

```
SET PRINTER TO [\\SPOOLER [\NB] [\F = <expN>]
 [\B = <expC>] [\C = <expN>] [\P = <expN>]
```

which has parameters similar to Novell's SPOOL or CAPTURE command. For instance, NB means no banner page, F refers to a form number, B specifies a banner name, C specifies the number of copies, and P identifies the network printer number.

The _pscode and _pecode system memvars, which define a printer initialization and deinitialization string, respectively, can be used to ensure that the printer is in the desired state for a given report. These memvars are particularly useful with the PRINTJOB/ENDPRINTJOB programming construct, which defines the environment for a print task. Unfortunately, since a typical network printer supports a multitude of applications including spreadsheet and word processing, users must agree on a standard printer deinitialization protocol so that users who either forget, or do not bother, to initialize the printer can expect to find the printer in a reasonably standard state.

Of course, this is easier said than done, and there is a better way. You could, for example, code a utility program that combines the functions provided by the Novell SPOOL or CAPTURE facility with your own printer configuration functions. Such a program would use a printer definition file that includes the escape sequences of all supported devices. The heart of the system is its ability to precede output from any workstation with user-specified printer control commands. Thus it does not matter in what state a previous network job leaves a printer—any report should print just the way you expect it to.

How is it done? Quite simply, by using two little-known DOS INT 21H extended functions. Function 5EH, Code 02H, is the Printer Setup function that takes a string of desired control characters and puts them at the beginning of every print job. Function 5FH, Code 02H, is the complement function that allows you to obtain the printer's "list entry index," from which you can identify the printer to which the control string will be sent. A printer with an entry index of 0 is the first printer on the list. Before invoking the Printer Setup function, you load the BX register with the entry index and the CX register with the length of the string.

Printjob and Endprintjob

Some system memvars (for example, _pcopies, _pecode, _peject, and _pscode) can be assigned values from the command window, but they can only be used in a program because they become active only with the PRINTJOB and ENDPRINTJOB commands. The PRINTJOB/ENDPRINTJOB commands are structured programming constructs that define the environment for a print task. The system memvars should be defined before the PRINTJOB statement. Output commands, including invocations of print procedures, should appear inside the PRINTJOB/ENDPRINTJOB construct. For example,

```
_pcopies = 2
_pscode = "<printer initialization string>"
_pecode = "<printer deinitialization string>"
_peject = "AFTER"
PRINTJOB
     ?/?? or DO <proc>
     .. other FoxPro commands including loops ..
ENDPRINTJOB
```

The PRINTJOB statement causes _pcolno (print column number) to be initialized to 0, the string assigned to _pscode to be sent to the printer, and the paper to be ejected if _peject has the value "BEFORE" or "BOTH." The ENDPRINTJOB statement causes the string assigned to _pecode to be sent to the printer, a page to be ejected if _peject has the value "AFTER" or "BOTH," and the statements within the PRINTJOB loop to be executed the number of times defined by _pcopies. Only the pages that are within the range specified by the _pbpage (begin page number) and _pepage (end page number) system memvars are output by the print job.

Chapter Summary

FoxPro has a powerful set of report writing and printing facilities to handle even the most intricate reports. Its built-in report writer, FoxReport, provides a WYSIWYG work surface with report bands that can be painted with database fields, text, lines, and boxes. The report writer's expression dialog facilitates the formulation and verification of report field expressions. Vertical stretch and floating band options permit maximum utilization of the 255 columns allowed in a report. With FoxReport, printing memo fields in a box and printing a column showing a numeric field's value as a percentage of the total are almost trivial exercises.

In this chapter, we described the format of a FoxPro report form (.frx) in detail. Unlike dBASE IV, FoxPro does not translate the report definition encoded in the file to a program that you can then customize further. Knowing the format of the .frx file is the first step you need to translate the report into a program. Here, we showed a program, ReadFrx.c, which gives you a headstart at developing such a utility that can be run from the DOS command line. We also described the format of a FoxPro mail label (.lbx) file in detail and showed a utility program, ReadLbx.c, to list the contents of the file.

FoxPro's page handler, activated by the ON PAGE command, eases end-of-page processing such as the handling of page headers and footers. It specifies the action to take when an EJECT PAGE command is issued or when a specified line number is reached during report generation.

In this chapter, we also discussed mailmerge reporting and the design of a generalized mailmerge system. We described a generic mailmerge routine that uses a set of delimiter pairs in a letter template to handle page format directives, processing directives, FoxPro commands and functions, field names, and expressions. We also discussed two strategies for snaked column reporting, including a technique that uses the facilities offered by the mail label generator.

Commands can be issued directly to the printer using the ??? command, which also leaves the printer row and column unchanged. Unlike FoxBASE+ and dBASE III Plus, FoxPro can send the null character to a printer. Thus, with FoxPro, we can create .bin files on the fly using only the ??? command with the output redirected to a file instead of a printer.

The SET PRINTER TO command allows output to be directed to a local device, network printer, or a file. The SET DEVICE TO command can redirect @...SAY output to a file. FoxPro's ability to redirect printer output to a file, including those generated by the @...SAY command, can be used to test programs even when a printer is unavailable. The presence of an unfilled print spool causes the PRINTSTATUS( ) function to always yield .T. and therefore can be used also to test a program in the absence of a printer.

FoxPro automatically maintains system memvars to control the appearance of printed output, including page margins and alignment. System memvars cannot be released by the RELEASE or CLEAR MEMORY commands, but they are initialized with default values on startup.

Chapter 12

Low-Level File I/O

FoxPro provides a set of low-level input/output (I/O) functions that offer the ability to manipulate files of any format. They are particularly valuable in accessing non-FoxPro formatted files. The functions are comparable to I/O functions available with the C programming language and, like C, can be used for buffered or unbuffered I/O. Although the set FoxPro provides is actually a subset of the functions typically found in a C compiler, the FoxPro functions offer a great deal of programming power and flexibility. The FoxPro low-level file I/O functions are summarized in Table 12-1.

Note that files opened with FoxPro's FOPEN (when opened for writing) and FCREATE functions open the file for exclusive use. If FOPEN is used to open a file with read-only privileges (<expN> is 0 or 10), the file is opened for shared use.

How does buffered file I/O compare to unbuffered I/O? Buffered I/O systems use a temporary storage area in memory called a buffer to store data being read from or written to a disk file. The program actually reads from and writes to the buffer. When data is read from disk, a fixed number of bytes are read and stored in the buffer. Thus a request for additional data does not require an additional disk read if the requested data is already contained in the buffer.

This method provides more efficient file I/O since it requires fewer disk accesses. However, since updates are written to the buffer and not immediately back to disk, the buffer must be "flushed" (written back to disk) before any updates will appear in the disk file. As Table 12-1 shows, the FCLOSE function, which should be called to close a file, flushes the associated buffer. Therefore, a program that terminates normally flushes all file buffers before

Table 12-1. FoxPro Low-Level File I/O Functions

Function	Description
FCHSIZE	Changes the size of the file and returns the final size in bytes. (The file must be opened with read/write privileges in order for its size to be changed.)
FCLOSE	Writes file buffers to disk and closes the file.
FCREATE	Creates a file for input and/or output and returns a numeric file handle.
FEOF	Returns .T. or .F., indicating whether the file pointer is at the end of the file (EOF).
FERROR	Returns a nonzero value if the last file function caused an error; otherwise, returns zero.
FFLUSH	Writes file buffers to disk.
FGETS	Returns a string of characters from the file. If a number is provided, returns the specified number of bytes (or fewer, if a carriage return is encountered); otherwise, returns all characters from the current pointer position until the next carriage return.
FOPEN	Opens a previously created file for input and/or output and returns a numeric file handle.
FPUTS	Writes the specified character string to a file, adding a carriage return and line feed, and returns the number of bytes that were written.
FREAD	Returns a specified number of bytes from a file.
FSEEK	Moves the file pointer in a file and returns the current pointer position.
FWRITE	Writes characters to a file, returning the number of bytes that were written to the file.

exiting. Updates that have not yet been flushed to disk are lost if a program terminates abnormally.

Unbuffered file I/O systems, on the other hand, do not use a buffer in memory, but perform all file I/O directly on the disk file. These functions are inherently less efficient than their buffered counterparts, but they have the advantage that the disk file will contain current updates even if the program terminates abnormally. By default, FoxPro opens files for buffered I/O, unless the file being opened is a communications port (COM1 or COM2).

Comparison with the C File I/O Functions

FoxPro's file I/O functions perform essentially the same processing as their C counterparts. However, experienced C programmers should note the minor discrepancies between the two. One difference is that FoxPro uses a numeric file handle, whereas the C buffered file I/O system uses a FILE pointer for a file handle. This should be transparent to the FoxPro programmer.

The file I/O functions in C and FoxPro have subtle differences. The return values differ for many of these functions. In many cases, FoxPro returns .T. or .F. to indicate the function's success or failure, whereas the C functions typically return a zero or nonzero value. C does not have a function equivalent to FCREATE. To create a new file in C, the FOPEN function is called with a specific file access mode parameter indicating that a new file is to be created.

C functions that return a string (for example, FREAD and FGETS) typically require a pointer to a buffer for storage of the string; the equivalent FoxPro functions simply return the string to the calling procedure. Also, some parameters that are required in C (such as the origin for the FSEEK function and the maximum number of characters for the FGETS function) are optional in FoxPro.

Formats for the functions differ significantly for the FGETS, FPUTS, FREAD, and FWRITE functions. Also, there is no FCHSIZE function in C.

These comparisons between FoxPro and C functions are based on the C functions found in the Microsoft C and Borland Turbo C compilers.

Uses of the Low-Level File I/O

So far we have just discussed the low-level file I/O functions and compared them to equivalent C functions. But how are they used normally? Primarily, these functions are used to read from and/or write to any non-FoxPro formatted file. They allow you to manipulate any file directly, regardless of its format.

The advantages to using these functions should become clearer after a few examples. You can manipulate text files as well as binary files directly.

Although there are alternatives to working with text and binary files from within FoxPro, the low-level functions are simpler and more efficient.

Manipulating Text Files

Sometimes an application system needs to read from or write to a file that was not created by FoxPro. For example, an application may need to report from an existing free-formatted text file. There are several ways to accomplish this in FoxPro.

One option is to create a "scratch" or temporary file and append data from the alien data file to the temporary .dbf. Since there is no means for selectively appending data records from a free-formatted text file, the entire data file would be appended to the .dbf. This could result in a very large temporary file. The use of the low-level file I/O functions saves both disk space and processing time. No temporary storage is required, and the record-by-record overhead is minimized by sequentially reading each line and determining whether further processing is required on a line-by-line basis.

For example, consider a 20,000-line text file in which you want to locate and process only 10 lines. Using the scratch .dbf method, you must create a temporary .dbf containing one character field of the maximum width of 254. You must allocate the maximum number of characters because you do not know the size of the longest line in your text file. Next, you must append the entire text file into the scratch .dbf because you have no way to selectively append data. This means that you will have 20,000 records in your scratch .dbf. Now, to locate the desired 10 lines, you search record by record through your .dbf.

To perform this same process using low-level functions, you simply open your text file directly and read each line until you locate the ones you want. No temporary storage is required, and the overhead of a record-by-record search through a database is eliminated. Once you locate the lines you want, you can process them further by perhaps importing only these lines into a .dbf file.

Another option for reading the text file uses a shareware program called MAKEMEM, written by Andrew Schulman. This utility accepts a text file as input and writes a series of memory variables to a .mem file. Each line in the file is written to a different memory variable. A FoxPro program can process each memory variable in turn in order to process the entire report file one line at a time. This alternative also has limitations. First, the maximum number of variables that can be created by MAKEMEM is 235, thus limiting the size of the text file to 235 nonblank lines. Second, temporary storage (memory) is required for each line of the file.

The following example shows how you might use MAKEMEM to import text data into a FoxPro application. Assume that you are writing a floppy disk catalog program and need to import the disk's filenames into your database. As long as you have no more than 235 files in any one disk, an efficient way to do that is to run the DOS DIR command and pipe the output to MAKEMEM. When you issue the command

```
!DIR | MAKEMEM -x disk
```

MAKEMEM creates a memory file, Disk.mem, containing one memory variable (named Var_1, Var_2, and so on) for each line of output from the DIR command, along with the memory variable MemNum which tells you how many memory variables the program created. For instance, the following lines from the DISPLAY MEMORY command show the values of Var_3 and Var_4:

```
VAR_3       pub  C    "FILES     LST     43092    1-01-90   12:42p"
VAR_4       pub  C    "CALCULON TXT       4992    1-01-90   11:42a"
```

Clearly the filenames that your disk catalog program needs can be extracted as substrings from the values of the memory variables.

The low-level file I/O functions eliminate some of the limitations imposed by these alternate methods by permitting direct access to the text file. With these functions, the FoxPro program may open the text file, read from and/or write to the file, and close the file without requiring additional temporary storage or the use of a utility program.

Let's consider the use of the low-level functions for reading a network system error file. A good example of this is the Net$Log.Msg file used on a Novell LAN (described in Chapter 14). The Net$Log.Msg file is available to programmers for recording system errors or for recording user access to particular applications. Assume that an application has written a series of messages to this file as errors occurred, as shown in Figure 12-1. A FoxPro program can be written to provide summary reporting of the error messages reported by a given application. The sample program shown in Listing 12-1 performs this function by reading the Net$Log.Msg file and determining for each record whether it was written by the application identified in the ApplName parameter. For each record found, the appropriate counter is incremented.

```
06/26/90 15:39 STN  8:   Inventory  Mod1 Error opening Stock.Dbf file
06/26/90 15:42 STN  8:   Inventory  Mod3 Error printing report
06/27/90 09:22 STN  2:   Financial  Mod2 Unable to obtain record lock
06/27/90 12:00 STN 12:   Sales  Mod1 Error writing to Comm.Dbf
06/27/90 12:54 STN 10:   Sales  Mod4 Error printing report
06/27/90 15:42 STN  8:   Inventory  Mod3 Missing Parts.Dbf file
06/28/90 09:22 STN  2:   Financial  Mod2 User abort
06/29/90 12:00 STN 12:   Sales  Mod2 Error writing to Customers.Dbf
06/29/90 12:54 STN  5:   Sales  Mod4 User Abort
06/29/90 13:00 STN  7:   Sales  Mod1 Unable to obtain file lock
06/29/90 14:54 STN 14:   Sales  Mod4 User Abort
06/29/90 15:00 STN 12:   Sales  Mod2 Corrupted Index
06/29/90 16:54 STN 10:   Sales  Mod4 Missing Comm.Dbf
```

Figure 12-1. Sample Net$Log.Msg file.

This simple example returns only a count of errors found and assumes that the application has exactly four modules. Of course, it could be enhanced to allow for a variable number of modules and to provide additional summary reporting. To do this, we could use an array to keep track of errors by module.

In addition to providing a count of errors by module, the program deletes the records as they are processed. Actually, to delete records, the program rewrites the Net$Log.Msg file to a temporary file, writing only those records not processed, and finally overwrites Net$Log.Msg with the new file. Note that in order to run this program, the user (presumably the network SUPERVISOR) must have full rights to the Novell NetWare SYS:SYSTEM directory, the directory where the Net$Log.Msg file resides.

A sample report from this program (using a parameter of Sales) is shown in Figure 12-2.

Another good use of the FoxPro low-level file I/O functions is for extracting data from a large text file. Data can be read from a non-FoxPro formatted file in order to respond to a user query or to be included in a .dbf file. For example, consider a system designed to report budget figures for a selected department. This application reads a large budget file (stored as a text file) containing figures for all departments within a company, and it returns only those numbers pertaining to the specified department. Figure 12-3 shows a sample portion of a company budget report stored as a text file used for this example.

To extract data from the budget report using the scratch .dbf method, the FoxPro program would have to append a potentially large company report to

Listing 12-1. RdNetErr.prg, procedure to read the NetWare Net$Log.Msg file.

```
PROCEDURE RdNetErr
****************************************************************
* Program: RdNetErr.prg
* Author : P. L. Olympia and Kathy Cea
* Purpose: Reads the Net$Log.Msg file on a Novell NetWare LAN and
*        : tallies the count of errors reported for the application
*        : identified by the ApplName parameter.  Also deletes the
*        : records it processes by rewriting the Net$Log.Msg file.
*        :
* Syntax : Do RdNetErr WITH <applname>
*        : where <applname> is the name of the application to be
*        : reported against.
*        :
****************************************************************
PARAMETERS ApplName

* Set up environment
SET TALK OFF
SET SAFETY OFF

*Open Network message file for reading and
* temporary file to rewrite messages not
* processed
handle = FOPEN("SYS:SYSTEM\NET$LOG.MSG")
newhand = FCREATE("TEMP.MSG")
IF (handle < 0) .OR. (newhand < 0)
        ?"Can't open message file"
        RETURN
ENDIF

* Process Application identified by ApplName, assuming
* exactly 4 modules

Repl_Msg = .T.
Mod1Cnt = 0
Mod2Cnt = 0
Mod3Cnt = 0
```

(continued)

Listing 12-1. Continued

```
Mod4Cnt = 0
DO WHILE !FEOF(handle)
        rec = FGETS(handle)
        IF UPPER(ApplName) $ UPPER(rec)
                DO CASE
                CASE "Mod1"$rec
                        Mod1Cnt = Mod1Cnt + 1
                CASE "Mod2"$rec
                        Mod2Cnt = Mod2Cnt + 1
                CASE "Mod3"$rec
                        Mod3Cnt = Mod3Cnt + 1
                CASE "Mod4"$rec
                        Mod4Cnt = Mod4Cnt + 1
                ENDCASE
        ELSE
                write_out = FPUTS (newhand, rec)
                IF write_out = 0
                        ?"Error writing to NET$LOG.MSG file."
                        ?"File not modified"
                        Repl_Msg = .F.
                ENDIF
        ENDIF
ENDDO

*Close the network message file and the temporary file
* The = allows you to call a function without assigning the
*  return value to a memory variable or field
= FCLOSE(handle)
= FCLOSE (newhand)

*If no errors occurred writing the temporary file
* make a backup copy of the network message file then
* overwrite it with the temporary file
IF Repl_Msg
        COPY FILE SYS:SYSTEM\Net$Log.Msg TO SYS:SYSTEM\Net$Log.Sav
        COPY FILE Temp.Msg TO SYS:SYSTEM\Net$Log.Msg
```

(continued)

Listing 12-1. Continued

```
        DELETE FILE Temp.Msg
ENDIF
SET CONSOLE OFF
SET PRINTER ON
SET PRINTER TO ErrSumm.Rpt
?
?"SUMMARY OF ERRORS REPORTED TO SYSTEM ERROR FILE" AT 1
?
?"Date:" AT 1,DATE() AT 8,"Application: " AT 24,UPPER(ApplName) AT 38
?
?"Module Number           Count of Errors" AT 1
?
?"1" AT 6,LTRIM(STR(Mod1Cnt)) AT 32
?"2" AT 6,LTRIM(STR(Mod2Cnt)) AT 32
?"3" AT 6,LTRIM(STR(Mod3Cnt)) AT 32
?"4" AT 6,LTRIM(STR(Mod4Cnt)) AT 32
?
SET PRINTER TO
SET PRINTER OFF
SET CONSOLE ON
```

```
  SUMMARY OF ERRORS REPORTED TO SYSTEM ERROR FILE

Date:  07/02/90        Application: Sales

  Module Number            Count of Errors
      1                          2
      2                          2
      3                          0
      4                          4
```

Figure 12-2. Sample RdNetErr output.

```
ABC Corporation
Budget for FY 1990

Department:      Sales

Staff                                   $ 200,000
Commissions                               220,000
Office Furniture                           50,000
Supplies                                   10,000


Department:      Accounting

Staff                                   $ 500,000
Temporary Staff                           100,000
Equipment                                 250,000
Office Furniture                           70,000
Supplies                                   40,000

Department:      Data Processing

Staff                                   $ 300,000
Office Furniture                           12,000
Supplies                                   20,000
Equipment                                 200,000

Department:      Support

Staff                                   $ 150,000
Office Furniture                           50,000
Supplies                                   15,000
```

Figure 12-3. Portion of a sample company budget file.

a temporary, or "scratch" .dbf, and then process record by record to find the desired department and associated budget figures. Listing 12-2 demonstrates a process to read a text file containing budget data into a scratch .dbf, determine if the department specified in the Dept parameter is listed on the

Listing 12-2. RdTxtScr.prg, procedure to process a text budget file by reading it into a scratch .dbf.

```
PROCEDURE RdTxtScr
*******************************************************************
* Program: RdTxtScr.prg
* Author : P. L. Olympia and Kathy Cea
* Purpose: Reads a budget report in text format into a "scratch"
*        : .dbf file.
*        :
* Syntax : Do RdTxtScr WITH <budgfile>,<dept>
*        : where <budgfile> is the name of the file containing the
*        : budget report, and <dept> is the name of the department
*        : to be reported.
*******************************************************************
PARAMETERS BudgFile, Dept

* Set up environment
SET TALK OFF
SET SAFETY OFF

*Use temporary dbf to store contents of budget file
USE SCRATCH
APPEND FROM &BudgFile TYPE SDF
GO TOP

*Search Scratch.Dbf record-by-record until find Dept or
* End-of-File
Found = .F.
SCAN WHILE (.NOT. Found)
        IF (UPPER(Dept) $ UPPER(Line_Item))
                Found = .T.
        ENDIF
ENDSCAN

*Check whether Dept was found
IF .NOT. Found
```

(continued)

Listing 12-2. Continued

```
        ?"Department " AT 1, UPPER(Dept) AT 12
        ??" Budget not available"
        ZAP
        RETURN
ENDIF

*Send report to file
SET CONSOLE OFF
SET PRINTER ON
SET PRINTER TO Dept + ".Rpt"

EndDept = .F.
*Write report header
?"Budget for Department: " AT 1, UPPER(Dept) AT 25
?
?"Date:  " AT 1, DATE() AT 9
?
*Print each line item until find next Department
DO WHILE .NOT. EndDept
        SKIP
        IF ("DEPARTMENT" $ UPPER(Line_Item))
               EndDept = .T.
        ELSE
                ?SUBSTR(Line_Item,1,20)
                ??SUBSTR(Line_Item,40,12)
        ENDIF
ENDDO

*Close report file
SET CONSOLE ON
SET PRINTER OFF
SET PRINTER TO

*Zap temporary Scratch.Dbf
ZAP
```

```
Structure for database: D:\FOXCODE\SCRATCH.DBF
Number of data records:        0
Date of last update   : 12/06/89
Field  Field Name  Type        Width    Dec
    1  LINE_ITEM   Character     254
** Total **                      255
```

Figure 12-4. Structure of a scratch .dbf file.

report, and print a small report containing the figures for that department. Although this method works, it can potentially consume a large amount of disk space to temporarily store the budget file into a scratch .dbf, and it incurs extra overhead by processing database records sequentially. Note that the scratch .dbf (shown in Figure 12-4) structure simply contains one character field with a width of 254 (the maximum). Since we do not know how long the longest line will be in the budget file, we must allocate the maximum amount of space. Although most of the space goes unused, it still requires disk storage.

Listing 12-3 demonstrates the same process using low-level file I/O functions. A scratch .dbf is no longer needed because we can open and read the report file directly. We simply search each line in the budget file for the desired department. If found, we produce the same report provided by the last program. This method saves us disk space by not requiring temporary storage for the scratch file, and eliminates the database processing overhead by reading the file directly.

These sample programs simply write the desired budget information to a text file that uses the Department as the filename and .Rpt as the extension. Alternatively they could write the extracted budget information to a separate .dbf file for processing at a later date.

Working with Binary Files

In addition to providing an easier way to read from and write to text files, the low-level file I/O functions allow us to work with binary files. Without these functions, it is very difficult to read or write to a binary file from within FoxPro.

Listing 12-3. RdTxtLow.prg, procedure to process a text budget file using low-level file functions.

```
PROCEDURE RdTxtLow
*******************************************************************
* Program: RdTxtLOW.prg
* Author : P. L. Olympia and Kathy Cea
* Purpose: Reads a budget report in text format using low-level
*        : file I/O functions.
*        :
* Syntax : Do RdTxtLow WITH <budgfile>,<dept>
*        : where <budgfile> is the name of the file containing the
*        : budget report, and <dept> is the name of the department
*        : to be reported.
*******************************************************************
PARAMETERS BudgFile, Dept

* Set up environment
SET TALK OFF
SET SAFETY OFF

*Open File containing the Budget
handle = FOPEN(BudgFile)
IF (handle < 0)
        ?"Can't open budget file"
        RETURN
ENDIF

*Read each record until find Dept or End-of-File
Found = .F.
rec = FGETS(handle)
DO WHILE (.NOT. Found) .AND. (!FEOF(handle))
        IF UPPER(Dept) $ UPPER(rec)
                Found = .T.
        ELSE
                rec = FGETS(handle)
        ENDIF
ENDDO
```

(continued)

Listing 12-3. Continued

```
*If End-of-File, Dept was not found
IF FEOF(handle)
        ?"Department " AT 1, UPPER(Dept) AT 12
        ??" Budget not available"
        = FCLOSE(handle)
        RETURN
ENDIF

*Send report to file
SET CONSOLE OFF
SET PRINTER ON
SET PRINTER TO Dept + ".Rpt"

EndDept = .F.
* Write report header
?"Budget for Department: " AT 1, UPPER(Dept) AT 25
?
?"Date:  " AT 1, DATE() AT 9
?

* Print each line item until find next Department
DO WHILE .NOT. EndDept
        rec = FGETS(handle)
        IF ("DEPARTMENT" $ UPPER(rec))
               EndDept = .T.
        ELSE
                ?SUBSTR(rec,1,20)
                ??SUBSTR(rec,40,12)
        ENDIF
ENDDO

*Close report file
SET CONSOLE ON
SET PRINTER OFF
SET PRINTER TO

*Close the budget file
= FCLOSE(handle)
```

For example, a useful utility for any FoxPro application would be one that identifies for each index file the index expression and the .dbf to which it belongs. Since FoxPro does not maintain in the index file any information regarding the associated .dbf file, this is a two-part process. The first part requires a program to write the .dbf name somewhere in the index header area. Of course, the user (or more likely, the program developer) must supply the .dbf name. The second part, executed after all the index files have the .dbf identified, is to read each index file, obtain the .dbf name and the index expression, and store the information in another .dbf.

As described in Chapter 10, the index file's header record is a 512-byte block, with most of the bytes currently unused. The TagIdx program shown in Listing 12-4 writes the .dbf name provided on the command line starting at byte offset 496. This program accepts the index filename (wildcards allowed) and the .dbf name as command line parameters as follows:

```
DO TagIdx WITH <Idx-Name>, <Dbf-Name>
```

The string identified in <Dbf-Name> is written to each .idx file named by <Idx-Name>. Note that the program does not verify the <Dbf-Name>—it is up to the user to provide a valid .dbf name. The string provided in <Dbf-Name> is written into the header record of each index file identified by <Idx-Name>, starting at offset 496. This string can be a maximum of 12 characters. This area in the header record is currently unused. If Fox Software changes the format of the .idx file in a future FoxPro release, you may have to adjust the starting offset.

Once the index files have been updated to contain the .dbf name in the header, you can read that information together with the index expression stored by FoxPro. In the ReadIdx program shown in Listing 12-5, each index file identified by <Idx-Name> is processed by reading the index expression (starting at byte offset 16, where FoxPro puts it) and the .dbf name (starting at byte offset 496, where we wrote it). Note that we remove the trailing NULLs (CHR(0)) on the index expression; FoxPro pads this area with NULLs, not spaces. The NULLs must be removed before the string is written into a database file because the TRIM function removes only trailing spaces. If the string were left containing NULL values, it might be impossible to use as part of another command. For example, if you wish to re-create your index with the INDEX ON <expr> TO <file> command, the string containing <expr> cannot contain NULL values.

The information obtained by this program is stored in the DbfIdx.dbf database (displayed in Figure 12-5) for later use. This database can prove very

Listing 12-4. TagIdx.prg, procedure to write a .dbf name into an index file header record.

```
PROCEDURE TagIdx
*******************************************************************
* Program: TagIdx.prg
* Author : P. L. Olympia and Kathy Cea
* Purpose: Writes the associated .dbf name into header record of
*        : index file.
*        :
* Syntax : Do TagIdx WITH <idx-name>,<dbf-name>
*        : where <idx-name> is the name of the index file(s) to be
*        : written to, and <dbf-name> is the .dbf filename to be
*        : stored in the index header.
*******************************************************************
PARAMETERS Index, DbfName

* Set up environment
SET TALK OFF
SET SAFETY OFF

* Define the byte offset and maximum string length
byte_off = 496
max_len = 12

init_val = SPACE(max_len)

* Check for wildcards in filename.
* The SYS(2000) function returns the name of the first
* file that matches the character expression.  This
* allows the use of wildcards in filenames.

IF ("*" $ Index) .OR. ("?" $ Index)
        IdxFile = SYS(2000,Index)
        IF IdxFile == ""
                ?"No matching index files found"
                RETURN
        ENDIF
ELSE
```

(continued)

Listing 12-4. Continued

```
                IdxFile = IIF(".IDX" $ UPPER(Index), Index, Index + ".Idx")
        ENDIF

        DO WHILE .NOT. (IdxFile  == "")
                * Open .idx file named in IdxFile
                handle = FOPEN(IdxFile,2)
                IF (handle < 0)
                        ?"Can't open Index file " + LTRIM(IdxFile)
                        RETURN
                ENDIF

                * Position file at byte offset
                = FSEEK(handle,byte_off)

                * Append the .dbf extension if necessary
                DbfFile = IIF( ".DBF" $ UPPER(DbfName), ;
                                UPPER(DbfName),UPPER(DbfName) + ".DBF")

                *Initialize the area with spaces
                write_out = FWRITE (handle, init_val)
                IF write_out < max_len
                        ?"Unable to write to index header record"
                ELSE
                        * Write the .dbf name into the index file
                        = FSEEK(handle,-max_len,1)
                        write_out = FWRITE (handle, DbfFile, max_len)
                        IF write_out < LEN(DbfName)
                                ?"Error - DbfName truncated"
                        ENDIF
                ENDIF

                * Close the index file
                = FCLOSE(handle)

                * Allow for wildcards in index name
                IdxFile = IIF (("*" $ Index) .OR. ("?" $ Index), ;
                                SYS(2000,Index,1),"")
        ENDDO
```

Listing 12-5. ReadIdx.prg, procedure to extract index expression and .dbf name from index file and store to a .dbf file.

```
PROCEDURE ReadIdx
******************************************************************
* Program: ReadIdx.prg
* Author : P. L. Olympia and Kathy Cea
* Purpose: Reads the index expression and associated .dbf name from
*        : the header record of the index file(s).
*        :
* Syntax : Do ReadIdx WITH <idx-name>
*        : where <idx-name> is the name of the index file(s) to be
*        : read.  Filename wildcards are accepted.
******************************************************************
PARAMETERS Index

* Set up environment
SET TALK OFF
SET SAFETY OFF

* Define the byte offsets
expr_off = 16
dbf_off = 496

* Define the maximum length of the index expression and .dbf name
max_expr = 220
max_dbf = 12

* Check for wildcards in file name
IF ("*" $ Index) .OR. ("?" $ Index)
        IdxFile = SYS(2000,Index)
        IF IdxFile == ""
                ?"No matching index files found"
                RETURN
        ENDIF
ELSE
        IdxFile = IIF(".IDX" $ UPPER(Index), UPPER(Index), ;
                        UPPER(Index) + ".IDX")
ENDIF
```

(continued)

Listing 12-5. Continued

```
* Open the .dbf containing index information
USE dbfidx INDEX dbfidx

DO WHILE .NOT. (IdxFile == "")
        * Open .idx file named in IdxName
        handle = FOPEN(IdxFile)
        IF (handle < 0)
                ?"Can't open Index file " + LTRIM(IdxFile)
                USE
                RETURN
        ENDIF

        * Position file at byte offset
        = FSEEK(handle,expr_off)
        expr = TRIM(FREAD(handle, max_expr))

        * Remove trailing NULL values
        nullpos = AT(CHR(0), expr)
        IF nullpos > 0
                expr = SUBSTR(expr,1,nullpos - 1)
        ENDIF

        = FSEEK(handle,dbf_off)
        dbfname = TRIM(FREAD(handle, max_dbf))

        * Close the index file
        = FCLOSE(handle)

        * Update the dbfidx.dbf file
        IF SEEK (UPPER(IdxFile))
                REPLACE Dbf with dbfname, ;
                        IndexExpr with expr
        ELSE
                APPEND BLANK
                REPLACE DBFIDX->IdxName with IdxFile, ;
                        Dbf with dbfname, ;
                        IndexExpr with expr
        ENDIF
```

(continued)

Listing 12-5. Continued

```
          * Allow for wildcards in index name
          IdxFile = IIF(("*" $ Index) .OR. ("?" $ Index), ;
                           SYS(2000,Index,1), "")
ENDDO
USE
```

useful for system maintenance and even for use in conjunction with a library routine designed to open all associated index files with any .dbf file that is opened. Chapter 14 describes in greater detail the use of such a library routine.

Although you can obtain the index expression of any index file by executing the SYS(14) function, the TagIdx and ReadIdx programs also allow you to store the .dbf name in an index file and to retrieve both the .dbf name and the index expression for permanent storage in the DbfIdx.dbf file. This can be done without using any .dbf or .idx file in any SELECT area.

Accessing Communications Ports

The file I/O functions may be used to write to or read from your computer's communications ports (COM1 and COM2). Communications ports are always opened for unbuffered I/O. There are two important requirements for working with the COM ports. First, the port must be initialized external to FoxPro. The easiest way to do this is to execute the DOS MODE command

```
Structure for database: D:\FOXCODE\DBFIDX.DBF
Number of data records:       3
Date of last update   : 01/02/90
Field  Field Name  Type        Width    Dec
    1  IDXNAME     Character      12
    2  DBF         Character      12
    3  INDEXEXPR   Character     220
** Total **                      245
```

Figure 12-5. Structure of the DbfIdx.dbf file.

prior to entering FoxPro. For example, the following command will initialize the COM1 port for 2400 baud communications, no parity, 8 data bits, 1 stop bit, and continuous retries:

```
MODE COM1 2400,N,8,1,P
```

Once your port has been initialized, you can open it with the FOPEN function.

The second important requirement is that you turn your modem's Echo capability Off. The current FoxPro release performs all communications I/O with a one-character buffer. For this reason, the port can easily become overwhelmed with data and you can lose input and output. Even with Echo turned off, you may still be able to communicate at relatively slow speeds, such as 300 baud, due to the one-character buffer.

Echo can be set Off for modems that accept the standard Hayes AT command set with the following command:

```
=FPUTS(handle,"ATE0")
```

The following code fragment demonstrates a capability to dial a number from your modem while in FoxPro 1.01. It assumes that the port has already been initialized.

```
PARAMETERS phonenum

handle = FOPEN("COM1",12)
IF handle < 0
     ?"Can't open COM1"
     RETURN
ENDIF
dialphone = "ATDT " + TRIM(phonenum)
=FPUTS (handle,"ATE0")

=FPUTS(handle, dialphone)
WAIT
=FCLOSE(handle)
```

This code sample opens the COM1 port, dials a phone number that is passed to the program in the PhoneNum parameter, waits for a keystroke, and closes the COM1 port. It could be integrated into a more sophisticated facility, for example, one that allows a user to select a person to call from a list, and dials the phone for them.

Chapter Summary

The FoxPro low-level file I/O functions provide an efficient means for reading any non-FoxPro formatted file. They let you directly manipulate text files without using temporary .dbf files or third-party utilities. In addition, they let you work directly with binary files. In short, they allow you to perform certain types of processing previously available only through C and assembly language programs.

The sample programs in this chapter demonstrate the power and flexibility available with these functions. The examples should give you some ideas for additional uses of the FoxPro low-level functions in your own application programs.

Chapter 13

Multiuser Procedures and Techniques

Local Area Network (LAN) installations are rapidly increasing—Novell alone estimates that four million workstations are installed currently, and this number is growing. As the opportunities for data sharing increase, so does the need for multiuser application development. FoxPro/LAN, the multiuser version of FoxPro, enables us to share data on a network. The multiuser version offers all the features of single-user FoxPro and also provides mechanisms for controlling shared data access.

This chapter introduces some of the unique issues that must be considered for multiuser applications and explores procedures and techniques for database design and programming with FoxPro/LAN.

Shared Files

In a single-user application, there is no contention for files or records; in effect, all files are opened for exclusive use. In a multiuser application, you have a choice of opening a file for exclusive or shared use. However, opening a file for exclusive use eliminates the ability to share data since no other user can open the file even for reading. For this reason, exclusive use of a file in a multiuser system should be used only when absolutely necessary.

Exclusive control of shared data results from, in order of progressively reduced concurrency, locking a record (RLOCK or LOCK), locking a file (FLOCK), or using a file in exclusive mode. Opening a file for shared use (through the SET EXCLUSIVE OFF command) requires that you control concurrent reads and updates through file and record locks. A user who has locked a record or file is permitted to write to the resource, and any attempt by anyone else to write to, or obtain a lock on, the record or file will fail. When a file is locked, other users can open the file for reading but not for update. When a record is locked, other users can view the locked record but not update it; however, other records in the file can be locked by other users.

Some operations such as PACK or REINDEX require that the data files be opened for exclusive use. Files that are so opened cannot be accessed by other users even for read-only operations.

Note that if you open a file that resides on a local drive, it is opened for EXCLUSIVE use even if SET EXCLUSIVE is off, unless you have loaded the DOS SHARE module at your workstation. If SHARE has been loaded, files residing on your local drive are opened for shared use by default. If you must load the SHARE module, the FoxPro/LAN documentation recommends that you open local files for EXCLUSIVE use.

To maintain data integrity in a multiuser system, locks are required for the duration of an update operation. This ensures that only one user updates any given data item at one time. Of course, these file and record locks reduce concurrency by denying other users access to the data. One of the primary goals in multiuser programming is to ensure data integrity (through file and record locks) while maintaining maximum concurrency. This requires determining the minimum amount of time during which files and records must be locked for update operations.

FoxPro Implicit Locking

In many cases, FoxPro/LAN automatically imposes a file or record lock when required for an update. This facility is particularly useful when converting a single-user system to a multiuser system. Whenever a file or record is locked implicitly by FoxPro, it is also automatically unlocked at the completion of the update.

There are times when you will want or need to specify the points at which a record or file is locked and unlocked. In these cases, the RLOCK( ) and FLOCK( ) functions are used to lock records and files, respectively. The UNLOCK command releases the record or file lock in the currently selected work area; the optional [IN <alias>] clause allows you to release a file or record lock in another work area. The UNLOCK ALL command releases all locks in all work areas.

Locks are also released when the locked file is closed with the USE command and when a program terminates normally. Unlike many of the other Dbase products, issuing another lock command for a different record of the same file does not necessarily release the lock on a previous record. If SET MULTILOCKS is ON, FoxPro, like dBASE IV, allows multiple records of the same file to be locked simultaneously.

With SET MULTILOCKS ON, a set of records in the same work area may be locked by either issuing a series of RLOCKs or by passing a set of record numbers to the RLOCK( ) function. An UNLOCK command will still release all record locks in the specified work area, even if SET MULTILOCKS is ON. If SET MULTILOCKS is OFF, locking a record will automatically release a previous record lock in the same work area. If MULTILOCKS is OFF and LOCK( ) is called with a string of several records, FoxPro successively locks and unlocks each record in the string until it reaches the last record, which it locks and leaves locked. Note that toggling the MULTILOCKS setting performs an implicit UNLOCK ALL.

Table 13-1 displays the minimum lock requirements for FoxPro and other Dbase family products for selected operations. This table shows only the minimum required locks without indicating whether the user must impose them or the software automatically imposes them.

As you can see from the table, FoxPro's general approach to shared use is not to lock files or records for operations that read, but do not modify, the data. This approach gives you more precise control of your applications. Thus commands such as REPORT FORM do not require a lock but you may impose one anyway if there is a chance that the data will change while the report is in progress.

Although Table 13-1 shows that BROWSE requires a record lock, FoxPro does not require one if the command is invoked with the NOMODIFY option. Like FoxBASE+ and dBASE IV, FoxPro performs automatic locks on commands that require them if you do not explicitly obtain the required locks yourself.

Note that the INDEX and JOIN commands do not require a lock. You should lock the file yourself before executing either one of these commands to ensure the integrity of the newly created file.

Deleting Records on a Network

Typically, when you delete records in a single-user FoxPro system, you plan to PACK the database at a later time in order to permanently remove the deleted records and recapture the space they occupy. In a multiuser system, the PACK command requires EXCLUSIVE use of the .dbf file, which presents a concurrency problem because all other users are locked out of the file for the duration of the PACK operation.

Table 13-1. Minimum Locks Required by FoxPro and Other Dbase Family Products

Command	FoxPro	FoxBASE+	dBASE IV	dBASE III Plus	Clipper	dBXL/ Quicksilver[8]
APPEND	Entire DBF[1]	Entire DBF	Current record	Entire DBF	N/A	Entire DBF
APPEND BLANK	DBF header	DBF header	DBF header	Entire DBF	Record[7]	Entire DBF
APPEND FROM	Entire DBF	Entire DBF	Entire DBF	Entire DBF	Record[7]	Entire DBF
AVERAGE	none	none	Entire DBF[5]	Entire DBF	none	Entire DBF
BROWSE	Current record[2]	Entire DBF	Current record[6]	Entire DBF	N/A	Entire DBF
CHANGE	Current record[2]	Entire DBF	Current record	Entire DBF	N/A	Current record
CHANGE NEXT 1	Current record[2]	Current record	Current record	Current record	N/A	Current record
CHANGE <scope>	Current record[2]	Entire DBF	Current record[6]	Entire DBF	N/A	Current record
CHANGE RECORD <n>	record <n>[2]	record <n>	record <n>	record <n>	N/A	record <n>
COPY	none	none	Entire DBF[5]	Entire DBF	none	Entire DBF
COPY STRUCTURE	none	none	Entire DBF[5]	Entire DBF	none	Entire DBF
COUNT	none	none	Entire DBF[5]	Entire DBF	none	Entire DBF
DELETE	Current record	Current record	Current record	Current record	Current record	Current record
DELETE <scope>	Entire DBF	Entire DBF	Entire DBF	Entire DBF	Entire DBF	Entire DBF
DELETE RECORD <n>	record <n>	record <n>	record <n>	record <n>	record <n>	record <n>
EDIT	Current record[2]	Entire DBF	Current record	Entire DBF	N/A	Current record
EDIT NEXT 1	Current record[2]	Current record	Current record	Current record	N/A	Current record
EDIT <scope>	Current record[2]	Entire DBF	Current record[6]	Entire DBF	N/A	Current record
EDIT RECORD <n>	record <n>[2]	record <n>	record <n>	record <n>	N/A	record <n>
INDEX	none[3]	Entire DBF	Entire DBF	Entire DBF	none	Entire DBF
INSERT [BLANK]	Exclusive use	Exclusive use	Exclusive use	Exclusive use	N/A	Exclusive use
JOIN	none	Entire DBF	Entire DBF	Entire DBF	none	Entire DBF
MODIFY STRUCTURE	Exclusive use	Exclusive use	Exclusive use	Exclusive use	N/A	Exclusive use
PACK	Exclusive use	Exclusive use	Exclusive use	Exclusive use	Exclusive use	Exclusive use
RECALL	Current record	Current record	Current record	Current record	Current record	Current record

Command	FoxPro	FoxBASE+	dBASE IV	dBASE III Plus	Clipper	dBXL/ Quicksilver[8]
RECALL <scope>	Entire DBF	Entire DBF	Entire DBF	Entire DBF	Entire DBF	Entire DBF
RECALL RECORD <n>	record <n>	record <n>	record <n>	record <n>	record <n>	record <n>
REINDEX	Exclusive use	Exclusive use	Exclusive use	Exclusive use	Exclusive use	Exclusive use
REPLACE	Current record	Current record[4]	Current record	Current record	Current record	Current record
REPLACE <scope>	Entire DBF	Entire DBF	Entire DBF	Entire DBF	Entire DBF	Entire DBF
REPLACE RECORD <n>	record <n>	record <n>[4]	record <n>	record <n>	record <n>	record <n>
SORT	none	none	Entire DBF[5]	Entire DBF	none	Entire DBF
SUM	none	none	Entire DBF[5]	Entire DBF	none	Entire DBF
TOTAL	none	none	Entire DBF[5]	Entire DBF	none	Entire DBF
UPDATE	Entire DBF	Entire DBF	Entire DBF	Entire DBF	Entire DBF	Entire DBF
ZAP	Exclusive use	Exclusive use	Exclusive use	Exclusive use	Exclusive use	Exclusive use

[1]During an APPEND, FoxPro actually locks just the DBF header and serially locks the records as they are APPENDed.

[2]During a Browse, Change, or Edit, FoxPro locks the current record and all records from fields in related databases (specified by alias) once editing begins.

[3]FoxPro does not require a lock to INDEX but will not index correctly if another user is updating the primary key field.

[4]FoxBASE+ automatically places a record lock during REPLACE RECORD <n>, but it requires a user to place a record lock manually for a REPLACE command.

[5]dBASE IV performs automatic locks with commands that only read data (e.g., SUM, COUNT, LABEL) if SET LOCK is on.

[6]dBASE IV BROWSE requires only a record lock even when adding new records. Records are locked one a time as they are edited or added. CHANGE/EDIT <scope> require a series of record locks.

[7]Clipper does not really require locks on APPEND BLANK/FROM.

[8]Quicksilver version 1.3, like Clipper Summer '87 version, does not support interactive commands. dBXL/LAN behaves like dBASE III PLUS except that it performs automatic locks on most commands. In Browse, for example, it locks a record or the entire file depending on what is being changed.

An alternative approach to the DELETE command can be used in a multiuser system to avoid locking everyone out of the files being PACKed. One such alternative is to recycle the record by first blanking it and then marking it as deleted. Later, when the application requires a record to be APPENDed, it may simply RECALL (undelete) the deleted record and return it to the requesting application as a new record. Of course, if you run out of blank, deleted records, you still need to APPEND new ones. When this time comes, the recommended technique is to APPEND a batch of blank records and then mark all of them as deleted except the one you are going to return to the application. This approach reduces the amount of time that the file is inaccessible to others because APPEND and APPEND BLANK require a lock on the header data.

Note that if you choose to implement this method for deleting and appending records, you should SET DELETED ON to ensure that your blank, deleted records are "invisible" during normal application processing.

To find an already blank record to use in an indexed database, make sure that you have SET DELETED OFF and then look at the top of the file. If there are any blank records, they will be at the top of the .dbf because these records have a blank key. When you find a blank record, mark it undeleted and return it to the calling procedure.

How do you blank a record that is about to be deleted? In FoxBASE+, the easiest way to do this is to use an undocumented feature known as the "phantom" record. This phantom record is a blank record found just past the end of the file (EOF). It is ideal for use in blanking another record. To get to the record, go to the bottom of the file and then perform a SKIP. The database pointer is now at the phantom (blank) record. Figure 13-1 shows a sequence of commands demonstrating the existence of the phantom record just past the end of the file.

Note that the record number is actually one greater than the count of records in the file. Also, notice that a display command shows a series of blank fields. Since FoxBASE+ supports arrays, the phantom record serves conveniently as a blank record that can be SCATTERed to an array.

Since dBASE IV does not provide a "phantom" record, it requires a different approach to blanking records. The recommended solution in dBASE IV is to retain a small set of blank records and then copy one of the already blank records to the record originally targeted for deletion. To do this, the already blank record is copied to an array using the COPY TO ARRAY NEXT 1 command, and the array is copied to the record earmarked for

```
. use employee
. ?reccount()
      45
. go bottom
. ?recno()
      45
. skip
. ?recno()
      46
.display
Record#  EMP_ID EMP_NAME HIRE_DT EMP_DEPT
```

Figure 13-1. Series of commands demonstrating the existence of the FoxBASE+ phantom record.

deletion using the REPLACE FROM ARRAY NEXT 1 command. You need the NEXT 1 clause because, without it, COPY TO ARRAY attempts to copy all records in the file beginning with the first record and continues until all array elements are exhausted, rather than copying just the blank record where the database pointer rests.

Although FoxPro also has the phantom record, you don't need it if you only want to blank a record. FoxPro has new options in both the SCATTER and GATHER commands that make blanking a record a breeze. For instance,

```
Alternative 1
   SCATTER TO x BLANK      && x will be an array with empty elements
   GATHER FROM x           && blanks the current record

Alternative 2
   SCATTER MEMVAR BLANK    && Creates set of empty memory variables
   GATHER MEMVAR           && blanks the current record
```

SCATTER MEMVAR creates a set of memory variables with the same name and type as the database fields, just like the useful AUTOMEM facility of dBXL and Quicksilver. As expected, this set of memory variables is empty if the BLANK option is used.

Controlling Concurrent Updates

As discussed previously, a multiuser system must impose locks on files and records in order to prevent two or more users from updating the same data at the same time. On a typical network, user requests for data involve copying the file from disk into the user's workstation memory. This can result in erroneous updates even if the records or files are locked. Several users can have copies of the same data in workstation memory. If one user modifies the data, writes it back to disk, and then unlocks the record or file, another user may now try to update the old copy of the data still residing on his or her workstation. This user's update will now be written to disk, overwriting the previous update. Thus a "lost update" is possible unless some measures are taken to control concurrent updates.

Some of the methods and techniques that deal with this issue of concurrent updates are as follows:

1. Open files exclusively.
2. Flag records in use.
3. Use NetWare semaphores.
4. Simulate the dBASE IV Convert utility.
5. Compare before/after values in arrays.

Open Files Exclusively

The simplest approach is to EXCLUSIVEly open the file(s) involved in an update action for the duration of the read/update cycle. This precludes any other users from even obtaining a read-only copy of the file while any update takes place within the file. Although this provides an effective means of controlling concurrent updates, it denies other users access to entire files for unnecessarily extended periods. For that reason, it is an extremely inefficient solution and would be difficult to justify or recommend.

Flag Records in Use

As part of an application, you can create a "master" .dbf that stores in each record the primary key and a flag indicating whether the record is in use. Any request for access (read or update) to a record must first check this .dbf to determine whether the record is in use. If so, the user is denied access to the

```
Structure for database: D:\FOXCODE\RECLOCK.DBF
Number of data records:       24
Date of last update   : 01/07/90
Field  Field Name  Type         Width    Dec
    1  REC_ID      Character       64
    2  IN_USE      Logical          1
    3  DATE_USED   Date             8
    4  USERID      Character        8
** Total **                        82
```

Figure 13-2. Sample "master" .dbf file structure.

record. This is more efficient than exclusively locking the file(s) because it effectively locks only the records in use and leaves the remaining records in the files available to other users. Its drawback is in programming overhead, particularly if the application already exists, because each request for record access must first call a routine to check the record's availability. If the record is available, the flag must be updated to indicate that it is in use; upon release of the record, the flag must again be updated.

A sample master .dbf file structure is presented in Figure 13-2. As you can see, this file contains fields for the primary key and a flag as well as fields for date and userid. The primary key is stored in this .dbf as a character string of up to 64 bytes. Although not required, the date and userid fields are useful for reporting back to the user if a record is not available.

Listing 13-1 demonstrates two simple functions: LockRec and RelRec. LockRec is called with the following syntax:

```
LockRec (<record-id>,<user-id>)
```

where <record-id> is a character string containing the primary key for the record to be checked, and <user-id> is a unique id for the user, probably the network userid. If the record is not already contained in the file, it is added and marked In-Use. If it is available, the In-Use flag is changed to .T. and the date and userid are written. If the record is not available (In-Use is .T.), the function returns .F.

The RelRec function marks a record available. This function is called as follows:

```
RelRec (<record-id>)
```

Listing 13-1. LockRec and RelRec functions.

```
FUNCTION LockRec
*********************************************************************
* Program: LockRec.prg
* Author : P. L. Olympia and Kathy Cea
* Purpose: Determines whether the requested record is available.
*        : If the record is not already in the database, adds the
*        : record, marks it In-Use, and returns .T.  If the record is
*        : in the database and not already In-Use, marks it In-Use
*        :  and returns .T. Otherwise returns .F.
*        :
* Syntax : LockRec (<rec-id>, <user-id>)
*        : where <rec-id> is the primary key of the record to be
locked
*        : <user-id> is the name of the user requesting the record.
*        :
* Notes  : The RecLock .dbf file with RecId .idx must be open in
*        : the current work area.
*********************************************************************

PARAMETERS mRec_id, mUserid

SEEK (ALLTRIM(mRec_id))
IF FOUND()
        IF RecLock->In_Use
                RETURN .F.
        ELSE
                REPLACE RecLock->In_Use WITH .T., ;
                        RecLock->Date_Used WITH DATE(), ;
                        RecLock->UserId WITH mUserId

        ENDIF
ELSE
        APPEND BLANK
        REPLACE RecLock->Rec_Id WITH mRec_id, ;
                RecLock->In_Use WITH .T., ;
```

(continued)

Listing 13-1. Continued

```
                RecLock->Date_Used WITH DATE(), ;
                RecLock->UserId WITH mUserid
ENDIF
RETURN .T.


FUNCTION RelRec
*******************************************************************
* Program: RelRec.prg
* Author : P. L. Olympia and Kathy Cea
* Purpose: If the record is currently In-Use, marks it available
*        : (sets In-Use to .F.) and returns .T.  Otherwise
*        : returns .F.
*        :
* Syntax : RelRec (<rec-id>)
*        : where <rec-id> is the primary key of the record to be
*        : released.
*        :
* Notes  : The RecLock .dbf file with RecId .idx must be open in
*        : the current work area.
*******************************************************************

PARAMETERS mRec_id

SEEK (ALLTRIM(mRec_id))
IF FOUND()
        REPLACE RecLock->In_Use WITH .F.
                RETURN .T.
        ELSE
                RETURN .F.
ENDIF
```

where <record-id> is the primary key of the record to be released. If the record identified by <record-id> is found, it is marked available (In_Use is set to .F.), and the function returns .T. Otherwise, the function returns .F. Note that both the LockRec and RelRec functions require that the RecLock .dbf be opened with the RecId index (indexed on the Rec_Id field) in the current work area prior to calling the function.

The following code fragment demonstrates the use of the LockRec and RelRec functions:

```
mRecId = "123-45-6789"
mUser = "J_SMITH"
SELECT 9
USE RecLock INDE RecId
IF LockRec(mRecId, mUser)
        * Process the record
        SELECT RecLock
        = RelRec (mRecId)
ELSE
        ?"Record is currently unavailable"
        ??" - please try again later"
ENDIF
```

Use NetWare Semaphores

For FoxPro/LAN applications running on a Novell NetWare LAN, the NetWare semaphore function may be implemented to control access to the records based on their primary key. A NetWare semaphore is a mechanism that associates a user-defined label (representing some resource) with a counter that may take a value from 0 through 127. It is used to control access to a resource. Table 13-2 lists the NetWare semaphore functions.

Each semaphore has an open count and a value associated with it. The open count is simply the number of processes that have the semaphore open, which means that it is the number of applications that have called OpenSemaphore and have not yet issued a call to CloseSemaphore. The open count information has very little use—it simply indicates the number of processes that may request access to the resource. The value is the number of resources still available; this number is set initially by the first process that calls OpenSemaphore for a particular resource. The semaphore value is maintained by the system, and it is the crucial element in controlling access to a resource. When the value becomes negative, a process must wait for the resource to become available—it must wait for one or more processes to release the resource with a call to SignalSemaphore.

Table 13-2. Netware Semaphore Functions

Function Name	Description
OpenSemaphore	Opens a semaphore; creates it if it does not already exist. A semaphore must be opened before any other call can be made to it.
ExamineSemaphore	Returns the current value and open count for a semaphore.
WaitOnSemaphore	Decrements the value of a semaphore. This function is called when an application requests access to the resource represented by the semaphore. A timeout is specified, which defines the maximum time that a process will wait for the resource to become available.
SignalSemaphore	Increments the value of a semaphore. This function is called when an application releases the resource.
CloseSemaphore	Closes a semaphore. This function is normally invoked when the application terminates.

An application using semaphores to control concurrent access to a record would call OpenSemaphore with the primary key as the label and an initial count of 1. It would then call the WaitOnSemaphore when it is ready to access a record; if the record is unavailable, the WaitOnSemaphore function would place the requesting program in a queue until either the record becomes available or the timeout limit (specified by the application) expires. When an application is finished using a record, it must call SignalSemaphore to increment the count and permit another user to access the record. Finally, the application must call CloseSemaphore before terminating. Of course, for this method to effectively control access to a record, all programs must recognize the same naming convention (assignment of semaphore labels) for the database records.

This solution is similar to the Flag Records in Use option described earlier in that it locks only the record(s) in use and leaves the rest of the file available

Table 13-3. Data Contained in the _DBASELOCK Field

_DBASELOCK Contents	Description
COUNT	A 2-byte hexadecimal value containing the number of times the field has been updated.
TIME	A 3-byte hexadecimal value containing the time the field was last locked. The time is stored in the format HHMMSS.
DATE	A 3-byte hexadecimal value containing the date the field was last locked. The date is stored in the format YYMMDD.
NAME	An 8-byte field containing the id of the user who locked the field.

to other users. It is an effective solution but may require significant program modifications in an existing system because a call to a .bin file would be required for each request to access a record (read, lock, or unlock).

Simulate the dBASE IV Convert Utility

CONVERT is a new dBASE IV command that, together with related functions called LKSYS( ) and CHANGE( ), provides multiuser lock detection features. CONVERT adds a field (named _DBASELOCK) to a .dbf, which is used to store resource locking information. The contents of the _DBASELOCK field are shown in Table 13-3.

Once a .dbf has been CONVERTed, you can run the CHANGE( ) and LKSYS( ) functions against it. The CHANGE( ) function returns .T. or .F. to indicate whether or not the record has been updated since it was read into workstation memory. It does this by comparing the Count values in the _DBASELOCK field on disk and in memory. This function can be used within an application to determine whether someone else has updated a record since it was read from the file. The record need not be locked until it is about to be updated; just prior to updating the record, the application should invoke the CHANGE( ) function to ensure that the record has not been altered by another user. If CHANGE( ) returns .T., the copy of the record in memory at the workstation is no longer current and must be reread from disk before the lock is applied and the record is updated. This requires special processing to notify the user that the record has been modified since it was last read, and that the user's changes are now outdated.

The LKSYS( ) function returns date, time, or user information based on the parameter passed to it. If a parameter of 0, 1, or 2 is passed, the time, date, or userid (respectively) associated with the current lock is returned. Note that a value is returned only if the record or file is currently locked. If a parameter of 3, 4, or 5 is passed, the time, date, or userid associated with the last lock placed is returned. If a record is locked, the lock information is stored in the _DBASELOCK field in that record. If the file is locked, the lock information is stored in the _DBASELOCK field in record 1.

CONVERT, CHANGE( ), and LKSYS( ) features are not currently available in FoxPro; however, Fox Software has indicated that they plan to implement these features. In the meantime, it is possible to write your own functions to simulate the processing. The CONVERT function is relatively straightforward; it simply adds a field called FoxLock (the equivalent of dBASE's _DBASELOCK) to the .dbf. A FoxPro CONVERT function is shown in Listing 13-2. This function is called as follows:

```
= Convert (<dbfname>)
```

where dbfname is the name of the .dbf file to be CONVERTed. The function first verifies that the file has not already been CONVERTed. If the FoxLock field is found in the file, the function returns .F. because it assumes that CONVERT has already been run. Of course, this means that you cannot have a field named FoxLock in any of the .dbf files you want to CONVERT.

If the CONVERT function does not find the FoxLock field, it adds the field and initializes the count field to zero.

Once a .dbf file has been CONVERTed, dBASE IV takes care of updating the _DBASELOCK field values. Of course, if you implement this feature in FoxPro, you have to handle the update of the FoxLock field values yourself. In dBASE IV, the Count value is incremented each time the record is updated. You must write a COUNT function equivalent to the dBASE COUNT function and ensure that it is called each time a record is updated. For example, you should call this function each time a REPLACE command is executed for any given record.

Listing 13-2. FoxPro CONVERT function.

```
FUNCTION CONVERT
*****************************************************************
* Program: Convert.prg
* Author : P. L. Olympia and Kathy Cea
* Purpose: Simulate the dBASE IV Convert utility by adding the
*        : FoxLock field to the database file.  Returns .F. if
*        : the FoxLock field already exists in the .dbf, otherwise
*        : adds the field and returns .T.
*        :
* Syntax : Convert (<dbfname>)
*        : where <dbfname> is the .dbf to be CONVERTed. The .dbf
*        : extension must be included.
*****************************************************************
PARAMETERS dbfname

USE (dbfname)
Found = .F.
* Check whether the FOXLOCK field already exists
FOR I = 1 to FCOUNT()
        IF FIELD(I) = "FOXLOCK"
                Found = .T.
                EXIT
        ENDIF
ENDFOR
USE

IF Found
* The FoxLock field already exists in the database
        ?"File already CONVERTed"
        RETURN .F.
ENDIF

SET SAFETY OFF
* Copy .dbf to a backup file
COPY FILE &dbfname TO Save.dbf
```

(continued)

Listing 13-2. Continued

```
* Use dbfname exclusively since you are modifying the structure
USE (dbfname) EXCLUSIVE

* Save data to a temporary file in text delimited format
COPY TO convtemp.txt DELIMITED

* Copy structure extended
COPY STRUCTURE EXTENDED TO convtemp

* Use the file containing the structure extended to
* add the new FoxLock field
USE convtemp
APPEND BLANK
REPLACE field_name WITH "FoxLock"
REPLACE field_type WITH 'C'
REPLACE field_len WITH 16
* Overwrite existing .dbf with new structure
DELETE FILE &dbfname
CREATE &dbfname FROM convtemp
USE (dbfname)

* Load data into .dbf from temporary file
APPEND FROM convtemp.txt DELIMITED

* Initialize Count to zero for all records
lockstr = CHR(0) + CHR(0)
REPLACE ALL FoxLock WITH lockstr
USE

* Delete temporary files
DELETE FILE convtemp.txt
DELETE FILE convtemp.dbf
RETURN .T.
```

In addition, dBASE IV writes current date, time, and user information into the _DBASELOCK field each time a record is locked. You must write a function to update these values, and you must ensure that the function is called whenever a lock (implicit or explicit) is placed on a record.

Once this processing is implemented in your system, you can write the CHANGE( ) and LKSYS( ) functions. CHANGE( ) requires that the count in FoxLock stored in workstation memory be compared to the count stored on disk. You can implement the LKSYS( ) function by passing a parameter into the function as described earlier. When the function is passed a parameter of 0, 1, or 2, it must ensure that a lock attempt has failed before it returns the requested data. When the LKSYS( ) function is passed a parameter of 3, 4, or 5, it simply returns the requested data from the FoxLock field in the appropriate record.

Although the CONVERT option and associated CHANGE( ) and LKSYS( ) functions can be implemented to some degree in FoxPro, it may not be worth your time given the limited benefit it offers. First, unlike dBASE IV, you cannot protect the FoxLock field containing the lock information from accidental or intentional updates. This is because the FoxLock field name does not begin with an underscore (to indicate that it is a system variable), as the dBASE IV _DBASELOCK field does. Second, to effectively implement these features, your application must ensure that the function to update the count is called anytime a record is updated, and that the function to update date, time, and userid is called anytime a lock is placed either implicitly or explicitly. This burden alone may be enough to dissuade you.

Additionally, to truly simulate the dBASE IV implementation, you must be able to determine whether a file or record lock has been placed because the file lock information is stored in record 1. This may not be possible. Finally, even if you are able to overcome all of these obstacles, the best you can do with the CHANGE( ) function is determine that an interim update has been made and disallow a user's update. This may be an unsatisfactory solution to end users, who will probably not be too happy to find that after entering several screens full of updates, their changes are invalid and they must now either start over or abandon the operation.

Compare Before/After Values in Arrays

You may implement your own procedure to verify that a record has not been modified by another user between the time the record is read into workstation memory and the time the record is updated. At the time you read a record, copy its contents into an array (using the SCATTER command). Then copy the record to a temporary file where a user may modify the data. Just prior to updating the record, copy the record into another array. Now, compare the first array with the new array; if there are any differences, you know that the record has been changed. This should be communicated to the user, who will have to reenter the edits. If the arrays match, write the updates contained in the temporary file to the permanent .dbf.

The following code fragment demonstrates this technique:

```
numfield = FCOUNT()
DIMENSION bef_changes(numfield), aft_changes(numfield)
SCATTER TO bef_changes
COPY TO tempfile NEXT 1
SELECT tempfile
* Process user updates in tempfile
* SELECT your permanent .dbf
* GOTO record to be modified
IF RLOCK()     && Lock record while comparison is made
     SCATTER TO aft_changes
     Changed = .F.
     fld = 1
     DO WHILE ((fld <= numfield) .AND. (.NOT. Changed))
          IF bef_changes(fld) <> aft_changes(fld)
               Changed = .T.
          ENDIF
          fld = fld + 1
     ENDDO
     IF Changed
          * Inform the user that data has changed
     ELSE
           SELECT tempfile
           SCATTER TO moverec
           * SELECT your permanent .dbf
           GATHER FROM moverec
     ENDIF
     UNLOCK
ELSE
     * Unable to lock record, perform alternate processing
ENDIF
RELEASE bef_changes, aft_changes, moverec
```

Note that this technique does not work if your database file contains memo fields because memo fields are not copied to the array during a SCATTER operation. In this example, memo fields would not be compared before and after because they would not be contained in the Bef_changes and Aft_changes arrays.

Deadlock

Once you introduce file and record locking into your multiuser application, you also introduce the possibility of a resource contention problem called deadlock. Deadlock occurs when two or more processes are in a wait state, each waiting to lock a resource (file or record) currently locked by one of the other processes.

Figure 13-3 demonstrates an example of deadlock resulting from file locking. Process 1 locks Customer.dbf, whereas Process 2 locks Sales.dbf. Process 1 requires a lock on Sales.dbf to proceed; Process 2 requires a lock on Customer.dbf before it can continue. When this happens, Process 1 and Process 2 will wait indefinitely unless the system detects and resolves the deadlock.

Figure 13-4 demonstrates an example of deadlock based on record locking. In this case, Process 1 locks record 1 in Customer.dbf, and Process 2 locks record 1 in Employee.dbf at the same time. Process 1 requires a lock on record 1 in Employee.dbf before it can continue; Process 2 requires a lock on record 1 in Customer.dbf in order to proceed. Again, both processes will wait indefinitely unless one of the processes is aborted.

The following alternatives can prevent deadlock situations:

1. Open files in a prescribed order.
2. Preassign files to specific work areas.
3. Lock all files and records needed at program initiation.
4. Use the FoxPro SET REPROCESS option.
5. Implement NetWare synchronization services.

Open Files in a Prescribed Order

An application system can adopt a standard calling for all .dbf files to be opened and locked in a predetermined order, regardless of the order in which they will be used. For example, an application program could be required to open .dbf's in alphabetical order. In this case, the deadlock situation shown in

Process 1	**Process 2**
`SELECT 1`	`SELECT 1`
`USE Customer`	`Use Sales`
`DO WHILE .NOT. FLOCK()`	`DO WHILE .NOT. FLOCK()`
`ENDDO`	`ENDDO`
`SELECT 2`	`SELECT 2`
`USE Sales`	`USE Customer`
`DO WHILE .NOT. FLOCK()`	`DO WHILE .NOT. FLOCK()`
`ENDDO`	`ENDDO`
`* Process`	`* Process files`
`UNLOCK ALL`	`UNLOCK ALL`

Figure 13-3. Two processes contending for file locks that result in a deadlock.

Figure 13-3 would not occur because Process 2 would have to be rewritten to open and lock the Customer.dbf before the Sales.dbf (since the letter "C" comes before the letter "S"). This solution eliminates the possibility of deadlock when opening and locking files.

Process 1	**Process 2**
`SELECT 1`	`SELECT 1`
`USE Customer`	`USE Employee`
`GOTO Record 1`	`GOTO Record 1`
`DO WHILE .NOT. RLOCK()`	`DO WHILE .NOT. RLOCK()`
`ENDDO`	`ENDDO`
`SELECT 2`	`SELECT 2`
`USE Employee`	`USE Customer`
`GOTO Record 1`	`GOTO Record 1`
`DO WHILE .NOT. RLOCK()`	`DO WHILE .NOT. RLOCK()`
`ENDDO`	`ENDDO`
`*Process records`	`*Process records`
`UNLOCK`	`UNLOCK`

Figure 13-4. Two processes contending for record locks that result in a deadlock.

This alternative can also be modified slightly to avoid deadlock situations when locking records. In this case, the application system must require that records be locked in an order based on the .dbf file to which they belong. For example, a program could be required to lock records from files in alphabetical order. In the example shown in Figure 13-4, records from the Customer.dbf file must be locked before records are locked from the Employee.dbf file (since "C"comes before "E"). Unfortunately this solution quickly falls apart if you are processing (and locking) records from multiple files in a serial fashion, or if you are locking multiple records from the same file.

The requirement that a program lock files or records in a prescribed order can very easily lead to an impractical and inefficient design. At best, it could require files or records to be locked in a way that does not exactly match the needs of the program. At worst, it could require files or records to be locked long before they are needed, thus keeping them locked for unnecessarily long periods of time.

Preassign Files to Specific Work Areas

This solution also requires that a standard be imposed on an application system. In this case, each .dbf may be opened only in a preassigned work area. Then, the work areas must be selected in numeric sequence.

This alternative has several major drawbacks. First, FoxPro allows a maximum of 25 work areas. Therefore, this alternative is unworkable for a large application that uses more than 25 .dbf's simultaneously. Second, the standard may be even more difficult to enforce than the solution described earlier where .dbf's are opened in a prescribed order. Every programmer involved in the application development must have access to some list indicating the work area assigned to each .dbf in the system. Maintenance of such a system is a burden when the preassigned areas must be changed or new .dbf's are added. Finally, this method is effective for avoiding deadlock when locking files (as in Figure 13-3), but it cannot prevent deadlock situations when locking records (as in Figure 13-4).

Lock All Files and Records Needed at Program Initiation

Another alternative to avoid deadlocks is to require that each application program in a system lock either all files or all records that it will need at the beginning of the procedure. If even one lock cannot be obtained, the program should release all its locks. This avoids the deadlock resulting from locking files as well as records because a program never waits for the availability of a file or record.

This solution would eliminate the file and record deadlock situations shown in Figures 13-3 and 13-4. These programs would have to be rewritten to eliminate the endless loop while waiting for a file or record lock. As soon as one file or record was unavailable, all locks would have to be released with the UNLOCK ALL command. For example, the programs in Figure 13-3 would be rewritten as follows:

Process 1

```
SELECT 1
USE Customer
IF FLOCK()
   SELECT 2
   USE Sales
   IF FLOCK()
      * Process files
   ELSE
      UNLOCK ALL
      ?"Unable to lock files"
   ENDIF
ELSE
   ?"Unable to lock files"
ENDIF
```

Process 2

```
SELECT 1
Use Sales
IF FLOCK()
   SELECT 2
   USE Customer
   IF FLOCK()
      * Process files
   ELSE
      UNLOCK ALL
      ?"Unable to lock files"
   ENDIF
ELSE
   ?"Unable to lock files"
ENDIF
```

This solution forces an application to know up front exactly what resources it will require. This can present a problem if the processing varies depending on data provided by the user. It could also make maintenance more difficult. This solution could also monopolize resources because all the resources (files and records) that the application needs are locked for the duration. On the other hand, if many resources are required up front, the program could wait a long time for all of them to be available simultaneously.

Use the FoxPro SET REPROCESS Option

FoxPro/LAN provides an option for specifying the maximum length of time a program should wait for a record or file lock. It can be used to specify either the maximum number of retries or the maximum number of seconds during which retry attempts will be made. This feature can be used in place of the

Table 13-4. Average Time Delays for Different Numbers of Lock Retry Attempts

Number of Retries	Seconds
1	1
10	1
100	7
1000	56
10,000	550

endless loop shown in Figures 13-3 and 13-4 to specify a maximum time period to wait for availability of a record or file lock.

Table 13-4 displays some average time delays associated with a number of retry attempts for record or file locks. These numbers were obtained on a Novell NetWare LAN with little or no traffic. The waits were the same regardless of whether the program was attempting to lock a record or a file. The numbers are not conclusive, but they can be used to determine relative waits experienced for different numbers of retry attempts.

Specifying a maximum wait for a lock eliminates deadlock possibilities by defining a finite time period during which a program will wait for a resource to be available. If the lock cannot be obtained within the defined period, the application's ON ERROR process takes over, allowing the programmer to define an alternative course of action. (Chapter 14 discusses ON ERROR processing in more detail.)

Implement NetWare Synchronization Services

Systems running on a Novell NetWare operating system have another alternative. The Novell APIs (Application Program Interfaces, available to developers) provide an option called synchronization services. The Synchronization Services offer facilities for both file and record locking used in conjunction with C and Assembly language programs. Programs written to take advantage of these services may be converted to .bin files for use in a FoxPro application.

The Novell APIs provide three types of synchronization services: File Locking, Physical Record Locking, and Logical Record Locking. The File Locking services use a log table that records all the files to be locked. Similarly, the Physical Record Locking services use a log table that stores information pertaining to each record to be locked. An application can then request that the set of files or records contained in the log table be locked. The set is either locked in its entirety or not at all. The application releases the set before it terminates. The log table concept is useful in that the set of files or records can be unlocked but kept in the table for later use. With Physical Record Locking services, the records are actually specified with a DOS file handle, the starting offset, and the record length.

Unfortunately the File Locking services and Physical Record Locking services cannot be easily implemented in a FoxPro application. Complex code is required to determine and monitor the file handles for open files. Another problem is that an update made by the C or Assembly routine to a field that is part of the database's primary key will not be reflected in the index file, resulting in an index file that is out of sync with the corresponding .dbf file.

The NetWare Logical Record Locking services present a more reasonable solution. These facilities do not actually place any physical locks, but rather they keep track of logical locks placed on names representing records. These features coordinate multiuser access to shared data without physically locking data. A greater degree of internal control is required of an application to effectively implement logical record locking. The key to using this facility is to establish a standard for assigning names to records to be locked. A logical record name can be a maximum of 100 bytes in length, including a null terminator. Thus a reasonable naming convention might be to assign a name consisting of the .dbf name plus the value of the key field(s) for the record to be locked. The FoxPro program could formulate the string value and pass it to the .bin files, which would then take care of the appropriate locking/unlocking function.

The Logical Record Locking services are similar to the File Locking and Physical Record Locking functions in that a log table is maintained to track the records to be locked; a set is either locked in its entirety or not at all. Table 13-5 shows the Logical Record Locking functions.

Chapter Summary

Multiuser programming introduces important issues that are not concerns in a single-user environment. Users may contend for the same data in a multiuser environment, so an application must ensure data integrity through appropriate

Table 13-5. NetWare Logical Record Locking Functions

Function	Description
LogLogicalRecord	Adds a logical record to the log table and optionally locks the record.
LockLogicalRecordSet	Attempts to lock all logical records in the log table.
ReleaseLogicalRecord	Unlocks a logical record, but leaves it in the log table.
ReleaseLogicalRecordSet	Unlocks all logical records currently locked in the log table, but leaves them in the table.
ClearLogicalRecord	Unlocks a logical record and removes it from the log table.
ClearLogicalRecordSet	Unlocks all logical records in the log table and removes the records from the table.

record and file locking. At the same time, we would like to maximize concurrency, that is, we want to provide as much access to shared data as possible. The tradeoff between data integrity and concurrency requires that programmers pay special attention to the locks imposed by an application.

FoxPro/LAN implicitly locks a file or record in many cases. However, a programmer can specify the points at which a record or file is to be locked or unlocked, thereby overriding the FoxPro defaults. In deciding when and how to place a lock, you should consider the problem of the "lost update" and potential deadlock situations. In this chapter, we discussed these problems and presented techniques for avoiding them.

We also presented an alternative approach to deleting records. Since a PACK requires exclusive use of a database file, a technique that eliminates the need to periodically PACK the database will increase concurrency. We discussed a method of deleting and reusing records.

The techniques presented in this chapter should help you avoid many of the potential pitfalls of multiuser programming.

Chapter 14

More Multiuser Techniques

In Chapter 13, we introduced some of the issues that must be addressed when programming in the multiuser environment. In this chapter, we will look at some additional concerns and alternative techniques.

Reporting

When a user runs a report in single-user FoxPro, data cannot possibly be updated while the report is generated. In a multiuser environment, however, there is always the possibility that another user is updating the database while the report is running. In some cases, this is not a problem. However, when you want to run a program such as an accounting summary where the figures must balance, you have to consider what will happen if a few of the numbers are changed between the time the report program begins execution and the time it completes.

If you require that the data remain static once the report run begins, you have several options:

1. Lock all .dbf files for the duration of the report run.
2. Copy .dbf files to temporary files.
3. Create temporary files by selectively copying records.

Lock All .dbf Files for the Duration of the Report Run

The obvious solution to the problem of a changing database during report execution is to lock all the files that the report program needs for the duration of the run. Then, although other users can obtain a read-only copy of these .dbf files, they cannot change the data until the report program completes and releases the file locks.

In most cases, this technique is too extreme to be considered viable. It eliminates the benefits of running in a multiuser environment because it monopolizes normally shared resources while the report runs. You should consider one of the other alternatives before looking at this option.

Copy .dbf Files to Temporary Files

Another method for ensuring that the .dbf files are not modified while a report program runs is to copy the .dbf files to another set of "temporary" files, for use only by the report program. The report program then deletes the temporary files before terminating.

Files may be copied using either the COPY or SORT command. If the report you will be running processes data in a prescribed order, SORT is preferable since it can create the temporary file in the required order.

Clearly this alternative provides greater concurrency. It ensures that data is not changed by creating temporary files for the report program's exclusive use. At the same time, it does not lock anyone out of the production .dbf files. To effectively implement this method, you must have a means of uniquely naming your temporary files. This issue is addressed later in this chapter.

This method also raises the issue of disk space usage. In addition to the disk space that the production files need, you now must have sufficient space for all the temporary files. This means that if several users run the report program concurrently, you will have several sets of temporary files.

If you consider implementing this option, you have two choices for the location of your temporary files. You may write them to a network disk or to a local hard disk. If you write to a network disk, the user contends with normal network traffic for all file I/O. You also risk monopolizing a large amount of network disk space if the files are very large or if you have a number of users running against temporary files simultaneously.

If you run the report against temporary files written to a local hard disk, you eliminate the network traffic factor. However, there is always a chance that a user will run the report from a workstation that has no hard disk. Also, unless all the workstation hard disk directories are standardized at your site, you do not have the advantage of knowing the directory structure, and thus you have to take your best guess as to where to write the temporary files. In addition, you have no way of centrally monitoring available disk space on local drives, whereas the system administrator typically has utility programs for monitoring network disk space usage. Finally, you must consider the average access speeds on the network drive versus the local drive. Often, network disk drives are faster than local disk drives.

Create Temporary Files by Selectively Copying Records

Rather than copying the contents of every .dbf needed for a report, you can use one of several different FoxPro options to selectively copy only those records you will be using. This reduces the size of your temporary files and may speed up the report process because many or all of the unneeded records have already been filtered out.

One option for selectively copying records is to use the SET FILTER TO option for your database files. You then use the COPY TO command to copy the records that meet your filter criteria to a temporary file. However, SET FILTER TO is normally very slow. If you must use it, you should release your indexes.

A better alternative could be to create a filtered index using the FOR clause of the INDEX command. This creates an index that acts as a filter by including only those records that meet the FOR criteria. You then use the FoxPro COPY TO command to copy the records that meet your selection criteria to a temporary file. Only those records that met the FOR condition when the index was created will be present in the temporary database file. This option has the added advantage of producing a temporary file in sorted sequence.

Finally, you can use FoxPro's COPY TO or SORT command options to limit the fields or records to be copied to the temporary file. This includes the FIELDS, FOR, and WHILE options. The SORT command has the advantage in that it can create a file in the order required by the report.

The disadvantage to using one of the alternatives described in this section is the time FoxPro requires to select the records that meet your specified criteria. If you expect to be using a lot of temporary files for application reporting, you may want to set up your own tests to determine which method is most efficient in your environment.

Network Conventions for Assigning Unique Filenames

If you choose to create temporary files for any of your application programs, and these files are written to the network disk, it is critical that you implement a procedure that ensures unique temporary filenames. Otherwise, you will have users overwriting each other's temporary files and running against each other's database files.

FoxPro provides the SYS(3) function to help you create unique filenames. However, you should use this function cautiously as it is based on the system clock. As described in Chapter 6, if two users happen to request filenames using the SYS(3) function at precisely the same time, they will receive duplicate filenames.

To ensure that your filenames are indeed unique, you can append some unique network identifier to each filename. For example, on a Novell NetWare LAN, you can use the STATION parameter. This parameter is unique for every separate user login, regardless of the userid or physical workstation logged into. To obtain the STATION id, you can set an environment variable in the System Login Script using a statement such as

```
SET STA = "%STATION"
```

Alternatively you can write a .bin routine to pick up the user's STATION id dynamically. You can then LOAD and CALL the .bin file from within your FoxPro application to obtain the NetWare STATION id.

The following code fragment assumes that the environment variable STA has been set in the System Login Script to the STATION id, and it generates a unique filename using the SYS(3) function combined with the STA information:

```
station = GETENV('STA')
rptname = SYS(3) + '.' + ALLTRIM(station)
```

This technique ensures the integrity of each user's temporary files.

Transaction Processing

In every network application, you must consider the possibility of a program terminating abnormally before it completes its processing. This could be the result of a program failure or a hardware failure. If this happens, will you be left with partial updates and database files out of sync? This is entirely possible unless you make use of a transaction processing facility.

In addition, there are times when you will have a series of related database updates that should either be made as a set or not made at all. If you successfully complete several of the updates and then are unable to complete one or more, perhaps because of the unavailability of a record lock, you need to be able to "undo" the related updates you already completed in order to leave the database in a consistent state. What you need is a way to abort your transaction.

In database terms, a transaction is a logical unit of work. It may be a single database operation or a series of update operations as defined by the application. These database operations must be made as a set in order to leave the database in a consistent state, maintaining data integrity. For example, a banking transaction may be made up of two operations: one to debit an account and one to credit another account.

Transaction processing ensures that a transaction is either completed in its entirety or is completely canceled. In the banking example, if the debit to one account is completed and then the system fails before the credit can take place, the transaction processing facility is responsible for undoing the debit, thus leaving the database in a consistent state. A transaction may be "rolled back," or aborted, before it completes, thereby restoring the database to the state it was in prior to the start of the updates. In addition to providing recovery from a hardware failure, a rollback feature allows an application to cancel a set of related updates that have already been made before they are written to disk.

FoxPro, unlike dBASE IV, does not provide a transaction processing facility. Therefore you must consider the alternatives of using a network-provided transaction tracking service or writing your own if you wish to implement transaction processing. Novell, for example, provides TTS (Transaction Tracking Services) on some of its NetWare operating systems. This section explores transaction processing alternatives in greater detail.

NetWare Transaction Tracking Services

NetWare TTS has a set of functions that can provide transaction processing to an application system such as one developed in FoxPro. Actually, two types of transaction tracking are available in NetWare TTS: explicit and implicit.

Implicit transaction tracking does not require any calls to the NetWare TTS functions; it works in connection with multiuser software that performs record locking. To enable implicit transaction tracking, the database files are simply flagged as Transactional.

Although this method is very easy to implement because it does not require any programming, it does not allow the developer to specify the beginning and end of a transaction. By default, NetWare starts a transaction when the first record is locked and ends the transaction when all records are unlocked. A utility is available to specify the number of locks required to start and end an implicit transaction. However, this will probably not provide enough flexibility to be used in a multiuser FoxPro application. In addition, the Novell documentation states that implicit transactions are not guaranteed to work with all multiuser applications. For these reasons, we do not recommend implicit TTS.

Explicit transaction processing, on the other hand, requires calls to NetWare functions defining the beginning and end of a transaction. This allows a developer to make the appropriate calls from anywhere within an application. Although it requires additional programming, it is the recommended approach. The function calls that pertain to explicit transaction processing are as follows:

Function Call	**Description**
TTS Begin Transaction	Signals the start of a transaction. The transaction remains open until either TTS Abort Transaction or TTS End Transaction is called.
TTS Abort Transaction	Backs out the transaction and returns the file to the state it was in prior to the beginning of the transaction.
TTS End Transaction	Signals the end of a transaction and writes the updates to disk. (If the file server fails before all updates are written to disk, the transaction is backed out when the server is rebooted.)

The remainder of this section addresses only the explicit transaction tracking functions.

You can take advantage of these functions by writing Assembly language programs that place specific NetWare calls. You must then convert the executable files to .bin files that can be LOADed and CALLed from within FoxPro. Three .bin files are needed: one to signal the beginning of a transaction, one to "commit" the transaction (write all updates to disk and make the update final), and one to "roll back," or undo, the transaction.

For example, in the banking transaction described earlier, you would implement transaction processing as follows:

1. LOAD the .bin files.
2. CALL the TTS Begin Transaction .bin file.
3. Perform the updates associated with debiting an account.
4. Perform the updates associated with crediting an account.
5. If all updates were successful, call the TTS End Transaction .bin file; otherwise, call the TTS Abort Transaction .bin file.

This sequence of events ensures that the database is left in a consistent state at the completion of the update cycle. In other words, either all the updates have been successfully applied to the database or none of the updates have been applied.

TTS Considerations If you decide to add transaction processing to your FoxPro application with NetWare TTS, you should consider several factors. First, there is the location of your transaction work files. These are the files that store your original data during an update. They are used to restore your database in the event that an update is incomplete and must be rolled back.

During NetWare installation, you specify the volume on which transaction work files will be stored. Novell recommends that the volume have sufficient disk space and that it be located on a separate disk channel from the database files. This allows the transaction data to be written simultaneously with database updates.

Record locks applied within a defined transaction are not released until the transaction is completed. This means that even if you issue an UNLOCK, the network operating system keeps the locks in place. This prevents other users from updating data within a transaction that is not yet complete, an important aspect since a transaction can always be "rolled back" before it completes. Be aware of this when defining a transaction because record locks may remain in force longer than you think. Also, since all record locks are held until the transaction completes, the possibility of deadlock increases. Refer to Chapter 13 for more details about deadlock and how to avoid it.

Be aware that a TTS Abort Transaction call is not the only way to roll back a transaction. The network will back out a transaction in any of several different circumstances. For example, if a workstation is rebooted or the application hangs in the middle of a transaction, the transaction will be backed out automatically. Also, there is the chance that even after a TTS End Transaction has been executed, the transaction will still be backed out. This happens if any of the disk updates associated with the transaction cannot be completed due to a system failure. Under this circumstance, the application thinks that the transaction completed normally, but the network actually backs out the entire transaction to avoid a partial update. When this happens, a message is displayed on the file server console.

Transactions may consist of as many updates as you want. However, you should keep your transactions as small as possible to make the sizes of the transaction work files manageable. Although transaction work files are reused after the transactions that belong to them are completed, a transaction work file continues to grow as long as updates take place and the transaction has not completed.

Any file flagged as Transactional cannot be deleted or renamed. Since all database files involved in a transaction must be flagged as Transactional, applications must be aware of this limitation. If it is necessary to delete or rename a file flagged as Transactional, you should first flag it as Non-transactional before attempting the rename or delete action.

Finally, remember that implementing the NetWare TTS functions slows down any application because each update requires two separate writes: one to the database and one to the transaction work file.

Implementing Your Own Transaction Processing

If a transaction tracking feature is not available on your network operating system, you can devise your own. Generally any transaction processing scheme you implement will be somewhat less effective than one that is provided by the operating system, but it can still offer improved data integrity.

The Simplest Approach: Make Updates to a Temporary File One very simple approach to transaction processing involves the use of temporary work files that you create. Once a record is locked, the contents of the record are copied to a separate temporary .dbf file. If several updates are involved in a transaction, each record is copied to its own file. All updates are applied to the temporary files while the database remains intact. Upon completion of all updates, the contents of the files are written to the database.

This approach allows you to abort a transaction (as defined by the application) and provides protection against a hardware crash. If the workstation or file server goes down while the updates are taking place, none of the updates are written to the database, and the database is left in a consistent state. The only risk of a partially updated database exists when the system fails (hardware or software) while the temporary files are being written to the permanent database.

The disadvantage to this approach is the overhead required by all of the writes to and from the temporary files. If quick response times are critical, this approach may not be feasible.

Another Alternative: Write Backup Data to a Temporary File Another approach to transaction processing is to store your data into temporary .dbf files prior to beginning the updates and to apply the updates directly to the database. This way, you only need to write the data from the temporary file to the database in the event of an aborted transaction. This alternative is a little more complex than the previous one.

The first requirement is that a field be added to each .dbf that will be involved in transaction tracking. This field should be able to hold at least 12 characters and is used to store the name of the temporary file while a transaction takes place. If desired, the field can be longer in order to hold additional information such as user name, module name, date/time of lock, and so on. We'll call this field Trans for our example.

In your program code, you execute an update or series of updates related to a transaction as follows:

1. Lock the required record(s).
2. Check the Trans field in each record to ensure that it is blank.
    a) If it is not blank, notify the user that the database is corrupted, release the record locks, and terminate the transaction. The database must be restored by a separate program, usually executed by a system administrator. This normally indicates that a system failure occurred while processing a transaction.
    b) If it is blank, continue to Step 3.
3. Copy the contents of each record involved in the update to its own temporary file. Write the name of the temporary file associated with the record into the Trans field.
4. Write the updates to the database.
5. Delete the temporary files when all the updates are complete.
6. Clear the Trans field in each record by overwriting it with spaces.

Although some processing overhead is still incurred with this approach, it is considerably less than with the previous alternative. Like the previous method, this method allows the application to abort a transaction as well as to back out a transaction in the event of system failure.

If an application needs to abort a transaction, the database updates are undone by reading the Trans field for each record to obtain the temporary filename and by copying the contents of that file back into the record. The Trans field should then be cleared by the application.

If a system failure occurs, the fact that the database is corrupted will be found the next time a user attempts to update one of the records involved in the failed transaction. As described earlier, if a record can be locked and yet it still contains Trans data, corrupted data is indicated.

A separate program is required to recover from a system failure and to resynchronize the database. This program must search each record in each .dbf looking for a nonblank value in the Trans field. When such a value is found, the program determines whether the record can be locked. If so, this record is part of the failed transaction and is restored from the data in the temporary file. If the record cannot be locked, we know that another user currently has the record locked and that the record is part of an active transaction. We do not need to concern ourselves with this record.

If you implement a transaction tracking procedure requiring the use of temporary files, you must ensure that your filenames are unique. (Network conventions for assigning unique filenames were discussed earlier in this chapter.)

This transaction processing technique can be modified slightly if your .dbf files do not contain memo fields. In this case, you do not need temporary files, but rather you add a memo field to each .dbf in your system—this memo field will be used to store the data prior to the update. This approach eliminates the need for a field in the .dbf to contain the name of the temporary file (the Trans field), since the data is stored right in the record. The data is cleared from the memo field when the update completes successfully. Thus the application checks whether the memo field (rather than the Trans field) is empty before starting a transaction. This approach is somewhat simpler than using an external temporary file, but cannot be used if any of the .dbf files already contain memo fields.

Maintaining Data Integrity in the Multiuser Environment

Controlling Access to the Database and Index Files

Multiuser applications often have many .dbfs and associated index files. It can quickly become a burden to ensure that all associated index files are opened each time a .dbf file is opened for update. Without a controlled means of opening .dbf and .idx files, you run the risk of corrupting your indexes by updating a .dbf without opening one or more of its indexes.

One option for controlling the use of your database files is to maintain a system .dbf with the names and index expressions of all your indexes. The DbfIdx.dbf file discussed in Chapter 12 is an example (Figure 12-5 shows the structure). As we discussed in that chapter, you can write your own procedure for maintaining this .dbf.

In this section we present two examples for using this .dbf in an application system. One is to call a system library procedure for opening a .dbf and its indexes. Listing 14-1 shows a function that uses the DbfIdx file to ensure that all associated indexes are opened with a .dbf. Of course, this approach relies entirely upon the data stored in DbfIdx.dbf—if this information is incomplete, the procedure will not work properly. The calling procedure must call the USEDBF function as follows:

```
USEDBF(<dbf-name>,<primary-index>,<mode>)
```

where <dbf-name> is the .dbf file to be opened, <primary-index> is the name of the .idx file to be used as the primary index, and <mode> is set to 0 if you want to open the file for shared use or 1 if you want to open it EXCLUSIVEly. The function then ensures that all other associated index files are opened with the .dbf. The .dbf and index files are opened in whatever work area the USEDBF function is called from, so it is up to the calling procedure to SELECT the correct work area before calling USEDBF.

A second example for using the data stored in DbfIdx.dbf is a program that rebuilds all your indexes. This is a very easy task once you have the index expression and the name of the index. Although the REINDEX command can do the job if your index files are simply out of sync, it does not do you any good if any of your indexes are actually corrupted (for example, the header record has become corrupted). Listing 14-2 demonstrates a procedure that rebuilds each index file found in the DbfIdx database file, based on the index expression that is stored in DbfIdx.

Limiting Access to Reindexing Facilities

While we are on the subject of rebuilding index files, we should discuss the use of such a facility in a multiuser environment. Since you should USE your

Listing 14-1. UseDbf.prg, procedure to open a .dbf with all of its associated indexes.

```
FUNCTION UseDbf
*******************************************************************
* Program: UseDbf.prg
* Author : P. L. Olympia and Kathy Cea
* Purpose: Opens a .dbf with all its associated indexes.  Uses the
*        : DbfIdx.dbf file to determine what indexes are associated
*        : with the .dbf passed in the dbfname parameter.
*        :
* Syntax : UseDbf(<dbf-name>,<index-name>,<mode>)
*        : where <dbf-name> is the .dbf to be opened, <index-name>
*        : is the primary index to be used, and <mode> is 0 to open
*        : the file for shared use, 1 to open the file exclusively.
*        : <dbf-name> is opened in the current work area.
*        :
*        : Returns .T. if successful, .F. otherwise
*******************************************************************
PARAMETERS dbfname, indexname, mode

* Program requires that a primary index be named in indexname

SET EXACT OFF
SET TALK OFF
SET SAFETY OFF

USE DbfIdx
*Create temporary index for DbfIdx.dbf
INDEX ON UPPER(ALLTRIM(Dbf)) + UPPER(ALLTRIM(IdxName)) to DbfDbf

* Append the file extensions if not already there
dbfname = IIF( ".DBF" $ UPPER(dbfname), ;
                 UPPER(dbfname),UPPER(dbfname) + ".DBF")

indexname = IIF( ".IDX" $ UPPER(indexname), ;
                 UPPER(indexname),UPPER(indexname) + ".IDX")
```

(continued)

Listing 14-1. Continued

```
* Make sure the .dbf and .idx names are in the database
SEEK (UPPER(ALLTRIM(dbfname)) + UPPER(ALLTRIM(indexname)))
IF .NOT. FOUND()
        RETURN .F.
ENDIF

* Build the string of index names
indexstr = indexname
SEEK (UPPER(ALLTRIM(dbfname)))

SCAN WHILE DbfIdx->Dbf = dbfname
        IF DbfIdx->IdxName <> indexname
                indexstr = indexstr + ", " + DbfIdx->IdxName
        ENDIF
ENDSCAN

IF mode = 0   && Open the database for shared use
        USE (dbfname) INDEX &indexstr
ELSE
        USE (dbfname) INDEX &indexstr EXCLUSIVE
ENDIF

DELETE FILE DbfDbf.Idx
RETURN .T.
```

.dbf EXCLUSIVEly before attempting to build an index (the REIND procedure shown earlier does this for you), you can monopolize your database resources while a major reindex is underway. Therefore, it is not a good idea to let all of your end users have access to a reindex facility. Under most circumstances, a reindex program should be provided only to the system administrator on a separate maintenance menu. This prevents users from unknowingly tying up database files and indexes for long periods of time while reindexing. The administrator should schedule this maintenance activity as necessary and notify users accordingly.

Listing 14-2. Reind.prg, procedure to rebuild all your index files.

```
PROCEDURE Reind
*******************************************************************
* Program: Reind.prg
* Author : P. L. Olympia and Kathy Cea
* Purpose: Rebuilds all of the index files found in the DbfIdx.dbf
*        : file, using the index expression and index name stored
*        : in DbfIdx.
*        :
* Syntax : DO Reind
*        :
* Notes  : TALK is not set OFF in this procedure in order to allow
*        : the user to see what indexes are created.
*******************************************************************

SET SAFETY OFF
LastDbf = SPACE(8)

SELECT 1
USE DbfIdx
* Create temporary index
INDEX ON UPPER(ALLTRIM(Dbf)) + UPPER(ALLTRIM(IdxName)) to DbfDbf

DO WHILE .NOT. EOF(1)
        SELECT 2
        * Open dbf only if it is not already opened from last record
        IF ALLTRIM(LastDbf) <> ALLTRIM(DbfIdx->Dbf)
                USE (DbfIdx->Dbf) EXCLUSIVE
        ENDIF

        * Store index name and index expr to memvars so
        * we can use macro substitution
        IndexName = DbfIdx->IdxName
        IndxExpr = ALLTRIM(DbfIdx->IndexExpr)
        LastDbf = DbfIdx->Dbf

        * Rebuild index
        INDEX ON &IndxExpr TO &IndexName
```

(continued)

Listing 14-2. Continued

```
        SELECT 1
        SKIP
ENDDO

USE IN 1
USE IN 2
DELETE FILE DbfDbf.Idx
```

The USE NOUPDATE Option

FoxPro has an option for its USE statement that prevents accidental changes when a module is intended to provide read-only access to .dbf files. Any attempted modifications to the data are denied when the file is opened with the NOUPDATE option. The syntax of this command is as follows:

```
USE <file> NOUPDATE
```

All the other options (such as IN and INDEX) are still available with the NOUPDATE option.

ON ERROR Processing

When you run a multiuser application, there is always a chance that a resource you need is unavailable. The application should handle these situations with an ON ERROR procedure.

Upon entering an application system, perhaps in the main menu routine, you should set an ON ERROR DO <procedure> statement, where <procedure> is the name of the error handling procedure. (We discussed the ON ERROR routine in some detail in Chapter 4.) Here we will look at multiuser specific error handling that should be included.

In handling errors in a multiuser environment, you should be most concerned with three situations: when a file is required for exclusive use, when a file is unavailable, and when a record is unavailable. Table 14-1 shows the three error messages (and codes) that are returned from FoxPro related to these error situations.

Table 14-1. Important Multiuser Error Messages in the Programming Environment

Error Message	Code	Description
Exclusive open of file is required.	110	Occurs when a command that requires exclusive use of a file is executed on a .dbf that was opened for shared use. Examples of commands requiring exclusive use of the .dbf are PACK, REINDEX, and ZAP.
File is in use by another.	108	Occurs if a user attempts to USE a file that is in EXCLUSIVE use by another user, if a user attempts to USE EXCLUSIVEly a file that is in use by another, or if a user cannot obtain a file lock because someone else has the file (or records in the file) locked.
Record is in use by another.	109	Occurs when a user cannot obtain a needed record lock, either because someone else has the record locked or because another user has the file locked.

Your users should not receive error 110 (Exclusive open of file is required) once your application is debugged; however, you may want to account for the possibility of this error while debugging.

The other two errors, 108 and 109, can happen anytime. The following code fragment demonstrates a way to handle these errors from within your ON ERROR procedure:

```
YN = .F.
DO CASE
CASE err = 108  && File is in use
        @20,1 SAY "File is in use by another"
        @21,1 SAY "Do you want to retry opening the file?" ;
              GET YN PICTURE 'Y'
```

```
        READ
        IF YN
                RETRY
        ELSE
                * Execute your close-out routine
                RETURN TO MASTER
        ENDIF
CASE err = 109  &&Record is locked by another
        @20,1 SAY "Record is currently in use by another"
        @21,1 SAY "Do you want to retry locking the record?" ;
              GET YN PICTURE 'Y'
        READ
        IF YN
                RETRY
        ELSE
                * Execute your close-out routine
                RETURN TO MASTER
        ENDIF
... (more CASE statements)
ENDCASE
```

Keep in mind that the ON ERROR procedure is called only after the system has retried to obtain the record or file for the duration specified by your SET REPROCESS value. If your user elects to retry the lock, the system again attempts to obtain the record or file lock until either it gets the lock or the SET REPROCESS period expires.

Maintaining a System Audit Trail

At times you might want to know who accessed what data or when and where errors were generated within your application. In these cases, you may want to maintain an audit trail that your programs write to during critical updates and/or as part of the error handling procedure.

If you have sensitive data or critical updates in your application, you may wish to record user access into a .dbf file. A sample structure used to record application name, module number, user name, date, time, and update indicator is shown in Figure 14-1. A simple library procedure can be written that is called from any application module for which you wish to monitor user activity. The calling procedure should pass the module number, user name, and whether updates were made; the library routine can determine the remain-

```
Structure for database: D:\FOXCODE\AUDIT.DBF
Number of data records:        0
Date of last update   : 01/13/90
Field  Field Name  Type       Width    Dec
    1  AUD_APPLNM  Character     20
    2  AUD_MODNUM  Numeric        4
    3  AUD_USER    Character     12
    4  AUD_DATE    Date           8
    5  AUD_TIME    Character      8
    6  AUD_UPDATE  Logical        1
** Total **                      54
```

Figure 14-1. Audit.dbf structure for maintaining system audit trail.

ing values and simply add a record with the information. You can then use the Audit.dbf file by browsing it, or you can develop a set of reports to run against it based on your specific criteria.

You may also want to establish a file for recording error information. You can automatically call a procedure from your ON ERROR procedure to write pertinent error information such as the calling module, the line causing the error, user information, date, time, and so on. This makes it easier for you to debug your system and may help your end users by not making them solely responsible for reporting error information. It also allows you to collect statistics for errors by module.

An alternative to recording this information to a .dbf file is to write to a network message file, if one is available to you. On NetWare LANs, the Net$Log.Msg file is a text file available to application programs for recording system information. This file is stored in the SYS:SYSTEM directory so it is ordinarily accessible only to the system administrator. However, by taking advantage of a NetWare function call (E3H, Log Function 13), any user can write to this file. This function allows you to append a message (maximum 79 characters, plus the null terminator) to the file. NetWare precedes the message with the date, time, and STATION id. A sample Net$Log.Msg file is shown in Figure 4-1.

To create a .bin file that will execute the function call and permit you to write to the Net$Log.Msg file, run the program shown in Listing 14-3. This program uses the ??? command, which allows you to write directly to the

Listing 14-3. Program to create a .bin file that can be LOADed and CALLed to write to the NetWare Net$Log.Msg file.

```
* Program to create the netmsg.bin file
* netmsg.bin is called to write to the NetWare Net$Log.Msg file

SET PRINTER TO FILE netmsg.bin
SET PRINT ON
???"{235}Z{2}{0}{13}{0}{0}{0}{0}{0}{0}{0}{0}{0}{0}{0}{0}{0}{0}{0}{0}{0}{0}"
???"{0}{0}{0}{0}{0}{0}{0}{0}{0}{0}{0}{0}{0}{0}{0}{0}{0}{0}{0}{0}{0}{0}{0}"
???"{0}{0}{0}{0}{0}{0}{0}{0}{0}{0}{0}{0}{0}{0}{0}{0}{0}{0}{0}{0}{0}{0}{0}"
???"{0}{0}{0}{0}{0}{0}{0}{0}{0}{0}{0}{0}{0}{0}{0}{0}{0}{0}{0}{0}{0}{0}{0}"
???"PSQRVW{30}{6}{139}{243}{14}{7}{191}{6}{0}{38}{198}{6}{5}{0}{0}{185}P"
???"{0}{172}{10}{192}t{13}{170}{38}{254}{6}{5}{0}{38}{255}{6}{2}{0}{226}"
???"{238}{14}{31}{190}{2}{0}{191}Z{0}{180}{227}{205}!{7}{31}_^ZY[X{203}"
SET PRINT OFF
SET PRINTER TO
```

printer. Once you have created the .bin file, you may LOAD and CALL it from any module from which you wish to write to the log file. You may want to record user access and/or error messages in this file.

Chapter Summary

This chapter presented some additional considerations and approaches for programming in FoxPro/LAN. When a report must be run against an unchanging database, special processing is required. We presented three alternatives for ensuring that data does not change: lock all .dbf files for the duration of the report run, copy the .dbf files to temporary files, and create temporary files by selectively copying records. We also presented a method for assigning unique filenames in the network environment.

Transaction processing is an important issue in multiuser programming. Without a transaction tracking facility, a database may be left in an inconsistent or invalid state. FoxPro does not currently provide a transaction tracking service, but you can still incorporate one into your application by taking advantage of a network transaction tracking service or implementing your own. We discussed TTS, the transaction tracking service offered by some Novell NetWare operating systems, and presented two general approaches for writing your own transaction tracking facility.

Some critical issues in maintaining data integrity were presented, and sample programs illustrated methods for controlling access to your application database and index files. Finally, we looked at maintaining audit trails and where you write your audit/error information on a network.

Chapter 15

Distributing a FoxPro Application

After you complete the design, coding, and testing of your FoxPro application, you are just about ready to distribute it. Regardless of the number of client sites where you expect to install the application, there are some things you can do to make the turnover easier. They include ensuring that your programs will perform optimally, providing or limiting access to certain system functions, protecting your investment by encrypting it, and creating an effective yet simple installation procedure. In this final chapter, we pull together many of the performance issues addressed throughout the book and discuss a few more techniques for successfully distributing an application.

Optimizing Performance

Even though you may have an efficient program design (for example, normalized database, modular program design, use of arrays where appropriate, and effective use of indexes), there may still be room for improvement in your application. Specifically there are final considerations relating to the application's environment that can impact performance.

Programming Techniques

In this book we have covered many techniques for improving application performance and for simplifying long-term maintenance. We do not attempt to list these here, but rather we emphasize a few last-minute code checks you should make.

1. Make sure you SET DOHISTORY OFF. Although this is the default setting, you should ensure that it is not left turned ON from your debugging activities. Leaving DOHISTORY ON will significantly slow program execution, as discussed in Chapter 4.
2. Ensure that you have removed any SET TALK ON commands that may have been left over from a debugging session. Clearly, setting TALK ON not only slows processing, but it may compromise your source code by allowing a knowledgeable user to reconstruct your program based on screen output.
3. Keep the use of macro substitution to a minimum. It is a good idea to search through your code for all occurrences of the macro character (&) and determine whether macro substitution can be replaced with something else such as indirect file referencing. For instance, a command such as USE &dbf is slower than the alternative command USE (dbf).
4. Check your SYSMENU setting. If you decide to permit access to the system bar menu during a READ, make sure SET SYSMENU is ON; otherwise, set it OFF.
5. Don't go overboard with your index files. Although you would normally want all index files for a database to be open so they remain updated, remember that keeping each one updated exacts a performance price. Index files that are used only rarely (for a sorted report, for example) may be better built as needed.
6. To minimize the cost of maintaining and supporting your application, consider including as part of your ON ERROR processing procedure a routine to record into a file every bit of information that will help you diagnose the source of the error. This includes a dump of the screen at the moment of error, the error message from FoxPro's MESSAGE( ) function, and the program nesting at the time, which you can get with the help of the SYS(16) or PROGRAM( ) function. You would also want to include the data provided by the LIST STATUS and LIST MEMORY commands. Chapter 4 demonstrates the use of many of these commands in a sample ON ERROR routine.

Using Procedure Files

Once all of your modules are tested, you should combine them into one procedure file. This can be easily accomplished with the FoxBind utility (discussed later), and it improves processing time by minimizing the number of files that FoxPro opens and closes. Recall that a procedure file consists of up to 1170 individual procedures and functions. If the individual procedures are maintained as separate files, each time one of the procedures is called, FoxPro may have to search the disk, open the file, and close it when exiting. A procedure file improves performance because FoxPro only needs to find and open it once, and then it remains in memory while your application runs.

Let's examine how FoxPro searches for procedures. Whenever a procedure (or function) is called, FoxPro looks in the following locations in the order indicated until it finds the requested procedure or fails to locate it.

1. In the currently executing program. If several related procedures are placed into one file, they are all read into memory when any one of the procedures is first called. This feature was not available in FoxBase+.
2. In a procedure file that has been opened with the SET PROCEDURE TO command (if there is one).
3. In any currently open program files, starting with the currently executing program and moving backward toward the initial, master file.
4. On the disk for a program file with a name matching the procedure name. Files on the search path (defined with SET PATH TO) are checked.

What all this means is that unless you store your procedures in the file containing your main routine, you should combine your separate procedures and functions into one procedure file and issue the SET PROCEDURE TO command as part of your initialization routine. Otherwise, your application will be slowed unnecessarily by the system searching for, opening, and closing files.

The FoxBind Utility

The FoxBind utility combines individual procedure programs into one procedure file. It takes each named input file and appends it to the named output file, prefixing each separate procedure with a heading that looks something like this:

```
************************************************************
*                        YourProg                          *
************************************************************
PROCEDURE  YourProg
```

where "YourProg" is the name of the procedure. The syntax for the FoxBind utility is as follows:

```
FOXBIND <outfile> <infile1> [<infile2>...<infilen>]
```

If you do not include an extension for the output file, .Prg is assumed. You must, however, include the extension for each input file. You can include the DOS wildcard characters * and ? in the input file list.

If a file already exists with the name specified for the output file, the procedures are appended to the existing file.

For example, assume that all your library routines are prefixed with L_. You may combine all the library procedures into a procedure file called ApplLib.prg with the following command:

```
FOXBIND ApplLib.prg L_*.prg
```

Using Files Exclusively in a Multiuser Environment

In Chapters 13 and 14, we discussed the implications of exclusive versus shared file use. Although it is not generally desirable to open a file for exclusive use, it can improve application performance and is an acceptable option when only one user will be running the application. For example, consider a nightly batch or reporting process. If the process is left running on just one network workstation, opening the files exclusively eliminates the overhead of checking file and record availability and improves performance.

Location of Temporary Files

If you are familiar with your client's hardware environment, you should be able to determine what options are available for alternate locations for overlay and temporary files. As we discussed in Chapter 4, the following configuration parameters in the Config.fp file specify the location of FoxPro overlay and temporary files:

Parameter	**Use**
OVERLAY	For FoxPro overlay files.
EDITWORK	For temporary files created by the editor.

Parameter	Use
SORTWORK	For temporary sorting and indexing work files.
PROGWORK	For the FoxPro cache file.
TMPFILES	For EDITWORK, SORTWORK, and PROGWORK files if not otherwise specified.

As discussed in Chapter 4, performance can be improved by specifying an alternative drive for the location of the overlay and temporary files. This is especially true in a multiuser environment, where many users contend for access to the network hard drives. In these cases, OVERLAY, EDITWORK, SORTWORK, PROGWORK, and TMPFILES should specify local drives whenever possible.

Obviously you cannot specify alternate locations if you do not know the client's environment. Even so, you can provide instructions with your program documentation to include these statements in the Config.fp file where sufficient hard disk space is available.

Added Hardware

Overall performance can be improved by executing the FoxPro application on equipment that has LIM 4.0 expanded memory. FoxPro can take advantage of as much EMS as it can get. A FoxPro application also shows performance improvements on machines equipped with a math coprocessor, even if the application is not computation-bound.

A RAM disk is the ideal location for FoxPro's PROGWORK (cache file), which does not grow as large as the sort work files. Of course, since a FoxPro application, like any other DBMS application, tends to be I/O bound, a hard disk with a fast access time is always a good investment. You may also encourage your clients to use a disk defragmenting utility on their local hard disks as part of their application maintenance routine.

Compiling an Application

Once you have assembled all your individual program files and procedure files, you need to compile them for use in a production environment. In this section, we summarize two very important COMPILE options and describe how to use the Fls utility and related utilities to perform batch compiles.

Batch Compiling

In the \FOXPRO\GOODIES subdirectory, you will find three files that are used to perform batch compiles: Fls.exe, ProComp.bat, and ProComp.fxp. Together, these files provide a utility for compiling a set of files from the DOS command line. Note that FoxPro does not currently offer a true command-line compiler, unlike FoxBASE+ which has the Foxpcomp utility. Instead, you need to invoke either FoxPro or FoxProln in order to compile your programs.

To compile one or more programs from the DOS command-line, make the \FOXPRO\GOODIES directory your current (working) directory and issue the following command:

```
ProComp [/s] <template>
```

where <template> is a DOS filename, with optional path name and/or wildcard specification. The optional /s argument specifies that subdirectories are to be processed. The following examples show typical ProComp usage:

```
*-- compile just one program file, MainMenu.prg,
*-- in the current directory
ProComp MainMenu.prg

*-- compile all program files with .prg extension,
*-- in current directory only
ProComp *.prg

*-- compile all program files with .prg extension in the
*-- C:\ApplProg directory and all its subdirectories
ProComp /s C:\ApplProg\*.prg
```

Any errors are placed in a text file with the same name as the program being compiled, but with an .ERR extension, if SET LOGERRORS is ON (which is the default).

You can examine the ProComp.bat and ProComp.prg files to review the compilation steps being executed. The Fls.exe utility is used to output to the screen a list of all filenames matching the template; the ProComp.bat file redirects the output to a file named $files.lst. The Fls.exe file can be used as a standalone utility to produce lists of filenames, if desired.

Note that the ProComp.bat file issued with the current version of FoxPro contains the following statement:

```
foxpro procomp
```

If you are running FoxPro/LAN, you must modify the statement to read

```
foxproln procomp
```

Also note that the ProComp.prg file compiles each file without the optional ENCRYPT and NODEBUG clauses. When compiling your programs for production, you may want to modify the ProComp.prg file statement that reads

```
compile &file
```

to

```
compile &file ENCRYPT NODEBUG
```

The ENCRYPT and NODEBUG Compile Options

When compiling your programs for distribution, you should include both the ENCRYPT and NODEBUG clauses. These options perform the following functions:

Option	**Description**
ENCRYPT	Encrypts your compiled code, providing additional protection against a user decoding the .fxp files of your application.
NODEBUG	Reduces the size of your compiled code by 8 bytes per source program line by removing source code cross-references. Once compiled with this option, the Trace and Debug facilities and the DOHISTORY option are no longer accessible, but you should not need such access in your production compiled code. Executing this option reduces the size of your program files for distribution, thus saving disk space and copying time. How much disk space you save with the NODEBUG compile option depends partly on the program but 30 percent or better is typical. For instance, Adduser.prg, which comes with FoxPro/LAN, is a 22,316 byte program that compiles to a 20,392-byte and 14,680-byte .fxp file without and with the NODEBUG option, respectively. Note that the LINENO( ) function always returns zero for a program compiled with NODEBUG.

Writing an Application Config.fp File

Every application should be distributed with a Config.fp file in order to ensure that your programs behave the way you intend them to. Even if all your settings are the FoxPro default settings, include this file to be sure that an extraneous Config.fp residing on your client's hard drive is not accidentally used.

In our discussion of optimizing performance earlier in this chapter, we mentioned several important settings that control application performance. It is a good idea to include every SET command that can potentially impact your application. This includes SET commands that affect screen display (SET COLOR, SET BORDER, and SET BLINK), date and time presentation (SET DATE, SET HOURS) as well as settings that control program functionality such as SET COMPATIBLE, SET EXACT, SET NEAR, SET HELP, SET RESOURCE, and SET UNIQUE. We recommend that you include all the settings, even if yours match the default, to ensure a correct setup. At a minimum, however, you should include those settings that are required for consistent and correct application execution.

Also note several settings that, if not assigned properly, can cause your programs to fail. These include SET INDEX, SET MVARSIZ, SET MVCOUNT, and SET REPORT. Refer to Appendix A for a complete listing and description of the configuration settings.

In addition to creating a Config.fp file for your application, you should consider any special requirements for the DOS Config.sys file. This includes the BUFFERS and FILES statements in the Config.sys file. The BUFFERS setting should be between 20 and 40 for optimal performance. The FILES statement should contain a number at least 10 greater than the maximum number of files open in your application at any one time. A minimum of 40 is recommended. If your clients do not have a Config.sys on their machines or if you are uncertain about the settings, you should supply one with your application.

Note that the FoxPro SYS(2010) function returns, as a character string, the FILES parameter in the Config.sys file or the files setting in effect. Thus your FoxPro installation or initial checkout program can determine whether this number should be raised and even modify the current configuration file. Note also that on a network such as Novell, the FILE HANDLES setting in the Shell.cfg file overrides the FILES parameter in the Config.sys file.

Compressing Files for Distribution

Your application distribution disk(s) likely will consist of system files and application files. System files include the FoxPro Runtime module (FoxPrort.exe, FoxPrort.ovl, and FoxPrort.rsc), the resource files (Foxuser.dbf and Foxuser.fpt), and configuration files (Config.fp and Config.sys).

The application files consist of the appropriate data (.dbf and .fpt) files, help, index, report form, format, or label files, along with the compiled (.fxp) programs.

Together, these files can take up a lot of room. You will be doing yourself and your clients a favor by minimizing the number of disks that you need to distribute. You can easily do this using a file compression program that not only compresses files to 50 percent or better of their original sizes but also puts related files together to ensure that your users get all the required files. Of all compression programs in use to date, the one that we consider to be best suited for the job is LHarc, written by Haruyasu Yoshizaki.

LHarc is a completely free program and has one of the most efficient compression ratios among programs of its type. It also is a small (31K) program that is a complete compression/archiving utility. You use the same program to compress files, decompress files, list the contents of an archived file, and produce a self-extracting file out of the archive. Because LHarc can produce self-extracting files (either .com or .exe), your entire application can be distributed, if you wish, as one self-installing .exe file that does not require LHarc or anything else for decompression. The complete LHarc package, along with the C and Assembly language source, is available from many electronic bulletin boards in the United States. It is also included in the program disk for this book for the convenience of its readers.

Ideally you would want to have at least two self-extracting .exe files produced by LHarc on your distribution disk. One .exe consists of the system files, and the other consists of the application files. To build the self-extracting .exe of system files, the appropriate commands are as follows:

```
LHARC a sysfile foxprort.* foxuser.* config.sys config.fp
```

This command creates a compressed archive file, Sysfile.lzh, containing the FoxPro runtime module, the resource file, and the DOS and FoxPro configuration files. It assumes that all files are on the default drive. If they are not, simply add the appropriate path to the file.

To turn the .lzh file into a self-extracting file, Sysfile.exe, give the command:

```
LHARC s sysfile.
```

Copy the Sysfile.exe file to your distribution disk. Your install program or batch file can then invoke Sysfile.exe to extract the individual files and store them in the appropriate subdirectory of your client's disk. A code fragment from a sample installation batch file is shown in the next section.

Follow a similar procedure for compressing the data and program files of your application. Depending on the size of your application, you may want to create separate self-extracting .exe files for program, data, and support files (including documentation, if any). Note that .dbf and text files compress very well with LHarc, sometimes up to 90 percent or better of their original sizes.

If any of the .exe files becomes too large to fit on one disk, you have two choices. You can reinvoke LHarc and create two or more files out of the large .exe, or you can use one of the many public domain programs such as Chop or Slice that split a file so they fit on a floppy disk and reassemble them later on your client's hard disk.

A Few Notes About LHarc

LHarc can create small and large self-extracting archive files. A small model archive is either a .com file (64K in size or smaller) or an .exe file, which theoretically can be as large as DOS's memory space of 640K, but ideally should not be much larger than 400K. A small model archive must be able to run (self-extract) within the machine's available RAM. So, creating a small model archive of 500K or more may fail to self-extract because a typical DOS machine's transient program area will probably be smaller than this. (Memory-resident programs such as a network shell, screen blanker, and others reduce the amount of memory available to the transient program.)

A large memory model self-extracting archive is limited only by available disk space. It is always an .exe file that runs under currently available RAM. Such a file can self-extract without regard for available RAM. To create a large memory model archive requires only the /x switch in the LHarc command line, for instance,

```
LHARC s /x sysfile
```

A large model archive has several additional features that facilitate the installation of its member files. If the archive is created with a "keyword," and if the archive contains a file named AutoLarc.bat, invoking the archive with the keyword causes the archive to self-extract and automatically executes AutoLarc.bat. For instance, if the keyword provided when the self-extracting file was built is "go", as in

```
LHARC s /x /kgo sysfile
```

then, giving the command

```
SYSFILE go
```

causes Sysfile.exe to self-extract and run AutoLarc.bat.

With a large model archive, you may also specify the target directory where the files should be restored. For example,

```
SYSFILE /ef:\myapp
```

restores all files in the Sysfile.exe archive to the F:\MYAPP subdirectory.

LHarc can also store full path information of the files in the archive and restore the files on the target machine to the appropriate subdirectories, creating the subdirectories as needed.

Installing Your Application

Your application should be "self-installing" in the sense that your clients need not have any intimate knowledge of computers to install the application from the distribution disks. Installation is greatly facilitated by having your applications in self-extracting files as we discussed in the previous section. The following code fragment is from an installation batch file that installs all the files in Sysfile.exe to your client's C:\Sysfile subdirectory:

```
echo off
REM Log into the directory where system files will be stored
C:
CD\SYSFILE
Echo Place Disk #1 on the A: drive
Pause
A:sysfile
```

Of course, if you are providing Config.sys, you should copy Config.sys to the boot drive and remind your users that the machine has to be rebooted after installation. In a multiuser environment, the resource files probably should also be copied to users' home directories.

One perennial issue during installation and one that affects the speed with which your application runs is where the files should be stored and how your search paths should be set. Given that DOS slows down the more files there are on a subdirectory, it is a mistake to place all the files that an application needs, including the runtime module, into one subdirectory. At the very least, consider placing system files into one subdirectory, the compiled application programs in another, and the application data files into a third subdirectory. This arrangement is particularly advantageous in a network because users normally should have read-only access to the subdirectories containing program and system files.

On a network, you may also consider altering the search path so that the subdirectories containing your application data and program files are searched ahead of the network system subdirectories. Your application should then restore the original search path before it terminates.

Application Adhoc Reports and Database Security

Like most applications, yours probably contains a report module consisting of a number of canned reports which users can select from a menu. The set of reports in the module likely were determined during the systems analysis phase when users communicated to you the standard reports they expected from the application. No matter how thorough you have been during the analysis and design phases of the application development work, it is virtually impossible to come up with a complete list of all the reports that your users would want. Thus your application should allow users to query the databases or create adhoc reports.

Since your users only have the runtime module, they cannot create their own query programs. Naturally you would not want them to have the FoxPro development package to access the application data files directly because that could easily compromise the integrity of the data. That would also be an undesirable option in a multiuser implementation because one user conceivably can monopolize all the data files of the application rendering them inaccessible by others for extended periods.

One solution is to provide users with a third-party query product that simply accesses data files without modifying them. Another solution is for you to supply, as part of the application, an adhoc query program that simulates an interactive FoxPro command session or a FoxBASE+ dot prompt. This would be a compiled program that FoxPro-literate users can use to issue database queries and other commands as though they were using the full FoxPro development package in an interactive session. To preserve the integrity of the application's data, the program has the responsibility for filtering out destructive commands such as ZAP, DELETE, or PACK and modifying certain commands so they no longer contain any clauses or options that would alter the data. For instance, the program could accept the BROWSE command but would automatically add the NOMODIFY option to it before the command is issued. Luckily, in FoxPro this problem is trivial because the USE command's NOUPDATE clause bars any modification to the .dbf file.

Listing 15-1 shows Adhoc.prg, a rudimentary program that simulates a Dbase-style dot prompt that accepts commands from a user but filters out any destructive commands or command options. It does not include all the commands that a full query package should have, but it can be easily modified so that the program will recognize additional commands. It is intended to allow users, knowledgeable in both FoxPro and the application's data dictionary, to compose adhoc queries. Note that the program still alters the BROWSE command to add the NOMODIFY, NOAPPEND, and NODELETE options even though it always appends the NOUPDATE clause to the USE command. This is necessary because the program allows the CREATE REPORT command which, when invoked when no .dbf file is in use, activates FILER that can open a file for unrestricted use.

You can modify the program to include additional commands that you are willing to accept as long as you ensure that the commands will not modify data in any way. The INDEX command is a good example of one that requires scrutiny. On the one hand, you don't want to filter it out because users need it for a sorted report. On the other hand, because the command creates a file, there is a possibility that users could use an index filename used by the application in a production environment. One solution is to adopt a convention that the query program will only allow index filenames that begin with a standard set of letters. Another solution is to enforce the rule that any files created by the query program can only be written in the user's home directory.

Adhoc.prg has the added feature of storing the last 20 commands issued by the user. Like the Dbase-style dot prompt facility, the program allows the recall and reexecution of previously issued commands with the up and down arrow keys. You must include your own ON ERROR and ON ESCAPE routines with Adhoc.prg.

Listing 15-1. Adhoc.prg allows user adhoc queries by simulating a Dbase-style dot prompt that filters out commands that modify data files.

```
*****************************************************************
* PROGRAM ......... : Adhoc.prg
* AUTHOR .......... : Original by Emmanuel Sigler
*                   : Mangled substantially by P. L. Olympia & K. Cea
* PURPOSE ......... : Provides a limited command line capability with
*                   : the FoxPro Runtime module. Permits
*                   : nondestructive query of databases
* NOTES ........... : The program keeps track of the last 20 commands,
*                   : recallable using the up and down arrow keys.
*                   :
*******************************************************************
*-- Save the view
CREATE VIEW BAdHoc

CLEAR ALL
CLOSE ALL

*-- Define your own Error/Escape routine
*ON ERROR DO Adhoc_Err
*ON ESCAPE DO Adhoc_Esc
SET ESCAPE ON
SET SYSMENU OFF
CLEAR

DIMENSION ComList(20)
ComList = SPACE(10)
LastCom = 1
ComPtr = 1
CurIntense = 'ON'
CurTalk = SYS(103)
PromptLine = '24'
Miss =  'Missing phrase/keyword in command.'
Playdumb =  'Unrecognized phrase/keyword in command.'

DEFINE WINDOW remind FROM 1,40 TO 2,79;
    TITLE "Type QUIT to exit Adhoc"
ACTIVATE WINDOW remind
```

(continued)

Listing 15-1. Continued

```
ACTIVATE SCREEN

DO WHILE .T.
   SET TALK OFF
   SET INTENSITY OFF
   UNLOCK
   ExitKey = 0
   NoError = .T.
   ComLine = SPACE(250)
   PrevPtr = LastCom
   CurDevice = SYS(101)
   SET DEVICE TO SCREEN
   @ &PromptLine,0 SAY '.'          && Give 'em Mrs. Dot
   SET DEVICE TO &CurDevice

   DO WHILE ExitKey <> 271 .AND. ExitKey <> 15
      @ &PromptLine,2 GET ComLine PICTURE '@S78'
      READ
      ExitKey = READKEY()
      IF ExitKey = 260 .OR. ExitKey = 4   && Pressed the up arrow key
         IF ComList(PrevPtr) <> SPACE(10)   && Not yet top of list
            ComPtr = PrevPtr
            PrevPtr = IIF(ComPtr = 1, 20, ComPtr - 1)
            ComLine = ComList(ComPtr) +;
            SPACE(250 - LEN(ComList(ComPtr)))
         ENDIF
      ELSE
         IF ExitKey = 261 .OR. ExitKey = 5   && Pressed the down
arrow key
            IF ComPtr <> LastCom
               PrevPtr = ComPtr
               ComPtr = IIF(ComPtr = 20, 1, ComPtr + 1)
               ComLine = ComList(ComPtr) +;
               SPACE(250 - LEN(ComList(ComPtr)))
            ELSE
               ComLine = SPACE(250)
               PrevPtr = LastCom
            ENDIF
```

(continued)

Listing 15-1. Continued

```
         ENDIF
      ENDIF
   ENDDO                 && while ExitKey

   IF ComLine = SPACE(250)
      ? ''
      LOOP
   ELSE
      LastCom = IIF(LastCom = 20, 1, LastCom + 1)
      ComList(LastCom) = TRIM(ComLine)
      ComList(IIF(LastCom = 20, 1, LastCom + 1)) = SPACE(10)
   ENDIF

   ModComLine = UPPER(LTRIM(RTRIM(ComLine)))
   SET INTENSITY &CurIntense
   SET TALK &CurTalk
   ? ''

 DO CASE

   CASE LEFT(ModComLine,MIN(4, LEN(ModComLine))) $
'AVER,CONT,COPY,COUN,DIME,DIR;
,DISP,EJEC,EXIT,FIND,LIST,LOCA,QUIT,REPO,REST,SAVE,SEEK,SKIP,SUM;
,TOTA,TYPE' .OR. ModComLine = 'GO'
         IF ModComLine = 'QUIT'
            CLEAR WINDOW remind
            EXIT
         ELSE
            IF ModComLine = 'REST'
               ComLine = TRIM(ModComLine) + ' Additive'
            ENDIF
            &ComLine
         ENDIF

    CASE LEFT(ModComLine,MIN(4, LEN(ModComLine))) $ 'USE ,SET '
         IF AT('EXCL',ModComLine) <> 0 .OR. AT('PROC',ModComLine) <> 0
         ELSE
            SET TALK OFF
```

(continued)

Listing 15-1. Continued

```
            ComClause = SUBSTR(ModComLine, MIN(5, LEN(ModComLine)), ;
              MIN(4, LEN(ModComLine)))
            SET TALK &CurTalk
            IF ModComLine = 'SET' .AND. ;
                 (LEN(ModComLine) = 3 .OR. ComClause $;
'ESCA,ECHO,PROC')
                         ? Playdumb
               RELEASE ComClause
            ELSE
               IF ModComLine = 'USE'
                  &ModComLine NOUPDATE
               ELSE
                  &ComLine
               ENDIF
            ENDIF
         ENDIF

     CASE ModComLine = 'BROW'
         &ModComLine NOMODIFY NOAPPEND NODELETE

     CASE LEFT(ModComLine,4) $ 'CLEA,CLOS'
         IF AT('ALL',ModComLine)=0 .AND. AT('PRO',ModComLine)=0 .AND.;
AT('MEMO',ModComLine)=0
            &ComLine
         ELSE
            ? Playdumb
         ENDIF

     CASE LEFT(ModComLine,4) $  'MODI,CREA'
         ClausePos = AT(' ',ModComLine)
         DO WHILE SUBSTR(ModComLine,ClausePos,1) = ' '
            ClausePos = ClausePos + 1
         ENDDO
         IF SUBSTR(ModComLine,ClausePos,4) <> 'REPO'
            ? 'Unrecognized command.'
         ELSE
            IF AT(' ', SUBSTR(ModComLine,ClausePos)) = 0
               ? Miss
```

(continued)

Listing 15-1. Continued

```
               ELSE
                  &ComLine
               ENDIF
            ENDIF
            RELEASE ClausePos

        CASE ModComLine = 'SELE'
               &ComLine

        CASE ModComLine = 'INDE'
            SET TALK OFF
            ClausePos = AT(' TO ', ModComLine)
            ClausePos = ClausePos + 3
            DO WHILE SUBSTR(ModComLine, ClausePos, 1) = ' '
               ClausePos = ClausePos + 1
            ENDDO
            SET TALK &CurTalk
            &ComLine
            SET TALK OFF
            CurIndex = NDX(1)
            SET INDEX TO
            SET INDEX TO &CurIndex
            SET TALK &CurTalk
            RELEASE ClausePos, CurIndex

        *-- We're going to allow DO and RUN
        CASE ModComLine = 'DO' .OR. ModComLine = '!'
            &ModComLine
            SET EXACT OFF
      ENDCASE

      IF ModComLine = 'SET' .AND. NoError
         DO CASE
            CASE LTRIM(SUBSTR(ModComLine,MIN(4, LEN(ModComLine)))) =
'STAT'
               SET TALK OFF
               PromptLine = IIF (RIGHT(ModComLine,2) = 'ON', '21', '24')
               SET TALK &CurTalk
```

(continued)

Listing 15-1. Continued

```
         CASE LTRIM(SUBSTR(ModComLine,MIN(4, LEN(ModComLine)))) =
'INTE'
            SET TALK OFF
            CurIntense = RIGHT(ModComLine,3)
            SET TALK &CurTalk
         CASE LTRIM(SUBSTR(ModComLine,MIN(4, LEN(ModComLine)))) =
'TALK'
            CurTalk = SYS(103)
      ENDCASE
   ENDIF
   IF (AT(' GET ',ModComLine) = 0 .AND. AT('@',ComLine) = 0) .OR. ''
= TRIM(ComLine)
      ? ''
   ELSE
      @24,0 CLEAR TO 24,79
   ENDIF
ENDDO

* Sets the environment back to where it was before
* ON ERROR DO L_ERROR
* ON ESCAPE DO L_ESC
SET VIEW TO BAdhoc
RETURN
```

Chapter Summary

Before you distribute your application, review your program code one last time. During this last pass, make sure that your code is optimized and that extraneous code and settings (such as those used for debugging) have been removed. Then, combine your separate procedures and functions into one procedure file and compile with the ENCRYPT and NODEBUG options.

Also review your client's hardware setup and, if appropriate, recommend the particular equipment that is best suited to host your FoxPro application. We summarized the hardware options that offer the most gain in performance.

Also consider assigning alternate locations for FoxPro's overlay and temporary files if the hardware is available.

Write a Config.fp file that supports correct and consistent operation of your programs, and distribute it with the rest of your files. It is also a good idea to include a standard DOS Config.sys file in your distribution. Use a file compression utility such as LHarc to package your application into one or more self-extracting files. This minimizes the number of disks required to distribute the application and helps ensure that all required files are distributed together. It also facilitates the installation of your application significantly. An easy-to-use installation program is absolutely necessary to ensure that your end users form a positive "first impression" of your application, and to minimize training and support requirements.

These final activities are well worth your time and effort because they can make the difference between a satisfied and dissatisfied client and ultimately define the success of your FoxPro application.

Appendix A

SET Commands

Table A-1. SET Commands That Can be Defined in Config.Fp

SET Command	Values	Description
ALTERNATE	<filename>	Direct screen or window output to a file.
ALTERNATE	**OFF**/ON	Disable or enable output to an ALTERNATE file.
AUTOSAVE	**OFF**/ON	Disable or enable periodic flushing of buffers to disk.
BELL	**ON**/OFF	Enable or disable sounding of the bell when a field is filled or when data entered is invalid.
BELL	<19 to 10000, 2 to 19<	Set the tone and duration of the bell. Default is 512,2.
BLINK	**ON**/OFF	Specify screen attributes and colors.
BLOCKSIZE	<expN>	Specify disk space allocation for memo fields. Default is 64.
BORDER	<attribute>	Define the border of menus, popups, windows and boxes created with the @...TO command. Default is SINGLE.

(continued)

Table A-1. Continued

SET Command	Values	Description
BRSTATUS	**OFF**/ON	Disable or enable the display of the status bar in a Browse window.
CARRY	**OFF**/ON	Disable or enable the ability to CARRY data forward to appended records.
CENTURY	**OFF**/ON	Disable or enable display of the century portion of dates.
CLEAR	**ON**/OFF	Enable or disable clearing of the screen when the SET FORMAT TO command is issued or when you QUIT FoxPro.
CLOCK	**OFF**/ON	Turn the system clock off or on.
CLOCK	<coord>	Specify the location of the system clock. Default is 0,69.
COLOR	<color attrib>	Define the colors for selected screen elements.
COLOR OF NORMAL| MESSAGES|TITLES| BOX|HIGHLIGHT| INFORMATION| FIELDS	<color attrib>	Define colors for various screen elements.
COLOR OF SCHEME <expN>	<ColorPairList>	Specify the colors of a color scheme.
COLOR SET	<ColorSetName>	Load a previously defined color set. Default is DEFAULT.
COMPATIBLE	**OFF**/ON (**FOXPLUS**/DB4)	Specify FoxBASE+ compatibility.
CONFIRM	**OFF**/ON	Disable or enable the requirement to press a key to exit a field during editing.
CONSOLE	**ON**/OFF	Enable or disable screen output.
CURRENCY	<char>	Specify the currency symbol. Default is "$".

(continued)

Table A-1. Continued

SET Command	Values	Description
CURRENCY	<position>	Position the currency symbol to the left or right of the currency value. Default is LEFT.
CURSOR	**ON**/OFF	Turn the cursor on or off.
DATE	<format>	Specify the date format. Default is AMERICAN.
DEBUG	**ON**/OFF	Enable or disable access to the Trace and Debug windows.
DECIMALS	<0 to 18>	Set the number of decimal places displayed in numeric results. Default is 2.
DEFAULT	<drive/dir>	Set the drive and/or directory for disk operations.
DELETED	**OFF**/ON	Disable or enable access or display of records marked for deletion.
DELIMITERS	**OFF**/ON	Disable or enable the display of field delimiters.
DELIMITERS	<expC>/DEFAULT	Specify field delimiter characters. Default is ":".
DEVELOPMENT	**ON**/OFF	Compare the creation date and time of a source program and its object file.
DEVICE	**SCREEN**/PRINT/ FILE <file>	Direct output of @...SAYs to the screen, printer, or a file.
DISPLAY	<type>	Specify a display mode. Default is Installed.
ECHO	**OFF**/ON	Deactivate or activate the Trace window for program debugging.
ESCAPE	**ON**/OFF	Enable or disable trapping for pressing of the Esc key.
EXACT	**OFF**/ON	Specify whether two strings must be of equal length in order to match when they are compared.

(continued)

Table A-1. Continued

SET Command	Values	Description
EXCLUSIVE	**ON**/OFF	Specifies whether database files will be opened for exclusive or shared use.
FULLPATH	**ON**/OFF	Specify whether a full pathname is included when a file name is returned from a command or function.
FUNCTION <num>	<char_str>	Assign a character string to a Function key(s).
HEADING	**ON**/OFF	Enable or disable the display of column titles for each field in the AVERAGE, CALCULATE, DISPLAY, LIST and SUM commands.
HELP	**ON**/OFF	Enable or disable the FoxPro online Help facility.
HELP	<filename>	Specify a Help file to be used when the FoxPro online Help facility is invoked. Default is FoxHelp.
HOURS	**12**/24	Specify a 12 or 24 hour format for time functions and the system clock.
INTENSITY	**ON**/OFF	Enable or disable highlighting of input fields.
LOGERRORS	**ON**/OFF	Specify whether compilation errors will be sent to a file.
MACKEY	<key>	Specify a key(s) that displays the Keyboard Macros dialog. Default is F10.
MARGIN	<**0** to 254>	Set the left printer margin.
MARK	<char>	Specify the date separator character. Default is "/ ".

(continued)

Table A-1. Continued

SET Command	Values	Description
MEMOWIDTH	<8 to 32,000>	Specify the width of memo field output and values returned by ATLINE( ), ATCLINE( ), MEMLINE( ), RATLINE( ), and MLINE( ) functions. Default is 50.
MOUSE	<1 to 10>	Specify the sensitivity of the mouse. Default is 5.
NEAR	**OFF**/ON	Specify placement of the record pointer after an unsuccessful database search.
NOTIFY	**ON**/OFF	Enable or disable the display of certain system messages.
ODOMETER	<1 to 32,767>	Specify the reporting interval for commands that return status information. Default is 100.
PATH	<path>	Specify a list of directories for FoxPro to search for files not in the working directory.
POINT	<char>	Specify the character to be used as a decimal point. Default is ".".
PRINTER	**ON**/OFF	Enable or disable output to the printer.
RESOURCE	**ON**/OFF	Enable or disable use of the FoxPro Resource file.
RESOURCE	<filename>	Specify a Resource file. Default is FoxUser.
SAFETY	**ON**/OFF	Enable or disable file overwrite protection.
SCOREBOARD	**OFF**/ON	Specify display of NumLock, CapsLock, and Insert keys.
SEPARATOR	<char>	Specify the character used as a numeric separator. Default is ",".

(continued)

Table A-1. Continued

SET Command	Values	Description
SPACE	**ON**/OFF	Specify if a space will separate fields or expressions in the ? and ?? commands.
STATUS	**OFF**/ON	Disable or enable display of the status bar.
STEP	**OFF**/ON	Specify whether to execute a program without pausing or to single step with pauses.
STICKY	**ON**/OFF	Specify the display of menus in the FoxPro menu system. Only mouse users are affected.
SYSMENU	**ON**/OFF	Enable or disable access to the system menu bar during program execution.
TALK	**ON**/OFF	Enable or disable display of command results to the screen.
TYPEAHEAD	<0 to 32,000>	Specify the number of characters to be stored in the typeahead buffer. Default is 20.
UNIQUE	**OFF**/ON	Specify whether records with duplicate keys will be included in the index file.

Table A-2. SET Commands That Can be Defined Only in Config.Fp

SET Command	Values	Description
COMMAND	<command>	Executes a FoxPro command after all other configuration settings are established.

(continued)

Table A-2. Continued

SET Command	Values	Description
EDITWORK	<dir>	Specifies where the text editor should place its work files.
EMS	**ON**/OFF/<expN>	Determines whether or not FoxPro will take advantage of EMS, or limits the amount of EMS for FoxPro's use.
INDEX	<extension>	Specifies the extension for FoxPro index files. Default is IDX.
LABEL	<extension>	Specifies the extension for FoxPro label definition files. Default is LBX.
MVARSIZ	<1 to 64>	Establishes the amount of memory, in K bytes, that is allocated for character strings stored in memory variables. Default is 6.
MVCOUNT	<128 to 3600>	Defines the maximum number of FoxPro memory variables. Default is 256.
OVERLAY	<dir>	Specifies where FoxPro should place its .OVL (overlay) and .RSC files.
PROGWORK	<dir>	Specifies where the program cache file will be placed.
RESOURCE	<pathname>	Specifies where the FoxUser resource file will be placed.
REPORT	<extension>	Specifies the extension for FoxPro report definition files. Default is FRX.
SORTWORK	<dir>	Specifies where SORT and INDEX operations will place their temporary work files.
TEDIT	<exp|expN>	Specifies the external text editor that is used when the MODIFY COMMAND command is issued.
TIME	<1 to 1,000,000>	Establishes the amount of time that FoxPro waits for the print device to accept a character. Default is 6000.

(continued)

Table A-2. Continued

SET Command	Values	Description
TMPFILES	<drive:>	Specifies a location (drive) for the EDITWORK, SORTWORK, and PROGWORK files if not otherwise specified.

Table A-3. Other SET Commands

```
SET CARRY TO [<field list> [ADDITIVE]]
SET DOHISTORY ON|OFF
SET FIELDS ON|OFF
SET FIELDS TO [[<field1>,<field2>...]]| ALL]
SET FILTER TO [<expr>]
SET FIXED ON|OFF
SET FORMAT TO [<file>| ?]
SET INDEX TO [<file list>| ?]
SET LOCK OFF|ON
SET MESSAGE TO [<expC>]
SET MESSAGE TO [<expn> [LEFT|CENTER|RIGHT]]
SET MOUSE ON|OFF
SET MULTILOCKS OFF|ON
SET ORDER TO [<expN>]
SET PRINTER TO [<file> | <port>]
SET PROCEDURE TO [<file>]
SET REFRESH TO <expN>
SET RELATION OFF INTO <alias>
SET RELATION TO [<expr1> INTO <alias> [ADDITIVE]]
                    [,<expr2> INTO <alias> [ADDITIVE]] ...
SET REPROCESS TO AUTOMATIC | TO <expN> [SECONDS]
SET SHADOWS ON|OFF
SET TOPIC TO [<expC>|<expL>]
SET VIEW ON|OFF
SET VIEW TO <file> | ?
SET WINDOW OF MEMO TO [<window name>]
```

Appendix B

Color Pairs for Each Color Scheme

Color Pair	Color Scheme Scheme 1	Scheme 2	Scheme 3	Scheme 4	Scheme 5
Color Pair 1	SAY field	Disabled	Disabled pads	Disabled option	Normal text
Color Pair 2	GET field	Enabled option	Enabled pads	Enabled option	Text box
Color Pair 3	Border	Border		Border	Border
Color Pair 4	Title, active	Menu titles			
Color Pair 5	Title, idle	Message			
Color Pair 6	Selected item	Selected option	Selected pad	Selected option	Select item
Color Pair 7	Clock		Hot keys	Hot keys	Hot keys
Color Pair 8	Shadow	Shadow		Shadow	Shadow
Color Pair 9					Enabled Control
Color Pair 10					Disabled Control

(continued)

Color Pair	Scheme 6	Scheme 7	Scheme 8	Scheme 9	Scheme 10	Scheme 11
	Color Scheme					
Color Pair 1	Disabled option	Normal text	Normal text	Disabled option	Other records	Text & B full
Color Pair 2	Enabled option	Text box	Text box	Enabled option	Current field	Report field
Color Pair 3	Border	Border	Border	Border	Border	Border
Color Pair 4			Title, active		Title, active	Title, active
Color Pair 5			Titles, idle		Title, idle	Title, idle
Color Pair 6	Selected option	Selected item	Selected text	Selected option	Selected text	Selected item
Color Pair 7		Hot keys	Hot keys		Current record	Band A, empty
Color Pair 8	Shadow	Shadow	Shadow	Shadow	Shadow	Shadow
Color Pair 9		Enabled Control	Enabled Control			Band A, full
Color Pair 10		Disabled Control	Disabled Control			Band B, empty

Appendix C

@...SAY/GET PICTURE and FUNCTION Codes

PICTURE Template Codes

A PICTURE expression may include any characters; only the defined template codes enforce editing on data entry or format the input and output data. Any characters other than the defined template codes that appear in a PICTURE expression are simply printed as such by FoxPro. For input operations, such characters appear in the field as comment information which is skipped over by the cursor.

A	Allows alphabetic characters only.
L	Allows logical data only.
N	Allows letters and digits only.
X	Allows any character.
Y	Allows logical Y, y, N, n only. Converts y and n to uppercase.
9	With character data, allows digits only. With numeric data, allows digits and signs.
#	Allows digits, blanks and signs.
!	Converts lowercase letters to uppercase letters.
$	Displays the current currency symbol (as defined with SET CURRENCY). May only be used in GET fields when SET CURRENCY is LEFT.

*	Displays asterisks in front of the numeric value. Use with a dollar sign '$' for check protection.
.	Specifies the decimal point position.
,	Separates digits left of the decimal point.

FUNCTION Codes

A	Allows alphabetic characters only.
B	Left-justifies numeric data within the output field.
C	Displays a CR (credit) after a positive number. May be used only with numeric data and only with the SAY clause.
D	Uses the current SET DATE format for editing date type data.
E	Edits date type data as a European (BRITISH) date.
I	Centers output text within the field.
J	Right-justifies output text within the field.
L	Displays leading zeros (instead of spaces) in numeric output. May be used with numeric data only.
M <list>	Specifies multiple preset choices where <list> is a comma-delimited collection of items. Individual items within the <list> may not contain embedded commas. If the GET variable does not contain one of the items from the <list> when the READ is issued, the first item in the <list> appears in the GET field. This function may be used only with character data, and only with a GET variable.
R	If used with a <format> string that contains characters other than PICTURE template codes, the non-template characters will be displayed but not stored. May be used with character data only.

S<n>	Limits display width to <n> characters, where <n> is a positive integer. Horizontally scrolls the field within the <n> columns specified. The Right Arrow, Left Arrow, Ctrl-F and Ctrl-A cursor-control keys may be used to bring hidden portions of the field into view. May be used with character data only.
T	Trims leading and trailing blanks from the field.
X	Displays a DB (debit) symbol after negative numbers. May be used only with numeric data and only with the SAY clause.
Z	Displays the field as all blanks if its numeric value is 0. May be used with numeric data only.
(	Encloses negative numbers in parentheses. May be used only with numeric data and only with the SAY clause.
!	Converts alphabetic characters to uppercase. May be used with character data only.
^	Displays numeric data using scientific notation. May be used with numeric data only.
$	Displays data in the currency format. The currency symbol appears before or after the field value depending on the current setting of SET CURRENCY. May be used with numeric data only. If CURRENCY is SET LEFT, may not be used with GETS.

Appendix D

FoxPro System Memory Variables

Memvar	Description, Syntax and Default Value
_alignment	Dictates the alignment (left-justified, right-justified, or centered) of output produced by the ?/?? command when system memvar _wrap is set to .T. _alignment = <"left" | "center" | "right"> (default="left")
_box	If set to .T., the boxes defined with the DEFINE BOX command will display. _box = <condition> (default=.T.)
_dblclick	Defines the number of seconds used to check for double or triple mouse click. _dblclick = <expN> (default = 0.5)
_indent	Indents the first line of a paragraph by the specified number of characters when _wrap is .T. The value of _indent may range from the negative value of _lmargin to (_rmargin - _lmargin - 1). _indent = <expN> (default=0)

(continued)

Memvar	Description, Syntax and Default Value
_lmargin	Defines the left margin of the page (0 through 254) for output produced by the ? command when _wrap is .T. _lmargin = <expN> (default=0)
_padvance	Defines how the printer advances the paper. _padvance = <"formfeed" | "linefeed"> (default="formfeed")
_pageno	Determines or sets the current page number. Allowed values range from 1 through 32,767. _pageno = <expN> (default=0)
_pbpage	Specifies the beginning page for a printjob. Pages with numbers less than _pbpage are not printed. Allowed values range from 1 through 32,767. _pbpage = <expN> (default=1)
_pcolno	Moves the output position to the specified column of the current line, or returns the current column number. _pcolno may be assigned an integer value between 0 and 255. _pcolno = <expN> (default=current column)
_pcopies	Specifies the number of copies (1 through 32,767) to print for a printjob. _pcopies = <expN> (default=1)
_pdriver	Activates the specified printer driver or returns the name of the current driver. This memvar is not active in version 1.0x. _pdriver = "<printer driver filename>"
_pecode	Defines the control string (up to 255 characters) to send a printer at the end of a printjob. _pecode = <expC>

(continued)

Memvar **Description, Syntax and Default Value**

_peject

Determines whether a sheet of paper is to be ejected before or after a printjob.

_peject = <"before" | "after" | "both" | "none"> (default="before")

_pepage

Specifies the ending page (1 through 32,767) for a printjob. Pages with numbers greater than _pepage are not printed.

_pepage = <expN> (default=32767)

_pform

Activates the specified print form file, or returns the name of the current .prf file.

_pform = "<.prf filename>"

_plength

Sets the length of the printed page. Allowed values range from 1 through 32,767.

_plength = <expN> (default=66)

_plineno

Assigns the line number for the streaming output, or returns the number of the line currently being printed.

_plineno = <expN> (default=0)

_ploffset

Defines the left offset of the printed page. It may be assigned an integer value from 0 to 254.

_ploffset = <expN> (default=0)

_ppitch

Specifies the printer pitch, or returns a string showing the pitch that is currently active.

_ppitch = <"default"|"pica"|"elite"|"condensed"> (default="default")

_pquality

Sets letter quality (.T.) or draft mode (.F.), or returns a logical condition showing the print mode currently defined. This will be supported when FoxPro supports printer drivers.

_pquality = <expL> (default=.F.)

(continued)

Memvar	Description, Syntax and Default Value
_pscode	Defines the control codes (up to 255 characters long) to send the printer at the start of a printjob. _pscode = <expC>
_pspacing	Defines whether output will be sent with single, double, or triple spacing. _pspacing = <expN> (default=1)
_pwait	Specifies whether or not the printer will pause between pages of output. _pwait = <expL> (default=.F.)
_rmargin	Defines the right margin of the page (maximum value is 255) for output produced by the ? command when _wrap is .T. _rmargin = <expN> (default=80)
_tabs	Sets the default tab stops for the word wrap editor or defines the tab stops for screen, printer and file output produced by the ?/?? command. _tabs = <expC>
_wrap	Sets word wrapping between margins on or off. _wrap = <condition> (default=.F.)

Appendix E

FoxPro Index (.Idx) File Structure

A FoxPro .idx file consists of a header record and one or more node records. Each record type is 512 bytes long. The structure of the header record is shown in Table E-1 (and also in Table 10-1) while the structure of a node record is shown in Table E-2.

The header record contains information about the root node, next available node, the length of the key, index options, the key expression and the index FOR expression (if used). Unlike dBASE IV, FoxPro does not store the type of the index key (for example, numeric) in the header record; FoxPro determines the index key type from the expression. When used as a key, numbers undergo an internal conversion process so they can be sorted using the same ASCII collating sequence as characters. FoxPro uses the following conversion algorithm for numeric keys:

1. Convert the number to IEEE floating point format.
2. Swap the order of the bytes from Intel 8086 order to left-to-right order.
3. If the number is negative, take the logical compliment of the number (swap all 64 bits, 1 to 0 and 0 to 1); else invert only the leftmost bit.

A node record contains information about the node type, the number of keys in the node, pointers to the left and right of the node, and the characters encompassing the key value. A node record may be a root, leaf, or index node. The root node is the top node in the tree, where a search begins. Leaf nodes are the bottom nodes of the tree and point to database records. Index nodes are indexes into other nodes, narrowing down the set of nodes to be searched as they are traversed.

Table E-1. The Structure of a FoxPro Index Header Record

Byte	Description
00–03	Pointer to root node. This value points to the entry location of the index file.
04–07	Pointer to free node list (-1 if not present). This value points to the next available 512-byte block in the index file.
08–11	Pointer to end of file (file size)
12–13	Length of the index key
14	Index options (may be one of the following, neither, or the sum of both): 1 A UNIQUE index 8 FOR clause used
15	Index signature (reserved for future use)
16–235	Key expression (in ASCII)
236–455	FOR expression (in ASCII; ends with null byte)
456–511	Unused

Table E-2. The Structure of a FoxPro Index Node Record

Byte	Description
00–01	Node type or attribute (may be one of the following or their sums): 0 Index node 1 Root node 2 Leaf node
02–03	Number of keys present (0, 1 or many)
04–07	Pointer to the node directly to the left of the current node on the same level (-1, if not present)
08–11	Pointer to the node directly to the right of the current node on the same level (-1, if not present)
12–511	Group of characters containing the key value for the length of the key, along with a four-byte hexadecimal number. The number contains the actual database record number if the node is a leaf node; otherwise, it contains a pointer to another block which contains either the actual pointers into the file or pointers to a lower node. The key value/hexadecimal number pair occurs as many times as there are keys in the node record as defined in bytes 02-03.

References

Barkakati, Nabajyoti, *The Waite Group's Turbo C Bible*, Howard W. Sams & Company, Indianapolis, IN, 1989.

Date, C.J., *An Introduction to Database Systems*, Volume I, Addison-Wesley Publishing Company, Reading, MA, 1987.

Freeland, R. Russell, "Binary Output," *Data Based Advisor*, Volume 7, Number 4, May, 1987.

Kernighan, Brian W. and Dennis M. Ritchie, *The C Programming Language*, Prentice-Hall Inc., New Jersey, 1978.

Novell NetWare Application Programming Interface (API) manuals, 1989.

Olympia, P.L., R. Russell Freeland, and Randy Wallin, *dBASE Power: Building and Using Programming Tools*, Ashton-Tate Publishing, California, 1988.

Russell, Craig, "Printing Labels in Snaked Columns," *Ashton-Tate Technotes*, March, 1989.

Schulman, Andrew, "Inside dBASE," *Data Based Advisor*, Volume 5, Number 5, May, 1987.

Tenenbaum, Aaron M. and Moshe J. Augenstein, *Data Structures Using Pascal*, Prentice-Hall Inc., New Jersey, 1986.

White, Chris, ed., *Secrets of dBASE*, Ashton-Tate Publishing, California, 1987.

Index

Developing FoxPro Applications
Program Diskette

Order Form

Please send me a disk containing the programs from *Developing FoxPro Applications* by P. L. Olympia and Kathy Cea. Enclosed is a check for $19.95 ($20.95 for Maryland residents).

____
Name

____
Address

____________________ __________ _________
City State Zip

____
Daytime Phone (with Area Code)

☐ 5.25-inch disk

☐ 3.5-inch disk

Please make your check payable to *Kathy Cea* and send it along with this order form to:

FoxPro Applications Disk
Darwin Systems, Inc.
17 Thorburn Road
Gaithersburg, MD 20878